PRESENTING JAPANESE BUDDHISM TO THE WEST

ORIENTALISM, OCCIDENTALISM,

The University of North Carolina Press • *Chapel Hill and London*

AND THE COLUMBIAN EXPOSITION

PRESENTING JAPANESE BUDDHISM TO THE WEST

by Judith Snodgrass

Designed by Gary Gore
Set in Schneidler and Minion
by Keystone Typesetting, Inc.
Manufactured in the United States of America

The paper in this book meets the guidelines for permanence and durability of the Committee on Production Guidelines for Book Longevity of the Council on Library Resources.

Frontispiece: The Parliament Assembly (Rossiter Johnson, *A History of the World's Columbian Exposition*, 4:249).

Library of Congress Cataloging-in-Publication Data
Snodgrass, Judith.
Presenting Japanese Buddhism to the West : orientalism, occidentalism, and the Columbian Exposition / by Judith Snodgrass.
p. cm.
Includes bibliographical references and index.
ISBN 0-8078-2785-1 (cloth: alk. paper)
ISBN 0-8078-5458-1 (pbk.: alk. paper)
1. Buddhism—Missions. 2. Buddhism—Japan—History—1868–1945. 3. Orientalism. 4. World Parliament of Religions (1893 : Chicago, Ill.)
I. Title.
BQ5925 .S63 2003
294.3′0952′091821—dc21 2002152516

Portions of this work appeared earlier, in somewhat different form, as "Japan Faces the West: The Representation of Japan at the Columbian Exposition, Chicago 1893," in *Japanese Science, Technology and Economic Growth Down Under* (selected papers from the Japanese Studies Association Biennial Conference, Sydney, July 1989), ed. Morris Low and Helen Marriott, 11–24 (Melbourne: Monash Asia Institute, 1996), reprinted with the permission of the Monash Asia Institute; "The Deployment of Western Philosophy in Meiji Buddhist Revival," *Eastern Buddhist* 30:2 (Spring 1997): 173–98, reprinted with the permission of the Eastern Buddhist Society; "Retrieving the Past: Considerations of Texts," *Eastern Buddhist* 31:2 (Spring 1998): 263–67, reprinted with the permission of the Eastern Buddhist Society; and "*Buddha no fukuin*: The Deployment of Paul Carus's *Gospel of Buddha* in Meiji Japan," *Japanese Journal of Religious Studies* 25:3–4 (Fall 1998): 319–44, reprinted with the permission of the Nanzan Institute for Religion and Culture.

cloth 07 06 05 04 03 5 4 3 2 1
paper 07 06 05 04 03 5 4 3 2 1

CONTENTS

	Introduction: Japan in Chicago	1
Chapter 1.	Japan Faces the West	16
Chapter 2.	Manifest Destiny: *Christianity and American Imperialism*	45
Chapter 3.	The Rules of the Parliament: *Securing the Truth*	65
Chapter 4.	Alterity: *Buddhism as the "Other" of Christianity*	85
Chapter 5.	Buddhism and Modernity in Meiji Japan	115
Chapter 6.	Buddhist Revival and Japanese Nationalism	137
Chapter 7.	Deploying Western Authority I: *Henry Steel Olcott in Japan*	155
Chapter 8.	Buddhism and Treaty Revision: *The Chicago Project*	172
Chapter 9.	Defining Eastern Buddhism	198
Chapter 10.	Paul Carus: *Buddhism and Monist Mission*	222
Chapter 11.	Deploying Western Authority II: *Carus in Translation*	245
Chapter 12.	From Eastern Buddhism to Zen: *A Postscript*	259
	Notes	279
	Bibliography	323
	Index	345

FIGURES

	The Parliament Assembly	*frontispiece*
1.	The Dome of Columbus	22
2.	The Ferris wheel	27
3.	The Court of Honor	28
4.	The Japanese Pavilion	30
5.	The Hōōden: interior of the north wing	31
6.	The Hōōden: a room in the south wing	32
7.	The Hōōden: interior of the central hall	33
8.	Bird's-eye view of the exposition	36
9.	A Buddhist temple	111
10.	Olcott in Japan	166
11.	The Japanese delegation	177
12.	Hirai Kinzō	183
13.	Christ is a Buddha	238

PRESENTING JAPANESE BUDDHISM TO THE WEST

INTRODUCTION

Japan in Chicago

The narrative of Zen in the West begins with the introduction of Japanese Buddhism by a delegation of Buddhist priests—representatives of the Meiji Buddhist revival movement—to the World's Parliament of Religions in Chicago, 1893. The Buddhism they presented was not Zen, but Eastern Buddhism, the product of this movement, shaped by the imperatives of institutional, social, and political crises of the early Meiji period, and by the desire to produce an interpretation of Buddhism appropriate for the modern state. It was further determined by the links between Buddhist revival and the emerging nationalism of the early 1890s. The representation of Buddhism at Chicago, as the delegates planned it, was a strategic statement in the discourse of Buddhist nationalism and was given shape by the tactics and strategies implicit in this project.

The representation was further determined by the event itself. The Parliament was an aggressively Christian event, born of American Protestant Christian confidence in its superiority and organized around unquestioned Christian assumptions of the nature and function of religion. It was governed by a set of rules for controlling discourse so permeated with Christian presuppositions that they effectively reduced all other religions to inadequate attempts to express the Christian revelation. The Parliament was, for all its undoubtedly sincere rhetoric of fostering universal brotherhood and international goodwill, an arena for the contest between Christians and the "heathen," with all that that implied in terms of late nineteenth-century presuppositions of evolution, civilization, and the natural right of the West to dominance over the East.

As I see it, the representation of Buddhism was simultaneously a strategy in a number of different but interdependent discourses brought together by this unique occasion. Locating the Parliament within the Columbian Exposition places the representation within a number of overt relations of power. The most immediate of these were the New World challenge to Europe as the United States emerged as an international power, and the tension between the dominant West and the Orient. This was even more evident in Chicago than at other expositions because the Columbian Exposition was consciously organized to present an "object lesson" in Social Darwinism displaying the rightful place of the people of the world in the hierarchy of race and civilization.[1] For Japan the reality of Western dominance was focused in the "unequal treaties" imposed upon it by Western nations, and by the perception that favorable modification of the treaties depended on demonstrating that Japanese civilization was "equal" to that of the West. (The problems of just what these terms mean is discussed shortly.) Japan's primary project at the fair was to challenge this Western presupposition of cultural superiority and protest the lowly position assigned to the Japanese in the hierarchy of evolutionary development.

These overt relations of power traversed the exposition and shaped the Japanese exhibit. Japan's bid for equality with Europe was most clearly articulated in the Hōōden, a stunning display of decorative art and architecture, but the religious delegation and its representation of Buddhism was also an important part of the project. The delegates believed that Buddhism, the Buddhism of Meiji revival, was the one area of knowledge in which Japan was not just equal to the West but superior to it. Buddhism was to be Japan's gift to the modern world and, as such, a source of national prestige. The Hōōden was evidence of Japan's "highly evolved" material civilization; Japanese Buddhism demonstrated concomitant intellectual achievement.

The exposition exercise overlapped that of Buddhist revival. In the simplest possible terms, revival leaders, attempting to attract the support of the Western-educated elite of Meiji Japan, argued that Japanese Buddhism embodied the truth and wisdom of both Western philosophy and Western religion. Aware of the perceived conflict between orthodox Christianity and nineteenth-century developments in scientific thought, they hoped to convince this domestic audience that Buddhism was the most appropriate religion for the modern world. Because their task was to bring this revelation to the attention of the Western-educated lay community and convince it of Buddhism's truth, the international platform of the Parliament in Chicago with its large and select audience of religious specialists was, in the words of the delegates and their supporters, a chance that came but once in a thousand years.[2] Although the papers were presented to display the superiority of Japanese Buddhism over all other religions to the Parliament audience, the desired result was to impress Japanese with the West's positive reception. The delegation to Chicago was also, therefore, a strategic intervention in the Meiji discourse on religion.

The importance of this aspect of the delegation to Chicago is signaled by its membership. There were six speakers in the Buddhist contingent: four scholarly priests and two politically active Buddhist laymen who also acted as translators.[3] The four priests were all highly educated Buddhist scholars and active participants in Buddhist revival. The two Buddhist laymen also had a long history of political activity and commitment to Buddhist revival, most notably in the instigation and organization of Henry Steel Olcott's tour of Japan in 1889.

The conjunction of national and international imperatives was also evident in the representation of Japanese Christianity. The Japanese Christian delegates, led by Doshisha College president Kozaki Hiromichi, were similarly ardent Japanese patriots, experienced campaigners seeking to shape the religious future of Japan. Like the Buddhists, they were opposed to Western interference in Japan and the impositions of the treaties, but saw the religion of the future in a Japanese interpretation of Christianity, which—in parallel with the Buddhist aims—would be proof of Japanese superiority and Japan's gift to the world. What they offered was a rationalized Christianity, Christianity brought to its fulfillment by the Japanese spirit. Following the claims of the Buddhist delegates, they offered an Eastern spirituality to compensate for Western materialism. As the Doshisha group had been among the most vocal opponents of Buddhist revival in Japan, the two contingents represented the major contenders in the debate over the religious future of Japan. Their participation at Chicago extended the local contest into the international arena.[4]

Although rivalry between Christianity and Buddhism was a significant factor in the restructuring of Meiji Buddhism and in the discourse at the Parliament, it was not simply a matter of confrontation between two clearly defined, monolithic opponents. For a start, it is vital to make the distinction between Japanese Christian converts and Western missionaries. The Japanese delegates—Christian and Buddhist alike—were united in defense of the nation against the Western imperialism of the Christian missions. They both saw Western Protestant Christianity as a model for the role of religion in modern society. Doctrine only entered the debate marginally, as each accused the other of being nonscientific, irrational, and therefore incompatible with the modern world view. The Christianity of Meiji Japanese nationalism, like Meiji Buddhism, was shaped by the need to conform to the latest intellectual developments in Europe; the latest ideas were eagerly imported and adopted by the Western-educated elite of the nation in its desire for modernization. Shifting alliances were apparent in Chicago as Buddhist and Christian delegates, opponents in the local arena, were allied as patriots, challenging the West and extolling *yamato damashii*, the spirit of Japan.

The international context of the exposition and shared opposition to missionary endeavors also aligned the Japanese Buddhist delegates with the religious representatives of Ceylon, Thailand, and India, thereby overriding Japan's attempts to dissociate itself from colonial countries, from other Asian races and cultures. Association with South and Southeast Asians also compromised Japan's attempts to distance Eastern Buddhism, Japanese Mahayana Buddhism, from other non-Christian religions, particularly from the Theravada Buddhism of the South. Consequently, the network of contests in which Buddhism was involved at the World's Parliament of Religions was complicated by the overlap of national, international, and doctrinal issues.

Buddhism and Orientalism

Not the least of the interconnected and diverse discourses in which Japanese Buddhism participated at Chicago was the alterity of Buddhism—the reified abstraction of Western discourse—to Christianity. The formation of "Buddhism" as an object of Western knowledge in the late nineteenth century typifies the processes of what Edward Said has called "Orientalism."[5] Buddhism was informed by Christian presuppositions from the time of the pioneering work of missionaries who described Asian religious practice by seeking answers to questions formed within their own belief systems.[6] The inappropriate parameters and vocabulary of translation established in this way were reinforced when Asian Buddhist apologists responded to missionary questions and criticisms in these terms. On this basis of compromised understanding, the study of Buddhism began in Ceylon in the early decades of the nineteenth century, initiated by a combination of the missionary imperative to "know the enemy" and the colonial administration's documentation of its subjects. In Ceylon, site of the first academic study of Buddhism, the interpretation of Buddhism, its definition, became a matter of direct political and economic importance by the mid-nineteenth century because of the particular relationship between the British government and the Buddhist *sangha* that arose out of their treaty agreement. The publications that emerged from this contest were subsumed into Orientalist knowledge when Buddhism moved from being a matter of restricted local interest to a subject of academic discourse. From the third quarter of the nineteenth century when it was deemed there were sufficient "correct opinions of Buddhism, as to its doctrines and practices,"[7] that is, to extract its "essence" by comparative study of local manifestations, Buddhism became a resource not only for the comparative study of religion and the racial, imperial, and evolutionary themes encompassed by this new field of academic endeavor, but for the crucial debates of the period over the conflict between religion and science, the search for a nontheistic system of morality, a humanistic religion. Once introduced to the academic arena, Buddhism was defined, the object of discourse formed, through the concatenation of its deployment in these contests of essentially Western concern. As a result it was thoroughly imbued with Western preoccupations and presuppositions.

The very term "Buddhism" is a consequence of Christian scholars following the biblical analogy of Christianity's relation to Christ and implies a distorting dependence on the historical existence of the Buddha as founder of the religion. Christianity depended on the life and teachings of Christ; Buddhism was assumed to depend on the life and teachings of Sakyamuni. That the title "Buddha" (literally, "Awakened One") is commonly used as Sakyamuni's personal name, is a consequence of this. Although the emphasis Christo-centric scholarship places on the particular historical teacher is at odds with the Asian focus on the *arya dharma*—the eternal teaching—it is nevertheless indicative of the role Buddhism played in late nineteenth-century Western thought.

More than any other non-Christian religion, Buddhism was the "other" of Christianity, not only because of its academic history but also because of the dilemma it posed. It was both superficially similar—its moral teachings almost identical—and fundamentally different. The significant "other," the external against which one defines oneself, is not simply radically different but also similar enough to make effective comparison: within a general frame of similarity, the self and other differ on the essential points of definition. At a time when scientific knowledge brought into question ideas of an immortal soul, of an interventionist God, Buddhism was discussed and thereby defined in terms of absence of soul, absence of a creator God, absence of divine wrath, absence of a Savior. For missionaries, these "absences" provided legitimation for their imperative to convert the natives. But for others the principal features of Buddhism reflected those aspects of orthodox Christian doctrine inconsistent with scientific knowledge.

Christian critics of Buddhism typically described it in terms of these negations, but so did Buddhism's Western supporters. They saw the doctrine of *anātman*, understood as a denial of the existence of soul, as evidence of Buddhism's concurrence with the new psychology. Buddhism's denial of a creator God accommodated evolutionary theory and materialist philosophy. The point is that, although the interpretations were contested, the characteristics themselves were not, and through their repetition in the ongoing debates, they were reinforced as truth. "Buddhism," as it was known in the West at the time of the Parliament, was constituted by the combination of statements emerging from points of contest in widely different fields, its truth determined not by its observed fit with any Asian reality but by the repetition and reinforcement of statements as they circulated and became "invested, colonized, utilized, involuted, transformed, displaced, selected by ever more general mechanisms" of the technologies of truth.[8] Because Buddhism was defined through this process of Christian soul searching and redefinition, it occupied a unique place in the Parliament, the exhibition of nineteenth-century religious development.

The process of circulation and reinterpretation of enunciations from which Buddhism emerged implies an ongoing contest, which keeps the object, like the discourse itself, in a state of flux, its shape momentarily dependent on the cumulative state of the innumerable and diverse contests. Its "permanence," the recognized general features amid the points of difference and dispute that always exist, depends upon the overall effect of the "mobilities," the points of contest. But this is neither a random nor chance accumulation. It is, as already indicated, dependent on the existing intellectual climate, the fields of discourse within which the statements circulate, and it is controlled, or at least directed, by processes that might broadly be called the role of social convention in the constitution of knowledge. These include the cult of expertise and the professions that determine the authority to speak on a subject, the protocols of scholarship and presentation that must be conformed to for a work to be taken seriously, the rules of the various academic disciplines that determine what subjects may be spoken about and what questions are suitable to ask. Rules such as these shaped Western academic Buddhism by directing the selection of the Pali texts as the source of Buddhist knowledge, directing the decision to translate sutras in preference to commentaries, and directing the choice of which sutras from the vast canon would be given priority. Rules of scholarship then determined which parts of the texts were to be taken as the Buddha's actual speech and, conversely, which parts were to be excluded as later interpolations and denied recognition as part of Buddhist belief.

Rules of Western scholarship had also determined that Japanese Buddhism remained virtually unknown as late as 1893, excluded from serious consideration by Orientalist emphasis on "essences" and "origins." Although Buddhism had been introduced into scholarly circles through Rhys Davids's Hibbert Lectures in 1881 (also published) and popularized through Edwin Arnold's immensely successful *Light of Asia* (1879), Japanese Buddhism was regarded as nothing more than a local expression of the universal essence captured by Western scholarship and its scientific study of the Pali texts. As a form of Mahayana Buddhism, it was necessarily a later and therefore aberrant form of the teachings of the historical Buddha. Challenging this assumption was one of the specific aims of the Japanese Buddhist delegation. It was also one of the difficulties the delegation faced as similar technologies of truth governed the conduct of the World's Parliament of Religions, determining, among other things, who might speak on Buddhism, what questions might be addressed by the speakers, and which parts of a speech represent its "essence" to be preserved in the official record. In the published record of the proceedings Japanese Buddhism was again marginalized by academic protocol governing how these representations were to be documented, presented, and assessed.

Of Orientalists and Orientalism

The Buddhist scholars T. W. Rhys Davids and F. Max Muller, and the various scholars of the Pali Text Society, were unquestionably great Orientalists in the pre-Saidian sense of dedicated scholars who devoted their lives to the serious and meticulous study of Asian-language texts. They provided the foundations of Buddhist studies to the present. They are, to use Hallisey's term, "inaugural heroes" to whom all of us in Buddhist studies owe a great deal. Their work was also, however, archetypically Orientalist. My examination of the genesis and circulation of the knowledge they produced in this period of unquestioned dominance and emerging Asian modernities is not intended to detract from their achievement, but to illustrate the effects of the technologies of truth and the dynamics of discourse.

Following the pattern identified by Said, the representation of Buddhism resulting from nineteenth-century Orientalist scholarship, including that of Rhys Davids and Max Muller, became part of the apparatus for dominating, restructuring, and maintaining authority over various Asian Buddhist states by defining the norm against which Buddhist practice was judged, and by which the relative value of Buddhist thought against European philosophy was measured. Western scholarship both created the object and assessed its value. Although the construct did not correspond with any Asian reality, it nevertheless functioned as the truth of Buddhism. It was an intrinsic part of Western knowledge actively participating in the ongoing religious debates. This was its reality. Paradoxically, however, this also gave it value to Asian Buddhist reformers.

Orientalist Scholarship and Asian Buddhist Modernities

Although the late nineteenth century was a period of unquestioned Western dominance, it was also a time of emerging Asian modernity. In Ceylon, Thailand, and Japan, the three Buddhist nations represented at the Parliament, Buddhist reform leaders, well aware of the limitations of the Western academic construct of Buddhism as a representation of their beliefs, used it to their own local advantage. Its most important function was in providing a model and basis for a rationalized interpretation of indigenous religion, an interpretation that reconciled traditional religion with the changes that had accompanied modernization. It was an interpretation validated by the standards of Western scholarship and therefore acceptable to the Western-educated elites of Asia, useful in attracting their support to Buddhist revival. Western Buddhist scholarship was also an aid in defense against Christian imperialism, a ready resource in countering Christian criticism, and in claiming the superiority of Buddhism as a religion compatible with a scientific world view. "Buddhism" as it existed in Western texts in the late nineteenth century was reinterpreted by Asian Buddhists to demonstrate the superiority of their religion over that of the West. Western scholarship gave them "proof" that Sakyamuni was a greater philosopher than any individual European, his system of thought more complete. It was evidence that Asia—here the term functioned to allow the delegates of Ceylon and Japan to share in the Indian achievement—had achieved this level of philosophical development two thousand years before Europe. Pali scholarship provided Theravada states with a rationalized, scientific interpretation of their religion.

Although this appropriation was not so readily achieved in Mahayana Japan, the techniques of this Orientalist scholarship and the model of its product were used in the formation of a new rationalized interpretation of Buddhism, *shin bukkyō* (new Buddhism). *Shin bukkyō* was yoked to nationalism by Inoue Enryō, a founding member of the nationalist organization, Seikyōsha, and of the more specifically Buddhist nationalist organization, Sonnō hōbutsu daidōdan. Both societies emerged in the late 1880s amid reaction against the previous period of indiscriminate Westernization and concern over Western encroachment. Both societies urged that defense against Western imperialism depended on developing a strong national spirit. The previous tendency to imitate the West would never win international respect. Only by maintaining an independent national identity could Japan hope to deal with world powers as equals. Modern Japan had to be defined in distinction from the West. The Seikyōsha therefore looked within Japanese tradition for something unique that would be internationally esteemed.

Inoue offered Buddhism. It was a logical candidate, he argued, because it had been the basis of Japanese culture for centuries but, more important, it was the one product of Japan that exceeded anything available in the West. It not only contained all the truth of Western philosophy but brought it to its full development. More than this, it resolved the conflict between religion, science, and philosophy. Inoue's study of contemporary Western thought convinced him that the truth contained in Japanese Buddhism was the culmination of Western intellectual evolution. His observation of Western interest in Pali Buddhism convinced him that Western intellectuals were seeking an alternative to Christianity and would welcome the greater profundity of Japanese Mahayana Buddhism. By taking Buddhism to the West, Japan would win international prestige and recognition of its spiritual and intellectual achievements. Reviving Buddhism would strengthen the Japanese spirit and defend the nation. To achieve this Inoue needed to enlist the support of "young men of talent and education" (his expression), the Western-educated elite of Japan, and this required that the Japanese Buddhism he offered was acceptable in terms of the dominant rational criteria of the time. Inoue wrote that he had gone to the West to find the truth, but that having found it there he then recognized that it had existed in the East for three thousand years. His stated mission was to share this revelation, to convince intellectuals that Japanese Buddhism was the equal of Western philosophy, superior to Western religion and completely in accord with Western science. This was also the mission of the delegation to Chicago.

The task that both Inoue and the delegates faced in conveying this message was to relate Japanese Buddhism to the Western construct that privileged the Theravada of the Pali texts. They needed to show that Japanese Buddhism encompassed all of the truth of the Theravada—that is, all those aspects of Buddhism which had attracted contemporary Western approval—but that Theravada, Southern Buddhism, was no more than a provisional and introductory expression of the Buddha's teachings, which were more completely expressed in the Mahayana texts, and specifically in Buddhism as it had been developed in Japan. For the delegates to Chicago addressing a Western audience, this also involved dissociating Japanese Buddhism from the then much maligned Northern Buddhism, the Mahayana of the Himalayan regions. Eastern Buddhism, a term coined for the occasion, was the culmination of Sakyamuni's teaching, and the most suitable candidate for the universal religion of the future.

Defining Eastern Buddhism

The Japanese delegation defined Eastern Buddhism as a new category of Buddhism but one that nevertheless depended on existing Western knowledge, which provided the discursive elements that were appropriated, reinterpreted, denied, extended. One problem, however, was that the Japanese delegates were not the only voices contributing to the representation of Buddhism at the Parliament. First there were other Buddhists: the Sinhalese lay preacher, Anagārika Dharmapāla, and His Royal Highness Prince Chandradat Chudhadharn of Siam, both presented papers on Theravada Buddhism with deliberate reference to the dominant Western interpretation as incorporated into their local Buddhist revival. As well as this, and in spite of the Parliamentary regulation that permitted only qualified representatives of each religion to speak, Buddhism—in its function as the "other" of Christianity—was discussed or referred to by Christian theologians, scholars of comparative religion, and Christian missionaries. Here again, the task of the Japanese delegates was to lift Japanese Buddhism above the criticisms of Christians and Western Pali-centered scholarship, not disputing, for example, Western descriptions of Theravada as nihilistic, pessimistic, and world-renouncing, but disclaiming these as characteristics of Eastern Buddhism. Nevertheless, because Eastern Buddhism was presented through its relation to existing knowledge of Buddhism, the accumulated result was that the Christian-related parameters of the existing construct were reinforced and validated by the Parliament. Mahayana Buddhism remained marginal, at least in the short term.

Oriental Participation in Orientalism

The Japanese Buddhist delegation did not succeed in arousing an interest in Eastern Buddhism among academics whose studies remained tied to the Pali and Sanskrit sources. Nor did the delegation alter the views of Christian proselytizers who remained content with the existing atheistic, nihilistic interpretation, which better served their purpose of demonstrating Christian excellence. One person whose attention it did manage to attract, however, was Paul Carus. Carus was inspired by the world-affirming, scientific presentation of Eastern Buddhism to return to existing Western Buddhist scholarship and compile his *Gospel of Buddha*, an archetypical Orientalist exercise using Buddhism to promote his post-Kantian Christian monism.

Carus's book, though a popular success, was treated with disdain by Buddhist scholars. Why, therefore, was this idiosyncratic interpretation of Buddhism translated into Japanese and published in Japan? The answer confirms the strategic value of Western Buddhist scholarship in the discourse of Buddhist nationalism. Japanese Buddhists, well aware of the limitations of the book as a source of knowledge of Buddhism, used it to their own indigenous advantage. The publication, however, had unforeseen repercussions in the West, where it was promoted as an endorsement of Carus's book by practicing Buddhists, giving the work an authority it could not otherwise have claimed. Consequently, the Japanese publication, intended in large part to convince a Japanese audience that Western intellectuals were interested in the Mahayana, reinforced the entrenched Pali construct. The Orient participated in Orientalism.

This incident, one of several dealt with on the theme, exemplifies one of the problems with much of the work on Western images of Japan, which typically reproduces the Eurocentrism it purportedly reveals by looking at Japan as an object of exclusively Western discourse, and consequently by neglecting Asian agency. The exclusion that was central to Said's concept—the idea that the dominant West spoke for the passive East, the West denied the East a voice, represented it in ways determined by the West—was only a partial description of the dynamics of discourse, one that was well suited to Said's own project of emphasizing the wrong done to the Middle East, but it has serious limitations. It misses the much more important function of Orientalism as a particular example of the consequences of a number of functions of alterity: the various ways in which one society uses, speaks about, and consequently forms images of others. Orientalism is not, after all, a particularly Western sin but a case study of the more general process of the way one culture forms images of another. This happens not so much as the result of consciously directed efforts to represent reality but as a consequence of multiple processes of discourse. Occidentalism, a term that might be used to describe Asian recourse to the West as a resource for various domestic strategies, was not simply an inversion of Orientalism. The crucial difference in Meiji Japan, as elsewhere in Asia in the late nineteenth and early twentieth centuries, was the importance of the West even in countries such as Japan that were not under colonial rule, as model and judge of the modern, and its prestige among the Western-educated Asian elites. Asian nationalist imperatives fostered Asian participation in Western discourse. Considering the formation of Orientalist knowledge as an engagement restores agency to Asia, and some of the complexity of the Foucauldian origins of Said's insights to the process. It makes the colonial domination a factor in the process rather than its determining mode.

Zen for Americans and Other Histories

Carus's interest in Eastern Buddhism had consequences far beyond the publication of *The Gospel of Buddha*. He is remembered most particularly for his part in fostering American interest in Buddhism through his own writings, through his continuing contacts with the Buddhist delegates, and in opening the way for D. T. Suzuki's long career as interpreter of Mahayana Buddhism and the transmission of Zen to the West. Suzuki's presence in La Salle and the work that he produced there, which led to the Zen boom of the 1960s and to the present strength and variety of Zen in America and overseas, were a direct consequence of the delegation to Chicago. This, too, is a story of politically determined discursive interventions, of East-West interaction, of an Orientalist gaze that sees only what is relevant to its present preoccupations, of appropriation, deployment, and interpretation. Until recently, it was usually told in hagiographic mode, the story of but one of the delegates, Zen Patriarch Shaku Sōen, and focusing on but one of the two papers he presented, "The Law of Cause and Effect as Taught by the Buddha."[9] The concern to elevate a spiritual leader above the "contamination" of politics reduced this important historical figure to little more than a link in the chain of transmission leading to American Zen. The narrative so focused overlooked the other members of the delegation, and the North American Protestant context of the Parliament. It was unconcerned with the significance of the delegation in Meiji Japan. It minimized the exposition context to enhance the seriousness of the Parliament as an international conference on religion.[10]

Japanese accounts of the delegation at the Parliament, like South Asian accounts of the Indian Vivekananda and the Sinhalese Dharmapāla, also neglected the exposition context, preferring to present the event as an academic conference, a serious gathering of religious specialists. The point of their accounts of the event was that the West took Eastern religion seriously; not that the thousands of people who packed into halls to hear the Asian representatives may have had no more interest in the Parliament than in any of the other novel and colorfully dressed exotic sideshows. The atmosphere of the Parliament was less than academic. Vivekananda's opening words, "Brothers and Sisters of America," brought on four minutes of applause and cheering, suggesting that expressions of brotherhood, not information on Hindu doctrine, was what America wanted to hear. This impression is confirmed by the total neglect of the much more informative paper by the official Hindu representative, Professor Manilal N. D'Vivedi. The most popular of the Japanese speakers was similarly not one of the high-ranking abbots explaining Mahayana thought, but the layman Hirai Kinzō. His attack on Christian missionary aggression and impassioned quotation of the American Declaration of Independence drew wild applause from the public visitors to the fair.

Although South Asian historians frequently refer to the role of the Parliament in South Asian nationalism, the idea that the Parliament may have played a similar function in Japanese history had not been considered until James Ketelaar's study.[11] This omission was partly a consequence of the preoccupation of earlier studies with Shaku Sōen and the transmission of Zen, but it was also part of the neglect of the political role of Japanese Buddhism in general, and the modern Western assumption that religion belonged to the private sphere, divorced from the realms of politics and economics. Buddhist clergy engaging in these activities were considered "secularized" or "corrupt."[12] The history of Buddhism, isolated by this inappropriate dichotomy from the society in which it functioned, became largely the history of Buddhist doctrine, a history of ideas, focusing on the development of schools and the teachings of the masters. This tendency is a feature of histories of religions in general but was exacerbated here by Western emphasis on Buddhism as an otherworldly tradition dedicated to personal salvation. As McMullin describes it, Buddhism, "possibly more than any other tradition . . . has been religionized, doctrinalized, spiritualized, 'otherworldly'ized, and individualized in ways and to degrees that simply do not fit the classical Buddhist case but that do fit the case of some modern Western views of religion."[13] The history of Buddhism, he continues, borrowing from Pierre Bourdieu's comments on art history, "finds in the sacred character of its object every pretext for a hagiographic hermeneutics superbly indifferent to the question of the social conditions in which works are produced and circulate."[14] The writings of McMullin, Herman Ooms, and Collcutt addressed this problem for Buddhism in the medieval and early modern periods;[15] Grappard, Collcutt, Thelle, Ketelaar, and Jaffe for the Meiji.[16]

The study of Meiji Buddhism was also marginalized by the emphasis on doctrine and its development, which direct focus to the points of "origin" recognized in the entry of schools from China (the Nara schools, Tendai and Shingon, Zen) or the development of new sects (the Pure Land Schools, Nichiren). Meiji Buddhism was dismissed as a deterioration or Westernization, of no relevance in the search for the "real" Japanese belief or its evolution. The first study of Meiji Buddhism was Kathleen Staggs's unpublished thesis on the writings of two leaders of the Meiji Buddhist revival, Inoue Enryō and Murakami Senshō, which dealt with their work as responses to the intellectual and doctrinal challenges to Buddhism at this time.[17] This was followed by Notto Thelle's *Buddhism and Christianity in Japan*, which situated Buddhism in Meiji history, showing its role in connection with the state and society, as he traced the transition in the relationship between Buddhism and Christianity in Japan from the bitter conflict of early Meiji to the development of tolerant dialogue in the late 1890s. Thelle includes a chapter on the delegation to the World's Parliament of Religions but sees little significance in the event for the dialogue in Japan apart from the confidence it gave Japanese Buddhists in the sincerity of the Christian belief in the brotherhood of religions, which contributed to an atmosphere of greater tolerance.[18] It was, for Thelle, yet another example of Buddhist action inspired by Christians.

Without doubt, the most significant work on the Japanese delegation to Chicago to date is Ketelaar's *Of Heretics and Martyrs in Meiji Japan: Buddhism and Its Persecution*. This work provides an account of the formation of Meiji Buddhism from the intellectual attacks of the late Tokugawa and early Meiji periods, when Buddhism was deemed a non-Japanese heresy, to the 1890s, when it became a resource for Japanese national identity, the spirit of Japanese civilization. Ketelaar deals with the Chicago delegation as an episode in the projection of Japanese Buddhism as a universal religion, a strategy in the reconstruction of Buddhism. His argument is that the delegation served as a performance, an opportunity for the delegates to "re-present" the event to the Japanese audience, to demonstrate that Japanese Buddhism, by its inclusion in the World's Parliament of Religions and its acceptance in the West, was a universal religion. It was, to use his term, a gesture of "strategic occidentalism" in the battle over the future of religion in Meiji Japan. This is very much my own position, but as my concern is with the formation of Western knowledge, I would like to push beyond this aspect of the delegation and consider it also as a serious and organized attempt to intervene in the Western discourse on Buddhism—an attempt to modify Western perceptions. I consider the delegation as a simultaneous intervention in both discourses; my focus is precisely the discursive interaction inherent in the project.[19]

The field has shifted since I first envisaged the project.[20] Ketelaar has situated the delegation to Chicago within the revival of Meiji Buddhism; Thelle has documented the political importance of tension between Christianity and Buddhism in Meiji history; and Seager has situated the Parliament in the context of the Chicago exposition and North American history. More recently, Prothero's book on Henry Steel Olcott's career in Asia and Martin Verhoeven's study of Paul Carus have taken their contribution to Western understanding of Buddhism seriously. My aim is to show how these various arenas of activity interacted to create Japanese Buddhism as an object of Western knowledge. How did the representation of Japanese Buddhism in Chicago 1893 relate to Meiji Japan, to Japan's changing position in the international arena, and to the particular event, the World's Parliament of Religions at the Columbian Exposition? What were the implications of this for Buddhism in the West?

CHAPTER

JAPAN FACES THE WEST

For the United States of America, the four hundredth anniversary of Columbus's journey to the New World marked the emergence of the modern nation as an international power. At the Columbian Exposition America projected the extent of its material achievement in the vast scale of the exposition with its monumental buildings, displays of art, manufacture, and technology. The exposition was consciously organized as an "object lesson" in Social Darwinism, popularizing and propagating evolutionary ideas of race and progress. The United States was placed in this display as the representation of modern achievement and the culmination of white, European racial superiority.[1]

Japan's project at the exposition was essentially to challenge its assigned place in this arrangement, distancing itself from the Western stereotype of Asian nations as colonial and undeveloped, and realigning itself among the sovereign nations of the international community. For Japan the reality of Western dominance was embodied in the "unequal treaties" that had been imposed upon it decades earlier by Western nations; in the continuing refusal of the treaty powers to grant concessions; and in the perception that favorable revision depended on demonstrating the "equality" of Japanese civilization with that of the West. Treaty powers not only controlled Japanese tariff rates but set the rules by which Japanese civilization was to be judged. Without overemphasizing the importance of the Japanese exhibition at Chicago in the campaign for treaty revision, I argue that it was a supplement to the long-term, intense diplomatic negotiations, an exercise in public relations.

Japan's challenge to nineteenth-century Western assumptions of cultural superiority was most clearly articulated in the Hōōden, the official Japanese Pavilion, a stunning display of architecture and art. The project, however, also informed Japan's extensive participation in other aspects of the exposition, including the representation of Buddhism at the World's Parliament of Religions. Although participation in this project only partially accounts for the aims of the Japanese Buddhist delegation, it was an important determinant in the representation of religion.

This chapter considers the representation of Japan projected in the Hōōden, considering the building as a statement, visual rather than verbal, but nonetheless an attempt at communication, planned as a tactical intervention in a number of simultaneous discourses involving Japan and its relationship with the West and with other Asian nations, and in establishing its position within the international arena. It indicates the parameters of Japan's project, identifies some of its principal aims, and indicates problems in communication. These parameters, aims, and problems, which are readily apparent in the planning, representation, and reading of the supposedly transparent communication of Japanese material culture, point to less easily identified parallels in the representation of Japanese Buddhism in the West.

Treaty Revision and the Chicago Exposition

Japanese speeches and publications connected with the exposition, from the first introduction by the Japanese commissioner at Washington to the dedication ceremony of the Hōōden, stressed the issue of the treaties and related the Japanese exhibit to Japan's desire for their revision. Revision of the treaty agreements between Japan and a number of Western nations, agreements inherited from the Tokugawa *bakufu*, had been the overriding concern of the Meiji government since it came to power in 1868, affecting both domestic and foreign policy.[2] The initial treaties had been drawn up at a time when the West considered Asian countries to be "beyond the pale of international law," that is, the law of the international Christian community.[3] The treaties with Japan followed the models of Western treaties with undeveloped and colonial states. Hence they not only imposed inappropriate restraints on Japan's judicial and economic sovereignty but also burdened Japan with a status inferior to that of the "civilized" nations of the world. Equal treaties were as much the mark of a modern state as political, social, and economic reorganization. They were the mark of international recognition. By the 1890s the powers concerned generally recognized that the treaties should be revised. This was partly because Meiji reforms had brought Japanese institutions such as government, education, law, and the military into line with Western requirements, but, at least in Great Britain's view, also because of Japan's strategic location as an ally against Russian expansion in the Far East.[4] By this time the discussion between Japan and the treaty powers was essentially a matter of negotiating concessions.

One of the main obstacles to treaty revision was the problem of extraterritoriality under which foreign nationals in Japan were not subject to Japanese law. Treaty powers were reluctant to withdraw this right of consular jurisdiction until Japan adopted and enforced a system of jurisprudence and judicial administration "in harmony with that of Christian powers." That is, they were reluctant to place their nationals under non-Christian law.[5] Extraterritoriality had originated from the West's desire to protect its nationals from punishments considered cruel and barbarous.[6] The clause therefore not only impinged on Japan's sovereignty but gave it little control and no legal rights over foreigners who were increasingly circumventing the restriction on travel outside treaty ports. It also carried the stigma of "barbarism." Unfortunately, law had proved to be a most difficult area of reform. The new code of civil law had been rejected in 1892 amid a public outcry against the inappropriate application of law based on the French theory of individual rights to a society where the idea of duty was paramount.[7] The exposition project, already under way at this time, became even more important as an exercise in public relations.

While fully aware of the economic advantages of participating in world expositions, such as the opportunity to increase trade and develop new markets, the Japanese government also saw participation in the Chicago fair as a chance to influence Western public opinion in its favor. As Tateno Gozo, Japanese minister to Washington, wrote in an introductory article preceding the fair, here was a chance to come into contact with "intelligent thinking people" and prove that Japan "no longer deserves to labour under the incubus which circumstances forced upon her."[8] The exercise was not without precedent. When Tateno explained that participation in previous expositions had demonstrated to the Japanese the power of public opinion in America, he may well have been referring to the American response to the exhibition of Japanese antiques at the Philadelphia

Centennial Exposition in 1876. As one visitor wrote, "We have been accustomed to regard that country as uncivilized, or half-civilized at the best but here we found abundant evidences that it outshines the most cultivated nations of Europe in arts which are their pride and glory."[9]

Neil Harris observes that Japan became a beneficiary of the cultural rivalry between America and Europe. "Americans seemed to take pleasure in the fact that Europe's boasted antiquity was dwarfed by this visitor from the East. The Orient could be used to strike back at the pretensions of the Old World, which for so long had reminded Americans of their youth and lack of cultivation." In the opinion of the visitors to the fair, the elegance and workmanship of eight-hundred-year-old Japanese crafts rivaled the highest achievements of Italian art, and moreover, Japanese crafts showed no evidence of the decline or degeneracy apparent in the later periods of European art. The display at Philadelphia stimulated some Americans to demand the return of the $750,000 indemnity paid to the United States when Japanese fired on an American ship at Shimonoseki.[10]

The invitation to participate in the Chicago fair arrived during the first session of the newly formed Diet and, as Tateno related, it was welcomed as an opportunity to make the statement that now, twenty-five years into the modernization of the Meiji period, Japan was "worthy of full recognition in the family of nations," and though at that time "determined to cut public expenditure . . . the Diet was prepared to immediately appropriate whatever sum might be necessary for the purpose."[11]

> Without challenging the rightfulness of the restrictions which were imposed upon them when the treaties were made, the Japanese people feel that the necessity for those restrictions has entirely passed away. The burden which still remains may seem light to others; to them it is an ever present reminder of the fact that all they accomplished is incomplete so long as this unnecessary, incumbering vestige of the past remains. Therefore, it is just that they welcome the Columbian Exposition as one means of proving that they have attained a position worthy of the respect and confidence of other nations.[12]

The Japanese presentation at Chicago was, from the beginning, strictly controlled by an imperial commission headed by Mutsu Munemitsu, initially as minister of agriculture and commerce, and then from August 1892 as foreign minister. According to Perez, Mutsu was said to have spent "virtually every waking hour" pondering the problem of treaty renewal and its possible solution.[13] Unfortunately, Perez does not mention Mutsu's role in organizing the Chicago presentation, but he does confirm that Mutsu held a strong belief in the power of public opinion to influence government action and skillfully used the press to develop it, characteristics that are evident in Mutsu's autobiography, *Kenkenroku*.[14] Although treaty revision depended on demonstrating that Japan was the equal of Western nations, the early 1890s of Meiji Japan was a time of intense reaction against the indiscriminate over-Westernization of the previous decade. The presentation of modern, technological Japan at the exposition was therefore accompanied by a very strong statement of the continuing vitality and high achievement of indigenous Japanese civilization. The Hōōden was the centerpiece of this statement. The Japanese were "above all, determined to maintain their national prestige."[15] Mutsu's role in this project was indicated by his announcement in the *Japan Weekly Mail*, October 1891, that no Japanese exhibit would be permitted unless authorized by the Japanese government to ensure that only articles "truly Japanese" would be displayed.

Japanese culture was to be seen as unique and equally "civilized," but what does being "civilized" mean? To the late nineteenth-century West, the targeted audience—its imperial power and confidence supported by belief in the theories of evolution that saw the races of the world in an ordered line of ascent from the primitive to the modern Western type—to be "cultured" or "civilized" meant to measure up to a European norm in standards of intellectual, artistic, and material achievement. This assumption of Western superiority was evident in all nineteenth-century expositions, but never more than at Chicago. The lesson of the fair, we are told by its chroniclers, was that each nation could see its position in the hierarchy thus displayed.[16] The clearest example of this hierarchy was the Midway Plaisance of the fair, which appears in the bird's-eye view as a long corridor to the side of the main concourse (see fig. 8). This was the popular carnival sector of the exposition. It was here, along with the sideshows and amusements, that most of the Asian and Third World countries were represented. Some of the more popular attractions were the street in Cairo, the Dahomey village, the Javanese village, and the Eskimos, living exhibits in an anthropological display that illustrated the "progress of man" through a racial hierarchy that culminated in the modern Western type.[17] The Midway Plaisance was "a world gallery," a "voyage round the world and down time," where "one could drop back through every stage of humanity, European, Asiatic, African until he reaches the animal in Hegenbeck's menagerie."[18] Or alternately, as the same writer observed, the Midway could be "viewed in ascending manner culminating in the Exposition proper."[19] The "Exposition proper" was, of course, the White City, evidence of America's supreme position in the hierarchy. The fair was a vast anthropological object lesson in the ascent of man and the Darwinian justification of Western dominance.

Japan's participation in earlier international expositions had already raised the problem of its rightful position in the hypothetical line of ascent. However, although the American public was willing to consider the idea that Japanese culture may be a "high" culture, approval was ultimately reserved. It was, after all, an Oriental culture, and in the words of one critic, "We must have standards, and Europe is that standard."[20] Japan's problem, therefore, was that in order to communicate to a Western audience the "equality" of Japanese civilization, that is, Japan's right to a position within the hierarchy of development as elevated as that of Europe, its statement had to conform to European categories of value. Perhaps the easiest way to illustrate the problem is to compare the American presentation at the fair with that of Japan. Both these nations used the event to challenge the assumption of European superiority. In Japan's case the term "European" was meant in the wider sense of "European" as opposed to "Oriental," a term that included America.[21]

America and the Westward Progress of Civilization

The Columbian Exposition was held to mark the four hundredth anniversary of Columbus's discovery of the New World.[22] For the United States of America, this anniversary marked a "coming of age." It was an opportunity to demonstrate that America was no longer a "country cousin," but a mature, independent, modern nation. In the vast edifices of the exposition and the displays of art, manufacture, and technology they contained, America showed that its material achievement was unequaled; by the inclusion of the Auxiliary Congresses, a series of conferences on matters of spiritual, intellectual, and social concern, the United States established its intellectual credentials. In a total commitment to prevailing views on progress, the exposition at large proclaimed America's material and technological supremacy, while the congresses, under the banner "Not Things but Men; Not Matter but Mind," claimed the necessarily accompanying spiritual and intellectual development.

The Columbian anniversary was also an appropriate occasion to celebrate America's divinely ordained place in world history, a vision encapsulated in a proposal for a commemorative Dome of Columbus (fig. 1). The scale of the

Figure 1. The Dome of Columbus (Cutler, *The World's Fair*, 531)

dome is vast, designed with more consideration for numerical symbolism than economy or function. The pedestal, 1,492 feet by 1,892 feet, linked the year of Columbus's epic journey to that of the exposition. That the occasion was the four hundredth anniversary of the journey was recorded in the four-hundred-foot radius of the hemisphere that rose out of the pedestal. A colossal figure of Columbus, more than six hundred feet above the ground, pointed down to his achievement, his journey represented by a line drawn across the map on the surface of the dome. The map itself was curiously oriented, inverting European primacy by placing the Americas at the apex of the world, or as close to it as possible while remaining in the view of a prehelicopter audience. Columbus's journey from Spain read as an ascent: European man reached his culmination in the United States of America. The juxtaposition of the Italian Renaissance–style pedestal and the Temple of Liberty surmounting the dome showed American civilization rising out of the pinnacle of European cultural achievement to attain even greater heights. America stood at the summit of the world, representing the accumulated accomplishments of European civilization, and declared its continuity with the classical tradition of Europe, the essential premise for the claim to represent its culmination, through the appropriation of architectural styles. "The new world was the heir of all ages."[23]

America had been charged by God with the task of assisting in the natural and preordained unfolding of providential history by carrying the benefits of its civilization—post-Reformation Christianity and its democratic institutions—westward, extending the path of Columbus's journey. America had been "kept intact" until "a new light for the social and political life of mankind began to ray out from the open Bible in the hands of Luther." In this pristine environment God taught the chosen people "through the life developed here." The result was the American republican ideal in which men were "free to govern themselves in the light of reason and Revelation."[24] In the earlier years of the colony the idea of divine mission had inspired and justified the pioneers in their conquest of the continent. In 1893—just two years after the Wounded Knee massacre—this "self-abnegating world responsibility"[25] directed American vision across the Pacific.

The Dome of Columbus depicted this expansionist interpretation of America's vision of Manifest Destiny, a literal depiction of John L. O'Sullivan's image of "establish[ing] on earth the noblest temple ever dedicated to the worship of the Most High. . . . Its floor shall be a hemisphere—its roof the firmament of the star-studded heavens."[26] Here the temple, the republican ideal, stands at the end of the Atlantic journey, claiming the Western Hemisphere as its domain. Within a decade Theodore Roosevelt was to declare that "the Mediterranean era died with the discovery of America; the Atlantic era is now at the height of its development and must soon exhaust the resources at its command; the Pacific era, destined to be the greatest of all, is just at its dawn."[27]

Pacific expansion was not a new idea. The Christian Gospel had been carried to Hawaii in 1820, accompanied by American secular institutions, schools, and the press. An American-inspired constitution was bestowed upon the islands in 1887. In January 1893, amid rhetoric of bringing "stability, honesty and vigor to government" accompanied by economic incentives such as privileged access to a subsidized sugar market, America was involved in the deposition of Queen Liliuokalani. Hawaii's annexation to the United States followed in 1898.

An editorial in the *Japan Weekly Mail* (July 15, 1893) strongly protesting the racial and legal injustice of the constitution shows how contentious American domination of Hawaii was in Japan at the time of the exposition. As the article explained, the constitution of 1887 abrogated conditions of the Japan-Hawaii treaty of 1871, which had unconditionally guaranteed Japanese residents in Hawaii all privileges enjoyed by the citizens or subjects of any other power. The new constitution restricted franchise to adult male residents of Hawaiian, American, or European descent. There was no justification other than racial discrimination for this exclusion of Japanese, a considerable proportion of the population of Hawaii. The American action in Hawaii was a forceful reminder to the Japanese of their second-class status in the eyes of the West, and also of American disregard for the conditions of treaty. One of the arguments for American intervention in Hawaii was the need to defend Hawaii against Japanese aggression: "Unless America annexes Hawaii Japan will do so, and that means that Hawaii would be brought under the domination of Asiatic rather than American civilization."[28] The concern to see Hawaii become "Americanized" reflected the American sense of mission, but to the Japanese it was a savage racial slur.

In the mid-nineteenth century Commodore Mathew Perry wrote of "the Japans" and "the many other islands of the Pacific" en route to the markets of China, as yet untouched by the "constant and rapid increase of the fortified ports," and the "possessions in the East of our great maritime rival, England," as America's last hope of gaining colonies.[29] Britain was perceived to be the greater threat to Hawaiian independence, but the idea of installing British civilization was less effective in stirring public reaction. Commodore Mathew Perry wrote in preparation for his expedition to Japan that expansion was imperative for "the honor of the nation and the interest of commerce." The Reverend Edward P. Baker, a missionary to Hawaii, pleaded for America to "assume control of the nation" because "if the United States does not act the part of the Good Samaritan, John Bull will," adding that "the possessor of the Hawaiian Islands will hereafter dominate the Pacific Ocean."[30] Commercial incentive, rivalry with European powers, and imperial ambition, so clearly apparent here and in the "unequal treaties" subsequently imposed upon Japan, were mingled with an ideological ambivalence toward imperialism. As a former colony itself, America was opposed in principle to imperialism, "a wicked European game."[31] In spite of the aggressive appearance of Perry's fleet, westward expansion was ideally not to be achieved through military conquest but by purchase, annexation, accession. Expansion should occur through the incorporation of states that recognized the advantages of the American republican system and desired union with it. Perry took with him a printing press as a means of counteracting "the discreditable machinations of the Dutch" and publicizing the "the extraordinary prosperity of the United States under their genial laws."[32] The expedition was to "[l]et them see from the first that [America's] coming among them is a benefit and not an evil to them."[33] Manifest Destiny, however, also carried "the responsibility of imposing upon other nations the benefits of our own,"[34] and because it was a divine mission, "savages and other enemies who resisted conversion could be righteously exterminated as creatures of Satan."[35] Territorial expansion was idealized by America's mission to share the benefits of its civilization, symbolized by the Temple of Liberty.

What does the statement of the Dome of Columbus mean when placed in the domestic context of labor wars, bankrupt farmers, the problems of post-emancipation blacks and displaced Indians, urban slums teeming with Jewish and Roman Catholic immigrants who could no longer be considered outside mainstream American life? The coherence and dominance of the white American Protestant tradition were being challenged. From this perspective the dome is a point of resistance, a reaffirmation of the triumph of America, the republican ideal, and also an exclusion of minorities from identification as American.[36] American blacks were denied participation in the fair. Their petitions for an exhibition, a building, or a separate department were all rejected. Their contribution was restricted to state displays and was subject to the approval of a white committee. American Indians were included in the ethnological department, part of the display of the customs of native peoples of the world. The dome reinforced the object lessons in racial hierarchy of the Midway. At the Chicago exposition, civilization was defined not only by the West, but by a white, Protestant Christian West.

The Dome of Columbus was not built, possibly because as Cutler, a contemporary commentator, rather sarcastically remarked, the estimated cost of $3 million "was hardly sufficiently expensive to meet the ideas of the World's Fair directors."[37] The statements it embodied were nevertheless conveyed by the actual structures of the fair, and in only marginally more subtle forms. America's Great Exposition challenged Europe's assumption of cultural superiority using the European idiom and merely attempting to outdo Europe on its own terms. The fair, held in the vibrant, new city in the heart of the American continent, rather than in the old, European-founded city of New York, was bigger and more spectacular than any previous exposition. The organizers quite specifically set out to surpass the standards set by the very successful Paris Exposition of 1889. "The country of P. T. Barnum was not about to be outdone by France."[38] The fairground was several times the area of the Paris exposition. It cost many times more. In the handbook distributed at the fair by the Department of Publicity, Europe was dwarfed by American statistics. The Manufactures Hall, the largest roofed structure ever erected, was three times larger than St. Peters, four times the size of the Colosseum in Rome, and the entire army of Russia could be mobilized on its floor.[39] Early plans to build higher than the Eiffel Tower were abandoned, and instead the first and largest Ferris wheel ever built was installed as the symbol of American ingenuity in engineering and, to an even greater extent than the dome, as the symbol of America's predestination to world supremacy.

The Ferris Wheel

For contemporary American philosopher Denton J. Snider, the Ferris wheel epitomized the spirit of America in a way that the tower could never have done (fig. 2). Towers, wrote Snider, relate to past ages, and to association with military surveillance. They are hierarchical rather than democratic, "connected with overlooking a subject people."[40] The wheel, by contrast, is the cause and symbol of democratic, political unity. The intricate construction of the Ferris wheel "hints [at] a complex social system, each little part of which fulfils its special duty and thereby works for the great common end . . . each giving and receiving aid from the whole."[41] The virtue of the American system of government, he believed, was confirmed in the existence of the wheel itself: "Only a society like the Ferris Wheel, complex, colossal, could produce the Ferris Wheel, making the same, as God made man, in its own image."[42] The Ferris wheel was also a symbol of "the grand cosmical order," its rhythmical ascent and descent in harmony with the Sun itself, "but made by human hands," and when illuminated by electric light it competed with the heavens. In all it affirmed the modern ideal, "the subjugation of physical forces to human control" through the development of science and technology.[43]

The Ferris wheel, like the Eiffel Tower, dominated the exposition site and was visible from afar, a vast symbol of the fair, the image of industrial progress, and a celebration of the ideal of independence, "the self-active spirit."[44] Snider devoted a full thirty-two pages to the symbolism of the Ferris wheel. It was for him "the culmination of the Fair," both a statement of America's ideals and its mission to world conquest in the unfolding of providential history. The great educational value of the wheel, he wrote, was that it reflected the progress of civilization. From its position on the central concourse of the Midway Plaisance—set to "roll" along its East-West axis—it looked down upon the exhibitions of other nations, its revolutions "taking a short journey around the world," a microcosmic representation of the great history of the westward progress of civilization. "In the midst of the Orientals of the Plaisance, the Ferris Wheel mounts skyward, sug-

Figure 2. The Ferris wheel (Witteman, *The World's Fair*)

gesting the triumph of the Occident and throwing out deep intimations of meaning of the New World and of the march of the Ages. . . . Do they receive from it any forewarnings of destiny, any significant foreshadowings of the World's movement?"[45]

Though accepting God's will in the inevitability of American domination across the Pacific, Snider was less insistent on the accompanying Protestant Christian mission: "The East may never take our religion, but it must take our wheel. The Orientals of the Plaisance, daily gazing and wondering at the Ferris mechanism, cannot help having some presentiment. The monster will crush them if they resist it; but it will carry them if they jump on and ride."[46]

The fair covered seven hundred acres of Jackson Park, a massive achievement in landscaping and architecture, with neoclassical buildings on a scale that could only be achieved through the use of the latest materials and engineering techniques, arranged around a system of man-made lakes and canals. Although the decision to build in the classical style did have its critics, most visitors to the fair

Figure 3. The Court of Honor (Rossiter Johnson, *A History of the World's Columbian Exposition*, 1:496)

agreed with Snider, for whom the architecture of the fair was "the last utterance of man's reason and sense of beauty."[47] The White City no less than the Dome of Columbus claimed that America, born out of the European Renaissance, was "the last word" in the development of the values of the European Enlightenment. As Snider saw it, "Little Greece had, on the whole, buildings in proportion to her size," and America's ability to master the colossal, to project the same sense of order, harmony, and moderation admired in classical Greece on this much greater scale, was clear evidence of the superiority of America, a "truly limit transcending country."[48]

On the canals of the White City Venetian gondolas, claiming the elegance and sophistication of Europe, paddled alongside the newly invented electric-powered motor launch. Ornate fountains and statuary decorated the public spaces, and sculptured figures were clustered over the facades of the vast steel-framed buildings. At night, when illuminated by electric lighting, the straw and plaster reality of the Court of Honor was transformed into a vision of marble. Technological progress compensated for America's lack of antiquity, and Chicago's White City seemed to have everything that could be found in the cities of Europe, as well as all that new technology could offer (fig. 3).

Japan and the West

The centerpiece of Japan's presentation, the object of greatest single expenditure and concern, was the Hōōden or Phoenix Pavilion (fig. 4), an exhibition of Japanese art and architecture on the Wooded Isle at the center of the fair site. The pavilion itself was planned as a historical representation of three different epochs of Japanese architecture spanning more than eight hundred years, but to borrow Ernest Fenollosa's image, the Hōōden was an "architectural casket" of Japanese art treasures.[49] The art and architecture together presented an image of the sophistication and elegance of Japanese civilization from a period four hundred years before the discovery of America to the present.

The pavilion was inspired by the Hōōdō, or Phoenix Hall, of the eleventh-century temple, the Byōdōin, at Uji, near Kyoto. The original temple is said to represent the mythical *Hōō* bird (phoenix) descending to earth, wings outstretched, the illusion of flight suggested by the combined reflection of the building and clouds in the pond immediately beside it. The pavilion in Chicago took advantage of the unusual plan, using each of the three distinct areas that constituted the building to exhibit the material culture of a different period of Japanese history, the Fujiwara, the Ashikaga, and the Tokugawa.

The pavilion, designed by the government architect Kuru Masamichi, was built in Japan and shipped to Chicago in numbered pieces for construction on site by Japanese craftsmen. The rooms did contain some representative items of antique furnishings and works of art, but the interior decoration as a whole—the painted screens, walls, ceilings, as well as many of the objects on display—was designed and executed by the Tokyo Fine Arts Academy under the direction of nationalist art historian Okakura Kakuzō. It was, therefore, not simply a historical exhibition of Japan's past achievement but also a display of the present skill and vitality of the Meiji period. The Tokyo Fine Arts Academy was an outgrowth of the revival and conservation of Japanese art that had begun a decade earlier with Ernest Fenollosa. Okakura, now more commonly known in Japan as Tenshin, had initially worked as Fenollosa's assistant and had traveled with him in 1886 on an imperial commission to study art history and museums in Europe and America. The Tokyo academy was founded to revive old techniques and develop new ones with which to express the Japanese spirit in its modern development. The Hōōden was an exhibition of "original contemporary work created for this occasion by Japan's great living artists," proving that Japanese art continued to thrive.[50] Okakura was to continue the project of the Hōōden in his

Figure 4. The Japanese Pavilion (Witteman, *The World's Fair*)

writings, *The Ideals of the East* (1903), *The Book of Tea* (1906), and *The Awakening of Japan* (1903–4).

Okakura spelled out the message of the Hōōden in the pamphlet distributed at the fair.[51] The north wing of the Hōōden (fig. 5) was constructed in the style of the Fujiwara period (897–1185) at the end of the Heian, a time when Japan was isolated from continental influence and when "the liberal patronage of the Fujiwara family brought about a renaissance of pure Japanese taste."[52] This period represented "a new development in Japanese art and culture which may be termed the *national*, in contrast to the predominating *continental* ideas of the preceding epochs."[53] The interior was copied from the personal apartment of a high-ranking courtier in the Kyoto Imperial Palace and was furnished with writing desk, incense burner, musical instruments, mirror stand and cosmetic cabinet, all articles of high culture, learning, and sophistication, suggesting a refined era when, as Okakura wrote, "the aristocracy . . . was occupied with the exchange of visits; musical and poetic gatherings, and other amusements."[54] The walls were entirely covered with paintings, and the rich brocades of the period were generously

Figure 5. The Hōōden: interior of the north wing (Okakura, *The Hōōden*; courtesy of the University of Delaware Library Special Collections)

displayed. This wing established the antiquity of Japanese sophistication by representing the state of Japanese culture centuries before the discovery of America.

The south wing (fig. 6) was in the Ashikaga style (1233–1568), the interior a reproduction "with but slight changes"[55] of rooms in the Ginkakuji in Kyoto, built in 1479. The two rooms, a library, a "place where the master of the household read, studied, or occupied himself with Buddhistic meditation,"[56] and a room furnished for the tea ceremony, show "the part played by Buddhism in restoring the tranquil state of mind to the people."[57] The Ashikaga period, Japan at the time Columbus discovered the New World, was characterized by its refined taste and exquisite detail. Paintings by the great Japanese landscape artist Sesshū, a contemporary of Christopher Columbus, were displayed in the *tokonoma*.

The central section of the pavilion was divided into rooms used for official receptions during the fair. The main space, the central hall, was a replica of a sumptuous room in Edo castle at the height of Tokugawa power (fig. 7). The other rooms were similarly ornate. The phoenix, "a decorative motive for objects of dignity and importance,"[58] was, Okakura explained, "emblematic of the peace-

Figure 6. The Hōōden: a room in the south wing (Okakura, *The Hōōden*; courtesy of the University of Delaware Library Special Collections)

ful reign of the Tokugawa Shoguns."[59] Paintings of flowers and fruit signified, the handbook tells us, progress in the arts and general prosperity.[60] These rooms projected Tokugawa Japan, Japan at the time of Commodore Perry's intrusion into Japan's isolation and the imposition of the unequal treaties, as a wealthy and peaceful nation with a flourishing, highly developed culture. The Japanese may have been willing to concede that Perry hastened Japan's entry into the modern industrial world, but these rooms challenged any American assumption that he had brought "civilization" to barbarians.

The intended historical message of the Hōōden predated the design of the building itself. An early notice of Japan's plans for the Chicago pavilion mentioned that "the building would be copied from the finest specimens of Japanese architecture extant at the time Columbus discovered America."[61] That is, the intention was always to show the high state of Japanese culture at the time of the birth of America, but in the final building the message was expanded to include the additional ideas of the great antiquity of Japanese civilization—the eight-hundred-year span is twice the period of America's celebration—and its

Figure 7. The Hōōden: interior of the central hall (Okakura, *The Hōōden*; courtesy of the University of Delaware Library Special Collections)

continuing vitality. The Fujiwara wing showed the elegance and sophistication of Japanese culture centuries before the discovery of America, the Ashikaga wing showed the state of Japanese development at the time of Columbus's discovery, and the Tokugawa wing showed the continuation of the high level of Japanese cultural tradition up to the arrival of Western influences. The ability of Meiji Japanese to recreate these achievements in Chicago was evidence that the same tradition survived in contemporary Japan.

The furnishings in each of the rooms emphasized Japan's high regard for cultural activities such as reading, writing, painting, and music, echoing the theme of the Auxiliary Congresses, "Not Things but Men; Not Matter but Mind." Japan, no less than America, wished to be known for its intellectual and spiritual achievements, the fundamental indications of "progress" and "civilization." Japan participated in a large number of congresses and also impressed the public with its displays of printing and educational textbooks. Because cultural achievements were indications of evolutionary development, Japan's message was that it had reached great heights long before Europeans arrived in the Americas.

Using art and architecture to establish its cultural credentials was only one aspect of the presentation. For Japan to align itself with the Western nations implied that it must disassociate itself from the general Western perception of "Asia," stereotyped as either undeveloped and backward or, as in the case of China, degenerate. One reason for choosing the Hōōdō, the Phoenix Hall in Uji, as a model for the pavilion may therefore be that its unique plan gave it claim to be the oldest building of indigenous Japanese inspiration.[62] If the antiquity of high culture in Japan were the only point to be made, then Hōryūji, built in A.D. 607—more than four hundred years before Byōdōin—would appear a more logical choice.[63] These earlier buildings were, however, like the Nara period in general, too easily associated with Chinese prototypes, the "continental" Okakura spoke of, rather than the "national" of the Fujiwara period.

That is, for the designers of the pavilion in Chicago, antiquity appears to have been secondary to the need to stress indigenous Japanese achievement and to separate Japanese culture from continental origins. This was not entirely possible, of course, as Okakura's guidebook acknowledges, but the presentation placed emphasis on the Japanese development of imported ideas. The complementary statement, Japan's alignment with Western nations, found physical expression in the siting of the pavilion on the Wooded Island, a coveted position at the center of the main exposition site, across the lake from the United States government building.

Positioning the Statement: The Statement of the Site

The Wooded Isle was a principal focus of the original exposition plan, to be left free of buildings, "an island in the middle of the lagoon covered with native wood, affording a charming natural landscape to relieve the formal treatment of other portions of the grounds."[64] A preserve of nature to accentuate the achievements of culture. True to this concept, the organizers resisted a number of requests for this particularly desirable space. They were, however, after a considerable amount of trouble and expense on the part of the Japanese government, persuaded to allocate an island site for the Japanese Pavilion.[65] The agreement involved undertaking to build a permanent structure worth at least $100,000 as a gift to the people of Chicago and included a Japanese commitment to maintain the buildings and their gardens permanently.[66]

Why was the site so important to Japan? The reason given in the *Japan*

Weekly Mail was that the site allocated to foreign nations was not large enough, and it was felt that the impact of the Japanese architecture would be lost if the building were to be included with European structures. Certainly the wooded setting beside the natural shoreline of the lake was a more appropriate site, but the island location did more than show the building off to advantage. Set apart as it was, but within the bounds of the central concourse of the fair, it reflected Japan's image of itself in the world as an independent and unique nation, not attempting to compete with the West in Western terms, but demanding recognition for its own achievements. Japan was different but equally civilized and, most important, was distanced from both Third World nations and the Midway Plaisance.

The central importance of the Wooded Island in the organization of the exposition is apparent in the "bird's-eye view" (fig. 8). The island is surrounded by the principal United States buildings adjoining the Court of Honor. The area designated for foreign nations lies beyond the canal on the far right of the sketch. The Midway, with the twin towers of the Chinese Pavilion in the far distance, can be seen extending from the horizon, the site of the dawn of civilization in the scheme of progress mapped by the exposition plan.

The Midway Plaisance, described earlier for its role in propagating and popularizing evolutionary ideas of race and progress, was under the direction of the exposition's Department of Ethnology, its anthropological displays scientifically validated by the participation of the Smithsonian Institute and the Peabody Museum. The displays provided ethnological sanction for the American view of the nonwhite world as barbaric and childlike.[67] It was, therefore, also an area of light relief. As an official publication put it: "The Midway Plaisance . . . offered an admirable location for the picturesque displays, characteristic of the customs of foreign nations . . . and has the advantage of isolating these special features from the grand ensemble of the Exposition ground, thus preventing the jarring contrasts between the beautiful buildings and grounds on the one hand and the amusing distracting, ludicrous attractions on the other."[68]

The only Japanese presence on the Midway was a tea shop and a bazaar selling souvenirs, a private enterprise set up by Japanese merchants.[69] It was not given official government approval. By building on the island Japan not only avoided the racial stereotyping of the Midway but placed itself within the main concourse, the representation of modern achievement. China, by contrast, had no official pavilion and was instead represented solely by an exhibition on the

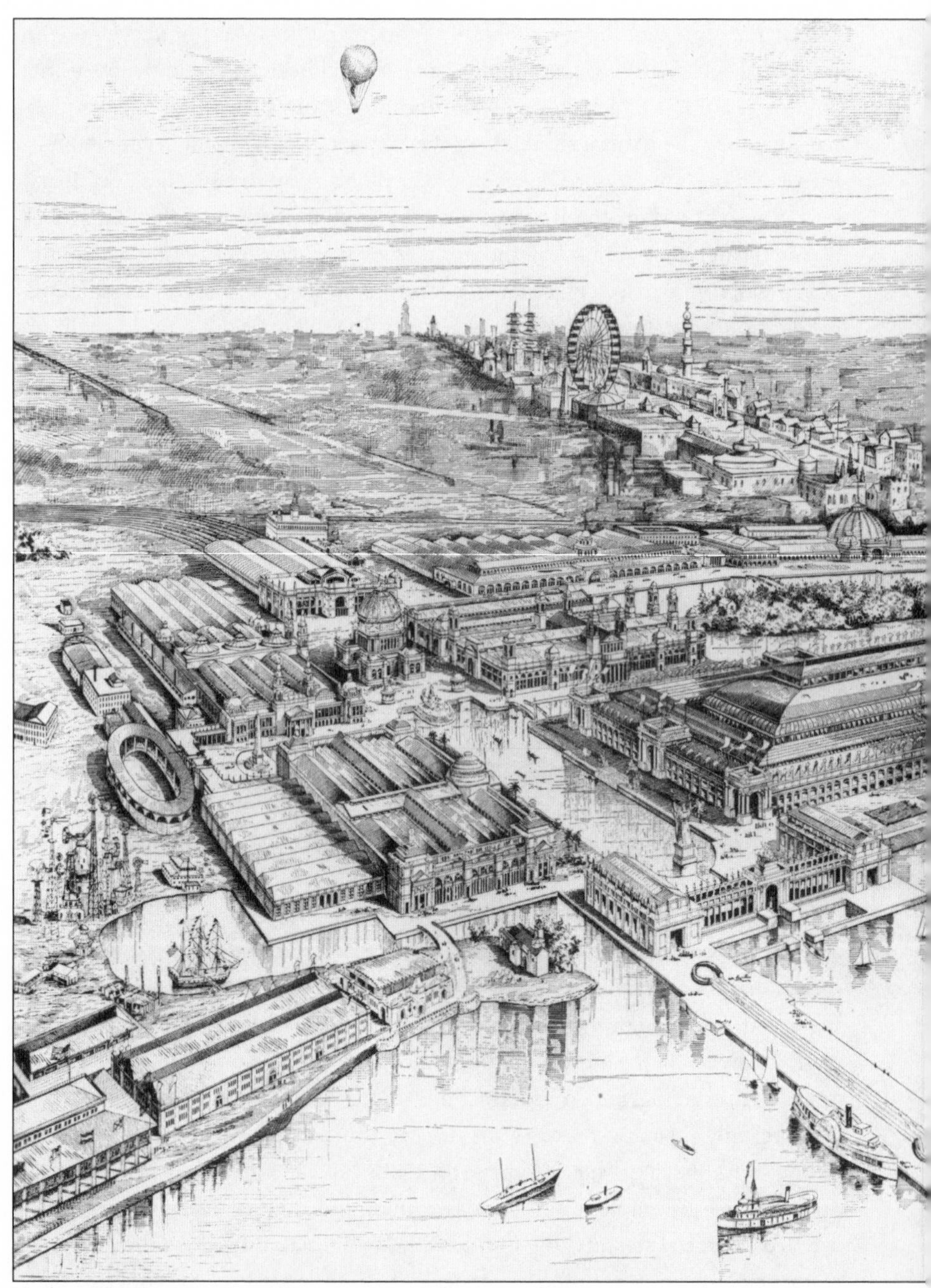

Figure 8. Bird's-eye view of the exposition (Library of Congress, Washington, D.C.)

Midway assembled by expatriate Chinese merchants. The Chinese display, sandwiched between entertainment facilities, itself became a source of amusement.[70] The success of Japan's project is indicated by Snider's account of the fair, which passed over Japan in the description of the progress of civilization, concentrating solely on the deficiencies of the Chinese as displayed on the Midway for an account of the East Asiatic type.[71] He discussed the Japanese exhibition along with those of England, Germany, and France. As Snider saw it, Japan had "joined the march of Western civilization."[72]

The symbolic significance of the exhibit and its association with treaty revision were made explicit at the dedication ceremony of the Hōōden held on Friday, March 31, 1893. The architect presenting the key to Commissioner Tejima spoke of the historical intention of the design, the plan to present the vast age and continuity of Japanese civilization in relation to American history. In his response, Tejima spoke of the significance of the timing, which explicitly linked the dedication of the ceremony to the signing of the first treaty with the United States on that same date forty years before. Using a coincidence of auspicious Fridays—the day Columbus sailed from Spain, the day the Japanese Diet signed the bill to fund the exposition participation—he further stressed the link between the Hōōden, the exposition, and the wish for treaty revision.[73] Meeting this very early deadline to make the point had been no easy task. The building began on October 29, 1892, but was interrupted by a winter unusually severe even by Chicago standards. A number of the large American buildings were crushed under the weight of snow; others could not withstand the gale-force winds. In spite of these setbacks the Japanese building was finished on time, even though the exposition itself was not due to open until May, and a great many of the other exhibits were not in place until much later than this.

In a cross-cultural play on the significance of the Hōōden, the "Phoenix Pavilion" in Chicago, "the Phoenix city" (a reference to its remarkable recovery after the devastating fire of 1871), he complimented the host city and invoked again the good wishes for the treaty project. As Okakura explained in the pavilion's guidebook, the Hōō bird only appears when a just ruler is on the throne and the nation is peaceful and prosperous, and its appearance is accompanied by tokens of success. Tejima also thanked the exposition authorities for assigning "the most favourable space for the historic buildings we are assembled here to dedicate," a reminder of the importance of the position of the building to the statement it made.

American Responses

The Hōōden was a popular exhibit and an excellent public relations project right from the time that the numbered pieces of precut timber arrived from Japan. Crowds turned out to watch the craftsmen work. One newspaper commented that it was a pity that they could not continue through the fair. The negative side of this was the patronizing tone of the appreciation. The workmen were like acrobats; their tools quaint; everything they did was "back to front." In general, public reaction was friendly and goodwilled but tended to reinforce the stereotype of the Japanese as small, dainty, polite, docile, and childlike. For the American public the Japanese represented the positive aspects of the "Oriental." The consecration ceremony of the Hōōden, unlike the Turkish ceremony, for example, did not involve a "barbaric blood sacrifice," though it was *no less interesting* to watch.[74] Japan was exotic, interesting, picturesque, but not barbaric. It was "inoffensively" foreign.

Certain messages such as the antiquity and continuing vitality of Japanese culture were communicated without difficulty. At the dedication of the pavilion, President Palmer of the National Commission for the Columbian Exposition, for example, with more enthusiasm than historical accuracy, admired Japan as "a nation which had a history when Abraham went wool gathering on the prairies of Mesopotamia . . . full of life, activity and enterprise, anxious to adopt all improvements and avail themselves of every influence that can keep them in the vanguard of progress." His concluding remarks, however, reflected the basically imperialistic attitude of the exposition, condescending and uncompromising. After some trite remarks on the efficient Japanese use of small resources, he warned that "[w]e have much of barbaric force which will astonish them if they do not accept its display as an attractive object lesson."[75]

Snider, whose account of the fair was essentially a reading of its architectural symbolism, was the most receptive commentator. As already mentioned, he accepted Japan's realignment, noticing also the "care with which the Japanese man explains that he is not a Chinaman," and that Japan was claiming a place among the progressive, modern nations. Snider was impressed by Japan's conspicuous effort to present itself at its best and realized that commercial reasons alone could not explain "the desperate struggle of the Japanese here at Chicago; there must be a national, perchance world-historical principle at work."[76] Nevertheless, he interpreted the message entirely in terms of Japan's success at modernization and concluded that Japan had "joined the march of Western civilization"; for Snider, the burden of its presentation was not its indigenous cultural integrity, but the reverse: "See how I have occidentalized myself in the last thirty years; I am one of you."[77]

Snider read Japan's effort at the fair in terms of his vision of America's divinely appointed responsibility to bring about world civilization. The movement of civilization, following the movement of the sun, was westward. "It has passed out of Western Asia to Europe, it is still passing from Europe to America, and now it seems to be tending toward Japan." Japan's adoption of the signs of Western progress—specifically "the railroad, the telegraph, the school, the printing press of the West"—was proof of the working out of the great movement of history, the unfolding of God's design. Japan had "made itself the bearer of Western civilization." The Japanese were "plainly the vanguard in the Occidental movement toward the Orient." Their success in Westernizing validated America's "mission" of expansion into the Pacific.

By Snider's account, Japan also solved America's ethical ambivalence toward imperialism. Westward expansion was not to be achieved through military conquest, but by purchase, annexation, accession, acts justified in self-abnegating terms of "messianic intervention," bestowing benefit, exerting a favorable influence. He read Japan's eagerness to impress as proof of its desire to adopt the American way and consequently as a request for alliance with America: "It allies itself with the nations of the West, especially does it appeal to the United States, the country that is behind it and next to it, in spite of, or rather by means of the ocean between."[78] Japan was inviting America to expand across the Pacific.

Snider reduced Japan's cultural exhibition to a claim for individuality. What was significant for him in Japan's presentation was evidence that the progress of Western civilization, which had passed from Europe to America, was now crossing the Pacific.[79] It was the Occidental in Japan that he admired. His extravagant appreciation of the Hōōden was condescending, relegating it to the stereotype of the quaint, the colorful, the garden ornament, a modern version of the fake pagodas in the landscape of Chinoiserie. It was the "the gem of the Wooded Isle."[80] As he saw it, "The little Japanese temple, delicate, light, with its wings almost ready to fly belongs to the garden . . . a humming bird among the flowers."[81] The Hōōden was a mere ornament on the island, and the island in the heart of the White City was part of the greater American imperial statement.

Of course, others saw the Hōōden differently. The human scale, harmonious composition, and honest use of exposed natural materials appealed to people reacting against the dominant pomposity of the period typified by the buildings of the White City. "The excellent proportions, superb craftsmanship, sensitive roof curves and structural honesty of the Hōōden set it apart from the surrounding hulks that concealed prosaic exhibition halls behind sham marble fronts."[82] Once again, however, the Hōōden was appreciated because it was recognized as conforming to an already emerging American aesthetic trend toward naturalism.

Neil Harris's survey of American reaction to the Japanese exhibition showed that, although some people undoubtedly admired the harmony, elegance, and restraint of Japanese art, the general public appreciated it for its profusion: its costliness and elaborateness, the intricacy of ornament, lavish use of materials, and for the immense amount of labor involved in the work.[83] All of these were abundantly evident in the interior of the Hōōden. Again, although the criteria are different, Americans judged Japanese art according to their own preoccupations and current fashion.

Accommodating Western Categories

Japanese organizers had, of course, expected this. Japan had been exporting decorative trade goods for many years—objects that suited the nineteenth-century vogue for eclectic bric-a-brac—and were therefore fully aware of the popular Western taste in Japanese decorative art. The pieces chosen for the exhibition at Chicago, however, had all been made specifically for the occasion, and unlike earlier mass exports—"curiosities . . . which are absolutely without prototypes in Japanese art" crudely and defectively made—each was of the highest quality. Nevertheless, many showed accommodation to Western needs. Lacquer was made to withstand the dry heat of American houses. Chikudō's acclaimed painting of a tiger was mounted not as a scroll but as a screen, which "will fit perfectly into the corner of a parlour and will be as striking a piece of furniture as any dilettante can expect to find."[84] Masterpieces of Japanese ceramic technique were produced in Western forms, such as a milk jug and sugar bowl. No doubt one purpose of these modifications was to make the articles more saleable, but there was more to it than that, as we can see in the example of the textile exhibits. Japanese tapestry, traditionally woven on a narrow loom, was for the first time produced in huge pieces (the largest twenty feet by thirteen) for the Chicago exhibition. The designs and techniques of the textiles remained the finest examples of the Japanese craft, the excellence of which had long been recognized in the West. But the size and presentation of the Chicago pieces lifted them out of the category of woven curiosities and placed them alongside the great tapestries of France and Italy. Not only was the product saleable, but the Japanese textiles were placed in deliberate comparison with those of Europe and, moreover, by increasing their size, gained recognition as fine art. Gobelin-type wall hangings were acceptable as art; an *obi*, the usual application of Japanese tapestry, no matter how exquisite, could not rise above the category of craft.

There may not seem to be any difficulty in communicating the worth and sophistication of Japanese civilization at the level of material culture. Gold and silk signify wealth and beauty in the West as they do in Japan. The beauty of a well-made lacquer box may be appreciated even if the culturally specific meaning of its design motif is not. American appreciation of Japanese aesthetic certainly had its limits, however. One of these was indicated by Mrs. Potter Palmer's decision to add chairs to the Japanese Ladies Association exhibit in the Women's Pavilion. The display, which reproduced three rooms such as would have been used by Japanese noblewomen of the Tokugawa period, was authentically furnished and fitted with heirlooms lent by members of the committee, which included their Majesties the Empress and the Empress Dowager. For Mrs. Potter Palmer, the president of the Board of Lady Managers, it seems, the room was incomplete.[85] According to nineteenth-century Western categories, a "furnished room" for example, could be rather narrowly defined. Rather, the definition was culturally specific. A room, no matter how exquisitely decorated, refined in its furnishings, or richly gilded, could not be "civilized" without chairs.

Rigid categories were a definite problem for the presentation of Japanese art at the fair. In spite of the fact that Japanese artists modified their work to conform to Western requirements, they were still underrepresented in the "high-art" painting and sculpture exhibitions. Most items were classified under the less prestigious label of "decorative art."[86] Japan contributed 270 of the total 291 items of decorative art in the Palace of Fine Arts, but only 24 of the 1,013 sculpture works, and 55 of the 7,357 paintings. One spectacular enamel triptych, a prize exhibit from the Japanese point of view, "being specially viewed and approved by the Emperor of Japan," was excluded from the art section entirely, relegated to the Hall of Manufactures, apparently because of the political content of its design.[87] The art exhibition was, of course, a competition; prizes were awarded, and Japan naturally wished to compete. What better way to establish superiority than to win in open, international contest? It was essential, however, that Japanese art be included in the highest categories. How could any nation ever be considered really "civilized" if it did not produce fine art?

For Japan to compete, and thereby establish the worth of its material culture, it had to select and modify its exhibits to conform to Western criteria. The statement of the Hōōden, intended to convey the less tangible concept of Japan's right to an elevated position on a perceived "ladder of social evolution," required a similar process of accommodation to Western categories. Okakura, the director, was well placed to organize the exhibit as his experience of Western museums and contacts with the Western art world, as well as his experience in collecting and cataloging Japanese art with Fenollosa, had given him a very clear idea of Western taste. It is not surprising therefore that the Hōōden exhibit provided for the main streams of Western vogue. The display of gold, strong colors, and rich ornamentation in the Fujiwara and Tokugawa suites would satisfy appetites for the rich and sumptuous. The elegant simplicity of the Ashikaga appealed to new tastes for elegant simplicity and appreciation of natural materials.

The representation could have been different. Although we are accustomed to consider the tea ceremony aesthetic of the Ashikaga period as typical of the period and classically "Japanese," as important as it was, it was only one of the possibilities.[88] The Japanese exhibition at the Seville Universal Exposition in 1992 showed reproductions of the screens and wall paintings by Kanō Eitoku of the sixteenth-century Azuchi Castle. Previously known only through descriptions in texts, the paintings were carefully planned to express the power and dominance of the great military leader Oda Nobunaga.[89] The exposition reproductions were prepared using authentic pigments and typically lavish amounts of gold. As the organizer of the exhibition commented, "[T]his exhibit will shatter the impression that Japanese culture is small in scale and subdued."[90] Even Japanese, accustomed as they are to seeing Eitoku's painting aged and darkened, he continued, will be startled. This will be a chance "to come into close contact with the energy and enthusiasm of Eitoku and his age. . . . The Azuchi screens and wall paintings do not have much to do with the quiet impressions of *wabi* (taste for the simple and sombre) and *sabi* (tranquility and elegant simplicity) peculiar to Japan."[91] Japan at Seville projected a new image of its aesthetic, an image to match its new prominence in the international world, showing that the energy of sixteenth-century Spain was matched by that of Japan.[92]

Conclusion

In Chicago, however, the overriding concern was to express Japan's cultural civilization. The importance of this in the issue of treaty renewal is illustrated by the way public reaction to the incidents at the start of the Sino-Japanese War just one year after the exposition jeopardized the ratification of the newly negotiated agreement. The negotiations for the revision of the treaty had been finalized on November 22, 1894, the day after Japanese troops occupied Port Arthur, but in accordance with the American Constitution, the agreement had to be approved by the Senate. The Senate was alarmed by reports of Japanese atrocities that appeared in the American press by November 28 and was hesitant about signing. Foreign Minister Mutsu Munemitsu personally intervened, assuring the United States that the reports were exaggerated, pointing to the past exemplary behavior of Japanese troops and suggesting that the victims were not civilians but Chinese soldiers out of uniform. He directed negotiators to "[t]ake action promptly to obtain swift senate approval of the new treaty before rumours arising from this affair spread further."[93] The treaty with America was passed by the Senate in February 1895, but as Mutsu noted in his autobiography, "the American press severely condemned the violent outrages of the Japanese forces and declared that Japan was in fact a barbaric savage with only a thin veneer of civilization . . . certain papers insinuated that the complete abolition of extraterritoriality proposed under the new treaty might be extremely dangerous."[94]

The degree to which Japan could be considered "civilized" was clearly of central importance to the abolition of the extraterritoriality clause and therefore to the whole issue of treaty revision. The one constant in the various American readings of the message of the Hōōden was that the American public appreciated things Japanese, accepted that the Japanese were "civilized," to the extent that they conformed to current American values. It was necessarily a partial and selective approval. Snider, for example, praised Japan's achievements in adopting Western customs and institutions rather than concede the worth of Japanese culture itself, which remained quaint and curious. The "real" Japan remained an Asiatic mystery concealed by the appearance of Westernization—hence the ease with which the civilization of the Japanese was deemed to be "nothing but a thin veneer" at the outbreak of war in the year following the great exposition and the warm reception there of Japanese culture by Americans.

CHAPTER

MANIFEST DESTINY

Christianity and American Imperialism

From the time of the Crystal Palace Exposition in London in 1851 the great expositions of the nineteenth century were preeminently displays of material and technical progress. The Chicago fair, symbolized as it was by the steel-supported structures of the White City and the engineering genius of the great Ferris wheel, was no exception. What made the Columbian Exposition unique was the inclusion of the "Auxiliary Congresses," an exhibition of the spiritual, intellectual, and social progress of mankind. The largest and most acclaimed of the Auxiliary Congresses was the World's Parliament of Religions, which not only epitomized the antimaterialist theme of the congresses but enshrined the motivating force of them all, American Protestant Christianity.

American rivalry with Europe might have been satisfied by an exhibition of material progress, but this material progress was itself subsidiary to and dependent on America's distinctive society and its resulting institutions. "The freest land must in the end create the most perfect machinery. . . . The American railroad is a product of the Constitution of the United States,"[1] and the Constitution, in turn, derived from the ideals of freedom, equality, and self-determination of Protestant Christianity brought to the New World by the early colonists. The Columbian Exposition, celebrating the four hundredth anniversary of Columbus's voyage, was permeated with a revived sense of America's predestined mission and an awareness of America's special place in the unfolding of Providential history. As Merril Edwardes Gates, delegate to the Auxiliary Congresses, explained in his paper "The Significance to Christianity of the Discovery and the History of America," God had kept the American continent undefiled until "the Reformation had taught the Christian world afresh the value of the individual man, standing erect, the Bible in his hand, fearless before priest and king, reverent before God. . . . When a new light for the social and political life of mankind began to ray out from the open Bible in the hands of Luther, God opened the way to the new continent."[2]

God had planted the seed of the new religion in the pristine soil of the new continent, had chosen the people and the government to bring it to fruition,[3] and had bestowed upon the people of America the duty to share the light of the Gospel and the benefits of the civilization "springing into life on the continent . . . here to grow until it should overshadow the kingdoms of the world."[4] Providence had ordained the Americanization of the world. The Auxiliary Congresses within the Chicago exposition demonstrated this interdependence of material progress, American civilization, and religion. The two hundred distinct congresses organized under twenty general departments "considering the greatest themes in which mankind is interested"[5] named the intellectual categories through which material progress was manifested.[6]

The World's Parliament of Religions, in spite of its name and the international recognition it subsequently acquired, was essentially an American event, both in its vision of evangelical mission and in its predominant concern with domestic issues. The Parliament grew out of a liberal Christian vision of U.S. Christian ecumenism (i.e., an ecumenical union of the Judeo-Christian religious communities of the United States), a bid to assimilate the rapidly increasing number of immigrants from diverse religious backgrounds into the Protestant ideal. It was a statement of Christian confidence, a bid for liberal Christian reform within the United States, and an exercise in reinforcing the dominance of Protestant Christianity in response to the rapidly changing social environment of the late nineteenth century.[7] The original proposal dealt exclusively with these essentially domestic issues but, once accepted, it was developed as the *World's* Parliament of Religions, an international event to match the international scope of the exposition of which it was an intrinsic part. The original domestic emphasis remained, but the Parliament also became a platform for the expansionist aspects of the American Protestant ideal, the "messianic heritage." In the early years of the colony, the sense of evangelical purpose justified continental expansion westward. In 1893, with American consciousness of its Pacific future revived by the takeover of Hawaii, the obligation was to share the light of the Gospel and American ideals with "those who are nearest to them but are without God and without hope in the world."[8] In the less generous terms of historical reality, the messianic heritage appeared to demand the Christian conquest of Asia.[9]

Asian delegates to the Parliament had long been familiar with aggressive evangelism. They anticipated its presence at the Parliament and came prepared to deal with it. It nevertheless contributed to the shaping of the representation of Buddhism by demanding reiteration of Buddhist apologetics, forcing the discussion of Buddhism toward topics raised by Christian attack. Far more difficult for the Buddhist delegates to accommodate was the essentially American preoccupation of the Parliament that set the parameters of the discussion. The themes suggested and officially endorsed by the organizing committee were directed toward encouraging Judeo-Christian tolerance in the United States, combating growing interest in materialist philosophy, and uniting the various religious communities to solve the social problems of the United States. The aim of the Parliament was to demonstrate the essential unity of human aspiration. In this project, the various religions were assumed to be related by a shared dependence on a patriarchal God and their hierarchically apportioned share in his revelation. These were Christo-centric assumptions of the essentially theistic nature and function of religion into which Buddhism could not easily be accommodated. The aspects of Buddhism that could be discussed at the Parliament were restricted by this American and Christian agenda of the program. The representation of Japanese Buddhism was constrained by the role assigned to it in a discourse generated by the religious debates and intellectual assumptions of nineteenth-century America.

The relations of power mapped in the previous chapter—New World challenge to Europe; the tension between the dominant West and the Orient; dominant white America's attempt to preserve the status quo against the challenge from social changes in the late nineteenth century; Japan's bid to disassociate itself from other Asian nations and establish itself in the international arena—also traversed the congress on religions. In spite of the organizers' professions of tolerance, of respect for other beliefs, and the stated aim of bringing about international understanding of religious ideas, the World's Parliament of Religions also provided evidence to support the themes of Social Darwinism so evident in the main exhibition. The Parliament, the first great attempt to bring together religious specialists of the world, was also a sideshow, an ethnological display of the various religions of the world. The non-Christian religions played a role parallel to the exotic displays of the Midway Plaisance and were similarly arranged as "object lessons" pointing to Protestant Christianity as the culmination of religious evolution.

The World's Fair Auxiliary Congresses

The Auxiliary Congresses were the inspiration of Chicago lawyer and civic leader Charles C. Bonney. His vision was of a series of conferences on matters of spiritual, intellectual, and social concern of the time, "a series of congresses for the consideration of the greatest themes in which mankind is interested."[10] His initial proposal, launched in the *Statesman Magazine*, September 20, 1889, argued that "the crowning glory of the World's Fair" should not be the material and industrial achievements of man, however magnificent that display may be. "Something still higher and nobler is demanded by the enlightened and progressive spirit of the new age." His proposal was for a series of international conventions in the areas of "government, jurisprudence, finance, science, literature, education and religion," discussed not by academics but by practitioners, "statesmen, jurists, financiers, scientists, literati, teachers, theologians." It was to be more widely representative of "peoples, nations, tongues" than "any assemblage which has ever yet been convened." The benefits as he initially perceived them would be nothing less than to "unite the enlightened people of the earth in a general cooperation for the great ends for which human society is organized." Although in Bonney's opinion "it would not be easy to exaggerate the powerful impetus given by [the material exposition] to commerce and all the arts by which toil is lightened, the fruits of labour increased, and the comforts of life augmented," the benefits of the congresses would be "higher and more conducive to the welfare of mankind."[11]

Bonney spoke for the United States, but his sentiments also reflected the particular concern of Chicago, the brash new commercial center that had very recently established its first university, to counter its aggressively commercial image. The congress theme, "Not Things but Men; Not Matter but Mind," stressed this reordering of priorities. Barrows, opening the Evangelical Alliance, observed that Chicago, "celebrated for its big warehouses, big railroads, big newspapers, big expectations and big achievements," would henceforth be known for its equally impressive spiritual achievement.[12] Addressing the Asian delegates, he said, "I want you to think of Chicago not as the home of the rudest materialism but as a temple where men cherish the loftiest idealism."[13] The Congress on Religions was not funded by the churches but by the U.S. government and the commercial community. It was, therefore, a platform for America rather than for Christianity, and the prominence of the World's Parliament of Religions reflected the centrality of religion in the American national vision.

The Chicago organizers planned to display the full progress of man. Here "the most comprehensive and brilliant display of man's material progress," the usual object of an international exhibition, was complemented by an equally extensive display of intellectual, social, and moral progress. There were congresses covering "all areas of intellectual and moral concern," the official history by Rossiter Johnson records, listing in order by way of example, "women, medicine, temperance, commerce, literature, education, religion, art, philosophy and evolution." (Other lists include such diverse subjects as the public press, engineering, government and law reform, religion and Sunday rest, public health, and agriculture.) The message of the Auxiliary Congresses was that America had reached maturity not only in industry and commerce but in social, intellectual, and spiritual development as well and stood poised to lead the world into the twentieth century.

Bonney expressed the millennial splendor of his vision, the United States as the culmination of post-Renaissance progress, at the opening of the first of the congresses on May 15, 1893: "A single week of years stands between us and the twentieth century. If the causes now in operation shall go on unchecked, the world will witness in these seven years the crowning glories of more than seven centuries of human progress."[14] He declared the event formally open with the hope: "To make the whole world one in sympathy; to make the whole world one in mental aim; to make the whole world one in moral power; learning and virtue passports to all lands."[15]

The sincerity of Bonney's desire for universal peace and brotherhood cannot be questioned. He was himself a Swedenborgian and spoke as representative of the goodwill of liberal Christianity. However, as any number of supposedly liberal papers showed, the assumption of a single, uniform human nature upon which this attitude of Eurocentric humanism is based leads too easily to interpreting the undeniable observable differences in the thought and action of other peoples as irrational or false versions of one's own—at the very least, as imperfect, preliminary attempts at achieving the same ends.[16]

The World's Parliament of Religions and Messianic Mission

The Parliament, though only one of the many Auxiliary Congresses, was generally perceived to be "the splendid crown," the epitome of the concept. Its prominence depended on more than religion's obvious position as the ultimate expression of "spirit," the natural opposition to mundane "matter" and the material world, the spiritual balance to the gross materiality of the general exposition that was so much commented on. The Parliament was as fundamental to the expression of American aspirations as the White City itself. Domestically, the Columbian Exposition was viewed by Americans as both Rome, the culmination of republican democracy, and the new Jerusalem, the site of religious renewal. Both images were intrinsic to the "enduring Protestant American dream" which was the dominant statement of the quadricentennial celebration.[17] America was not simply the site of post-Reformation progress and achievement, but also the divinely appointed *agent* of its universal dissemination. Bonney, opening the Congress on Women, introduced this recurring theme: "The nineteenth century, richer in manifold wonders than any which has preceded it in the august procession of the ages, crowns its greatest achievements by establishing in the world the sublime idea of a universal fraternity of learning and virtue. This idea, long cherished by the illuminati of every clime, descends at last from the luminous mountains of thought to the fertile fields of action, and enters upon the conquest of the world."[18]

Bonney here articulated the ideal of American mission and the fundamental problem of American imperialism, the tension between the ideal of converting the world through a self-denying "messianic example," providing a living demonstration of the advantages of its civilization that would inspire emulation and desire for membership in the union, and the more aggressive alternative, "messianic intervention," which was associated with the European model of imperialism that America, as a former colony, rejected. Evangelism—offering the gift of Light—provided a justification for territorial expansion and very frequently aided in the process. The quadricentennial celebration of Columbus's voyage revitalized the American Christian sense of predestined mission. America, the theater for achieving millennial perfection, was the model for the rest of the world, the "chief motor" for the conversion of the world to Protestantism.[19] Ideally, then, the mission depended on realizing the objective within the United States.

The first problem with this vision was that, as Seager remarks, "the World's Parliament of Religions marked the passing of an era in which the United States could be called, however inaccurately, a Protestant or even a Christian nation."[20] The optimism of these ideals was in contrast with the reality of increasing labor opposition to the growing power of industrial capitalists, disruption due to the breakdown of the traditional rural economy, the racial problems of recently emancipated blacks (whose form of worship was not orthodox although they were Christian and even Protestant), and the urban slums teeming with Jewish and Roman Catholic immigrants. While liberal and fundamentalist Christians attempted to consolidate their position, Roman Catholics, Jews, and black Americans were staking a claim as legitimate heirs to the prerogatives of the Republic.[21]

The visions that emerged from the rhetoric of the Parliament—"a blueprint for the kingdom of God on earth," a "latter day Pentecost," the "New Jerusalem," "the Babel tongues of the world . . . coming back to speak the one dialect of Heaven"[22]—are those of subsuming and assimilating all religions within the dominant Anglo-Saxon Protestantism. American delegates spoke of "manufacturing a republic—taking the black material of humanity and building it up into noble men and women; taking the red material, wild with every savage instinct, and making it into respectable men."[23] With the increased immigration of the late nineteenth century, American society similarly, at least in theory, transformed immigrants from diverse cultures into a citizenry supporting and enhancing the essentially Protestant ethos of a Christian American republic. The guiding principle of the Parliament, in which the majority of organizers and delegates was of the dominant Protestant groups, was that all the religions of the world would find their completion and fulfillment in the spiritual values of Protestant Christianity.

One of the problems at this time, however, was the failure of the ideal within the United States itself. The difficulty, from the point of view of at least one Protestant leader, was not just the increase in the volume of immigration but the different type of people involved by this time. In a paper on "The Problems of Our Multifarious Population and Their Probable Solution," the Reverend Wm. C. Roberts, D.D. LL.D., wrote:

> If it were made up, as in former years, of people from the British Isles, Holland, Germany, France and Northern Europe, the increase in numbers would probably excite no special alarm, for multitudes of them spoke our language, professed the Christian religion, admired our civil

> and social institutions, revered our Bible and respected our Sabbath. *They came in order to be of us.* But those who flock hither in these days are largely different in character and purpose. They are Jews from Russia, Italians from the Siciles, Bohemians, many of whom are of the baser sort, Poles, long taught to dislike every kind of regularly constituted government, Hungarians looked upon as revolutionaries, Armenians, Greeks and Bulgarians who have had the best elements of their nature stamped out by the iron heel of Turkey, British trade-unionists, French socialists, Austrian nihilists, German anarchists, and idol worshippers from China, India and the Islands of the Sea.[24]

The speaker clearly associated religious diversity with the social problems of the time, and the "material of humanity" he described was less malleable than he desired. The presence of these large numbers of Jews and Roman Catholics in the society, if not the nihilists, socialists, and "idol worshippers," forced debate on the interpretation of the constitutional guarantee of freedom of religion. Did it allow a denial of God? Expressed from a Protestant point of view in the previous century, the controversy had been whether the Constitution guaranteed freedom from all old religions and the establishment of a new universal (Christian) faith, or the freedom to persist in a false or partial religion until the establishment of the universal reign of Christ on earth.[25] Both of these interpretations assumed that all religions would be assimilated into Protestantism. This was, after all, part of the perceived reason for the existence of America. It was the site of the growth of the new revelation and the place of refuge for all those who sought its consolations. Under the still dominant Protestant ideal, as the Reverend Roberts put it, *they came in order to be of us.*

Bonney's Vision: The Origin of the Plan

The Parliament, as it was originally conceived by Bonney, was essentially a Christian conference, a gathering of the various religious communities of the United States, which, as a generous gesture of brotherhood and a recognition of the growing importance of Judaism in America, included believers in Jehovah as "Old Testament Christians."[26] The Christian parameters of the discussion are clear from the first four of the twenty-two themes proposed for discussion, which were: "a. The idea of God, its influences and consolations. b. The evidences of the existences of God, especially those which are calculated to meet the agnosticism of the present time. c. That evils of life should be shunned as sins against God. d. That the moral law should be obeyed as necessary to human happiness, and because it is the will of the Creator."

The capital "G" and references to God as "Creator" guaranteed the Christian connotations of the term. Another of the proposed themes demanded acceptance of the Christian revelation, the "influx from God into the mind of everyman teaching that there is a God and that he should be worshipped and obeyed." The final and culminating theme indicated the Judeo-Christian limits of Bonney's liberal vision of the Parliament: "That those who believe in these things may work together for the welfare of mankind, notwithstanding they may differ in the opinions they hold respecting God, His revelation and manifestation; and that such fraternity does not require the surrender of the points of difference. The Christian believing in the supreme divinity of Christ, may so unite with the Jew who devoutly believes in the Jehovah of Israel; the Quaker with the High Church Episcopalian; the Catholic with the Methodist; the Baptist with the Unitarian, etc."[27]

There can be no question of Buddhists being included among "those who believe" in Bonney's vision. His concern was for the religious tolerance among the major religious groups represented in the United States in the late nineteenth century and for contemporary, local problems, which included, as point b noted, increasing agnosticism. The proposals for topics for discussion were all concerned with the value of religion as a social force in North America. They specifically excluded discussion of doctrine except where "common aims and common grounds for union may be set forth." Among his proposals he stressed the importance of religion for "virtuous and pure" family life and in answering "the alleged prevalence of infidelity." For Bonney, the substantial fruits of sincere religion included "improved personal character, better business methods; nearly all works of charity; improved domestic order; greater public peace" (point j). The "indispensability of the weekly rest day," another of the proposed topics, was a matter of such contention among Americans at the time that the financial viability of the exposition was threatened by protests against opening the exposition on Sundays and an entire congress was eventually given over to the issue. Temperance was also considered of sufficient importance to deserve a separate congress.

Regardless of this domestic focus, several of the proposals were of direct and particular concern to the Buddhists. The first was the basic assumption that religion must necessarily be theistic. Japanese Buddhists targeted this as the point to which they must pay particular attention.[28] It was a familiar point of Buddhist vulnerability. Because Buddhism was not based on theistic principles, it risked being excluded from the category of religion altogether and linked instead with Western philosophic atheism, an association they vehemently protested. Because the proposal actually listed this as an important point "calculated to meet the agnosticism of the present time," there was a real risk that Buddhism would be called upon, as it frequently was in missionary literature of the time, to stand as the example of the fundamental error of such a view.[29] On the other hand, it was precisely the promotion of Buddhism as an example of the viability of a non-theistic system of ethics that had brought it prestige and respect. Consequently, point p, "the actual harmony of science and religion; and the origin and nature of the conflict between them," was also of particular relevance to the Japanese Buddhist delegates. This was a critical issue in Christian debate during the second half of the nineteenth century. A religion that depends on revelation was incompatible with science's denial of the supernatural. The form of Bonney's proposal here suggests that by the time of the Parliament, liberal Christians at least had resolved the issue. Nevertheless, it was on this point that the Japanese Buddhists perceived Christianity to be most vulnerable. Their confidence was increased by the knowledge that Western scholars had already established the harmony of Buddhism with science and modern philosophy.

North American Ecumenism to Christian Universalism

Once the initial proposal was accepted, the Parliament was organized by a committee of sixteen representatives of the various religious communities of the United States—including one Catholic archbishop and one rabbi—under the direction of the Reverend John Henry Barrows, D.D., a liberal Christian pastor of the First Presbyterian Church of Chicago.[30] As chairman, Barrows exerted a strong influence over the organization of the Parliament, particularly in the management of the non-Christian religions. He personally hosted the Asian delegates, edited and in several cases delivered their papers, and after the Parliament compiled and published the official version of its history, an act that has consequences in knowledge of the event to the present time.[31] Although Bonney's American and Christian vision of the World's Parliament of Religions still formed the core of the proceedings, under Barrows and his committee the event was expanded, given a universal scope in keeping with the world's exposition context. In this process, the Protestant Christian ideal of Westward progress was extended beyond the bounds of continental America to the vision of universal Christianity.

The Parliament, as described in its published objectives,[32] sought answers not simply to domestic issues but to "the great problems of the present age," although even here the centrality of America is apparent in the repetition of Bonney's listing of, as examples, "temperance, labour, education, wealth and poverty." It aimed not just for domestic harmony but for "securing permanent international peace." The World's Parliament of Religions had grown from Bonney's vision of a fellowship of liberal, humanist theists to a great international event bringing "together in conference, for the first time in history, the leading representatives of the great historic religions of the world." He specifically desired representatives not simply of Judaism but of "the Brahman, Buddhist, Confucian, Parsee, Mohammedan" faiths as well. In this expanded vision the heathen were now welcome, but for what purpose? The text adopted for the World's Parliament of Religions had been suggested by the Reverend H. Adler, chief rabbi of the British Empire: "Have we not all one Father? Hath not one God created us?"[33] It confirmed Bonney's ecumenical vision for the United States of America but did nothing to accommodate Buddhists.

Although representatives of most religions, Christian and non-Christian, came from all over the world, the Parliament was essentially an American Christian event. Foreign Christians played their part by contributing to ecumenical discussion, by clarifying points of difference between denominations, and, most important, by simply coming from all corners of the world and thereby giving witness to Christianity's claim for universality.[34] Non-Christian delegates were invited for a number of reasons, none of which, in spite of high-minded protests to the contrary, involved a serious desire to learn what they might offer. The stated aim, "To inquire what light each religion has afforded, or may afford to other religions of the world,"[35] must be weighed against the chairman's reassurance that "[t]he non-Christian world . . . has nothing to add to the Christian creed."[36] The aim of the organizers might more accurately have been rendered to the general public as it was to the Christian congregation: "To inquire into what light Christianity has afforded, or may afford, to other religions in the world." After his experience of the Parliament, Barrows, now claiming to know Oriental religions, "both ideal and practical," concluded that "the very best which is in them, the very best which these well meaning men have shown to us, is often a reflection of Christianity, and that which they lack, and the lack is very serious, is what the Christian Gospel alone can impart."[37]

Quite clearly, when Christianity was used as a measure of worth, not only did other religions necessarily fail to measure up but, to the extent that they did, they were unoriginal and derivative. Anything Barrows admired in Buddhism he assumed to be the result of its contact with Christianity. The idea that a new universal faith, a new religion for the twentieth century, might emerge out of the debate, an idea that Asian delegates spoke of frequently, convinced that they did indeed have "light" that they could contribute, was not envisaged by the chief promoters of the Parliament. They believed that "the elements of such a religion are already contained in the Christian ideal and the Christian scriptures." Their attitude allowed for reinterpretation and reform within Christianity but afforded no opening for intellectual input from Asian religions.

Exhibiting Spiritual Progress

The nineteenth-century study of comparative religion, whatever it may be now, was unashamedly Christo-centric and closely allied with the imperative of Christian missions to know the enemy. The presence of non-Christian religions was, of course, essential to give the event its international status. As Barrows himself recognized, "A World's Parliament of Religions in which only a few were interested would be a misnomer."[38] Asian religions were also essential as a contrast: "[S]uperiority cannot be shown without comparison."[39] Their presence was deemed necessary to display the relative excellence of Christianity. The difference in the quality of the exhibits would demonstrate the progress of Christianity.

The evolutionary lesson of the fair, the place of each nation in an international hierarchy, was most definitely also to be drawn from the Parliament. Ninety-seven nations participated in the Columbian Exposition, including "aborigines from the arctic circle and the Pacific" and other such materially undeveloped countries as Venezuela and the French Congo. The organizers had decided to arrange the exhibits throughout the fair in categories rather than by nation so that the relative merit of entries from different nations placed side by side would be apparent. It was considered one of the valuable lessons of the fair, Johnson records, that each nation could see its position in the hierarchy thus displayed.[40] At the World's Parliament of Religions "each country was, in the same spirit, invited to exhibit their [*sic*] religions."[41] Or as Barrows himself expressed it, employing the frequently used metaphor of reflections of the light of truth, the Parliament aimed "to study all the exhibits in the spectrum."[42] The result was that the "products displayed by the United States, Great Britain and Germany were immensely superior."[43] Spiritual superiority was established through the dubious authority of democratic competition and scientific comparison. Note that the claim to immense superiority is restricted to the three Protestant nations of the West, explicitly connecting material advancement with the Protestant Christian vision of spiritual progress.

Exhibiting the Exotic

The Parliament was a microcosm of the fair. Its exotic delegates provided the Midway Plaisance component, the object lesson in evolution, the color, entertainment, light relief, the picturesque, and like the Midway, the Parliament drew large crowds. Attendance apparently exceeded expectations as a second hall had to be opened to accommodate repeat sessions. The Hall of Columbus alone held four thousand people and was regularly packed. Newspapers reported, however, that there was little discrimination in the audience's response to Asian speakers, and much waving of handkerchiefs and throwing hats into the air—more the behavior of a music hall than of an academic conference. Indian delegate Vivekananda's opening words, "Brothers and sisters of America," brought on four minutes of applause and cheering. Vivekananda and the other photogenic and articulate South Asian delegate, Anagārika Dharmapāla, the Buddhist delegate from Ceylon, were lionized in the press, but the coverage gave much more space to their appearance and theatrics than to the content of their papers. The Parliament was part of the fair and the Asian delegates were a spectacular attraction. Neglect of more informative if less outgoing speakers on Hinduism such as Manilal D'Vivedi[44] suggests that these expressions of brotherhood were what the audience wanted to hear rather than information on Oriental thought. The other question that arises is just how much of any unamplified speech would be heard in an auditorium of that size. Front-row seats were reserved for registered participants. For many of the general public in attendance the visual spectacle must have been the principal satisfaction, and in spite of actually having been present at the Parliament and witnessing the pageantry and the sincerity of the delivery, their knowledge of the content of the speeches would have depended on the press reports and the published record: the voices of the Asian delegates, edited and interpreted by their Christian hosts.

Just how important was the carnival aspect of the Asian presence and how calculated was it? W. F. Warren, president of Boston University, wrote in response to the idea of the Parliament, apparently confirming a suggestion made to him in

Barrows's letter, that "even a museum of idols and objects used in ceremonial worship would attract beyond any other museum. Models and illustrations of the great temples of the world and of the world's history would be in a high degree instructive. Add to these things the living word of living teachers, and the whole world may well pause to listen."[45] Is it mere coincidence that Barrows subsequently invited these "living teachers" of exotic religions? Or that the official record was profusely illustrated with photographs of ritual objects, great temples, and Oriental practitioners? Of the nonportrait illustrations only twelve are Christian, and these are the great monuments: St. Paul's Cathedral, Westminster Abbey, St. Peter's in Rome, and the cathedrals of St. Petersburg, Worcester, Milan. Non-Christian religions are also represented by major buildings, among which is the Pearl Mosque in Delhi, Mandalay Pagoda, and the Temple of Heaven in Peking. There are rather more photographs of "heathen" curiosities such as those labeled "The Burning Ghat at Calcutta," "A Group of Fakirs," "A Chinese Idol," "Hindus at Devotion," and of assorted poorly dressed Oriental devotees. The abiding impression from thumbing through the volume is one of contrast between the cathedrals soaring toward heaven and the earthbound and materially backward heathen. The illustrated history echoed the message of the Midway, the object lesson in the transition from the primitive to the sublime.

The Congress as Parliament

The imbalance of the relationship between the American Protestant hosts and the non-Christian guests was simultaneously concealed and strengthened by the conception of the event as a "parliament." This is a powerful metaphor, carrying as it does the fundamental political relationships of majority government and the minority right to be represented and heard and to contribute to the legislative process, which is ultimately under the control of the majority. The hierarchical relationship of religions, which was the lesson of the sideshow aspect of the event, was reinforced by the lesson of this reference to democratic structures. Christianity, which had an overwhelming majority of delegates, was clearly cast in the role of universal religion, a message also projected by the presence of Christian delegates from such far-flung outreaches as Africa, Japan, and India. Buddhism, alone or as part of the larger Oriental, non-Christian contingent, and in spite of its actual vast Asian following, was here cast as a minority party. The function of its delegates was principally to be present, validating the democratic principle of representation—this was the *World's* Parliament after all—and to illustrate the democratic respect for the right of minority groups to be heard.[46]

The equality implied by calling the event a "parliament" upset orthodox sections of the Christian community and forced Barrows to clarify the intentions behind his expansive rhetoric of brotherhood. The Anglican archbishop of Canterbury led the objection. He wrote refusing to participate on the grounds that he did not understand how the Christian religion, "which is the one religion," could be regarded as a member of a parliament of religions "without assuming the equality of the other intended members and the parity of their position and claims."[47] In response Barrows explained that the term was certainly not intended to imply that the various religions were equal in doctrine or truth. Calling the event a "parliament" in no way compromised the Christian claim to superiority and unique revelation. It was only intended to guarantee the parliamentary privilege of equal right to speak and to present opinions. "There was no suggestion on the part of the Christian speakers that Christianity was to be thought of on the same level with other religions."[48]

In the most commonly reproduced photographs of the Parliament the Asian delegates appear as a handful of colorfully attired representatives contrasting with the sober, dark-suited Christians.[49] Their prominent position at the center front of the stage makes the most of their presence, bestowing an impression of religious diversity. Barrows describes the "most picturesque and pleasing spectacle" of the gathering on stage and delights in the "colour and movement" of the Oriental delegates with their "many coloured raiment" and especially the "most gorgeous group," the Chinese and Japanese, "arrayed in costly silk vestments of all the colours of the rainbow."[50] Consciously or not, the contrast among the Parliamentary delegates paralleled the planned contrast between the serious side of the fair, the White City, and the entertainment and amusement appeal of the Midway Plaisance.

The Invitation and the Limits of Tolerance

The Parliament, in the expansive terms of the call for papers, was to be a gathering of "the leading representatives of the great historic religions of the world, to show to man in the most impressive way, what and how many important truths the various religions hold and teach in common." It aimed to "promote and deepen the spirit of human brotherhood among religious men of diverse faiths, through friendly converse and mutual good understanding, while not seeking to foster the temper of indifferentism, and not striving to achieve any formal and outward unity."[51] Letters of response to the idea suggest that this vision was considered disturbingly liberal by considerable segments of the society, those whom even Barrows disparagingly described as "good bigots who imagine that God will not cease working until he has made all men Presbyterians."[52] But even the liberal view uncompromisingly placed Christianity at the pinnacle of evolutionary development that all other religions were destined to reach. In Barrows's words, "[I]t is not true that all religions are equally good; but neither is it true that all religions except one are no good at all." The invitation, for all its professions of mutual respect, was to come and be measured: "Christianity . . . will assign to each its place in that work of evangelical preparation which the elder doctors discern in heathenism itself and which is not yet completed."[53]

Hierarchies of Race and the Light

Embedded here are the interrelated assumptions that there is but one God whose plan unfolds in the progress of the world, and his revelation is universal, but unequally bequeathed. "God hath not left himself without witness" was a constant refrain, elaborated on by metaphors of Light—"the white light of Heaven," "the Light of Truth"—all implying that other religions are but a dim reflection of the Christian Light of the World. Christianity was "the sun among candles." Christians who "have the full light of the Cross should bear brotherly hearts towards all those who grope in a dimmer illumination."[54] The "twilight" state of others was variously explained. In Bonney's opening address we find that "God necessarily reveals himself differently to a child than to a man, to a philosopher than to one who cannot read." God gave two revelations, one in nature, which historically has been the preoccupation of the "Oriental" religions, and the higher revelation, the Christian revelation of the word.[55] A scientifically expressed variation on the theme was overtly racist: the revelation was given equally to all but was "broken into many coloured fragments by the prisms of men." Non-Christian races were unable to perceive the truth or to hold on to its brilliance. The white light shone upon them was defracted into the many hues of partial truths, "gropings after God."[56] One of the most frequently stated objects of the Parliament of Religions was to "change this many-coloured radiance back to the white light of heavenly truth."[57]

Acts 10:35—"God is no respecter of persons: but in every nation he that feareth Him, and worketh righteousness, is acceptable to Him"—was also quoted with great enthusiasm as an example of Christian magnanimity and tolerance. It seems to have been forgotten that it was a reply to Peter's question of whether the Gentiles could receive the Holy Spirit and offers only that men of all races may be converted. It has nothing to say about Christian tolerance for other religions to exist. The liberal inspiration of the Parliament notwithstanding, it was a Christian event both in the proselytizing aspirations of people such as Barrows and in the unquestioned assumptions upon which it was based.

While Barrows quite understandably presented the Parliament as welcoming and attractive to non-Christian delegates in the official invitation intended for international distribution, in publications intended to circulate among Christians—and in sermons before his congregation—he was less guarded and spoke more specifically of the function of the Parliament in converting the world to Christianity. News of one such sermon reached Japan with serious consequences for the Japanese delegation.[58] Conservative Japanese already opposed to the idea of Buddhist participation at the Parliament were confirmed in their suspicions that the event was a Christian trap and that non-Christian religions, far from getting a fair hearing, would be used.[59] Supporters of the delegation countered that such suspicions showed lack of confidence in Buddhism. They did concede that the circumstances of the Parliament, a Christian event held in a Christian country and controlled by a Christian chairman, were less than ideal, but that, properly managed, the benefits for Buddhism in Japan could be profound and that the risks were well worth taking.[60]

Barrows's sermon focused Buddhist rhetoric on the need to combat Christian imperialism. From the Japanese delegates' point of view, because Barrows had declared war, it was now possible to plead for support in terms of attack. The Parliament was an opportunity to "make the truth known and assail the evil teaching." Employing the rhetoric of Social Darwinism, they argued that Japan must send a delegation for the sake of Buddhism and for the sake of Japan. "The survival of the fittest is the general trend of society," they argued, and Japanese Buddhists had an obligation to the civilization of the future. Evolution of religion depended on competition between species, and among the world religions—which they identified as Buddhism, Christianity, and Islam—Buddhism alone is a sufficiently different "species," the one world religion "entirely different from Christianity in nature, organization, doctrine and means of propagation." Therefore, they argued, "the racial contest is between yellow and white; the contest of religions is between Buddhism and Christianity."[61] After years of conflict and rivalry with Christians in Japan, Japanese Buddhists were not predisposed to take Barrows's protestations of brotherhood at face value.

Tolerance: Assimilation or Plurality?

The Theravada Buddhist delegate, Dharmapāla, also expressed his suspicions of the Christian motive in inviting non-Christian delegates, admitting that he meditated for a year before deciding to attend. His opening address challenged the Parliament to match the tolerance of religious plurality, the tolerance demonstrated by the great Buddhist king Asoka "twenty-four centuries ago," recognizing and supporting the right of different religions to coexist. Experience of missionary attitudes in Asia warned delegates that this ideal of tolerance was unlikely to be what the organizers had in mind. Even liberal missionaries who showed respect for certain non-Christian religions held instead an ideal of assimilation in "fulfilment." Dharmapāla offered only conditional approval: "[I]f you are serious, if you are unselfish, if you are altruistic," the Parliament would be a success, and Barrows would shine forth as the American Asoka.[62]

The problem was a fundamental one: acceptance of the possibility of different religions coexisting in mutual respect, rather than mere rhetorical generosity. The difference in Christian and Asian views, of assimilation versus plurality, became clear at the closing ceremony in the audience reaction to two speakers, both of whom spoke on the theme of tolerance and religious unity. The first was the Reverend George T. Candlin, an English missionary to China, who showed his own admiration and sympathy for China by dressing in Chinese clothes and, according to the Japanese delegate Shaku Sōen, "speaking with such enthusiasm that foam flew from the corners of his mouth."[63] Candlin was given an enthusiastic ovation. He encapsulated the liberal Christian project of considering non-Christian religions as partial revelations of the Christian truth, their followers children of a lesser light. Chicago's achievement, as he saw it, was that it had opened the way for a new period of missionary enterprise in Asia. Christianity, which was not achieving expected results in Asia, would henceforth succeed more rapidly by adopting a less confrontational approach, by overcoming the "conventional idea" that

> Christianity is true and all other religions false; that Christianity is light, and other religions dark; that Christianity is of God, while other religions are of the devil, or else with a little more moderation that Chris-

> tianity is by revelation from heaven while other religions are manufactures of men. You know better, and with clear light and strong assurance you can testify that there may be friendship instead of antagonism between religion and religion; that so surely as God is our common Father our hearts alike have yearned for him, and our souls in devoutest moods have caught whispers of grace dropped from his throne.[64]

Candlin was followed by the Indian Hindu speaker, Vivekananda, who also called for tolerance and brotherhood, but in terms of acceptance and coexistence rather than conversion. The lesson of the Parliament was, he claimed, that holiness and purity were not the exclusive possession of any one faith. "Much has been said of the common ground of religious unity. . . . But if anyone here hopes that this unity would come by the triumph of any one of these religions and the destruction of the others, to him I say, 'Brother, yours is an impossible hope.' Do I wish that the Christian would become Hindu? God forbid. Do I wish that the Hindu or Buddhist would become Christian? God forbid. . . . The Christian is not to become a Hindu or Buddhist, nor a Hindu or Buddhist to become a Christian. But each must assimilate the others yet preserve its individuality."[65]

As Barrows observed, Vivekananda was one of the most popular speakers at the Parliament, "but very little approval was shown to some of his sentiments expressed in his closing address."[66] It was apparently acceptable that we all have one Father, that all religions are reflections of the one light (shining on different surfaces, fractured by the prisms of different minds), provided that the implications of this were not taken so seriously as to appear to validate the differences. All were ultimately to be subsumed in the One, and the Lord was ultimately to be called Jesus. The Christians in the audience showed by their disapproval that they understood only too clearly the implication of Vivekananda's quotation of Visnu's claim that whosoever makes offerings or prayers to any God makes them to him. For Candlin the tolerance of differences was a temporary stage on the road to ultimate conversion to Christianity as the universal religion. For him the Parliament heralded "a new era of missionary enterprise and missionary hope."[67] For Vivekananda, plurality was a permanent and desirable condition.

Conclusion

Although the Christian intention of the Parliament is evident enough in the official records, when Barrows wrote about the event in 1897, outside the protocol of the official publication intended for international distribution, he summed up his vision of the Parliament's purpose even more directly: "Christianity should be choked down no man's throat, but . . . all men should be invited to receive it for their own good, intelligently invited to an intelligent reception."[68]

The organizers of the Parliament were motivated by a dream of universal Christian supremacy that was to be achieved by bringing lesser beliefs to their fulfillment. In their view Christianity was already the perfect religion, and the point of the conference was to provide an opportunity for Eastern leaders to realize this. That their Asian colleagues might just as sincerely view the Parliament as an opportunity for the West to recognize the superiority of their religion was not conceivable.

Barrows entertained his Oriental visitors in the week before the Parliament by taking them to one of his Sunday services at the First Presbyterian Church of Chicago. Barrows reported that the Buddhist delegation, after witnessing two ceremonies of entry into Christianity, a baptism and the reception of three Chinese converts, "reverently listened to a sermon on 'Christ the Wonderful.' " "It appeared," to Barrows at least, "as if the Parliament had already opened beneath the splendor of the Cross."[69] The opening ceremony of the Parliament began with the singing of Psalm 100, a hymn rejoicing in having dragged the heathen into court.

Before Jehovah's awful throne,
Ye nations bow with sacred joy,
Know that the Lord is God Alone,
He can create, and He destroy.[70]

Although this scarcely seems an appropriate choice of anthem for an event meant to encourage religious tolerance and reassure non-Christian delegates of open-minded reception, the reception and hospitality the Asian delegates received were more tolerant than they had expected.[71] They had considerable experience with Christian attitudes, were forewarned of the possibility of Christian aggression, and came prepared to deal with it. Nevertheless, the attempt to make Japanese Buddhism acceptable and relevant in this North American Protestant Christian arena imposed certain determinants on its representation and consequently on Western knowledge of Japanese Buddhism.

CHAPTER

THE RULES OF THE PARLIAMENT

Securing the Truth

The invitation to participate in the World's Parliament of Religions was accompanied by a ten-point list of the objects of the event and a set of "specific rules and regulations . . . promulgated for the conduct of the proposed conference."[1] The rules specified that delegates would "state their own beliefs and reasons for them with the greatest frankness" and would refrain from criticism of others. The Parliament was to be "a grand international assembly for mutual conference, fellowship, and information, and not for controversy, for worship, for the counting of votes or for the passing of resolutions."[2] These specific rules for the conduct of the Congress of Religions were supplemented by the rules governing the Auxiliary Congresses in general, which Charles C. Bonney proudly described as the "the actual working machinery," the controls under which, the author boasted, "even congresses on labour and religion were conducted with such order, decorum, peace, and success, as were never surpassed and probably never equalled."[3] Under the general headings of "Themes, Speakers and Limitations" and "Discussion of the Subjects Presented," these rules controlled what might be spoken of, who might speak, the conditions under which speech might be heard. "By far, the most important of all these rules and regulations," Bonney declared, "was that which excluded controversy and prohibited strife."[4]

The documents exude the rhetoric of tolerance and universal brotherhood and were frequently quoted by contemporary commentators, the Japanese delegates included, to exemplify the spirit of the event.[5] The World's Parliament of Religions was "to bring together in frank and friendly conference, the most eminent men of different faiths, strong in their personal convictions, who should strive to see and show what are the supreme truths, and what light religion has to throw upon the important problems of the age—the labour problem, education, social problems."[6] The Parliament was "a royal feast to which the representatives of every faith were asked to bring the richest fruits and the fairest flowers of their religion."[7] "Each representative was asked to present the very best things he could offer for those in whose behalf he spoke, and was admonished that nothing was desired of him in the way of attack on any other person, system or creed."[8] The integrity of the proceedings as a serious search for the light of the world was further protected by being "rigidly purged of cranks," and there was "neither time nor fitness for minor sects."[9]

Although they appear to guarantee a generous and all encompassing tolerance, the objects of the Parliament, which emerged from and reinforced American and Christian dominance, and the rules of conduct of the Parliament that safeguarded them, conditioned the way non-Christian religions were represented. They controlled the discourse, effectively reducing all other religions to inadequate attempts to express the Christian revelation. They determined what was said of Buddhism and what authority was accorded the speech of its representatives.

This is, however, but one side of the Parliament's organization. No less important was the function of these rules in validating the knowledge that emerged. If only genuine authorities were allowed to speak, and they were allowed to speak freely, the event would produce the truth of all religions. This was then to be preserved in the official record, a "permanent record to be published to the world, an *accurate and authoritative account* of the present condition and outlook of religion among the leading nations of the earth."[10] Writing after the event, Bonney was explicit in confirming the authority of Barrows's version: "[T]he Parliament must be judged by its official record, edited by its Chairman, the Rev. Dr. John Henry Barrows, and not by any nor all of the very numerous fragmentary and distorted reports of it, *which have misled portions of the public at home and abroad*."[11]

The book, extensively edited and embellished with photographs—not artists' impressions but captured instances of "reality"—was the true record of the Parliament. In a certain sense, the point of the Parliament was to produce the text:

"[T]he chief object is to procure the maturest thought of the world on all the great questions of the age, in a form best adapted to universal publication."[12] It was the organizers' stated plan that it would become a source of reference and debate, a record for the next century to judge—and, indeed, though other records are available, it remains the authoritative source.[13] This chapter first considers the way in which the rules of the Parliament conditioned the presentation of Buddhism and the Japanese delegates' participation. It then looks at the way our memory of the event was further shaped by Barrows's record of it.

Absence of Debate

The rule of conduct most praised by the Parliament's chroniclers was that "no provision was made for any free debating society in the whole range of the Congresses."[14] Johnson confidently identified this as the fundamental condition of the success of the event.

> Strict regulations were made and enforced for the exclusion of the volunteer address, and of every form of random talk. The entire time at disposal was allotted to those who were supposed to be the most competent to instruct and advise. Controversy was prohibited and the passing of resolutions of approval and censure was forbidden. The writers and speakers were asked not to attack the views of others but to set forth with as much cogency as possible the merits of their own. The theory of the Congresses was that those who spoke in them were addressing the intellectual and moral world through the medium of the Congresses, and that *the views expressed would be afterward widely discussed in pulpit, forum, public press, and private conversation* . . . participating countries were earnestly requested . . . to recommend for the Congress speakers and writers of the highest qualifications and abilities.[15]

The overriding concerns of the organizers in calling the Congress of Religions a parliament appears to have been first, to convey the principle of the equal right to be heard and, second, that each of the speakers was a legitimate representative of his constituency. The event diverged from the parliamentary ideal most significantly on precisely the point regularly identified as its greatest achievement, the absence of debate. It was this, said one critic, that reduced it from a true parliament to a mere "World's Fair of Theological exhibits with a sort of Midway Plaisance attachment for the *bric à brac* of creeds."[16]

For most commentators, the lack of controversy at the Parliament was considered one of its greatest achievements. "Random talk"—unexpected and uncontrolled outbursts and address on unwanted issues—arose only on one or two occasions, such as when a speaker on Islam inspired "a sudden and unpremeditated outburst of feeling" by "what was taken for an attack on the fundamental principle of social morality."[17] Control of what could be spoken of began from the time that Barrows, as chairman and organizer of the program, read and approved papers. He disapproved of Hirai's first paper, but Hirai persisted, demanding the right to speak. Debate was prohibited under the banner of tolerance and fair hearing, allowing no room for the "malignant enemy of human progress . . . that vindictive spirit which finds delight in assailing others instead of presenting something meritorious of its own."[18] There was, however, another side to the prohibition. In the control of "volunteer address and random talk" the only questions or comments allowed during the sessions were under the control of the presiding officer, who could call upon the "most eminent persons present,"[19] invariably leading Christian theologians. The right of rebuttal of parliamentary debate was denied. Votes of approval or censure were also specifically forbidden, but significantly only during the proceedings, and because, as Bonney explained, the subjects treated were too important to be "submitted to the vote of those who happen to be present." This is what made the published record of the proceedings so important. It was to offer the papers "for subsequent deliberate examination by the enlightened minds of all countries; for unrestricted discussion in the forum, the pulpit, and the public press; and finally for that exalted public opinion which expresses the consensus of such minds."[20] The organizers intended that the discussion would take place in forums effectively closed to the foreign delegates. The non-Christian delegates would have no right of reply, no possibility of engaging in the discourse, or of intervening in the formation of its objects.[21] This may have been less a deliberate ploy to control discourse on non-Christian religions than a consequence of the extrapolation of Bonney's original vision of an essentially North American ecumenical harmony. It was nevertheless effective in excluding Buddhists from the discussion of Buddhism, from the public forum where they might answer criticisms or questions and clarify meanings.

As a consequence, the Parliament provided Christian sermon writers with a whole set of "straw men" authenticated and validated by the status of the delegates as chosen representatives of their faith and the assurance that they presented the "finest fruits" of their belief. Barrows's writings and sermons after the Parliament show that he at least used the Parliament in this way. Having hosted the delegates and attended the Parliament, he prefaced his still uninformed attacks on Buddhism by claiming he knew Oriental religions "both ideal and practical."[22] Under the banner of tolerance, free speech, and fair play, discourse was controlled and held tightly within the confines of Christian domination. There were no criticisms or questions in the one public forum where they might have been answered, where meanings might have been clarified. Buddhists had no control at all over how the information created under these restrictive conditions was then diffused.

Authorizing Speech

One of the most consistently repeated of the regulations was the assurance that all representatives were to be "persons of strong and vigorous convictions who would be acknowledged by their organizations as worthy to speak on their behalf."[23] The truth was guaranteed by controlling the speaker, and the constant reiteration of this rule and its enforcement were fundamental to the authority of the record. Nevertheless, we find that the Buddhist delegates were not the only "authorities" to speak on Buddhism. The number of Christians speaking on Buddhism at least equaled the number of authorized Buddhists. Apart from the Christian missionaries who directly attacked Buddhism in apparent disregard for the rules of the Parliament, a number of Christian theologians spoke of Buddhism within papers on the main themes. The imbalance is even greater if we consider that Buddhism was implicated in the discussion of nihilism, atheism, and materialist philosophy (see Chapter 4).

If we leave aside for the moment the problem of considering Buddhism as a single entity, Buddhism first entered into the proceedings in a paper by Professor Milton Valentine, D.D., president of a theological college and scholar of comparative religion. Valentine argued the universality of the notion of God, an argument that required he explain the apparent anomaly of Buddhist "atheism." Other non-Buddhists who contributed to the discussion included Professor M. S. Terry. The argument of his paper, "Sacred Books of the World as Literature," was that for those brought up under Christianity, there was little that was attractive in the writings of Buddhism, which, as he described it, was negative, life-denying, and pessimistic.[24] Mrs. Eliza Sunderland, Ph.D., speaking on hierology, confirmed for the audience that Buddhism was a "stiflingly ascetic ethical system." Buddhism, she declared, "neglects the divine, preaches the final salvation of man from the miseries of existence through the power of his own self-renunciation, and as it was atheistic in origin, it soon became infected by the fantastic of mythology and the most childish of superstitions."[25] Isaac T. Headland presented an illustrated firsthand account of idolatry and superstition in Chinese Buddhism and the degradation of its priesthood under the title "Religion in Peking." Each of these speakers was apparently "qualified" to speak, in spite of their obvious antagonism to Buddhism and lack of endorsement by any Buddhist community, by their training in Christian theology or the Western science of comparative religion.

Among the Christian missionaries speaking on Buddhism was the Reverend Dr. S. G. McFarland, veteran missionary from Bangkok. While not overly critical—Buddhism's moral code compared favorably with the Christian Decalogue—he nevertheless confirmed the atheistic, pessimistic, and selfish image of the Theravada.[26] The Reverend M. L. Gordon, missionary at Doshisha in Japan, with less sympathy, spoke on "Why Buddhism Is Not a Universal Religion."[27] The authority of these missionaries apparently depended on their firsthand contact with Asian religions, but on no account could they be considered accepted representatives of the Asian communities, and surely the condition of strong and vigorous commitment demanded of speakers by the rules of the Parliament implied commitment to the religion they spoke on. The prevailing attitude of the missionary contingent was indicated by the refusal of pioneer Chinese scholar Dr. Legge, himself a missionary, to attend a mission conference "where he would be compelled to listen to a continual violation of the Ninth Commandment [Thou shalt not bear false witness against thy neighbor] against those who would have no opportunity of defending themselves."[28] Legge, at least, recognized the importance of the right to rebuttal, denied at the Parliament in service of harmony.

The Parliament papers were given in three main divisions. Apart from the central forum, supposedly devoted to the great questions of religion, there was the parallel Scientific Section, which was given over to papers described as of "a more scientific and less popular character," and the Denominational Congresses, which encompassed such diverse discussions as the Congress on Missions and Sunday rest. In the Scientific Section of the Parliament, in contrast to the control of the main sessions, "papers were often followed by free conversation"[29] and the rules of qualification and commitment were so frequently flouted that they may not have applied at all. It was here that Christians spoke on Buddhism, Hinduism, Shintō, and every other religion controlled only by the "scientific" rules of comparative religion, a field of study itself imbued with Christian preoccupations. Whatever the distinctions made between papers presented in this category in the application of the "rigidly enforced" controls on authority, they were published along with those of the main presentations with nothing more than a subheading to indicate any change of perspective or authority.

The end result of these exceptions to the rigid enforcement of the rule of authority is that Gordon, missionary to Japan, was given equal status with Buddhist abbots. Barrows himself, summing up the Buddhist conception of God, referred with equal deference to the papers of Professor Valentine and of Shaku Sōen, the Buddhist "bishop," and of Dharmapāla, the Theravada representative. He ignored the contributions of the other qualified Buddhist authorities—all of whom addressed the issue of theism. Most significant, this essentializing stance overlooked any distinctions Japanese made between the teachings of their religion and the Buddhisms of other parts of Asia they were at pains to distance themselves from.

Extending Authority: The Solicited Prize Essay

Barrows had solicited papers attacking the religions of East Asia. He wrote to a missionary in Japan requesting a paper on Taoism, the "Demon in the Triad of Chinese Religion: Dragon, Image and Demon" (Confucianism, Buddhism, and Taoism), offering "an opportunity to present the dark features of a heathen system."[30] The paper on Confucianism presented to the Parliament by the eminently qualified Chinese diplomat and Confucian scholar Pung Kwang[31] was put against an essay by a Chinese Christian convert solicited in competition for which Barrows offered a prize of "a premium of gold."[32]

Introducing the paper, Barrows highlighted the fact that it was a "prize essay"—a paper proved by competition to be the best information on the subject—and an up-to-date opinion, because it was written especially for the Parliament and had been translated just a few months earlier (May 1893). As English is presumably the native language of the translator, the Reverend Timothy Richard of the English Baptist Mission, China, one can only assume that the decidedly quaint English in which the essay was written—"this doctrine is all important, like as the hinge of a door"—was meant to signal its authentic Chinese origin; that the translator made himself as transparent as possible, taking care not to impose the rules of English grammar on the work. Barrows, as editor, apparently followed his example. The essay did not criticize Confucianism as such, only its contemporary manifestation. It reinforced the message projected by Christians since the time of Matteo Ricci, that Confucianism is a system of civil organization with a monotheistic world view that is not antagonistic to Christianity. It was, however, critical of Taoism and Buddhism, to which were attributed the apparent flaws in observable practice. A third paper on Confucianism by Dr. Ernst Faber, "Genesis and Development of Confucianism,"[33] confirmed this general attitude. Faber presented Confucius as a fundamentalist reformer urging modern Chinese to throw out such evil accretions as foot binding, to return to his original teaching, and to learn from the West. Putting aside the sympathy shown here with Barrows's own mission, the point I want to make is not how Confucianism was represented but the discrepancy between the professed rules governing who may speak and the actual freedom of platform and overt encouragement given to critics of non-Christian religions. We should also note how the implication of Japanese Buddhism in essentialized notions of "Asia" and "Asian religions" contributed to what was said of it at the Parliament.

The Rule of Time

The possibility of presenting a coherent account of non-Christian religions was also restricted by the organization of the event. Like all well-run conferences, the World's Parliament of Religions placed firm restrictions on the length of time available to each speaker, assuring equal opportunity and encouraging its speakers to be concise and to the point: "[L]engthy papers are neither necessary or desirable."[34] This may indeed be the case for the Parliament as Bonney originally envisaged it, a forum for establishing Judeo-Christian ecumenism in which mainly Christian speakers would argue points of contention within a generally agreed body of doctrine, rehearse familiar controversies, and at most publicize ongoing institutional issues. Twenty minutes, the allocation, is ample time to express platitudes of fraternity and shared visions of the future. It may even be an appropriate period in which to present an explanation of a point of doctrinal difference between denominations within the shared ground of belief in the Holy Trinity. However, it totally removed the possibility of Buddhists establishing the parameters of their discussion.

The Buddhist explanation of their alternate view of the world could not be dealt with in a twenty-minute paper, especially because it was delivered in a foreign language, one that restricted the vocabulary for translation of Buddhist technical terms to either Christian terms or the terms of materialist philosophy, to an unprepared and largely uninterested audience. Curiosity is not the same as actually wanting to work at understanding what other people believe. A short paper, regardless of its desirability in other circumstances, could not allow the presentation of a total and totally unfamiliar belief system in any meaningful way. Presented under these circumstances, non-Christian religions must necessarily have seemed shallow, incomplete, and no doubt incoherent. The rule of time served to preserve and perpetuate the mystery and apparent irrelevance that surrounded them. Because there was an existing body of Western scholarship on Buddhism, the short papers prevented a real assault on the aspects of Western knowledge the Buddhists delegates perceived as error. Here, again, the organizing rules of the Parliament acted to reinforce the existing construct.

The Finest Fruits

What could be said, and was understood, about non-Christian religions was also conditioned by the apparently benevolent attitude that "the so-called heathen religions must not be judged solely by their idolatries and cruel rites any more than apple trees should be judged by their worst fruits."[35] The rule branded non-Christian religions as cruel and idolatrous in its very enunciation, reminding the audience that however reasonable the representation at the Parliament may seem, it is only one side of the picture. The other, darker side remained unspoken but was not to be forgotten.

Preserving the coexistence of good and evil in Buddhism was fundamental to the mission campaign of its eradication. The Reverend Spence Hardy, for example, one of the first missionaries to write on Buddhism, explained that to overcome Buddhism, Christians had to admit that there was undoubtedly much that was good in it. This was because it could not be denied, if the teachings alone were considered, that it had much in common with Christianity. The point of difference to be stressed, he argued, was that Buddhism is atheistic and nihilistic, and these faults outweigh all else.[36]

Discrepancy between the ideal teachings of a religion and its actual practice was also exploited. This again was a familiar argument against Buddhism. Because Western scholars had created the Buddha Sakyamuni as a historical, humanist philosopher, the lack of fit between the "Pure Buddhism" of their construct and Asian practices was explained by the inadequacy of such an austere philosophy to meet the needs of the people or, alternately, in racist terms, the inadequacy of the people to live up to the precepts. Barrows, qualifying the representation of Buddhism by the Japanese delegates, concluded that "the oriental speakers were, on the whole, fairly representative of the higher ideas of their own faith, if not of the popular religions."[37] His message was a clear reminder to his readers that what they had heard on Japanese Buddhism was partial. While it is certainly true that the Japanese presentation of Buddhism did not deal with popular Japanese practice, the same could certainly be said of the papers on Christianity.

The rule demanding that only the "finest fruits" of each religion be displayed opened the opportunity for the play of comparison between ideal and actuality. This was a familiar missionary practice in which biblical ideals were taken as the measure of existing Asian practice, usually as it could be observed among the poor and socially deprived.[38] The paper on Buddhism in Japan by Gordon exemplified the practice.[39] His "irrefragable" evidence of the immorality of Japanese priests came from rumors circulating in Christian missionary circles, from statistics of admissions to the mission clinics for treatment of "immoral diseases," and from the rhetoric of Meiji Buddhist reform, which followed the usual practice of enlisting public support for change by emphasizing present decay. One must ask not only why Gordon, as a Christian, was allowed to speak on Buddhism but what place his information had under the rules of the Parliament? Why, also, did it deserve inclusion in the Parliament proper rather than the smaller, less public Scientific Section? And, because Barrows tells us that he found it necessary to be quite severe in his selection and editing of the material to preserve in the two-volume record, why was this paper preserved against all the rules for securing the truth?

Like so many of the rules of the Parliament, this much repeated insistence on presenting only the best of each religion was at best selectively applied. Gordon's paper was devoted to what he believed was wrong with Buddhism, arguing in essence that its principal defect was that it was not Christianity. It has no concept of soul, an inadequate concept of deity, no sense of a personal sin against God, and an unsatisfactory doctrine of salvation. As well as this, he claimed, it is pessimistic, holds women in contempt, lacks homogeneity and unity, and is not exclusive or, as he put it, fails "to command the exclusive reverence of the human heart."[40] One would not expect this last observation to be ground for criticism amid the professions of brotherhood of the Parliament. With similar disregard for the much-lauded rules of the Parliament, missionaries discussing Hinduism did not hesitate to refer to *sati*, infanticide, child marriage, and *devadasi*.[41] These were familiar targets of criticism and, as such, were consequently also discussed by the Indian representatives of the Brahmo Samaj, because reform of these practices was essential to the foundation of their society,[42] and Jain delegate

Virchand Gandhi, who felt they reflected on Indian society as a whole. The point is that the reiteration of the existence of these practices, even in the statement of their reform, consolidated their association with Hinduism.

We have already discussed the implications of the rule insisting on the presentation of all that was good in each religion. Johnson's record, rephrasing it in the familiar terms of fundamentalist reform, of separating the essence of the religion from "any pernicious practices that had grown up through the centuries and claimed protection under its name,"[43] opens the possibility of a further interpretation. Asian religions were to be rationalized in the post-Enlightenment sense of the word by order of the organizing committee. Johnson avoided Barrows's hint of skeletons in the closet but nevertheless inappropriately imposed Christian and post-Enlightenment criteria of acceptability on what may be said about non-Christian religions. He enshrined the constructs of Western Orientalist scholarship, which were formed by this rationalization of severing "pernicious practices," "accretions of time," from Oriental religions to reveal the "true" doctrine. In Buddhist scholarship this meant stripping away all practice, ritual, mythology—and the whole of the Mahayana—to reveal the supposed essence of Sakyamuni's teaching, preserved in the oldest texts. Most important for the Japanese delegates, under this rule Japanese Buddhism, which did not exist in any form until more than a thousand years after the birth of the Buddha, could be dismissed as not really being Buddhism at all. This was, however, a familiar challenge to the Japanese delegates, and one that they set out prepared to meet.

Language and Authenticity

The rules of the Parliament specified that the proceedings were to be conducted in the English language. Apart from the difficulty the delegates faced in translating Buddhist concepts into English, there was also the problem of actual spoken delivery, of being audible, intelligible, and convincing while speaking to an audience of several thousand people in an unamplified hall. Dharmapāla and Vivekanada, both of whom lived under British domination in South Asia and therefore were familiar with both the English language and Western modes of public address, managed most effectively. This no doubt had a great deal to do with their popularity and their prominence in the press. Malalgoda comments on the importance of effective public speaking in Buddhist revival in Ceylon in the second half of the nineteenth century.[44] Buddhists, compelled to engage in debate with Christian missionaries, gave up the time-honored Buddhist mode of quiet, spoken, seated address in favor of the Protestant standing harangue with great success. The Japanese priests had not made this transition. Among the Japanese Buddhists Hirai and Noguchi alone had sufficient command of the language to speak before the audience.[45]

These problems aside, the more important aspect of the rule was that although the organizers deliberately sought out delegates with a knowledge of English,[46] the ability of the delegates to speak English was used to undermine their credibility as authentic representatives of non-Christian religions. The very fact of being learned and understanding English, Barrows argued, proved that they had come into contact with Western philosophy and Christian thought; consequently, whatever appeared to be positive aspects of their religion he dismissed as reflections of the power of these influences. His travels in India, China, and Japan subsequent to the Parliament apparently confirmed him in this belief because in 1899 he again declared that "Christianity has become so pervasive that it is difficult to find scholarly men who have not been touched by its brightness."[47]

The Published Record

The Parliament generated a profusion of literature,[48] but as the quotation from Charles Bonney at the head of this chapter states, only Barrows's edition was to be considered authoritative. It alone preserved the "truth" as generated by the event. Of the other publications available, the nearest challenger was *Neely's History of the Parliament of Religions*, the only other work that offered a "complete" record of the papers presented. *Neely*'s edition was compiled from original manuscripts supplemented by notes of the proceedings taken by "an expert stenographer who attended every session,"[49] whose certification of accuracy, completeness, and authenticity appears immediately behind the title page. Comparison of the two works reveals considerable discrepancies between them.

In general, the papers in Barrows's official edition tend to be shorter and more heavily edited, especially in the second volume where many of the papers on Buddhism appear. Hirai's paper, "Synthetic Religion," for example, is about four hundred words long in Barrows but closer to two thousand in *Neely's History*. Shaku Sōen's controversial "Arbitration Instead of War" in Barrows has been reduced to about half the length of the paper published by *Neely*. A minor casualty of the desire to preserve the seriousness and harmony of the event was Shaku Sōen's opening quip on the sixteenth day, a Congress on Buddhism, expressing the joy in having no one but "we heathen" on the platform.[50] Some papers, such as "Man from a Catholic Point of View,"[51] were omitted entirely, but then Barrows openly admitted that some interesting papers had to be "retrenched" for lack of space.[52] Barrows's editorial policy was not to record the total proceedings as *Neely's History* claimed to do. He had a higher purpose. He explained in a notice to readers in the front of the first volume that although it is rich with valuable materials, "it would be even more valuable if parts of it had been rigorously condensed."[53] The second volume therefore was to be carefully pruned "to furnish a book of 800 pages, in which the gold will be even more abundant than in the first volume." The selection and reduction of papers rested on what Barrows considered to be "gold," and this was clearly his vision of the triumph of future Christian universality to which he devoted his remaining years,[54] and he seems to have had few qualms about editing contributions accordingly.

As in the Parliament itself, the truth of the papers rested on the authority of the delegates speaking under Parliamentary protection, but here the image of harmony was even more controlled. Barrows modified the language of the papers, softening views that may have been considered critical. He eliminated contentious language and ideas such as Hirai's provocative call for religious unity: "Stop your debate about the difference of religion. Kill Gautama. . . . Do not mind Christ. . . . Tear up the Bible."[55] Although the sentiment may have conformed to the Parliamentary ideal of the nonsectarian pursuit of the truth, Hirai's expression jarred the harmony of the record and, no doubt, would have assailed Christian sensitivities. Violent rhetoric conformed to the image of neither men of religion nor gentlemen of the Orient. The publication of such a statement would also have made it rather difficult for Barrows to present Hirai, as he did, as a candidate for conversion. The purging of discord was again used as a device of control.

Ashitsu Jitsuzen's paper was edited to less than half its length in Barrows's edition.[56] The first three pages of the six that appear in *Neely's History* were heavily condensed. The paper was cut short, avoiding Ashitsu's criticism of Western scholarship and his suggestion that there might be more to Buddhism than the West had yet realized. The paper, as it appeared in *Neely's History*, continued, observing that although many Europeans and Americans had studied Buddhism, they had never heard of Mahayana and, consequently, "they too hastily concluded that the true doctrine of Buddhism is Hinayana, and that so-called Mahayana is nothing but a portion of Indian pure philosophy. They are wrong. They have entirely misunderstood. They have only poorly gained with their scanty knowledge a smattering of Buddhism. They are entirely ignorant of the boundless sea of Buddha's doctrine rolling just beyond their feet."[57]

Other cuts in this paper include Buddhist technical terms in Japanese, Sanskrit, and Chinese, and their explanation. These may not have meant much to the general reader Barrows had in mind, but their absence in the record may go some way toward explaining why scholars using this source dismiss the paper as a vague gesture toward the aims expressed in the Japanese.[58] With the aid of a dictionary of Buddhist terms to decipher it, the paper appears as a desperate attempt to convey a great deal of doctrine. It was, if nothing more, an indication that there was a great deal of Japanese Mahayana Buddhism that the West knew nothing of—the "boundless sea" he had referred to—a verbal gesture equivalent to the gift of the four hundred volumes of sutras in Chinese the delegation placed before the Parliament on the opening day. Compare, for example, the two discussions of the Three Bodies of the Buddha (Japanese: *sanshin*; Sanskrit: *trayah kayah*). In Barrows we get merely: "Buddha has three personalities. The first is entirely colorless and formless, but at the same time, it has the nature of eternality, omnipresence, and unchangeableness." In *Neely's History* the equivalent passage reads: "The Buddha has three personalities, namely Hosshin, Hoshin and Wojin. Now in Hosshin, Ho means law, and Shin means personality, so it is a name given to the personality of the constitution after the Buddha got the highest Buddhahood. This personality is entirely colorless and formless, but at the same time, it has the nature of eternality, omnipresence and unchangeableness. Hosshin is called Birushana in Sanskrit, and Honissai-sho in Chinese, both meaning omnipresence."

Granted the version in *Neely's History* was probably no more comprehensible to the audience at the Parliament, but by giving the Buddhist terms it indicated that there was indeed a Japanese doctrine dealing with the nature of the Buddha—that the concept of "Buddha" was far more subtle and complicated than the Western assumption of a human historical figure. Because the target audience for the Japanese delegation was Western scholars, a group that included people with knowledge of these languages, correlating the Japanese with the Sanskrit and Chinese opened the way for comparative study, and perhaps even a share of the admiration granted Sanskrit philosophical works. The effort to communicate is apparent even if the gesture was ineffective.

The significance of radical editing of the papers is also apparent in the debate over Shaku Sōen's paper "Arbitration Instead of War."[59] It is clear from the introductory passages available in *Neely's History* that the title is a reference to the opening address and proposes that the various religions of the world follow the example of international law, recognizing existing differences, protecting the weak against aggression. This was a core theme of the Japanese project in support of treaty revision at Chicago. In his closing remarks to the Parliament Hirai returned to the issue, congratulating the hosts as "the pioneers of human history. You have achieved an assembly of the world's religions, and we believe your next step will be toward the ideal goal of this Parliament, the realization of international justice."[60] As it appears in Barrows's edition, Shaku Sōen's paper is reduced to a rather woolly statement of brotherhood and peace. The longer version proposed that just as nations of the world settle their differences through international law—a law they all agree to, although it is not the national law of any of them—there should be an agreed common belief that all could uphold though none need claim as their own. The theme for the day on which he presented the paper, the sixteenth day of the Parliament, was the attitude of Christianity toward other religions. With typical Japanese concern for the appropriateness of the occasion, Shaku Sōen put in a gentle plea that the attitude displayed at the World's Parliament of Religions be generally applied; that differences be put aside under the general law of truth.[61] It was a call for coexistence in religious plurality rather than conversion.

The Parliament Illustrated

The visual spectacle of the World's Parliament of Religions was reproduced in the official publication. Portraits throughout conveyed the essential message of the global representation of religious opinion, and Protestant Christian universality was asserted by the prominent display of portraits in exotic costume of Christians from all corners of the world,[62] including portraits of Christian converts from India and Japan. A distinctively turbaned Honorable Maya Das, who, although not a delegate, was "a leading native Christian," appears on page 30, and on page 37 we find "that earnest Christian, Hon. Harman Singh, uncle of His Royal Highness Jatjat Jit Singh, the Maharajah of Karputhala." The rank of these men countered the accusation that Christianity was only successful among the lower classes of Indian society, a matter discussed at length in the Congress on Missions.

Christian converts were depicted well dressed, clean, alert, straight-backed, in two-thirds profile, as were the Christian delegates. These formal portraits were in distinct contrast to photographs of subjects such as the Brahman Pundits, depicted sitting on the floor in round-shouldered slouch.[63] The clearest example of what appears to be a mirror of the lessons in Social Darwinism of the Midway Plaisance was the photograph of "A Mendicant Dervish" (p. 712), slouched, slack-jawed, shifty-eyed, and barefoot, a stereotypical "Oriental" in what appears to be a staged studio portrait taken against a painted backdrop and foregrounded with exotic flowering plants. Christianity, the photographs of the converts claimed, was a force for civilization.

Portraits of the Asian delegates in the publication, as in the Parliament itself, provided the exotic, the picturesque, "arrayed in costly silk vestments of all colors of the rainbow."[64] The dignity of the delegates reflected on the event itself; of course, these were men who, as Barrows pointed out, had been touched by the civilizing influences of Western education and Christianity. However, the contrast between the portraits of these men and the photographs of native priests, native pilgrims, and scenes of native practice paralleled the contrast already stressed by Barrows and the rules of the Parliament between the "finest fruits" and the reality of Asian practice. The two illustrations accompanying Toki Hōryū's article make this point. The first is a portrait of Toki himself, captioned with a quotation "time to remodel Japanese Buddhism" (p. 545); the second is a curious photograph of an itinerant priest accompanied by a young child assistant ("A Buddhist Priest Carrying a Portable Idol Shrine," p. 553). The juxtaposition of the illustrations proclaimed Barrows's caution of the darker side of non-Christian religions, the discrepancy between ideal and reality and, in this case, a reminder of the persistence of idolatry in Japan.

Japan nevertheless fared comparatively well in Barrows's selection of images. Japanese Buddhism was also represented by several ornate buildings and a studio portrait of a "pilgrim" standing before a portrait of Mount Fuji (p. 629). By far the greater number of photographs depicted Shintō subjects, reflecting the assumption that Shintō, the indigenous religion of Japan, was more typically representative of Japanese religion than the "foreign" imported Buddhism. The Shintō priest, a venerable bearded figure ornately clothed in voluminous white robes, conveyed the very image of Oriental respectability. This general message of "non-barbaric heathenism" was expanded by the Shintō couple, the Shintō gateway, and the Shintō shrines, all of them exotic but inoffensive.

The privileging of Shintō evident in the illustrations reflected the marginalization of Japanese Buddhism by Western academics. For Barrows the Buddhism of Japan remained firmly within the general category of later aberrations of the original teachings of the Buddha, even after he had actually visited the country.[65] The Buddhism of Japan was but one of the present manifestations in various Asian countries, which were but aberrant forms of "real" Buddhism, lumped together into some sort of monolithic entity as a consequence of this common origin. Whatever was said of Buddhism in whatever form, therefore, contributed to the image of Japanese Buddhism, and illustrations such as those of "idols" in temples in Rangoon and Bangkok reinforced the notion of Buddhist idolatry in which the Buddhism of Japan shared.

Japan's place in the general Western category of "Asian" or "Oriental" also meant that depictions of other Asian religions, especially Hinduism, reflected on Japanese Buddhism. It was, after all, only a few decades before this that Emerson had referred to the Upanishads as Buddhist. The distinction was not widely recognized. Barrows reported that during the Parliament "even the omniscient newspapers were all the while confusing the faiths of the world."[66] Hinduism was represented by its architecture, its icons, and its people. One cannot accuse Barrows of misrepresentation, because all of the photographs are authentic, but the accumulated effect of scenes such as "Hindus at Their Devotions before Partaking of Food," which shows men, typically dressed with bare chest, seated on the ground about to eat (p. 315); of "Burning Ghat at Calcutta," showing a corpse exposed on the ground (p. 173); of *sunnyasis* with matted hair covered in ashes (p. 329); of "Shiva's Bull Carved out of Solid Stone" (p. 111)—which incidentally included two men, again "half-naked" in Indian fashion in postures of worship—was nevertheless to reinforce the "uncivilized," "heathen," and "idolatrous" images of India. Barrows's readers were no doubt as unimpressed by the display of skin in Asian dress as were their contemporary Western visitors to the East. The nineteenth-century West was affronted by uncovered bodies.[67] Uncovered bodies were primitive. Other aspects of the scenes—eating on the ground, public bathing, mass ritual, death unconcealed—would also fail to conform to audience proprieties. Other illustrations included multilimbed deities such as the sculpture of Siva slaying the Elephant Demon (simply captioned as "Interior of Hindu Temple," p. 321). Such images were still unacceptable to the Western aesthetic well into the twentieth century. Even for V. A. Smith, whose pioneering work *Fine Art in India and Ceylon* (1911) was the first to grant that India actually produced "Fine Art," they were "grotesque and absurd." "Additional limbs are put on as prescribed, whether or not they destroy the balance of the composition or excite a feeling of disgust at monstrous growths that call out loudly for amputation."[68]

The overall effect of the illustrations of India was to reinforce the missionary image of the idolatrous, heathen Oriental, and the contrast between this and the depiction of Japan in this publication accurately reflected Barrows's later statement of his feelings toward the two countries. India was for him "a great banyan tree, spreading out dark, wide, and gloomy, with many of its trunks decayed, a resting place of unclean birds, and sombre with clouds that cover both the zenith and the horizon." Japan, by contrast, was "a wild-cherry blossom, gleaming in the morning light of Western civilization." While his India represented the decaying past, "Japan represents the present and the future, and her brave, intelligent people abound with national hope and self-confidence."[69] The problem for the Japanese Buddhist delegation, however, was that for Barrows the Japanese religion that accompanied this positive image was not Buddhism but Confucianism, Shintō, or even Christianity. The relationship of Western attitudes to the two Indian religions, Hinduism and Buddhism, is dealt with in the following chapter, but the attitudes evident in the illustrations to the official record of the Parliament justify the Japanese project of distancing Japanese Buddhism from the Buddhism of the South.

The publication of the official record also gave Barrows the right of commentary. Although the work was ostensibly a record of the proceedings, that is, the papers of the delegates, large sections of both volumes were given over to Barrows's interpretation of the proceedings, his summaries of the most important issues, and comments from a variety of sources selected by him. In these sections he distilled the knowledge produced on such themes as "what the various faiths had to say concerning God" and "what the various religions reported in regard to the nature of man." In his summary of what Buddhism has to say concerning God Barrows referred only to Valentine, Shaku Sōen, and Dharmapāla, and as mentioned earlier, against all the rules of the Parliament he gave non-Christian authority equal weight with the authority of these selected Buddhists, ignoring other genuine Buddhist authorities such as Toki Hōryū, Ashitsu Jitsuzen, and Yatsubuchi Bunryū. In his desire to capture the essence of Buddhism he ignored differences and merged the Theravada and Mahayana. Barrows had the final say in defining what was said of Buddhism at the Parliament.

The Priority of the Text

The Japanese were very aware of the importance of the published record of the conference to Western understanding of their religion. Supporters of the delegation argued the need for the All Sects Buddhist Union to send an official Buddhist delegation to Chicago for this reason. They argued that the official body needed to take control of what was said at the Parliament because this would be recorded and would be regarded as the truth of Japanese Buddhism. Representation should not be left to an independent, because "what he says and what he does will be recorded as the principles of Buddhism, will be published in magazines and spread all over the world."[70] It is therefore most important, they argued, that what is said by the delegates agrees with what the union wished published. Once in print it would be impossible to change. The delegates and their supporters not only prepared their papers with this in mind but prepared a number of books on Japanese Buddhism for distribution.[71] These were especially written for the occasion and were then circulated among the Buddhist community, published in journals for discussion before being translated and printed for distribution. The decision to publish books was presumably to overcome the limitations of the short papers given on topics directed by the Christian organizers of the Parliament. Delegates also avoided the constraints of the official edition by publishing versions of their papers in Paul Carus's journals.[72] Each paper in Barrows carried his 1893 claim to copyright.

Max Muller wrote congratulating the organizers on the success of the World's Parliament of Religions, admitting that it had succeeded beyond his expectations.[73] Muller had not attended but had contributed a paper, though not, as one might expect, on Asian religions. Muller was generous in his praise of the American achievement, but in his view the real parliament of religions had occurred some time before with the publication of the "forty silent volumes" of his Sacred Books of the East series. As Muller saw it, the Parliament was a success because the world had been prepared for it through this work.[74] These volumes, he declared, were more authoritative than the Chicago Parliament because they contained the truth of the ancient texts rather than the well-intentioned but frequently erroneous accounts of Asian religions in their modern distortions. Muller criticized certain speakers—singling out Buddhists for his example—for putting forward statements that could not be substantiated by "chapter and verse from their own canonical books."[75] "It was the absence of this authority, the impossibility of checking the enthusiastic descriptions of the supreme excellence of every single religion, that seems to me to have somewhat interfered with the usefulness of that great ecumenical meeting at Chicago."[76] The rules of truth of the time gave ultimate authority to the written text. Muller's project—capturing the real and original essence of Eastern religions—was not that of the Parliament, which claimed to describe instead their present state, to encapsulate the living truths of the world's religions by having them delivered firsthand by the highest authorities. The authority of the World's Parliament of Religions nevertheless resided in its textual record.

Conclusion

There was a significant discrepancy between the statement of the rules governing the conduct of the World's Parliament of Religions and their implementation. The Parliament was to encapsulate the truth of each religion, truth that was guaranteed by the eminence and strength of conviction of the delegates, their presence and authority, given the fair and equal opportunity to speak, unconstrained by hostility, criticism, or debate. The rules successfully controlled "dangerous" speech, random and voluntary speech. They acted nevertheless to limit what could be said about Buddhism and to undermine the authority of what was said when it contradicted Christian expectations. The rules, however, remained flexible enough to allow the dominant Christian opinion to be expressed throughout. Most important was the effect of their frequent declaration that assured the truth of the proceedings. The publication was presented with the guarantee that it contained the truth of the present state of religion in the world. In particular, it contained the truth of Buddhism as presented by properly qualified "true believers" speaking in an atmosphere of professed tolerance without fear of contradiction, argument, or censure.

CHAPTER

ALTERITY

Buddhism as the "Other" of Christianity

Buddhism held a unique place at the World's Parliament of Religions. More than any other non-Christian religion it was the "other" of Christianity. Its function was not *xenos*, the radically different and totally "not-us" of the "heathen," "idolatrous" Hinduism of missionary rhetoric, or of Islam, which at this event remained beyond the pale,[1] but that of alterity. Buddhism was recognizably similar, a religion comparable with Christianity, but differing from it precisely on those points at issue in the debates of the time. The crucial issues were the nature and existence of God, the divinity of Jesus, the immortality of the soul, and the contingent questions of morality and ethics. The centrality of these issues to the World's Parliament of Religions is apparent in Barrows's summary of the proceedings. The first three topics listed for discussion were "What the Various Faiths Had to Say concerning God," "The Nature of Man," and "On the Importance of Religion," a forum that provided an opportunity for most speakers to expound upon the impossibility of morality and ethical society without a Christian sense of Deity and belief in the immortal soul of man.[2]

This Buddhism was not the religion of any Asian practice but the reified product of Western discourse. The very term "Buddhism" is a Western invention. High Priest Hikkaduvē Sumangala drew the Parliament's attention to the fact that the Sinhalese were followers of the *arya dharma*, "miscalled Buddhism by

Western scholars."[3] The term itself signals the way that Christian presuppositions informed Buddhist studies, focusing on the life of the Founder and his actual teachings as recorded in the sacred texts. The Buddha was the human counterpart of Jesus.

By the time of the Parliament, the preceding decades of debate and scholarship had established and agreed upon certain facts: Buddhism was founded by a historical man, Sakyamuni, who had taught a system of ethical philosophy that had later (for variously contended reasons) developed features of a religion. This Buddhism was atheistic or at least agnostic, denied the existence of an immortal soul, and taught self-reliance rather than reliance on a savior. Both supporters and detractors also agreed that the teachings of the Buddha had much in common with contemporary Western philosophy. The division of Southern and Northern Buddhism was generally accepted. Southern Buddhism was the Buddhism of the Pali texts, associated with the Buddhist practices of Ceylon, Siam, and Burma. These preserved the "essence" of Buddhism, variously referred to as "Pure Buddhism," "Original Buddhism," or "Real Buddhism." Northern Buddhism was the Buddhism of Sanskrit texts and their derivatives in the languages of northern Asia. This was the Mahayana, considered to be a later corruption of the Founder's teachings. Southern Buddhism was "Protestant"; Northern Buddhism was "Romish."

So well established were these "truths" of Buddhism that Western scholars quite confidently corrected Asian Buddhist authorities who attempted to modify them. The Reverend Dr. F. F. Ellinwood, for example, wrote at length explaining the real meaning of nirvana to Japanese Buddhist abbot Shaku Sōen.[4] Eminent Pali scholar T. W. Rhys Davids also criticized Japanese delegate Ashitsu Jitsuzen's understanding of this key term. According to Rhys Davids, Ashitsu's paper at the World's Parliament of Religions demonstrated "how astounding is the gulf on all sides between popular beliefs and the conclusions of scholarship."[5] Western scholars alone possessed the truth of Buddhism. Asian practitioners became "merely nominal Buddhists who know little if anything about *genuine Buddhism as elucidated in the texts*."[6]

Little was known of Japanese Buddhism at this time except for the dismissive assumption that it was nothing more than a local bastardization of this "real" Buddhism. These existing Western assumptions of the nature of Buddhism were consequently central to the representation of Japanese Buddhism. The Japanese delegates, aware of Western Orientalist scholarship, aimed to attach to their religion all that was admired of this Buddhism, such as its rationality, its compatibility with science, and its prefiguring by two thousand years the ideas of contemporary Western philosophy. They aimed to correct it where they felt they were unjustly slandered, such as in the assumption that Japanese Mahayana could not be the actual teachings of Sakyamuni; to modify it where they felt that Mahayana Buddhism improved upon the Theravada, as in the assumption that Buddhism was pessimistic; to expand it, because they recognized how little of the great teachings was known in the West. The Japanese representation of Buddhism pivoted on this construct, and because of the close relationship of Western understanding of Buddhism with the debates of Christianity, so too did its reception.

This chapter traces the emergence of interest in Buddhism from the exoticisms of travelers, through the early attempts of colonial administrators and missionaries to catalog their charges, to the installation of the academic construct, showing how the information produced in the early, isolated exercises, elaborated upon and given credence through Orientalist scholarship, became a resource for discussions beyond these limited specialist fields, as intellectual journals and intellectuals plundered them for evidence of the strength and weaknesses of alternatives to orthodox Christianity. Buddhism was defined in terms of alterity to the crucial issues of the nineteenth-century Christian West: absence of a creator God, absence of divine wrath, absence of a Savior, absence of soul.

The point I want to make is that Buddhism, the Western object of knowledge, had very little to do with Asian reality. In spite of the insistence of scholars on rigorous methodology and strict adherence to the most reliable texts, early assumptions about the nature of Buddhism—assumptions that predate any academic study of the religion, and features of interpretations with explicit political intent—persisted into the academic period. The resulting knowledge had more to do with nineteenth-century Western intellectual history than with its purported Asian object.

Buddhism of Travelers' Tales

Buddhist scholarship, which in the late nineteenth century was considered to be authoritative interpretation based on a study of texts,[7] dates from as recently as the second quarter of the nineteenth century when missionaries and colonial administrators moved into Buddhist Asia.[8] Knowledge of Buddhism prior to this depended on reports of travelers and Jesuit missionaries. Consequently, in contrast to the later privileging of the Theravada, the most extensive accounts were of the Mahayana Buddhism of China and Japan. What is surprising is the extent to which preacademic assumptions of the nature of Buddhism derived from these sources persisted and informed the later academic interpretations. Valignano, the Jesuit "Visitor" or inspector of missions in sixteenth-century Japan, was the first of many to compare Pure Land Buddhists with Lutherans and to speak of Zen priests as the philosophers of Buddhism.[9] Matteo Ricci, first Jesuit scholar in China, spoke of the degradation of Chinese priests but also recognized similarities between Buddhism and Christianity. Ricci proposed the idea that Chinese Buddhism was a corruption of Christianity.[10] The Dutch doctor Englebert Kaempfer, who lived on the island of Deshima in Japan in 1690–91, was the most frequently quoted source on Buddhism in Japan before the 1880s.[11]

Although the knowledge of Buddhism derived from these sources was not authoritative in the nineteenth-century sense of being based on philological analysis of original, edited texts, these early descriptions were extremely influential in the formation of presuppositions of Buddhism that persist to the present. Dumoulin, for example, traces the idea that Buddhism is pessimistic and nihilistic in German thought from Hegel's reading of early travelers' reports in terms of his own interests, through the work of Schopenhauer and Nietzsche.[12] Although Nietzsche wrote after a considerable body of work on Buddhism was available to him, he apparently paid little attention to it, depending instead on Schopenhauer.[13] Nietzsche, like his predecessors, was impressed with the self-reliance of the Buddha but propagated a nihilistic, pessimistic, and passive image of Buddhism. The persistence of these features through the period of academic scholarship in the face of evidence to the contrary implies that an impression formed of Buddhism by German sources was absorbed into a general vocabulary of images and propagated along with German philosophy. The formation of knowledge did not depend solely on academic criteria of truth acting on a body of authenticated texts but on the circulation of collectively held images. Herman Oldenberg's influential work on the life and teachings of the Buddha derived from Pali texts confirmed these early images in opposition to Rhys Davids's more optimistic reading of the same texts.[14]

The Buddha as Anti-Hindu Hero

The early British writings on Buddhism in Burma and Ceylon also show presuppositions that persist and inform later academic study. The most significant is a predisposition to favor Buddhism over Hinduism. Eighteenth-century Orientalists had found much to admire in the literature of Indian religion, but when missionaries gained access to India after 1813, public perceptions of Indian religion depended less on their work that circulated through learned societies than on the image projected through mission journals and other less elite publications. Here Hinduism was described as vile heathenism, "the most puerile, impure and bloody of any system of idolatry that was ever established on earth,"[15] an impression consolidated by works such as James Mill's criticism of Indian religion in *The History of British India* (1817). Although Orientalists still praised certain aspects of the Brahmanic texts, Hinduism was generally seen to be the pattern of heathen idolatry, living proof of the evils of ritual and a dominant priesthood, idolatrous, polytheistic, and pagan. Hinduism was the "other" of Christianity in the sense of representing the totally "not-Christian."

In this context the Buddha emerged as a hero. Although the chronological priority of Brahmanism had not at this time been decided, Buddhism was recognized as part of the continuity of the development of Indian religion. Scholars argued whether Buddhism was the pure teaching of which Hinduism was a later corruption, or a protest against the ritualism, caste hierarchies, and other perceived excesses of Brahmanism. Both schemes affirmed Buddhist superiority and attributed to it all that was considered good in Indian thought. The link between Buddhism and Lutheranism reemerged, but this time without reference to the Japanese Pure Land doctrine of salvation through faith in Amida Buddha. In Southern Buddhism, the Buddha Sakyamuni was likened to Luther himself for his reform of the excesses of the Brahmanic clergy.

Colonialists were also impressed by the contrast between the circumscriptions of Hinduism and the openness and accessibility of Buddhist priests and temples in Ceylon. Captain Anderson of the Nineteenth Infantry (1843) extolled the virtues of Buddhism in verse:

Where free to range the temple through,
No hallowed shrine withheld from view . . .
Oh, how unlike in each degree,
The Hindoo's foul idolatry,
Whose pond'rous pyramidal pile,
What strange disgusting rites defile!
Where crafty Brahmins guard those shrines
On which no lively sunbeam shines,
Where never strangers' searching eyes

Can pierce their horrid mysteries . . .
May never such a horrid creed,
To Buddha's simple faith succeed.[16]

Since Ceylonese Buddhist temples, like their Hindu counterparts, also contain images to which similar offerings of flowers, food, and incense are made, Anderson's preference for Buddhism over Hinduism would appear to depend on predisposition and the absence of opportunity for letting his imagination run free on the possibilities of pagan rites behind locked doors.

British predisposition toward Buddhism was further enhanced when James Prinsep deciphered the Brahmi script in 1837 and translated the Edicts of "Devanampriya," recognized by George Turnour from his work on the *Mahāvamsa* as Asoka Maurya.[17] This anchored Buddhist chronicles and legends in Indian history, making it possible to estimate the date of the Buddha's death.[18] The process of historicizing Sakyamuni had begun, and the content of the Asokan inscriptions was used to confirm the Protestant, humanist image of Buddhism. This was, for Rhys Davids and others, Buddhism before it was corrupted into a religion.

The identification of Devanampriya was also important in determining the evolution of Indian religion. Once it was established—to the satisfaction of some scholars at least—that the Buddha had lived in the fifth or sixth century B.C., the Brahmanic texts were given chronological priority. It was then possible to arrange the Sanskrit texts of Brahmanism in order, on the assumption that religion evolved from nature worship through to monotheism. This arrangement is no longer as obvious as it appeared to be over the past century. Indeed, the Hindu delegate to the World's Parliament of Religions, Professor Manilal N. D'Vivedi, disputed the scheme, particularly the reduction of the "highly rational thought of the Vedas" to the "outpourings of the minds of pastoral tribes ignorantly wondering at the grand phenomena of nature" and the idea that monotheism is "the acme of intellectual development."[19] It was nevertheless fundamental to the important position Buddhism was to hold in the later academic scholarship of Max Muller and T. W. Rhys Davids. For these scholars, Indian texts provided a record of the evolution of religion, and in this scheme Buddhism represented a point of protest. The Buddha was declared the opponent of Hinduism.

By the middle of the nineteenth century—that is, before any academic translation of the Buddhist texts—the Buddha had already become a hero of religious reform, a great human teacher, a man of virtue, and a moralist. He was both

Luther and the human counterpart of Christ. Identifying him with Luther implied a relationship between Buddhism and Hinduism parallel to that of Protestantism and the Roman Catholic Church. Comparing him to Christ implied that Buddhism held a position in relation to Brahmanism as Christianity to Judaism. In the predominantly Protestant Christian context of English-language scholarship, both schemes favored Buddhism.

The Scholarship of Imperialism

Prinsep and Turnour, both colonial civil servants, typified the new scholarly interest in Buddhism that accompanied nineteenth-century expansion of colonial domination into the Buddhist countries, continuing the Orientalist work of seeking knowledge for the more efficient control of their subjects.[20] Turnour translated the Buddhist chronicle *Mahāvamsa* (1830) in his search for the history of Ceylon. Alexander Csoma worked on Tibetan Buddhist texts to produce a Tibetan-English dictionary. Brian Houghton Hodgson, a civil servant posted to Nepal in 1821, produced the earliest informed accounts of Northern Buddhism. From 1813, when missionaries were first allowed into India, these Orientalists of civil administration joined forces with Christian missions in the cause of spreading civilization and moral improvement. As an early evangelist and director of the East India Company put it, British power in India was God's will: "[T]hose distant territories . . . providentially put into our hands . . . were given to us, not merely that we might draw an annual profit from them, but that we might diffuse among their inhabitants, long sunk in darkness, vice and misery, the light and benign influence of the truth, the blessings of a well regulated society, the improvements and comforts of active industry."[21]

Although there were politicians, administrators, and Orientalists committed to a policy of noninterference in matters of religion, the prevailing view was that "Christianity is the best known means of producing good and useful citizens." It was therefore "the duty of a Christian government . . . to promote the conversion of its heathen subjects."[22]

The two streams of scholarship, one devoted to understanding the native to rule more efficiently, the other understanding his religion the better to replace it, together contributed to the mosaic of information available. Each remained, however, a local project with specific local objectives. The Pali translations of the Wesleyan missionary D. J. Gogerly circulated no further than the mission journal, *Friend of Ceylon*. The results of Hodgson's research reached the readership of

Transactions of the Royal Asiatic Society, but the vast quantities of Buddhist manuscripts that he collected and deposited with various learned societies for translation remained untouched for decades.[23] There was little general interest in Buddhism at this time.

Defining Northern Buddhism

Hodgson's work demonstrates a number of the characteristic features of the early scholarship: a desire to know the colonial subject; a predisposition toward Buddhism; and, most important, an unquestioned assumption of post-Enlightenment Christian expectations of the nature and function of religion. To obtain his "scientific" "Sketch of Buddhism," Hodgson presented a written set of questions to a local Buddhist authority who had already shown his willingness to share his knowledge by presenting Hodgson with a "large collection of important *Bauddha* scriptures."[24] The informant answered all questions with frequent reference to Buddhist texts. How and when was the world created? "[W]hat was the origin of mankind?" "[W]hat is matter, what is spirit?" "[W]hat are the attributes of God?" "Is Buddha God, or the creator, or a prophet or saint? born of heaven or woman?" "[D]id God ever make a descent to earth?" "[W]hat is the name of your sacred writings and who is their author?"[25] Clearly, for Hodgson and his colleagues, religion was by definition theistic and dealt with questions of creation, immortality, and revelation. It was assumed that Buddhism, because it was manifestly a "religion," could be understood by its responses to these issues.

The article that consisted of the questions and answers, edited and annotated by Hodgson, equated God and Adi-Buddha, affirmed that Buddha is one of the names of God, and consequently that if Buddhism is not actually theistic "they have reduced the difference between theism and atheism almost to a nominal one." Buddhism, Hodgson surmised from the results of his inquiry, has a conception of matter and spirit virtually indistinguishable from the Christian. "Body, as created out of the elements, perisheth; soul as a particle of the divine spirit, perisheth not; body is subject to change . . . soul is unchangeable."[26] For Hodgson, Buddhists—at least the Buddhists of the North—almost had a God and definitely had an immortal soul. To what extent did reports such as this reinforce the separation of Northern Buddhism from that of the South, which was understood to be so emphatically atheistic?

The problem of Christian presuppositions was compounded by the Christian connotations of the European languages of these scholars and the lack of appropriate words to express the unfamiliar concepts of a radically different world view. Even those aware of fundamental conceptual differences were forced by the exigencies of translation to match foreign concepts to familiar expressions. The problem arose, for example, when missionaries attempted to teach Christianity. Although unquestionably committed to preserving the uniqueness of the Christian God, they had a choice of using biblical terms that would convey very little to their audience or of using terms from the local language, which necessarily compromised Christian exclusivity because it implied a correlation between the Christian Deus and local deities. Calling Jesus "Son of Isvara" might have effectively conveyed the sense of his religious supremacy to Hindus, but it also inserted him into the existing Hindu pantheon. Was God married to Uma?[27]

The missionaries faced with these decisions of translation were frequently also the first to describe Asian religions and Asian concepts to Western audiences, and similarly resorted to ill-fitting Christo-centric terms. Trying to fit Buddhism into English, the Japanese delegates to Chicago complained, was like attempting to scratch one's foot with one's shoe on, clearly suggesting that they found it an ineffective approach to communication. Distinctions became blurred, and comparison inevitable. Later scholars such as Rhys Davids advised against translating terms such as "nirvana" on the grounds that any word borrowed from the vocabulary of Christianity would inevitably bedevil the discussion with Christian connotations.[28] But this simply raised the question of identifying which Buddhist terms could not be successfully translated. Rhys Davids himself translated the equally difficult concept *bodhi* with the English word "Enlightenment," introducing connotations, which, though not Christian doctrine, were no less foreign to Buddhist teaching.[29]

Translating "nirvana" caused such difficulty that the term was readily recognized as outside Christian experience. The most egregious misreadings of Buddhism occurred precisely in those areas where authors felt confident that they "were in possession of applicable categories of interpretation."[30] The *Paticcasamuppāda*, normally translated as the Doctrine of Dependent Origination, for example, was "recognized" as an expression of the law of "cause and effect." It was subsequently found to be incoherent, inadequate, and self-contradictory because it failed to satisfy the expectations of this "law" and consequently became further evidence of the inferiority of the Oriental Mind.[31]

Failure to realize that not even the basic European categories of religion and philosophy applied to Buddhism led to debate. Was Buddhism a philosophy, an atheistic religion, or, as one Christian critic decided, "a case of philosophy gone mad; for it is a philosophy assuming the prerogatives which can only belong to a heavenly religion."[32] The constant was Buddhism's failure to be adequate to Western categories formed upon Christian assumptions. The work of Conze, Clausen, Welbon, Brear, Coward, and others all point to the inadequacies of nineteenth-century interpretations of Buddhism as representations of Asian belief and practice. Their criticisms show how European language, cultural presuppositions, existing paradigms, and contemporary intellectual concerns worked to shape the authors' interpretations.

What Is a Buddha?

Underlying the whole structure of Western interpretations of Buddhism is the question of the nature of the Buddha himself. From a Christian viewpoint, the alternatives were that he was a God, and therefore a heathen deity, or a man, a human philosopher later deified by his followers.[33] The work of Prinsep and Turnour favored the latter position, but from the evidence of Buddhist scholarship available in 1854, H. H. Wilson, the director of the Royal Asiatic Society, concluded that the historical existence of the Buddha Sakyamuni was far from established. "It seems possible, after all, that Sakya Muni is an unreal being, and that all that is related of him is as much fiction as is that of his preceding migrations, and the miracles that attended his birth, his life and his departure."[34]

Wilson's statement directly contradicted the two principal authorities on Southern Buddhism of the time, the Reverend Robert Spence Hardy and Sir James Emerson Tennent. For these authors, though for different reasons, the Buddha was unquestionably both historical and human. Both interpretations can be directly related to their respective positions on the politically charged questions of the relationship between the British colonial government and the religion of Ceylon. Hardy's work is particularly important because it became a basic reference. In spite of their overt political intent and consequent bias, his publications remained the authoritative source of information on Southern Buddhism until Rhys Davids's translations of the Pali texts three decades later. By that time the public discourse was well under way.

The Politics of Buddhism in Ceylon

Hardy was a Wesleyan missionary working in Ceylon in the nineteenth century. His interest in Buddhism was professional and explicit, as he explains in the introduction to *Eastern Monachism*: "I began the study of the native books that I might ascertain, from authentic sources, the character of the religion I was attempting to displace . . . [and] to afford assistance to missionaries living in countries where Buddhism is professed. . . . I ask for no higher reward than to be a humble instrument in assisting the ministers of the cross in their combats with this master error of the world, and in preventing the spread of the same delusion, under another guise, in regions nearer home."[35]

This book, the first academic account of Theravada Buddhism, was written with the dual purpose of undermining Buddhism by presenting it as an example of the error of materialist philosophy and using Buddhism to warn against the inadequacy of agnosticism. The missionary situation in Ceylon at the time, however, was complicated by political and economic issues, both of which centered on the treaty arrangement between Britain and Ceylon, the Kandyan convention of 1815, and it was this political controversy that actually brought the results of Hardy's study to print and popular distribution.

Briefly, Ceylon had not been conquered by Britain but ceded to it by the combined authority of the Buddhist *sangha* and the Kandyan chiefs on the clear understanding that the British government would, in return, maintain and protect their religion. The agreement was, in effect, that the British government would fulfill the traditional role of the state in Buddhist polity. The sign of the relationship was the British possession of the Tooth Relic in Kandy, the palladium of the state. The actual demands on the government were not onerous. It was required to validate appointments of priests to positions within the *sangha*, to supply small amounts of money for temple upkeep and ceremonial purposes, and to preside at certain ceremonies such as those associated with the Tooth Relic. The costs for the Kandy Perahera in 1840 was £15.19.9½.[36] It was a connection so undemanding that the British government and the missionaries could not understand why it was so important to the Kandyans.

But even this minimal honoring of the treaty offended the missionaries and was the subject of Hardy's first publication on Buddhism, a pamphlet, *The British Government and Idolatry in Ceylon* (1839), which called for the end of this "unnatural, sinful, and pernicious connexion between the British Government of Ceylon and idolatry."[37] Arguing from the premise that the world moved according to the design of God, Hardy saw a comparison between the great extent of the Roman Empire at the time of the birth of Christ with the extent of British power in the nineteenth century. Because the wide influence of the Roman Empire had been instrumental in the initial propagation of Christianity, it was clear to Hardy that God had placed nations under British authority to facilitate the conversion of the world. In an explicit statement of the connection missionaries perceived between Christianity and colonial expansion, he declared that it was time to inquire "whether our authorities in the east were carrying into effect the intention for which they have been raised by God to their present anomalous position."[38] For Hardy, as for Charles Grant, already quoted, conversion was the reason and purpose of empire.

Christian conversion was not making much headway in Ceylon, and Hardy believed one reason for this was that honoring the treaty gave the people the impression that the government approved of Buddhism. Consequently, he argued that if this government support were removed, Buddhism would collapse. To this end, he attacked the principle of a Christian government's connection with an idolatrous religion. Hardy's move was no doubt encouraged, if not inspired, by the British government's decision in 1838 to disassociate the East India Company from similar obligations to temples in India.[39]

Hardy's attitude to the treaty was also complicated by the relationship between Anglicans and other Christian groups in Ceylon. With few exceptions, most conversions were for reasons not connected with religious belief, but with the legal registration of births and marriages needed for property title, or for access to jobs in the colonial administration. The state-supported Anglican Church had advantages over the nonconformist missions in the job market and in establishing schools, the main arena of successful conversion. Consequently, the treaty issue became a focus for the disestablishment movement in Ceylon.

This debate on whether Britain could maintain its treaty obligations continued over the next decade, further complicated by a lobby of colonial plantation owners who wanted access to the large tracts of valuable Hill Country that belonged to the Buddhist *sangha*. The definition of the treaty term "the religion of the country," which the government had undertaken to maintain, was no longer simply the concern of religious specialists but became a central political and economic issue. It hardly seems coincidental, therefore, that in 1850, at the height of the controversy, both Hardy and Sir James Emerson Tennent, the spokesmen and advisers to the Colonial Office for the two main factions involved, should each publish a book on religion in Ceylon.[40]

Hardy and Tennent had much in common. They were equally ardent in their desire to see Ceylon converted to Christianity, and differed only in their view of how this should be achieved. The source material for both works was the same, and at first reading their interpretations appear very similar. The points of difference are significant because they relate to their respective positions on the treaty question, and of interest because, for different reasons, they are perpetuated throughout the discourse on Buddhism of the second half of the nineteenth century. Both agreed on the original secular and philosophical nature of Sakyamuni's teachings. For Tennent this was Buddhism. Buddhism was a philosophy. For Hardy, however, Buddhism—"the religion of Ceylon," the definition of which determined the interpretation of Britain's treaty obligations—was an atheistic religion that had developed out of Sakyamuni's teachings, proof of the inadequacy of a system without divine inspiration to satisfy human need. Their respective positions foreshadowed those of later debate.

Buddhism: Atheistic Religion

Hardy began his *Eastern Monachism* with a statement that encapsulated his image of the Buddha: "About two thousand years before the thunders of Wycliffe were rolled against the mendicant orders of the west, Gotama Budha [*sic*] commenced his career as a mendicant in the east, and established a religious system that has exercised a mightier influence upon the world than the doctrines of any other uninspired teacher, in any age or country."[41] By opening with an implied comparison between the Buddha and the fourteenth-century reformer Wycliffe, Hardy immediately introduced two features of what came to be the dominant Western interpretation: the origin of Buddhism as a reaction against the priestly and ritualistic excesses of Brahmanism, and the role of the Buddha as a social reformer. He also fixed him in human—Western—history. But most significant is his insistence that the Buddha was "uninspired." Gautama's teaching was, for Hardy, necessarily without divine inspiration. Gautama was nothing more than a mortal teacher.[42]

Although these features are now commonly accepted as the truth of Buddhism, it was not so for the Sinhalese whose beliefs Hardy was supposedly trying to present. Nor was it necessarily so, as Wilson demonstrated, on the evidence available to Hardy.[43] Hardy's own work contains evidence to the contrary. There is a considerable discrepancy between the image of Buddhism contained in the meticulously reproduced text, which projects his scholarly objectivity, and that of the author's commentary in the accompanying introduction and extensive footnotes that direct the reader to what Hardy saw as the "elaborations," "inconsistencies," "corruptions," and "absurdities" of the Sinhalese. These notes effectively exclude all mythological and supernatural aspects of his sources.

The fundamental justification for missionary activity was the belief that the Christian revelation is unique and exclusive. This was particularly so in Ceylon, where missionaries found it hard to justify conversion on social grounds alone. As one newly arrived missionary observed, the Sinhalese were such "thriving and well-to-do looking people" it was necessary to remember that they were "atheists" who supply the need for the supernatural by "demon worship."[44] Hardy and others readily conceded that Buddhism's moral and ethical system was comparable with Christianity's own. The failure of the teaching was rather that the system of ethics was so ideal it was beyond the possibility of most men, "left to [their] own unaided efforts in the great work of freeing [themselves] from the defilements of evil!"[45] Without the threat of divine retribution, "the Lightening of the Divine Eye, the thunder of the Divine Voice . . . the principle for good in man will soon be overwhelmed. . . . With these radical defects," Hardy confidently concluded, "it is unnecessary to dwell on the lesser."[46]

With Hardy's insistence that the Buddha was merely an uninspired mortal, Buddhism became in essence an atheistic system of ethics, and its practice—as observed by Hardy in Ceylon, where rituals were performed and offerings made before images—idolatrous. The discrepancy between the purity of the ethics of the Founder and the idolatrous practice of the people was proof for him of the inadequacy of an atheistic system to meet the needs of man, and consequently of the Sinhalese need for Christianity. "From no part of heathenism do we see more clearly the necessity of a divine revelation than from the teachings of the Buddha. The moral code becomes comparatively powerless for good, as it is destitute of all real authority."[47] The Buddha was a man; his teaching was "not divinely inspired" but "was formed by a man or men, who were liable to err, and have erred, in innumerable instances; consequently it cannot teach the way to purity or peace, or save from wrath and destruction."[48]

Such is Hardy's argument against Buddhism, and it clearly depends upon establishing the historical humanity of the Buddha. For Hardy Gautama was a man, but, as his opening paragraph suggests, he was an exceptional man. Having eliminated the possibility of revelation, Hardy assumed that the Buddhist religion developed from the progressive deification of its revered Founder. In echo of Protestant Christian belief, the example of the life of the teacher and the words he actually spoke constituted for Hardy the "true Buddhism." The fault with Buddhism, Hardy claimed, was not with the philosopher himself but with the inadequacy of an atheistic system to satisfy the religious needs of man. Whatever the merits of the Buddha's original teaching, for Hardy, the Ceylonese practice was idolatrous. Buddhism was atheistic in ideal and idolatrous in practice. The charge of atheism justified missionary activity; the charge of idolatry provided the ground of Hardy's political action. If Buddhism in Ceylon was idolatrous, Hardy believed, the government's obligation to the treaty of 1815 was "contrary to the Laws of God" and therefore not binding on a Christian government. By Hardy's definition of Buddhism the treaty simply need not be upheld because it was unconstitutional.

Buddhism: Philosophical Humanism

The close association of Hardy's interpretation of Buddhism with his professional and political objectives was paralleled by Sir James Emerson Tennent, whose book *Christianity in Ceylon* also appeared in 1850. Tennent arrived in Ceylon in 1847 as colonial secretary to Governor Torrington. As an administrator, Tennent believed that the British government should honor its treaty obligation, but this did not imply his support for Buddhism, which he was as keen as Hardy to see supplanted. Not only was the government legally bound to honor the treaty, but doing so was a means of avoiding measures that would increase the power of Buddhist groups. If the treaty were severed, he argued, the administration of *sangha* affairs would most likely pass to a council of Kandyan officials, an unattractive idea for the government as it would create an organized center of power among the Sinhalese. Under the existing arrangement, as Tennent pointed out, the duty of ratifying *sangha* appointments gave the government some control over the choice of Buddhist leaders. In general, Tennent's views seem consistent with those of Governor Torrington, who advised the Colonial Office in 1849 that the treaty should be upheld if only as a means of avoiding having to legislate on the relationship between Buddhism and the state, which could only serve to strengthen Buddhism. Torrington believed that by returning to the loose obligations of the original treaty, Buddhism would "sink of itself whereas legislation would only perpetuate it."[49] Tennent's interpretation of Buddhism consequently offered a response to the missionary agitation for disestablishment, justifying the continuation of government participation in Buddhist affairs and the political expediency of fulfilling the terms of the treaty.

Tennent shared Hardy's assumption of the historical reality of the mortal Gautama, and his opinion that the modern practice was a degeneration from the Founder's original teaching. Tennent's Buddhism was not, however, an idolatrous religion but a system of rational philosophic morality. For Tennent, the idolatry and excesses of Ceylonese practice had less to do with the failings of the teaching or the absence of divine wrath than with the racial inadequacies of the Sinhalese people. "The self reliance which Buddhism inculcates, the exaltation it proclaims, and the perfection of wisdom and virtue which it points to as in the reach of every created being" failed to overcome the "torpid and inanimate genius of the Sinhalese."[50] "The Sinhalese are lethargic and slothful to an excess beyond even the extreme of most Southern Asiatics."[51] Buddhism itself is a force for good, a rational philosophy: it was "less a form of religion than a school of philosophy," and its worship is "an appeal to reason" rather than a matter of "rites and parade."[52] Tennent did not attempt to deny the existence of ritual and image worship in Ceylon but simply to distance them from what he presented Buddhism to be. They were non-Buddhist accretions, the result of the weakness of mind of the people; a perpetuation of Hindu practice introduced by the conquering Hindu kings; features not intrinsic to Buddhism but "associated" with it over time.[53]

Tennent's association of the corruption of Buddhism with Hinduism, his frequent favorable comparisons of Buddhism against Hinduism, removed the Ceylonese situation from the legal precedent established in India. Tennent began his discussion of Buddhism with the proposition that assumed Buddhist superiority. Buddhism was either the "original doctrine of which Brahmanism became a corruption, or Brahmanism the original and Buddhism an effort to restore it to its pristine purity."[54] Buddhism denied the efficacy of ritual, and "salvation is made dependent upon moral qualifications, not upon the practice of ceremonies." Buddhism "utterly disclaimed" the "supremacy of 'caste' "[55] and "exhult[s] in the idea of the infinite perfectibility of man, and the achievement of the highest attainable happiness by the practice of every conceivable virtue."[56] Buddhism was far from being idolatrous. The Buddha was "in fact a deification of the human intellect."[57]

The essential features of Tennent's interpretation of Buddhism were that it is a system of ethics consistent with Christianity, that it does not share Hinduism's preoccupation with ritual, that the Buddha is not worshiped as a deity but merely revered as a teacher and guide. For Tennent Buddhism was not an idolatrous system. Consequently Tennent points out that Buddhist ceremonies are "less religious than secular, and that the Perahera in particular, the chief of their annual festivals was introduced not in honour of Buddhu [*sic*], but as a tribute to the Kandyan kings as patrons and defenders of the faith."[58] This is a crucial passage in understanding Tennent's position. The Perahera is the ritual procession of the Tooth Relic, palladium of the state and symbol of the mutually dependent relationship between the ruler and the *sangha* in Buddhist polity. Participation in the Perahera was the British government's principal and most visible connection with Buddhism and therefore at the center of the intense debate over this relationship. If, as Tennent claimed, the Perahera was a secular ceremony, and one honoring the ruler, there would be no objection to the government's participation. If Buddhism was really a philosophical system rather than a religion, Hardy's argument of the impropriety of a Christian government's connection with a heathen religion was undermined. The state's obligation to verify *sangha* appointments was not a religious question but an "indisputable civil right" because, Tennent explained, the *sangha* was "a clergy of reason" and the *bhikkhus* not priests but "teachers of ethics."[59] In 1852 Tennent was instrumental in framing the Colonial Office legislation that was to form the basis of settlement of the treaty problem, because it managed to reassure the Buddhist *sangha* and at the same time appease the missionaries.

Although Hardy and Tennent differed on points of interpretation vital to the immediate issue of treaty revision, they agreed on the essential features of the construct, the human historical existence of the Buddha, the absence of revelation, the essentially atheistic character of Buddhism, the absence of ritual or worship in "original" Buddhism. The Buddha had been a philosopher who taught an elevated system of ethics and self-reliance. The Buddha's teachings were a reaction against and reform of Brahmanism. Both Hardy and Tennent dismissed as later developments the mythological and soteriological aspects of the Buddhist texts that were the basis of alternative interpretations denying their essential argument of the human historical existence of the Buddha.[60]

In the four decades from the time of these first publications to the time of the Parliament, a distinctly Western conception of Buddhism was formed and propagated, and because much of the output at this stage depended on existing sources in European languages rather than on new translation, the impact of these early texts was considerable, and supplemented the influence they had through their direct readership. Hardy's *Eastern Monachism* was an important book for the American Transcendentalists Emerson, Thoreau, and Alcott, and therefore in introducing sympathy for Buddhism to America.[61] Hardy also made a significant, if less direct contribution to knowledge of Buddhism through Edwin Arnold's *Light of Asia* (1879), which went through more than thirty official editions in England by 1885. This extended romantic poem, based on the life of the Buddha given in Hardy's *Manual of Budhism*, did more than any other single book to popularize Buddhism in the West. There were numerous pirated editions in both countries and the book was translated into several other languages. It is estimated to have sold between five hundred thousand and one million copies in the United States alone.[62] Many of the other books and articles written on Buddhism between 1850 and 1880, when Rhys Davids's books began to appear, also relied to a considerable extent on Hardy's earlier publications. His interpretation of Buddhism, born of explicit political intent, was basic to the institutionalization of Buddhism, the creation of the construct that constituted the knowledge of Buddhism available to the audience at the World's Parliament of Religions.

Buddhism: Materialist Error

The next major work on Buddhism to appear was J. Barthélemy Saint-Hilaire's *The Buddha and His Religion* in 1860, which not only relied on Hardy for its knowledge of Southern Buddhism, but shared his project of using Buddhism to combat the increasing European interest in materialist philosophy.[63] For him, as for Hardy, Buddhism demonstrated the inadequacy of materialist philosophy to meet the needs of man.

Interest in materialist philosophy had increased as a consequence of the crisis in religion, the perceived incompatibility between Christianity and the implications of natural science. Christianity in its orthodox form no longer fitted the known facts of the nature of the world and human history. The tensions that had begun to be felt from about 1830 with the publication of works such as Charles Lyell's *Principles of Geology* (1830–33) and Robert Chambers's *Vestiges of Creation* (1844) reached a crisis in the third quarter of the century with Comte's *Catechism of Popular Religion* (1858); Charles Darwin's *Origin of Species* (1859); Bishop Colenso's *The Pentateuch Examined* (1862–63); Ernest Renan's scientific rewriting of the life of Christ, *La vie de Jesus* (1864); and Darwin's later book, *The Descent of Man* (1871).

The fundamental issues were, first, the incompatibility of concepts of revelation, divine intervention, and the miracles of Christ with the scientific world view that denied recourse to the supernatural. As Renan observed, "[T]he miracles and messianic prophecies which were formerly the basis of Christian apologetic were now an embarrassment to it."[64] Second, theories of evolution and human origin challenged the idea that humans were of a different order of being from the animal world, distinguished from the rest of creation by God's gift of an immortal soul. The denial of the existence of the soul undermined orthodox ethics. Darwin suggested that the social behavior observed among animals might be interpreted as an earlier stage of the social and moral capabilities of man, that morality was also subject to evolutionary development,[65] but Christians such as Hardy and Saint-Hilaire were outraged. Without the aid of divine wrath and the threat of eternal suffering to deter him from evil, the comfort of salvation and the inducements of rewards in heaven to encourage virtue, man is "thrown upon his own resources" and the moral code becomes "powerless for good."[66]

Saint-Hilaire is representative of those concerned about the threat to orthodox belief posed by growing interest in materialist philosophy among his contemporaries. For him, as for Hardy, Buddhism exemplified "the fate of man when he relies on himself alone." He states in the introduction that the sole purpose of the work is to bring out "in striking contrast the beneficial truths and the greatness of our spiritualistic beliefs" against "the strange and deplorable doctrines which it professes, the explanation for its powerlessness for good."[67] Buddhism, as he projected it, was a demonstration of the indispensable necessity of divine interference. Its value to him was the crucial difference of Buddhism from Christianity on the question of God and the immortality of the soul in an otherwise comparable system of values. He spoke of the Buddha and his teaching with the highest praise—the Buddha was second only to Christ in his perfections, "irreproachable" in the personal example of his life[68]—but only to stress that no matter how perfect a moral code, it is inadequate without divine interference. The principal fault he found in the religion was that "in the whole of Buddhism there is not a trace of the idea of God. Man, completely isolated, is thrown upon his own resources."[69] Saint-Hilaire echoed Hardy's position but extended the authority of his argument with reference to Sanskrit sources. In his defense of Christian orthodoxy against its European opponents, Saint-Hilaire reinforced the image of the Buddha as a human teacher, teaching an atheistic, pessimistic, nihilistic philosophy. Mahayana Buddhism was a falling away from the teachings of the Founder; the idolatry and ritual that it had developed, proof of man's need for religion.

Saint-Hilaire's message was endorsed by Bishop Bigandet's *Life and Legend of Gaudama* (1860) and by Samuel Beal's works from Chinese sources (1871, 1875), but the number of books available on Buddhism before 1880 was not large.[70] Nevertheless, articles discussing Buddhism appeared increasingly frequently in journals, both specifically Christian journals such as the *Christian Remembrancer* and the *Church Quarterly Review*, and in more general intellectual journals such as *London Quarterly Review*, *Intellectual Observer*, *Atlantic Monthly*, *Westminster*

Review, *Saturday Review*, *Dublin University Magazine*, and even the *Times*. The number increased dramatically after 1880. Thomas Huxley and Herbert Spencer wrote on Buddhism. Hardy, Tennent, and Saint-Hilaire were frequently cited. But before attempting to summarize the image of Buddhism created in the public domain, it would be useful to look at the Buddhism of T. W. Rhys Davids which articulated the other side of the positivist debate. The message Rhys Davids wished to convey was that an effective moral system—a liberal humanist religion—was possible without the orthodox Christian belief in an interventionist God and immortal soul. Rhys Davids used Buddhism to argue that the latest developments in European philosophy, far from being in conflict with Christianity, were the culmination of its evolution.

Buddhism: The Religion of Self-Reliance

By the time of the World's Parliament of Religions, the unassailable authority on Buddhism was T. W. Rhys Davids, Pali scholar and founder of the Pali Text Society (1881). Rhys Davids, like so many before him, first became interested in Pali while serving in the Ceylon Civil Service (1864–72). His interest in Buddhism at that time was incidental. To learn Pali he had to study with a *bhikkhu*. His first translation, typical of the historical bias of the time, was in numismatics and epigraphy, and led to his *Ancient Coins and Measures of Ceylon* (1877), which contained an attempt to date the death of the Buddha.[71] Moreover, the book that established his reputation as a Buddhist scholar, *Buddhism* (1878), was not the result of his own translation but was compiled from "materials then available," including the work of Hardy.[72] During the influential Hibbert Lectures in which he elaborated the results of this study, Rhys Davids announced the founding of the Pali Text Society, which was to become the vehicle for propagating his interpretation with the full apparatus of academic scholarship. Rhys Davids and his society colleagues dominated Buddhist scholarship until the early twentieth century.[73] Their pioneering work in collating, editing, and translating almost the whole of the Pali canon and in producing a dictionary, as well as their scrupulous adherence to the principles of "the science of religions" gave their interpretation indisputable authority within the academic parameters of the time.

While in no way detracting from the immense value of this great scholar's work, it is instructive that the inspiration for undertaking the task, Rhys Davis tells us, was his belief that study of the Pali texts could shed light on the evolution of religious thought in general and consequently on the changes that Christianity was undergoing in the nineteenth century. His aim was to establish that contemporary trends in philosophy represented the culmination of Christian evolution.[74] Buddhism, Rhys Davids declared, was "a religion whose development runs entirely parallel with that of Christianity, every episode, every line of whose history seems almost as if it might be created for the very purpose of throwing the clearest light on the most difficult and disputed questions of the origin of the European faith."[75]

A similarity between Buddhism and Christianity was fundamental to Rhys Davids's argument but so was the difference between them. Rhys Davids describes the shared moral doctrines; the shared concern for charity, sincerity, purity, meekness, gentleness, truth, and love—the humanistic aspects of religion so highly valued at the Parliament; and even the similarity in mode of teaching of the two "revered Teachers." The significance of these similarities, however, depended on the crucial difference, the question of God: "[I]n the midst of all this likeness, there is a difference no less unmistakable arising from the contrast between the Theistic creed which underlies the Christian and the Agnostic creed which underlies the Buddhist doctrines."[76]

Buddhism's value was its alterity. It was not the radically "not us" of Hinduism, but a religion that was recognizably similar, differing on precisely those points at issue in the current debates: the nature and necessity of God, the existence of the immortal soul, the divinity of Jesus. Rhys Davids underlined the similarities and took care to eliminate any question that either religion might have influenced the other. The resemblances were not due to borrowing in either direction but to "the same laws acting under the same conditions"[77] and were therefore evidence of a universally applicable, scientific law. As he saw it, both religions were born out of reaction against formalism and priestcraft, both owed their origin and insight to a "hero of humanity."

He also valued Buddhism because its texts preserved a complete record of the process of the elaboration of Gautama, the revered human teacher, into a divine personage, which provided the scientific evidence for a similar development in Christian orthodoxy. The similarities in the lives of the Buddha and the Christ are explained, he argued, by their shared humanitarian aims. The similarity in the elaboration of the texts—the miraculous birth, wonderful infancy, and supernatural powers—are alike caused by the similar stage of cultural development of their respective followers and their similar desire to give expression to a deeply felt reverence. Gautama was elevated by association with the Brahmanic concept of *cakravartin*, which conferred upon him all the legendary attributes of the World Ruler, his life embellished with "hallowed sun-stories" of the "half-converted Hindus."[78] When we realize this, Rhys Davids argued, we can see how Jesus was similarly associated with the Judaic concept of Messiah and thus became known as the Christ. The example of Buddhism provided an argument by analogy for the fabrication of the divinity of Jesus and, by extension, an argument against the Trinity. Through the study of Buddhist texts, he argued, we can clearly see the process of elaboration that gave rise to "stories miraculous and incredible"; to the development of powerful orthodoxies with new dogma and new deities; and, finally, to "the powerful hierarchies of modern Christianity and Buddhism."[79] For Rhys Davids, Christianity, like any other religion, should be able to stand scientific scrutiny.[80] Buddhism was the mirror that allowed Christians to see themselves more clearly. The mythological and miraculous that was no longer acceptable to the scientific world view could be disregarded, restoring Christianity to a place of respect in the modern world.

Rhys Davids saw another lesson to be learned from the history of Buddhism and its lack of dependence on the divine: pantheistic or monotheistic unity will always give rise to "a school to whom theological discussions have lost their interest," to thinkers who will seek "a new solution to the questions to which theologies have given inconsistent answers, in a new system in which man was to work out here, on earth, his own salvation."[81] His point was once again that Buddhism mapped the universal path of religious evolution that Christianity was to follow, so that the Pali texts help us to understand "how it is that there is so much in common between the Agnostic philosopher of India, the Stoics of Greece and Rome, and some of the newest schools in France, Germany, and among ourselves."[82] Here again, Rhys Davids argued, the path of Buddhist development indicated that the new developments in European philosophy represented the highest evolution of Christian thought.

In this context, Rhys Davids associated the Buddha with such philosophers as Spinoza, Descartes, Berkeley, Hobbes, Locke, Comte, Mill, and Spencer and, consistent with his view that Buddhism is a totally rational religion, spoke of the attainment of Buddhahood as "the crisis under the Bo-tree,"[83] interpreting it as a psychological experience rather than a religious one. In his Pali dictionary Rhys Davids wrote that "Nibbana is purely and solely an *ethical* state to be reached in this birth by ethical practices, contemplation and insight. It is therefore not transcendental."[84] To supplement this, Rhys Davids translated *bodhi* as Enlightenment, now accepted as standard.[85] The word comes from the root *budh*, to be awake, and the Buddhist commentaries explain that it denotes the acquisition of the Four Truths and is identical with the realization of nirvana.[86] They distinguish deductive and learned knowledge—the knowledge of the European Enlightenment—with which Rhys Davids wished to associate the Buddha, from this direct knowledge.

The theme of parallel development was propagated in Rhys Davids's extremely influential book *Buddhism* (1878) and repeated explicitly in the Hibbert Lectures of 1881 (also published) that did so much to introduce academic knowledge of Buddhism to the public. This project did not pass unremarked. To Arthur Lillie, whose book on Buddhism was written to "assail" Rhys Davids's interpretation, "it is very patent from the Hibbert lectures that the perversions of Dr. Rhys Davids are due to his sympathies with Comtism."[87] Rhys Davids, like Paul Carus, whose post-Parliament interpretation of Buddhism is the basis of a later chapter, looked to Buddhism for answers to the religious questions of the day in the new study of comparative religion. This, not Buddhism per se, but what Buddhism could contribute to his particular theory of the evolution of religious thought, was Rhys Davids's object. In spite of the vast quantities of meticulous translations of sacred texts, it was part of an academic discourse that had no interest at all in existing Asian practice or belief.[88] One of the more perverse assumptions of the "scientific" analysis of the texts was—as Max Muller, the most eminent of scholars in the field, explained—that the actual teaching of the Buddha was most likely different from Buddhism as it was practiced. In cases where there is a discrepancy between texts, the text "which least harmonizes with the later system of orthodox thought" was to be taken as the original one, the one peculiar to the Buddha.[89]

For Rhys Davids, the guiding principle in this process of selection was the assumption of the rational humanist nature of the Buddha's teaching, which could be extracted from the Pali texts. The process of uncovering it was first to establish which of the versions available was the earliest, then to eliminate all that "could be explained by religious hero-worship, mere poetical imagery, misapprehension, the desire to edify, applications to Gautama of previously existing stories, or sun myths and so on."[90] It is no surprise, therefore, that the Buddhism revealed by his scholarship contradicts the image of Buddhism derived by missionaries from observation of contemporary belief: "The Buddhism of the Pali Pitakas is not only a quite different thing from Buddhism as hitherto commonly received, but is quite antagonistic to it."[91] This was a strong platform from which to contradict the negative missionary interpretations, but it also excluded existing Asian practices just as effectively and with greater authority.

The Defining Debate: Rhys Davids versus Saint-Hilaire

Rhys Davids was of course one voice among the many contributing to the discussion on Buddhism, a voice representing liberal humanism, advocating rational, scientific belief. Saint-Hilaire represented the other side of this debate—that concerned about the threat to orthodox belief posed by materialist developments in contemporary Western thought. Though radically opposed, what Rhys Davids and Saint-Hilaire argued was the meaning and significance of a shared perception of the general features of Theravada Buddhism. The features themselves were not disputed, and their repetition in the discussion confirmed them. Buddhism as an object of discourse existed as a core of agreed assumptions within the ongoing debate. Buddhism was atheistic or, at least from the more positive interpretations of Rhys Davids in the 1880s, agnostic. The absence of a concept of Deity was fundamental to Saint-Hilaire's demonstration of the inadequacy of Buddhism, but, on the other hand, it was also an example of the possibility of a religion without an interventionist God. It questioned the orthodox claim, frequently reiterated at the Parliament, that belief in the Creator or higher authority is fundamental to all men. Buddhism appeared to offer examples of many different nations operating on this basis. Accounts of the observed ritual and worship of local deities in Buddhist practice fell into line with either Hardy's view that it was the natural result of man's craving for religion, or Tennent's view that they were merely accretions, evidence of the racial weakness of its followers. Both confirmed the reified textual Buddhism of Western scholarship as "real" Buddhism.

Abbé Grossier wrote of Buddhism in 1795 that "the whole of holiness consists in ceasing to exist, in being confounded with nothing, the nearer man approaches to the nature of a stone or log, the nearer he is to perfection."[92] Since that time, absence of a concept of God had been interpreted to mean that Buddhism was pessimistic, nihilistic, and world-denying. As we have seen, this image was propagated by German philosophers working from travelers' records such as Grossier's, and was repeated by the *Encyclopedia Britannica* in 1810.[93] The interpretation depended on translating nirvana, the ultimate goal of Buddhist practice, as annihilation, or utter extinction. The Triple Refuge of Buddhism then became, as Hardy put it, trust in a being annihilated (the Buddha), in a law without sanction or revelation (the dharma), and in the "partakers of sin and sorrow" (the *sangha*), a bleak outlook confirmed by a simplistic reading of the Four Noble Truths.[94] From this position, the pessimism of Buddhism was contrasted with the optimism of Christianity, which offered salvation through Jesus and eternal life in heaven. In opposition to this, Rhys Davids argued that Buddhism was more optimistic than Christianity because it offered salvation here in this world in the self-reliant pursuit of Enlightenment (his translation of the word *bodhi*, the prerequisite to attaining nirvana), whereas for Christians, this world was a place of probation. Rhys Davids explained that nirvana was not annihilation but the cessation of craving, lust, and desire, which hindered the pursuit of Enlightenment,[95] and that nirvana was "purely and solely an ethical state to be realized in this birth by ethical practices, contemplation and insight."[96] Edwin Arnold projected a similar view in his *Light of Asia*. Both presented the Buddha Sakyamuni as a prototypical humanist.

Karma and Rebirth

The other great issue of the period, the discussion of the nature of man, focused on the doctrine of karma and the related concept of rebirth. Karma was repugnant to many because, like Darwinism, it destroyed the theological uniqueness of the human species. All life belonged to the same interdependent continuum within *samsara*. Not only was there no immortal soul, but a human might be reborn as a beast. For others, however, it offered a view of the human position in the world that was compatible with evolutionary theory, "an anticipatory Asiatic Darwinism."[97] The doctrine of codependent origination (*paticcasamuppāda*), which explained the basis for moral action, also offered an explanation of the human condition that did not rely on an interventionist deity. This was the subject of Shaku Sōen's paper at Chicago. While argument continued over the implications of the Buddhist notion of the nature of man, reflecting the community's ambiguous feelings about nineteenth-century developments, the debate confirmed the premise that Buddhism had a great deal in common with "the latest speculations among ourselves."

Buddhism: Northern Decadence

An agreed feature of Buddhism—one most significant for the Japanese delegation—was that Mahayana or Northern Buddhism was a decadent development of real Buddhism. For Rhys Davids the Buddhism of "Nepal, Tibet, China, Japan and Mongolia" is "exceedingly interesting, and very valuable from the similarity it bears to the development that has taken place in Christianity in Roman Catholic countries."[98] That is, it confirmed his thesis of religious evolution. It was the result of "the overpowering influence of sickly imaginations." As theories grew and flourished, filling the sky with "forgeries of the brain . . . the nobler lessons of the founder of the religion were smothered beneath the glittering mass of metaphysical subtleties." It was not just a falling away, but a fetid growth, the negation of the real teaching: "As the stronger side of Gautama's teachings were neglected, the debasing belief in rites and ceremonies, and charms and incantations, which had been the special object of his scorn, began to live again, and to grow vigorously, and spread like the Bīrana weed warmed by the tropical sun in marsh and muddy soil."[99]

Max Muller's apologetic introduction to the first Mahayana texts published in his Sacred Books of the East series, Takakusu Junjirō's translation of the *Amitāyur-Dhyāna-Sūtra*,[100] testifies to the strength and persistence of these attitudes at the time of the World's Parliament of Religions. Muller was "so much disappointed with the contents of the Sūtra, that [he] hesitated for some time whether [he] ought to publish it," and only decided to do so at the persuasion of his "friends in Japan" and his own respect for the truth "that nothing should be suppressed that might lead us to form a judgement of Buddhism in its Mahāyāna dress, as professed by millions in China and Japan." The main value of the work in his view was not the teaching itself but that the Chinese translations could be dated "with considerable accuracy" and therefore act as "a new sheet-anchor in the chronology of Sanskrit literature."[101]

Muller's denigration of the Mahayana only confirms what one could deduce from his attitude to the highly trained and specially selected Japanese priests sent to study with him. Instead of seeing their presence at Oxford as a unique opportunity to expand the scope of his study of religion into a new area, he wanted only their skill in reading Chinese. Nanjō Bun'yū, the first Japanese priest sent by the Nishi Honganji to study Sanskrit with Muller in 1876, was put to work cataloging the Chinese Tripitaka in the India Office library, again principally for its value in dating Sanskrit literature.[102] For Muller, Mahayana Buddhism was simply beyond the pale. Japanese Buddhism was "a corruption of the pure doctrine of the Royal Prince" depending on the "degraded and degrading Mahāyāna tracts . . . the silly and mischievous stories of Amitābha and his Paradise."[103] In his opinion, "[I]f the Japanese really mean to be Buddhists, they should return to the words of the Buddha as they are preserved to us in the old sutras." He saw himself helping them along this path.[104]

Max Muller was not alone in his disdain. Western publications on Japan

Figure 9. A Buddhist temple (MacFarlane, *Japan*, 203)

which included descriptions of the religion of the country appeared from mid-nineteenth century, but all reproduced the assumptions of existing Western scholarship, relying most particularly on the early seventeenth-century observations of Kaempfer. Charles MacFarlane's *Japan: An Account, Geographical and Historical*, published in 1852, was typical, compiled, the author tells us, from "a critical assessment" of existing European-language sources.[105] The accompanying illustration (fig. 9) encapsulated expectations of the as yet secluded country. Japan in this vision is composed of elements borrowed from depictions of China. Note, for example, the hairstyle of the native and the roofline of the buildings.

The exotic vegetation is more typical of tropical Asia—stereotypical Asia, the Asia of Rhys Davids's Bīrana weed—than of temperate Japan. Japan was a land of heathens prostrated before a multilimbed idol.

What is more remarkable than the image presented by McFarlane prior to the opening of the country to Westerners is the absence of new material on Japanese religion afterward, particularly given the number of missionaries who flocked to Japan.[106] Nothing of significance was published until William Elliot Griffis's *The Mikado's Empire* in 1876, and although it included valuable observations on the social and institutional state of Buddhism at that time, the strength of the temples and their reform activity, it did not add any information on doctrine or teaching, which was still assumed to be essentially "pure" Buddhism smothered under unnecessary elaboration and local custom.[107]

Griffis's account of Japanese Buddhism is typical. It combined Orientalist scholarship on Pali Buddhism—its seventeen-page section on the subject began with an unattributed quotation from one of the standard works on the Theravada construct—with his own experience in Japan. On the one hand, he offered that the "three great distinguishing characteristics of Buddhism are atheism, metempsychosis, and absence of caste,"[108] a definition that clearly placed Japanese Buddhism back in the Orientalist field of the evolution of Brahmanism, but, he added, with some perspicacity, "the popular Buddhism of Japan, at least is not the bare scheme of philosophy which foreign writers seem to think it is."[109] He described two of the Japanese sects, the Nichiren, "the Ranters of Japan," and the Jōdoshinshū, using both to demonstrate the futility of the Christian project of conversion in Japan. Followers of the Nichiren sect, "the most vigorous and persistent" opponents to conversion, could not be converted, he predicted, because of the characteristics they shared with Christians, the "intolerance and bigotry" due to "the precision, directness and exclusiveness of the teachings of their master."[110] The Jōdoshinshū, on the other hand, did not need to be converted. They were "the Protestants of Japanese Buddhism." Their highly educated priests marry and live among the people, teaching in the vernacular. They "tabooed" penance, fasting, amulets, and charms. They taught salvation through faith.[111] Jōdoshinshū was already, "in a word, Protestantism in its pure sense."[112]

Once published, Griffis's work quickly became the standard and was quoted by later writers such as Reed (1880).[113] Reed also began with an introduction to Buddhism from Western Orientalists, equating Japanese Buddhism with the Buddhism of Western scholarship, but his book was distinguished by its inclusion of the first attempts by a Japanese Buddhist to intervene in the Western discourse: a history of Buddhism in Japan composed from Japanese texts, and a summary of the principles of the Jōdoshinshū faith. These were both translated by the Nishi Honganji priest, Akamatsu Renjō, who had traveled to England in 1873, "preparing the way," Reed commented provocatively, "for the conversion of Europe to the Shinshu faith." The Japanese vision of Buddhist universality and of Buddhist fulfillment of Christianity predated the World's Parliament of Religions by at least two decades.[114] There were Western scholars who studied Japanese Buddhism for personal interest, but who did not publish until much later. Most important among these are the Americans Ernest Fenollosa and William Sturgis Bigelow, who studied Tendai together under Abbot Sakurai Keitoku of Miidera. The work of Griffis, Reed, and Akamatsu did not impinge on academic knowledge. Although Reed and Griffis added local color and observed detail to images of Japanese Buddhism, they perpetuated the assumption that Buddhism in Japan, as elsewhere, was essentially that of the Western construct, which was by this time well established. They confirmed its alterity with Christianity.

Conclusion

Once introduced to the domain of public interest, Buddhism was defined through its participation in discursive contests of essentially Western concern. For all the positivist emphasis on the authority of original texts, what was widely accepted as Buddhism depended less on the results of the labors of translation than on a more general discussion. This is apparent in the persistence of images from travelers' tales "confirmed" by the selective use of sources in the face of equally plausible possibilities. It was most significant in the period leading up to the formation of the Pali Text Society when Buddhism was discussed in writings from Sherlock Holmes to Spencer. The role it played here persisted in the prefaces, introductory essays, and footnotes to the classical works of translation, Max Muller's Sacred Books of the East series and the volumes of the Pali Text Society, and helped determine which texts would be translated and given prominence. How many people read Buddhist texts in translation? How many more were content to read only the interpretations that accompanied them, or the more popular articles of scholars such as Max Muller and Rhys Davids, where they, too, related Buddhism to the concerns of the times? It was these interpretations that were further disseminated through repetition in the popular travel books of the late nineteenth century.

Buddhism, as it was known in the West, was thoroughly imbued with Western preoccupations and presuppositions. The term "Buddhism," following the analogy of Christianity's relation to Christ, implied an essential interdependence between the validity of the religion and the historical existence of its founder, a stress at odds with the Asian focus on the *arya dharma*, the teaching, rather than the teacher. From the earliest known records, the Buddha in India was not considered to be a Founder but one of a series of Buddhas who appear in the world to revive the dharma. This fundamental fact of Buddhism was recorded by Hardy in his translation of Sinhalese sources and by Rhys Davids's translations of Pali sutras and is evident in the stone sculptures of Sanchi (first century B.C.). The association of the Buddha and the Christ is nevertheless indicative of the role Buddhism played in late nineteenth-century Western thought. More than any other non-Christian religion, Buddhism was the "other" of Christianity. A crucial factor in this was, paradoxically, a perceived similarity with Christianity: even the most dedicated Christian missionaries found it difficult to criticize on moral grounds. Buddhism had an effective ethical system that, they admitted, compared well with their own, a shared sense of humanitarian ethics. The significant "other," the external against which one defines oneself, is not simply radically different but also similar enough to make effective comparison. Within a general frame of similarity, the self and other differ on the essential points of definition. Buddhism was discussed, and thereby defined, in terms of absence of soul, absence of a creator God, absence of divine wrath, absence of a Savior. Buddhism as the "other" of Christianity reflected the "diseased," discarded, disowned, or disputed parts of the nineteenth-century Christian self. It therefore occupied a unique place in the Christian exhibition, the World's Parliament of Religions.

CHAPTER

BUDDHISM AND MODERNITY IN MEIJI JAPAN

The Japanese Buddhist delegates did not enter the arena of the World's Parliament of Religions as naive innocents passively fulfilling the role assigned them by the conference organizers. The delegates were all active in Meiji Buddhist reform and went to Chicago as part of their ongoing campaign for the revitalization of Buddhism, welcoming the invitation to participate in spite of their realistic assessment of the Christian limitations of the event. These, they believed, would be outweighed by the opportunities it offered.[1] The Buddhism they presented was "Eastern Buddhism," a repackaging for a Western audience of *shin bukkyō*,[2] a philosophical, rationalized, and socially committed interpretation of Buddhism that emerged from the restructuring of Buddhism and its role in Japanese society necessitated by the religious policy of early Meiji government. *Shin bukkyō* was the New Buddhism of Japanese modernity, formed in an intellectual climate in which the West was recognized as both model and measure of modernity; shaped and promoted in reference to the West. Taking it to Chicago was an extension of earlier episodes in this process, as will be discussed in later chapters. First, it is necessary to sketch the development of Meiji Buddhism, showing how the conditions of the formation of *shin bukkyō* created an interpretation of Buddhism well prepared to meet the challenges of this celebration of Protestant Christian supremacy. The chapter concludes with a brief account of the events of the Meiji

Twenties that provided the opportunity to bring *shin bukkyō* to popular notice through an emerging nationalist movement, contextualizing the following chapters and establishing my claim that the delegation to Chicago was simultaneously a strategic intervention in both the Western discourse on Buddhism and in the Japanese contest for the religious identity of the modern nation.

Domestic Crisis and Criticism

Neither reform nor revival adequately describes the processes of the formation of Meiji Buddhism. It was not a matter of restoring purity or breathing new life into a tired, neglected, or degraded tradition but of total redefinition of the institutions and their relationship to the state and to the lay community.[3] The attempt of the early Meiji government to create a united Japanese state centered on the divinity of the emperor through the construction of State Shintō had cast Buddhism as a foreign religion, a pollution, inimical to the Japanese mind. The radical separation of Shintō and Buddhism after more than a thousand years of syncretic coexistence forced a redefinition of Buddhism.[4]

Buddhism's problems did not begin with the Meiji Restoration. It had been under intellectual attack from various quarters during the Tokugawa period. The strongest opposition came from nativist scholars whose pursuit of the original, undefiled Japanese spirit rejected all foreign influences and, with them, Buddhism. In strongly nativist areas this had led to persecution of Buddhism and attempts to eliminate temples. In the Mito domain, for example, Buddhism had been severely regulated in the mid-seventeenth century and again in the 1840s. Ketelaar argues that the pattern established by Mito served as a model for the post-1868 persecutions, such as the complete elimination of Buddhist institutions from Satsuma between 1868 and 1870.[5]

If Mito provided the ideological paradigm for Buddhist persecution, the Satsuma example demonstrated its economic logic and the extent of the threat. In Satsuma, temple landholdings represented an independent income of fifteen thousand *koku*. Their metal wealth was several hundred thousand *ryō*. Their support drained ten thousand *koku* from the domain. The destruction of Buddhism redirected all of this to domain coffers.[6] Priests forcibly returned to the lay community increased both the labor force and the taxes collectable from it. Young priests under eighteen were returned to their families, those eighteen to forty-five years of age were drafted into the new conscription army, and those over forty-five became teachers in the domain schools. The temple buildings themselves were used to house soldiers. Temple bells and metal sculptures were converted to cannon. Satsuma had Japan's first large blast furnace and was a leading domain in the production of military hardware.

By the mid-nineteenth century, a time of economic hardship and external threat, Buddhism was resented for its privileged and protected position and for the burden its support placed on the domains and people. As support for the *bakufu* government waned, the administrative association between Buddhist temples and the Tokugawa regime provided an opening for anti-*bakufu* rhetoric to spill over into anti-Buddhist sentiment. The national program of defense against Western imperialism, *fukoku kyōhei*—building a wealthy nation with a strong army—provided a utilitarian justification for a strong anti-Buddhist stance. The coincidence of difficult economic conditions, the introduction of scientific rationality, and the political insecurity of the times presented an opportunity for nativist leaders to act out their anti-Buddhist rhetoric, to eliminate what nativist ideology had designated the "foreign religion," the "evil heresy." Pragmatists argued that the nation would be better served by melting the temple bells and images to make cannon and by conscripting the priests into secular activities. Priests who learned a "useful trade" contributed to the prosperity of the nation. Others, it was apparently considered, did not.

The consequent persecution of Buddhism that had begun in domains such as Satsuma gained official sanction when the Meiji Restoration placed prominent anti-Buddhists in positions of power.[7] Following the models of Tokugawa nativist scholars such as Motoori Norinaga (1730–1801) and Hirata Atsutane (1776–1843), separation edicts (*bunri rei*) were issued, ordering the radical separation of Shintō and Buddhism (*shimbutsu bunri*), and officially ended the syncretism of the two religions. Although the government disclaimed any intention of destroying Buddhism, the implementation of the separation, particularly in those domains where anti-Buddhist attitudes were strong, presented an opportunity to vent anti-Buddhist feelings and developed into *haibutsu kishaku*, an attempt to eradicate Buddhism.[8] As a result, Buddhist institutions had entered the Meiji period devastated by persecution, confiscation of property, withdrawal of patronage, forced retrenchment of a large part of their clergy and stripped of the connection with the state that they had enjoyed for over a thousand years. The Meiji restructure of Buddhism took place in response to these extensive institutional, economic, political, and social upheavals.

Focal issues of the anti-Buddhist rhetoric were that it was a foreign religion, that it was not taught by the Buddha, that its cosmology and sacred texts were irrational and inconsistent with the findings of science, and that it was an anachronistic vestige of the past, of no benefit to modern society. The overlap between these criticisms and those leveled at Buddhism in the Western discourse is clear, as is the shared vulnerability of Buddhism and orthodox Christianity to the rational, scientific measure of truth. By responding to these issues of domestic attack, Japanese Buddhism was prepared to refute criticisms leveled at it in Chicago.

Buddhist reformers countered the nativist charge that Buddhism was un-Japanese by extolling Buddhist universality. It was not simply an Indian and therefore foreign religion, they argued, but one that applied to all people at all times and in all places. Although their need was to establish that Buddhism was, therefore, an appropriate religion for modern Japan, this was a message readily transported to the Christian arena of the World's Parliament of Religions. Reformers responded to the domestic charge that Buddhism was an irrelevant burden on modern society by promoting philanthropic works. By 1893, through this program and an accompanying reinterpretation of the bodhisattva ideal that established commitment to social welfare within the Buddha's teachings, *shin bukkyō* was equipped to refute the dismissive Western characterization of Buddhism as "otherworldly," concerned only with the future life and not with the living world.

Seeking Knowledge Abroad

The Meiji restructure of Buddhism might be dated from the formation of the transsectarian Association of Buddhist Sects (Shoshū kaimei) in 1869.[9] The association's proposals for reform indicated the two main areas of concern: to establish a new relationship between Buddhism and the state, and to redefine Buddhism to meet the needs of the modern nation. Along with the conventional reform demands for "expurgation of evil habits" and exhortation of sects to return to their doctrines and texts, the association called for "the establishment of a new type of school to produce men of ability," the founding of Buddhist colleges, the "encouragement of popular education," and the "discovery of new ways to use exceptionally qualified priests."[10]

Buddhist institutions followed the Meiji Charter Oath in seeking knowledge from abroad to strengthen the nation. Both the Nishi Honganji, which had strong links with the government through its support of the Restoration effort, and the Higashi Honganji sent delegations abroad as early as 1873, the fifth year of the Meiji era. Among the first priests to travel abroad were Shimaji Mokurai and Akamatsu Renjō, prominent throughout this history of the delegation to Chicago. The Nishi Honganji had hoped to send Shimaji with the Iwakura mission in 1871 to observe the condition and techniques of religion in the West in the same way that other high-ranking experts in various fields of endeavor were to gather firsthand knowledge of their portfolios.[11] The mission was characterized by a pragmatic recognition of Western superiority in many areas Japan wished to develop and an accompanying realistic evaluation of the folly of trying to impose inappropriate aspects of Western culture on Japan. When Shimaji did make his journey to the West, he gathered information for the modernization of Buddhism but also bought—and later translated—Henry Ball's *Self Contradictions in Christianity* and Renan's *Life of Christ*. He published a refutation of Christianity, "New Thoughts on the Resurrection," in 1875.[12] The study of Christianity was not new. In 1867–68 the Honganji sent twenty priests to study with missionaries in Nagasaki and report on their activities, and Christianity was incorporated into the curriculum of the Honganji seminaries in 1868.[13] By the 1870s, however, the object was less to gain doctrinal knowledge of Christianity than to see how it functioned within Western societies. The enemy was already familiar. The object was to discover the basis of its success in society, to learn from its example.

This was also part of the brief for the Buddhist priests, Kasawara Kenjū (1852–83) and Nanjō Bun'yū (1849–1927), who were sent to study with Max Muller in 1876. They arrived at Oxford in 1879 after three years in London studying English, and, as Muller recalled, their command of the language was still so rudimentary that "at first they could hardly explain to me what their real object was in coming all the way from Japan to Oxford, and their progress was so slow that I sometimes despaired of their success."[14] Indeed, one might wonder if Muller ever did discover their purpose: he consoled himself with the thought that by training these priests he was assisting Japanese Buddhists to adopt the Western Theravada construct, to "return to the words of the Buddha as they are preserved to us in the old texts."[15] He wrote to Takakusu Junjirō that he had gladly given of his time "in the hope that a truly scholarlike study of Buddhism may be revived in Japan, and that your countrymen may in time be enabled to form a more intelligent and historical conception of the great reformer of the ancient religion of India."[16] Even when condescending to a pupil, Muller could not bring himself to concede any value to Mahayana Buddhism.

In spite of Professor Muller's assumption that the Japanese priests had come to him to learn what Buddhism was really about, their brief was to observe the Western religion in its modern social context, and to study the science of religion, the philological and historical techniques of Orientalist scholarship. These were to be used to present Japanese Buddhism in a manner acceptable by the standards of Western scholarship, and therefore acceptable to the Western-educated elite of Japan. Mastering Sanskrit and Pali was part of this process, the essential return to original texts that characterized acceptable practice. Nanjō established a place for himself in Western Oriental scholarship with his *Catalogue of the Chinese Translation of the Buddhist Tripitaka* (1883).[17] Philological training eventually produced the collected and edited publication of the canon and compendiums of Buddhist knowledge, which began to appear from the turn of the century. Nanjō Bun'yū's *Bukkyō seiten* appeared in 1905 and volumes in Takakusu Junjirō's definitive edition of the canon from 1924.[18]

Of more immediate importance in these early years of Buddhist restructuring and for the delegation to Chicago was that through such students (these were only the first) Japanese Buddhist scholars obtained entry to the Western discourse on modern religion, in both its Christian and Orientalist aspects. By participating at the highest levels of Western academia, the Japanese priests obtained academic credentials and access to appropriate Western academic societies. They contributed to these societies as full members with appropriate Western training, and were listened to and taken seriously within professional circles, their interpretations validated by the same processes as those of Western authorities. The full value of this postdated the Parliament. Takakusu ("M.A. Litt. D. Ph.D. and W.S.") presented a paper to the Japan Society, London, speaking as an authority among peers, and his paper, published with the legitimation of the society, circulated among experts in the field.[19] Asian voices contributed to the Western academic discourse on Buddhism, and through their participation in the legitimating processes of Western academia Japanese scholars managed to maintain considerable control over Japanese Buddhist studies.[20]

Membership in academic societies was also part of the information-gathering exercise. Biblical criticism provided both a weapon against Christianity and a guide for Buddhist reform. Most significant, however, was the knowledge they gained of developments in both Western Buddhist studies and the current intellectual debates with which Buddhism was implicated. Nanjō and Kasawara subscribed to the *Journal of the Pali Text Society* from the first volume.[21] The information the priests gathered was channeled back to Japan and disseminated through journals such as the *Hansei zasshi*, founded in 1887 by Nishi Honganji.[22] In

October 1891, for example, the Buddhist press carried articles on Comte's humanitarianism, Spencer's philosophy, Max Muller's "Science of Religion," a translation of Dr. Clark's "Ten Great Religions," and a review of Monier-Williams's *Buddhism*.[23]

The juxtaposition of interests apparent here indicates the importance for Buddhist revival of training priests in Western secular thought and the importance of Western philosophy in the validation of Buddhism. The new Buddhism was to be the religion of the new, modern society. Priests in contact with Western Orientalists were aware of the vogue that Buddhism enjoyed among certain Western intellectuals at this time because of the perceived similarities between the teachings of the Buddha and contemporary Western thought, and of Rhys Davids's work in promoting Buddhism as a religion compatible with science and philosophy. They were also aware that this was based on Western knowledge of the Pali texts of Theravada Buddhism, which they regarded as preliminary preparation to the greater truth of the Mahayana. They were therefore confident that they held the answers to the religious problems of the West.

The mission to seek knowledge abroad also sent Buddhist priests to study Southern Buddhism. In 1887 Chicago delegate Shaku Sōen went to Ceylon to study Pali, Sanskrit, and Western writing on Buddhism. He observed and participated in the local practice, walking barefoot with his begging bowl, eating with his fingers, and enduring other severe cultural disruptions. This voyage also gave him firsthand experience of the arrogance of Westerners toward Asians and the injustices of colonialism in Ceylon. He began his work for Buddhist revival and strengthening Japan against Western encroachment soon after his return in October 1889, shortly before he became abbot of Engakuji.[24] The point of all this is that there can be no doubt the delegates to Chicago were aware of the extent and nature of Western knowledge of Buddhism and its function in Western discourse; they went to Chicago armed against expected criticism, confident of building upon existing approval of Buddhism.

Modernization and the Western Religion

The distinctive pattern of Christian conversion in Japan also forced Buddhist reformers to engage with Western knowledge. In the early Meiji period many Japanese turned to Christianity on the assumption that adopting the Western religion was a necessary step on the path to modernization. The catchcries of the period, *fukoku kyōhei* (wealthy nation, strong army) and *bunmei kaika* (civilization and enlightenment), associated the independent future of Japan with the attainment of Western knowledge. Modernization was initially identified with Westernization, and the young elite, the future leaders of the nation, looked to Western education and even to the Western religion as the necessary concomitant of this. Kozaki Hiromichi, the president of Doshisha and leader of the Japanese Christian delegation to Chicago, was quite explicit about this in his autobiography. He and many other patriotic young men became Christian "for the sake of the nation."[25]

Enthusiasm for Western education, and for Christianity, reached its peak in the mid-1880s when the government encouraged Westernization in the hope of convincing Western treaty powers that they had assimilated Western civilization. At this time Fukuzawa Yukichi, leading Enlightenment intellectual and promoter of Western learning, wrote that, "although I am personally entirely indifferent to religion, I believe that from the point of view of statesmanship we cannot avoid adopting the most influential creed of human society, *in order to give our nation an independent position among civilized countries* by boldly adopting their distinguishing characteristics."[26] He pragmatically estimated that a conversion by 1 percent of the population would be sufficient, if they were of the middle and upper classes—that is, if they were sufficiently prominent in Western notice. Fukuzawa's attitude here reflected the belief at this time that favorable treaty revision depended on becoming like the West, or at least appearing to do so. At the World's Parliament of Religions, Kozaki described how Christianity made "unprecedented strides" in the years 1882 to 1888 as "people poured into Christian churches."[27] Moreover, Kozaki explained, Japanese Christians were "predominantly educated young males of the shizoku or military class." "They have been, and still are, the very brain of the Japanese people . . . they are far superior, both intellectually and morally, to other classes."[28] These were precisely the people the Buddhists needed to attract to their cause if they were to install Buddhism as a force in the society. The important confrontation between Buddhism and Christianity in Japan at this time was not between priests and missionaries. It was the contest between reform Buddhists and Japanese Christians for the allegiance of this young elite.

Doshisha and the Kumamoto Band

The Japanese Christian delegates, the Kumamoto Band of Doshisha, typify the class. The Doshisha School (now one of Japan's leading universities) had been founded in 1875 by Niijima Jō (1845–90). Niijima had stowed away on a ship to the United States in 1864 when travel overseas was still forbidden. He was befriended by the ship's owner, who sponsored his study at Amherst. He returned to Japan in 1874 after acting as guide and interpreter for the Iwakura mission. He founded the school with the assistance of the American Board of Missions. Niijima himself became a Christian for the sake of the country, and following his vision, Doshisha was to teach Western learning and English language, to educate young men and women "who will devote themselves to the future of the country." Doshisha became a university in 1888. By the time of Kozaki's presidency the pedagogical balance of the university was strongly toward Western learning.

Kozaki and others of the Kumamoto Band had become Christians as the fulfillment of Confucian patriotism, adopting the ideology of the modern state they wished to bring to fruition.[29] They were introduced to Christianity while students at the Kumamoto Yōgakkō (School of Western Learning), which had been established by the Daimyō in the belief that Western learning was the key to rebuilding the strength of the domain and a means of installing its retainers in positions of bureaucratic power under the new regime.[30] The students were chosen by competitive examination, and all who entered the school, recalled Kozaki, aimed at a political career. An American teacher, Captain L. L. Janes, employed to teach at the school because of his Western military background, was specifically forbidden to teach Western ethics or religion. Janes nevertheless convinced his most promising students that because Western institutions and ideas were rooted in Christianity, adopting this ideology was a necessary concomitant to the modernization of Japan. Comparing Japan's position in the world with that of Switzerland, he convinced them that the country's independence and strength depended on its being both highly educated and Christian. Hence, he assured his students, "if any one wished really to sacrifice his life for his country choosing one of these roads [education or religion] was the ideal way."[31] Religion and education were "the two agencies for producing men" upon whom the future of the nation depended. Thirty-five of his students became Christians in an act of mass conversion on January 30, 1876.[32] Though consequently cast out of the school and disowned by their families, they were able to combine careers in both religion and education when they moved to Kyoto and took control of Doshisha. One convert recalled, "I turned my back on my parents and chose this way for the sake of my country."[33]

The converts characteristically adopted Christianity as part of a thoroughgoing modernization. They wanted "not just the externals of civilization but the essence of it."[34] Kozaki expressed this very forcefully in his paper "*Tōyō no kifū o dassezaru bekarazu*" (We must rid ourselves of Oriental traits): "We must not, in the progressive reform movement, simply adopt the extensive Western customs; we must go further and reform people's minds as well."[35] As Tokutomi Sohō put it, society was like an organism, all its parts mutually bound and inseparable. Therefore if Japan wanted to adopt the strong points of the West it must accept the whole civilization.[36] As universalists, these converts believed that the evolution of all races of man must pass through the same stages. Hence for Japan to reach full modern development it must emulate the West, which had simply been the first to travel along the path of progress, the path for all mankind. Following Spencer's concepts of evolution, they saw the change from Tokugawa to Meiji Japan, the transition from the militant, aristocratic phase of society to the industrial, democratic phase, as evidence of the irresistible process impelled by universal historical forces.[37] They believed that it was inevitable that Japan become like the West. The question was only how to facilitate the process.

The Kumamoto Christians had adopted Christianity with the specific purpose of hastening the modernization of Japan. Consequently, the Christianity they adopted was equally specifically the new theology of Western scientific scholarship, the latest Western development, not that of orthodox evangelists, under attack from science in its own country. They had become Christians, Kozaki recalled, at a time when the Bible was being questioned, "so the first difficulty that confronted us was the question of the relation between Christianity, especially theism, and science."[38] Everyone interested in Western learning, he tells us, took as his daily companions John Stuart Mill, Herbert Spencer, and Thomas Huxley.[39] Concepts of the "divinity of Christ and the efficacy for us of the death of Christ on the cross" were, along with the miracles of the Bible, "stumbling blocks to acceptance." Japanese Christianity was to be totally free of superstition and myth. Kanamori Tsūrin, another of the Kumamoto converts, spoke of the surprise of the educated Japanese when, on opening the Bible, they met with stories more incredible than anything they had yet heard from a Buddhist priest. Kanamori here reveals the anti-Buddhist prejudice typical of the elite who had been educated in Confucian schools. They knew nothing of Buddhism apart from what they had observed of local practice among the *gumin* (the stupid folk). As they saw it, it was a superstitious religion for people of lesser intellect, an anachronistic link with the past. Hence, even when the tide of opinion turned against Westernization, this prejudice had first to be broken down before they would even consider Buddhism, and the Buddhism they were introduced to had to be rational and scientific. Because this elite was the target audience for *shin bukkyō*, the task of its promoters, and a major factor in its formation, was for the New Buddhism to be "entirely consonant with reason and science" and to be distanced from the stigma associated with traditional Buddhist practice. Some sign of the success of *shin bukkyō* is that in 1891 Yokoi Tokio, also one of the original Kumamoto converts and by this time a leading Christian theologian, warned that in Japan "Christianity was confronted by a faith which is at least not inferior to it in profoundness of doctrine."[40]

Not all pro-Western Japanese turned to Christianity. Japanese Buddhism also had to be rational and scientific to attract others among the Japanese elite who saw Western materialist philosophy as the answer to the problem of how to become modern without adopting the foreign religion. Western philosophy appealed especially to those concerned about the apparent conflict between religion and science, and interest in it grew to such an extent that missionaries complained their strongest opponent was "not the religion and superstitions of old Japan but the skepticism of modern Europe."[41] To reach these people, Buddhism also needed to be presented as a rational philosophy.

The Question of Access

The need to compete with Western philosophy and Christianity also directed Buddhist reform to produce an introductory literature. Western philosophy and Christianity were readily accessible through books written in the vernacular. Although Buddhism possessed a vast literature, it was intended for specialists and was written in an archaic form of language densely scattered with technical terms that required doctrinal elucidation. The target audience for Buddhist revival was precisely the Western-educated generation who found it "easier to read the novels of Scott than to read the *Genji Monogatari*."[42] Consequently, even when this generation felt the need to assert a distinctive national character in indigenous cultural terms, it found Buddhism largely inaccessible. *Shin bukkyō* addressed this problem by presenting selected Buddhist teachings in the contemporary vernacular. One of the first and most successful of these was Inoue Enryō's *Bukkyō katsuron joron* (1887), an introduction to Buddhist philosophy directed to "young men of talent and education,"[43] which will be discussed in the following chapter. Inoue's slogan *gokoku airi* (defend the nation and love the truth) called for a redirection of the patriotic spirit and international vision that had inspired Christian conversion to the revival of Buddhism. Inoue invited "these talented young men" who had fallen "victim to this untruth" to seek the truth in Buddhism: "[I]f they know that the clergy's ignorance and lack of intelligence make them unfit to map out the revival of Buddhism, why do they not plan for the revival of the religion without the clergy?"[44] Inoue himself provided the model of active lay support and lay promotion of Buddhist philosophy by severing his institutional ties. His work is the subject of the following chapter.

Buddhism in Society

The encouragement of lay supporters, *koji* Buddhists, and the promotion of non-institutional lay practice, *zaike bukkyō*, was a distinctive feature of Meiji Buddhist reform. Advocates of *zaike bukkyō*, like Inoue, publicly described institutional Buddhism as "feudalistic, anti-social and impractical,"[45] but because they included such eminent institutional priests as Hara Tanzan, Fukuda Gyōkai, Shaku Unshō, Shimaji Mokurai, and Chicago delegate Ashitsu Jitsuzen, the thrust of the movement should be understood as providing lay access to Buddhism parallel to the continuing institutional forms rather than replacing them. *Zaike bukkyō* offered a variety of paths. The temples were open to intellectuals. Chicago delegates Hirai Kinzō and Noguchi Zenshirō took a lay initiation. Hirai studied at the Rinzai Zen temple Kenninji in Kyoto with an ordained master. D. T. Suzuki and novelist Sōseki Natsume studied with Shaku Sōen at Engakuji. Alternative paths were offered to other sections of the community by *zaike bukkyō* activists such as Ōuchi Seiran, who gave public lectures, wrote tracts, and designed daily observances suitable for domestic practice. Taking the tonsure was still a noble path but it was no longer the only one. Intellectuals needed a philosophical Buddhism. Ordinary people needed ordinary people's Buddhism, Buddhism that had been socialized.[46]

Buddhism was also given social relevance through the promotion of philanthropic works. This was in part a response to the charges that Buddhism was otherworldly, its support a drain on society. Christian social activities were both a model and a stimulus for this. Reform leaders, aware of the importance of establishing a broad base of support in the community, urged the Buddhist community to observe the growing goodwill that Christian missions were establishing among the general population through such efforts as their hospitals, charities, and famine relief and to emulate their model.[47]

The Christian model also inspired other innovations directed toward increasing lay community involvement with Buddhism. A network of youth organizations in the style of the Young Men's Christian Association (YMCA) was established and formalized by the founding of the *Dainihon bukkyō seinenkai* in 1894.[48] Buddhist marriage ceremonies were created from 1887;[49] Shimaji Mokurai performed a marriage ceremony in Tokyo in June 1892. A short description of the new ritual in the *Japan Weekly Mail* (July 1892) remarks on the similarity with the Christian form. Although the model was Christian, a possible domestic precedent for this was the early Meiji government's experiment in creating and installing Shintō funerals. Both cases were attempts to establish binding ties with the community through control of the rights of passage.[50]

Many of the most prominent Meiji Buddhists and supporters of the delegation remained laymen, practicing a nonsectarian and socially oriented Buddhism. One of particular relevance to this study was Ōuchi Seiran, whose Buddhist promotional activities ranged through such diverse projects as education for the blind and mute, printing, publishing newspapers, forming a society for the protection of animals, and establishing a life insurance company. He worked with Inoue Enryō to forge links between progressive leaders of the Buddhist and secular worlds, actively campaigned for government support of Buddhism, and stood as a candidate for election to bring Buddhist representation into the Diet.[51] In Ōuchi's writings Shōtoku Taishi, the sixth-century regent credited with establishing Buddhism in the Yamato state, provided the Buddhist paradigm of lay participation and government support.

Strengthening Imperial Rule

The Meiji government policy of *shinbutsu bunri* severed the relationship between Buddhism and the ruling powers that had existed in various forms since Buddhism had been first introduced to Japan. Throughout Japanese history religious institutions had shared in the exercise of political authority through a coalition of the major temples with the court and the military. Buddhism had been protector of the state since the emperor Shōmu had established Tōdaiji at Nara as the head temple in a network of state-sponsored provincial temples (*kokubunji*) in the eighth century. In these temples sutras were to be read for the prosperity and protection of the state. Tendai and Shingon, the oldest of the sects active in the Meiji period, had both been founded with imperial support, and both declared pacification and protection of the state (*chingo kokka*) to be their primary duty. In the Kamakura period, as Collcutt has shown, the military rulers established networks of Zen temples to parallel the Tendai and Shingon temple-based power systems of the courts.[52] In the Tokugawa, the use of temples to register and control local populations established Buddhism as a de facto state religion. Ooms's account of the use of religion by Nobunaga, Hideyoshi, and Tokugawa Ieyasu in the legitimation of their rule attests strongly to the importance of the relationship between the state and religious institutions.[53]

The ideal of the mutually supporting and reinforcing relationship between the state and Buddhism was formalized in the expression *ōbō-buppō*, the Japanese formulation of the Buddhist polity of the interdependence of the *sangha*—the community of Buddhist specialists—and the state. Though usually translated as "imperial law—Buddhist law," as McMullin explains, *buppō* must be understood to designate the Buddhist-Shintō and even Confucian composite of the living Japanese religion.[54] *Ōbō* (imperial law) is not simply "secular law" but *rāja dharma*, the duty of the righteous king, which implies a reciprocal relation with religious specialists and, in Japan, the sanction of the Shintō kami. Although the balance of the relationship between *ōbō* and *buppō* was in constant tension and regularly reinterpreted, the various sects of Japanese Buddhism, amalgamated doctrinally, ritually, and institutionally with Shintō and incorporating Confucianism, enjoyed the prerogatives of the de facto state religion of Japan until the Meiji period.

Consequently, renegotiating a relationship between Buddhism and the state was an overriding concern of Meiji reform. The first three "topics for study" the Association of Buddhist Sects listed in 1869 as areas for reform action were "The indivisibility of Imperial and Buddhist law; The study and refutation of Christianity; The co-operation between and perfection of the three Japanese faiths: Shintō, Confucianism, and Buddhism."[55] The juxtaposition is significant. The three issues were explicitly linked by the Shingon Buddhist leader, Shaku Unshō, in a formal petition to the government calling for a reversal of the policy of separation, to "save the people from the foreign barbarians." He argued that the emperor could not continue omnipotent unless the three faiths—Confucianism, Buddhism, and Shintō—were united. "*Haibutsu kishaku* will estrange the people from Buddhism, they will doubt Shintō, and Christianity will try to exploit this doubt."[56] The security of the nation depended on restoring the relationship between Buddhism, in its long-established fusion with other aspects of Japanese religiosity, and the state.

As Shaku Unshō's petition shows, regardless of the actual extent of the Christian threat to Japan in the early years of the Meiji, it was most useful as the specter of disruption in reform rhetoric. It was the religious specialists' focus of Western incursion, and their reference to it might be compared with the Meiji Restoration activists' use of the Western threat in the *sonnō jōi* campaign (revere the emperor, expel the barbarian). The Nishi Honganji, the institution most active in post-Restoration reform, had supported the Restoration movement under the slogan *sonnō gohō* (revere the emperor, preserve the dharma).[57] The symmetry of the slogans associated expelling the barbarian with the protection of the dharma. Evidence of Christianity's disruptive influence was ready to hand in the national memory of the Iberian Christian incursion of the early seventeenth century and the consequent disruptions that led to the proscription of Christianity for over two hundred years. The memory, kept alive by Tokugawa rhetoric of the "evil religion," was evoked at Chicago by Hirai Kinzō, who explained to his audience at the Parliament that this early contact had convinced the Japanese that "Christianity is the instrument of depredation." As he described it, "Christian missionaries, combined with the local converts, caused a tragic and bloody rebellion against the country, and it is understood that those missionaries intended to subjugate Japan to their own mother country. . . . it took the government of the Shogun a year to suppress this terrible and intrusive commotion."[58] History, or rather the national "memory" of events two hundred years earlier, justified Buddhist rejection of Christianity as part of its role as protector of the nation. The rhetoric of Christian aggression was part of the Meiji Buddhist attempt to reclaim a position as defender of the nation.

In the early Meiji years of Buddhist persecution, restoring links with the state was vital for the defense of the religion. The campaign remained a crucial issue in 1893, and consequently in the representation of Buddhism at Chicago, but by this time the emphasis in the rhetoric had shifted. The change in Buddhist priorities as the Meiji period progressed is indicated by the change of name of the Buddhist journal *Dampō* (Defender of the faith), which became *Gokoku* (Protector of the nation) in 1892.[59] Buddhist reformers promoted Buddhism as the spirit of the nation and called for support not to protect the religion but to strengthen the nation against Western aggression.

Buddhism and Japanese Identity

By the 1880s the radical reforms enforced on the institutions had produced new interpretations of Buddhism intended to answer the needs of the transforming society and to provide a role for Buddhism under the new regime. Following the lead and methods of Western Orientalist scholarship, a Buddhist philosophy was isolated from the ritual, mythology, and folk belief of actual practice. This New Buddhism was a noninstitutional lay practice accessible through the vernacular language. It was nonsectarian, "progressive, democratic, spiritual, social and rational," an indigenous alternative to the Western materialist philosophy and Protestant Christianity to which many Western-educated Japanese of this generation had turned. It was available when events of the late 1880s focused a growing reaction against the previous indiscriminate adoption of things Western and ushered in a search for an ideological basis for modern Japan. Buddhist reform leaders seized the opportunity to propagate *shin bukkyō* by linking it to the search for Japanese national identity.

The change in attitude to the West culminated in the failure of the 1887 attempt to revise the Ansei Treaties. The Japanese had been confident, given the progress of reforms and the degree of Westernization in Meiji Japan, that the treaties would be revised. The attempts at this time ultimately failed not because of Western rejection but because of internal reaction against what were perceived as humiliating concessions demanded by Western powers. Because the treaties symbolized the asymmetry of the relationship that had existed between Japan and Western powers three decades earlier when they were originally signed, revision on terms of equality would equally strongly symbolize Western recognition of Japan's sovereign status. Western intransigence on revision was interpreted as a threat to national independence. Failure to revise the treaties in spite of the progress that had been made in social and institutional reform discredited the previously widespread belief in Westernization as a path to revision. New strategies were required, and one proposal came from the Seikyōsha, a society formed in 1888 "for the preservation of Japan's cultural autonomy."[60] The Seikyōsha was not a specifically Buddhist organization—its membership encompassed a wide range of religious and nonreligious positions—but its founding members included the familiar reform leaders Ōuchi Seiran, Shimaji Mokurai, Inoue Enryō, and Ashitsu Jitsuzen.

The Seikyōsha argued that Japan's defense against Western imperialism depended on developing a strong national spirit. As Inoue wrote, imitation was poor political strategy because it would lead the West to despise the Japanese as lacking energy, strength, and independent spirit. Imitation was the behavior of slaves and flatterers. If the Japanese continued to adopt customs and ideas from those in the West indiscriminately, "they will consider us as simple and despicable, and they may regard us as a vassal state . . . but never, by any stretch of the imagination, look upon us as equals."[61] The Seikyōsha argued instead that Japan should follow the model of the smaller European states such as Hungary and Italy, which were at that time at a similar stage of development. These countries took pride in preserving their individual languages and cultures and coexisted with the more powerful and better developed nations in mutual respect. Only by maintaining an independent national identity could Japan expect to deal with world powers as equals. The Seikyōsha therefore looked within its own tradition for something uniquely Japanese that would be internationally esteemed and which Japan could contribute to the modern world. Buddhism, which had been the basis of Japanese civilization for fifteen hundred years, seemed a logical candidate.[62]

In the increasingly nationalistic atmosphere of the 1880s, the Seikyōsha search for the basis of national identity meshed with Buddhist reform initiatives, providing a platform and impetus for the propagation of *shin bukkyō* in the wider community. Inoue Enryō propagated the message of Buddhist nationalism through the journal *Nihonjin*, arguing that "the best way Japanese can be made Japanese and Japan can remain independent" was to preserve and propagate Buddhism.[63] He argued that Buddhism was the means by which Japan could gain the respect of the world and contribute to international welfare. Buddhism was Japan's "special product," its "strong point," a source of national identity and international recognition, a source of international prestige. It was a means of gaining recognition as a "civilized" nation and thereby affecting treaty revision: "Everyone knows that we must look to the West to supply models not only for all kinds of commodities and utensils, but also for models of government, law, the military system, education, the physical sciences and technology. However, there is one thing that Japan can transmit to foreign countries and win fame; that thing is Buddhism."[64]

Prestige did not require a mass contribution but one of quality, a point of strength and distinction. For Okakura Kakuzō, organizer of the Japanese Pavilion and the exhibition of Japanese art at the Chicago exposition—and author of the classic *The Book of Tea*—it was the Japanese aesthetic sensibility. Inoue and the Japanese delegates offered Buddhism: "Buddhism is now our so-called strong point. If we merely nurture it in our own country and do not export it abroad what else can we transmit to other countries? Material commodities are an advantage of the West. Scholarship is also one of their strong points. The only advantage we have is religion. This fine product of ours excels those of other countries."[65]

In 1889, shortly after the founding of the Seikyōsha, Inoue Enryō, Ōuchi Seiran, Shimaji Mokurai, Ashitsu Jitsuzen, and others concerned about the impact of the constitutional government on Buddhism formed the more specifically Buddhist organization Sonnō hōbutsu daidōdan (The Great Society for Revering the Emperor and Worshiping the Buddha). The society was "a union of all those who wish to protect our land and our religion from the contempt of the foreigner," principally by excluding Christians from public office and installing Buddhists in positions of influence. Its policy statement declared that by "selecting our representatives to the national parliament, to provincial assemblies, to town councils, or local offices, in the distribution of honors, in appointing school teachers, officials of societies and business companies etc., we pledge ourselves to carefully exclude all those who are disloyal to our Emperor or untrue to Buddhism."[66]

The society not only was specifically Buddhist but was overtly political, concerned to seize the opportunity of the promised representational government to gain a voice for Buddhism in governing the nation.[67] This was one of its strategies for reestablishing ties between Buddhism and the state. Inoue and Ōuchi also formally petitioned the government to this end. The organization's journal, *Daidō shinpō*, explained that the perpetuation of the Japanese race depended on a state religion that advocated "revering the Emperor," who represented the blood lineage, and "worshipping the Buddha," the spiritual lineage of the nation.[68] Adapting the ideal of Buddhist polity to the processes of representational government in a secular state, the organization attempted to mobilize the considerable voting power of the community of Buddhist priests to political action, fielded candidates for election, and campaigned against Christian candidates. Ōuchi himself stood for election and urged Buddhist priests to do likewise, arguing that more could be achieved for Buddhism at this time by leaving the priesthood to enter politics.[69]

The Discourse of the Meiji Twenties

Inoue Enryō's *Bukkyō katsuron joron* was published in 1887, Meiji 20, the start of a decade of intense activity in Buddhist revival. The formation of the Seikyōsha in 1888, the Sonnō hōbutsu daidōdan in early 1889, and the promotion of their political positions through their respective journals were indicative of the growing importance of Buddhism in the Meiji sociopolitical arena. Apart from the factors already mentioned—the changed attitude to the West and growing nationalist sentiment that caused interest in Buddhism as a repository of national identity—certain political events, such as the introduction of constitutional government in 1889, had a direct bearing on religion in Japan. Article 28 of the Constitution granted Japanese citizens a rather conditional "freedom of religion" and placed Christianity on the same legal status as Buddhism.[70] The boost of confidence the Christian community received from this was dampened by the Imperial Rescript on Education, issued November 3, 1890, and its subsequent interpretation, which raised doubts about the possibility of being both Christian and a loyal Japanese citizen.[71] Another major factor in increased activity among Buddhist leaders at this time was the successive failure of the attempt to install first State Shintō and then the Daikyō as the binding ideology and social ethic of the nation. These failures had created a national ideological space for possession of which Buddhism and Christianity were principal contenders. The battle, however, was not a simple confrontation. Buddhism and Christianity together contended against the perceived threat of Western imperialism, religious indifference, and "the forces of materialism." Their relationship was further complicated by government attempts to form a "civil religion." As Christian delegate to Chicago Kishimoto Nobuta described the situation in his paper "Future of Religion in Japan":[72] "Japan at present is the battlefield between religion and no religion, and also between Christianity and other systems of religion. . . . The prevailing attitude of our educated classes toward any system of religion is one of co-indifference if not strong antagonism. Among them the agnosticism of Spencer, the materialism of Comte, and the pessimism of Schopenhauer and Hartmann are the most influential. To them, God is either the product of our own imagination or, at most, unknowable. . . . The religions of Japan, whatever they may be, have to contend with these no-god and no-religion doctrines."[73]

Christianity had been favored among the intellectual elite during the period of the early 1880s when Westernization had been actively encouraged, but the change in attitude toward the end of the decade brought with it a search for an indigenous ideological basis for modern Japan. Interest in Buddhism was no longer confined to the religious institutions. For their part Japanese Christians—equally opposed to foreign domination—responded to the changed environment by distancing themselves from Western missions financially, institutionally, and doctrinally, creating and promoting an indigenous interpretation of Christianity. The victor in this contest would be whoever succeeded in attracting the support of the young, Western-educated elite, the future leaders of the nation. The discourse on religion of the Meiji Twenties was a contest for the allegiance of this audience. The nature of the discourse—particularly the political and social relevance of religion—and the sense of crisis within it during the months preceding the Parliament are apparent in an editorial in the *Japan Weekly Mail*, March 4, 1893: "If we are to judge from the intellectual vigour and variety displayed in the periodicals of the month, we should be sure that religion is fast becoming one of the most active concerns of the Japanese people. Especially noticeable is the attempt now being made on all sides to settle the problem of religion in its political and social bearings. The stake at issue is of vital importance—possession and guidance of social development in the empire."

The diversity of opinion and the importance of the discourse in the early 1890s are reflected in the profusion of new publications. Although many of them were short-lived, 2,767 journals and periodicals appeared between 1889 and 1894.[74] In October 1891, in recognition of the extraordinary activity in religious publications in the recent past, the Yokohama-based English-language newspaper, *Japan Weekly Mail*, introduced as a regular feature its "Monthly Summary of the Religious Press." There were at that time more than 400 Buddhist journals alone, as well as numerous Christian journals, and journals such as the *Daidō soshi*, which represented a union of Shintō, Confucianism, and Buddhism, proposed as the basis of a new religion.[75] Although the "Summary" was conceived in the recognition that religious groups of this time were vitally concerned with political and social issues, the intensity of this involvement seems to have surprised the editor, who wrote in July 1892: "It is a noticeable feature of the Japanese religious journals, Buddhist as well as Christian, that much less space is devoted in this country to doctrinal exposition than in the West. . . . There are a few conservative magazines of [the Buddhists] in which one finds from time to time a lecture on the mystifying doctrines of the sacred books; but as a rule, the entire press devotes itself to news, and to the discussion of the topics of the day. Speculative and technical disquisitions do not seem to meet the needs of the people, if the contents of the press are any index of those wants."

The space that progressive journals did devote to doctrinal matters was, however, crucial. It was the forum for the formation, presentation, and propagation of the new interpretations of Christianity and reform Buddhism. Doctrinal disputation between sects was not only irrelevant at this time of intense social concern but counterproductive. The important issues of the discourse were what each religion could offer the nation and the compatibility of each with modern science, Western philosophy, and Japanese identity, "settling the problem of religion in its political and social bearings" for the "possession and guidance of social development in the empire."

Although for the editor of the *Mail* doctrinal disputation may have been an essential characteristic of religious journals, it was actively discouraged by both reform Buddhists and the Doshisha Christians[76] (the Buddhist and Christian delegates to Chicago respectively), who were intent on strengthening their positions by uniting the various sects and denominations, not in emphasizing their differences. The Buddhist All Sects Council commissioned a "bible," a text that would encapsulate nonsectarian belief. Japanese Christians, while not all in agreement on what exactly they believed, preferred to consider themselves as members of the Church of Christ in Japan than as members of different denominations. "In essentials unity; in non-essentials liberty; in all things charity."[77] Although Buddhists and Christians each attempted to form a united front against the other, they united as "men of religion" (*shūkyōsha*) against the forces of materialism and especially of foreign encroachment. On September 2, 1893, the *Mail* commented that "the religious papers say nothing of politics; but what they say of religion is coloured through and through with that spirit of independence of foreign control which is so manifest in the political world."

The intensity of debate these articles aroused contradicts the *Mail*'s suggestion that the Japanese were less interested than their Western counterparts in "speculative or technical disquisitions." Such interests were simply of less immediate concern. The *Mail*'s surprise at the content of the journals of religious associations arose from an inappropriate stereotyping of "religious" journals. Unlike the Christian journalists of England and America, the Japanese journalists, particularly those I am concerned with, were not writing for a committed audience, but attempting to form one.[78] Religious journals such as these promoted modernization and social change by educating their readers. Conversely, the Seikyōsha journal *Nihonjin*, which was not Buddhist but contained articles by Buddhist writers such as Inoue Enryō, Ōuchi Seiran, and Ashitsu Jitsuzen, became an important channel for presenting Buddhist views on social and political issues to the wider public precisely because it reached a different audience from the religious journals.

The delegates to the World's Parliament of Religions were all active in reform movements and contributors to religious journals. The journals these delegates and their respective associates published, their books, the lectures and meetings they held, and their attendance at the Parliament were directed toward influencing the opinions of the contemporary intellectual elite, the active and influential Western-educated minority group of Meiji society concerned with social and political issues involved in the formation of the modern nation. The delegation to Chicago was an extension of this project, a strategy in this discourse contesting the religious basis of modern Japan. The leaders of Buddhist revival believed that the best way to convince pro-Western Japanese of their claim that Buddhism was superior to Christianity, that it was the answer to the religious problems of the modern world, was to win the support of Western intellectuals and religious leaders. They were confident that Japanese Buddhism, formed out of the contests of nineteenth-century skepticism, as alive in Japan as in the West, was a stronger candidate than Christianity to be the universal world religion. They were well rehearsed in defense against the standard Christian criticisms. *Shin bukkyō*, though the product of domestic imperatives to reform, had been shaped by the religious debates that informed the World's Parliament of Religions. Taking it to Chicago would show that it was the most suitable religion for the modern scientific world.

The anti-Buddhist movements of mid-nineteenth-century Japan gave rise to an interpretation of Buddhism prepared to meet its Christian critics. Domestic criticism included the charges leveled by various anti-Buddhist factions that the Mahayana was not taught by the Buddha, that Buddhism was irrational and incompatible with the age of science, that Buddhism was otherworldly and irrelevant to modern society, that Buddhism was un-Japanese—criticisms that clearly overlap with principal issues of the Western discourse on Buddhism. The charge that Buddhism was a foreign religion gave rise to its claim for universality.

Shin bukkyō was also prepared for Chicago by Meiji Japan's resort to the West as measure and model of the modern. In the Meiji spirit of seeking knowledge throughout the world to strengthen imperial rule, Buddhist reform leaders were among the first to travel to Europe and America, observing the condition and function of religion in Western societies, studying the methods of Orientalist scholarship and biblical criticism, and observing the European debates between religion, science, and materialist philosophy. Consequently, proponents of *shin bukkyō* knew of Buddhism's function in Western discourse, particularly the approval the Theravada construct enjoyed among certain intellectuals at this time because of the perceived similarities between the teachings of the Buddha and contemporary European thought. Japanese Buddhism, they believed, offered even more than this, as we will see in the following chapter. It contained all the truth of German idealism, held in great esteem in Japan at the time, and, moreover, transcended the conflict between religion, the scientific world view, and philosophy. It was therefore better suited than Christianity to be the future world religion. This belief was vital in making Buddhism acceptable to the Western-educated elite of Japan, the future leaders of the nation.

CHAPTER

BUDDHIST REVIVAL AND JAPANESE NATIONALISM

Meiji Buddhist revival and Japanese nationalism were united in the work of Inoue Enryō (1858–1919). His widely read and influential book, *Bukkyō katsuron joron* (1887),[1] did much to promote interest in Buddhism among the Western-educated elite of the Meiji Twenties, bringing a new interpretation of Buddhism, the product of two decades of Buddhist reform, out of specialist circles and linking it to the surge in nationalist sentiment of this time. Although Buddhism entered the Meiji period under attack, the foreign heresy against which Shintō was defined, by the 1890s, through the efforts of Inoue and others, it had become a major resource for defining modern, national identity. The apparent paradox is that to promote Buddhism, Inoue gave up his status as a Buddhist priest and took the title of philosopher (*tetsugakusha*). The word *tetsugaku* had been introduced into the Japanese language around 1870 by materialist philosopher Nishi Amane. It specifically denoted Western philosophy and carried the post-Enlightenment European connotation of the opposition between religion and philosophy.[2] Philosophy was a secular activity.

The previous chapter showed how Buddhist reformers, including Inoue, used the West as a resource in the formation of *shin bukkyō*. They adapted the methods of Orientalist scholarship and biblical criticism to their needs. They domesticated Christian institutions in the formation of a local Young Men's

Buddhist Association (YMBA), in instigating a Buddhist marriage ceremony, in using Christianity as a model of the role of religion in modern society. They used Western constructs of scholarship to present Meiji Buddhism as the religion of the modern nation. In *Bukkyō katsuron joron* Inoue elaborated on the theme of pro-Buddhist Western scholars who promoted Buddhism as a religion compatible with science and modern thought. He adapted Western philosophical theory to present an analysis of Buddhism. He reinterpreted evolutionary theory to show that Christianity needed Buddhism to reach its full development. This chapter investigates *Bukkyō katsuron joron* to reveal an additional function of the West in Buddhist revival, Inoue's deployment of the authority and prestige of Western philosophy in support of Buddhist revival.

Given the reality of Western dominance at this time and the overriding concern to revise Japan's treaties with the West, Japanese modernity would be measured against the West, and the treaty powers negotiating the terms of revision would be the ultimate assessors of what was acceptable. Consequently, in the battle for the "possession and guidance of social development in the empire," as the *Japan Weekly Mail* described the religious debates of the time,[3] the important issue was convincing the Western-educated class of Japan of what the Buddhist religion could offer the modern nation. Evidence of this had to stand scrutiny in the terms of the modern West. Inoue used the authority of Western philosophy to argue the case for Buddhism.

By speaking for Buddhism as a philosopher, Inoue assumed the voice of universal rationality. He distanced himself from his Buddhist affiliations and attached the authority of impartial reason (*kōhei mushi* in his terminology) to his speech. He used this claim to unbiased and objective authority to continue the imperatives of Buddhist reform: to denounce Christianity, but also to argue that Japanese Buddhism was the Buddha's teaching, that Buddhism was not irrational, not otherworldly, nor an anachronistic vestige of the past, but the one religion in the world compatible with science and modern thought.

Because Inoue was a founding member of both the Seikyōsha and the Sonnō hōbutsu daidōdan, his work links Buddhist revival with Japanese nationalist sentiment and the political issues of the Meiji Twenties. Most important, the *Manifesto*, an open letter to the Buddhist community calling for support for the delegation to Chicago, was an echo and a summary of the arguments he presented at length in *Bukkyō katsuron joron*. The delegation to the Chicago World's Parliament of Religions emerged from the same stream of Buddhist activity.[4] Summarizing Inoue's arguments can map the field of Buddhist revival discourse at this time. Inoue's *Bukkyō katsuron joron* located the various initiatives of revival—the need to win the support of the new generation, the need for Buddhists to undertake social and philanthropic work, the refutation of Christianity, the reestablishment of Buddhism's links with the state—within the nationalist program for the future of Japan.

Inoue Enryō

Inoue Enryō (1858–1919), born the son of a Jōdoshinshū priest, was ordained at an early age and received a Buddhist education. From 1878 until he graduated as a Bachelor of Arts in Philosophy from Tokyo Imperial University in 1885, his education was funded by the Higashi Honganji as part of its revival program for educating its most able priests. At Tokyo University Inoue studied under the young American professor Ernest Fenollosa, who taught classes in the history of modern Western philosophy, specializing in Hegel and in Herbert Spencer's theories of social development and evolutionary sociology.[5] Such was the interest in Western philosophy among the Japanese elite at this time that Fenollosa was nicknamed *daijin sensei* (teacher of great men),[6] a recognition that many who attended his classes already held positions of responsibility and others were later to become leaders of the nation. Through his study of philosophy Inoue came into contact with this influential elite, and from 1882 he actively worked to promote contact and understanding between Buddhist and secular intellectuals.

Inoue's period at Tokyo Imperial University coincided with indications of a growing interest in Buddhism among intellectuals. In 1881 Fukuzawa Yukichi, one of the foremost popularizers of Western studies, declared his support for Buddhism and called upon "priests who were amenable to reason" to defend their religion.[7] Two years earlier Fukuzawa's colleague in the Meirokusha (Meiji 6 society, formed to promote Western learning), Katō Hiroyuki, then president of Tokyo University, had appointed Sōtō Zen priest Hara Tanzan to lecture on Buddhism, thereby setting the precedent of teaching Buddhism as an academic subject within a secular institution, as a system of thought divorced from its ritual and practice. Buddhist philosophy was extracted from Japanese religion and placed in context with Western philosophy and science as a branch of knowledge. It was endowed with the prestige of university recognition.

Although Westernization continued strongly throughout the 1880s, the beginnings of a change of mood, a swing away from adulation of all things Western, at least among the elite, was evident from the early years of the decade. One sign of this was the immediate and generous response to Fenollosa's plea in 1882 for the preservation of Japanese art. His speech, delivered to the aristocratic Ryūchikai, apparently crystallized an already existing sentiment. Fenollosa received both financial and official support that allowed him to access and catalog surviving collections and train Japanese to continue the work. The emperor showed his personal support by bestowing official court rank on Fenollosa and awarding him several imperial decorations, including the Order of the Sacred Mirror. By 1886 this promotion of Japanese heritage had been officially sanctioned.[8]

One of the consequences of this revival was the establishment of the Tokyo Fine Art Academy under the direction of Okakura Kakuzō.[9] The art this institute promoted was not the result of a nostalgic revival of the past, but a modern application of long-established Japanese expertise. Traditional styles were studied for their universal principles, and the techniques of past eras were applied to make objects suited to contemporary lifestyles. The revival of art, like that of Buddhism, exemplified the Seikyōsha ideal of adapting aspects of Japanese heritage to enhance the modern nation. The movement to revive Japanese art indicated both the changed attitude to Westernization and also the functional value of Western authority in validating and promoting the project. Fenollosa led the campaign testifying to the universal value of Japanese art from the perspective of, and in the vocabulary of, Western aesthetics. Invoking the authority and prestige of Western philosophy and his own academic rank as philosopher was the nearest approximation to this voice of Western authority available to Inoue in his revival of Japanese Buddhism.

Inoue the Philosopher

Inoue had established his identity as a philosopher not only through scholarship but also through his activities at university. The Tetsugakkai, the Philosophy Society (1884), developed out of a society Inoue formed in 1882 for the study of Kant, Hegel, and Comte, bringing together progressive leaders of both the Buddhist and secular worlds. Core members of this society included Buddhist reform leaders familiar from the previous chapter (Ōuchi Seiran, Shimaji Mokurai, Hara Tanzan, Kitabatake Dōryū, Kiyozawa Manshi) and other such prominent Meiji intellectuals as Inoue Tetsujirō, Shiga Shigetaka, Miyake Setsurei, Tanabashi Ichirō, and Katō Hiroyuki. A number of these people would later become prominent in the Seikyōsha.[10] In 1886 the group began publishing a journal, *Tetsugaku zasshi* (Philosophy magazine), and in 1887 founded the publishing company

Tetsugaku shoin (Philosophy Press). This same year Inoue founded his school of philosophy, the Tetsugakkan (later to become Tōyō University), teaching Western philosophy but also Chinese and Japanese thought, resuscitating the "pale shadow of Eastern philosophy."[11] In 1889 Inoue traveled to Europe and America to investigate means of teaching Eastern thought there.[12] Inoue diligently cultivated his image as philosopher through this constant repetition of the term in his activities.

Inoue made the decisive statement in 1885 when he gave up his Buddhist robes and distanced himself from institutional Buddhism. This in no way diminished his effort to propagate Buddhism, but from this time he worked as an independent citizen. He thereby became an example of the ideal he espoused in *Bukkyō katsuron joron*, the educated layman committed to Buddhism as a personal philosophical religion, studying Buddhism in the intellectual pursuit of truth and reviving Buddhism to preserve this truth and defend the nation. He worked without the restrictions of a conservative institutional bureaucracy,[13] free to emphasize the nonsectarian aspects of *shin bukkyō* and to criticize the existing state of Buddhism. The greatest advantage, however, was the authority and objectivity of the title "philosopher." The author's preface to *Bukkyō katsuron joron* explained that as a philosopher his discussion of Buddhism was essentially different from that of a priest. The title allowed him to proclaim that his preference for Buddhism and rejection of Christianity was not based on prejudice but on a rational consideration of the issues. He would "judge on the basis of philosophy which is just and takes no sides."[14] This in no way moderated his criticism. Part 2 of *Bukkyō katsuron* was entirely devoted to denouncing the "evil religion." But by denouncing it from the supposedly impartial stance of philosopher, Inoue enlisted the support of an audience beyond Buddhists. He did not simply dismiss it as evil but analyzed it as irrational, conceptually untenable, prescientific, deleterious to Japan.[15] By taking the title "philosopher" Inoue was able to promote Buddhism and undermine Christian influence from a pedestal of rationality and objectivity. His arguments were made more palatable, he believed, "because my discussion of Buddhism is based on the impartial judgements of philosophy it is essentially different from the explanations of priests in the world."[16]

Hōsui, the Paradigmatic Meiji Intellectual

Inoue wrote *Bukkyō katsuron joron* under the pen name Hōsui and opened with an account of his search for truth, which positioned Hōsui, the autobiographical subject, as the paradigmatic Meiji intellectual.[17] He recalled how, prior to the Restoration of 1868, he, like the nation in general, had followed Buddhism as a matter of course with little knowledge of its doctrines and little commitment, "secretly believ[ing] that there was no truth in Buddhism," and had seized the opportunity offered by the incoming government's attack on Buddhism (*haibutsu kishaku*) to "put aside his clerical robes" and seek truth elsewhere.[18] Hōsui described how he then turned to Confucianism and even Christianity but this brought him nothing more than the conviction that all the traditional religions were inadequate. Hōsui, like so many of the Meiji generation, rejected religion because, as he perceived it then, it was not "in accord with the principles of truth." He was still at the vanguard of intellectual trends in 1873 when he took up Western learning—1873 was Meiji 6, the year of the formation of the Meirokusha, the society for the promotion of Western learning—and again in the early 1880s when he rejected religion altogether and came to the conclusion that "[t]he truth that I had been struggling for for over ten years was not in Confucianism or Buddhism, nor was it in Christianity; it could only be found in the philosophy that was being taught in the West."

Unlike others who had followed this path, however, Hōsui did not rest here. He turned again to Japanese Buddhism and, with his mind sharpened by his training in philosophy, was finally able to see and understand the truth he had previously failed to notice. "Having discovered the truth within the world of philosophy, when I made one more review of the various religions of the past, it became increasingly clear that the truth is not within Christianity. It was also easy to prove that the truth is not within Confucianism. Only the Buddhist religion is largely in accord with philosophical principles. Then I reviewed the Buddhist scriptures again, and gradually came to know the truth of their theories; I was overjoyed. Who would have thought that the truth that was the product of thousands of years of study in Europe already existed three thousand years ago in the East."[19]

The year of this revelation was 1885, the year of Inoue's graduation, three years after Fukuzawa's call for the protection of Buddhism, and the year that Ernest Fenollosa, Inoue's professor of philosophy at Tokyo University, took Buddhist ordination. Whether this is purely coincidental, Fenollosa's commitment to Tendai, which he described as offering "all the color and texture that Hegel lacked," would have reinforced Inoue's confidence in the appeal of Buddhist philosophy to modern Western intellectuals.[20] *Bukkyō katsuron joron*, the record of Inoue's discovery of the preeminence of Buddhism, was published in 1887.

Inoue's timing coincided with growing reaction against excessive Westernization, and Hōsui's search for the truth mapped the path for patriotic Meiji intellectuals. Inoue vowed to "reform Buddhism and make it a religion for the enlightened world."

The realization of the preeminence of Buddhist truth was the cornerstone of Inoue's project. Buddhism alone was in accord with the teachings of modern philosophy and with modern scientific principles. Inoue argued that the Buddha's highest teaching, the truth of the Middle Way, existed only in Japan because it had died out in India and China. Consequently Japanese Buddhism is the sole source of the truth that Western philosophy has taken "thousands of years of study" to realize. More than this, Japanese Buddhism contains the truth that Western philosophy is only now approaching but does not yet possess. Inoue therefore believed that Western scholars would now welcome Japanese Buddhism and that Buddhism was the one great and unique contribution Japan could make to the modern world. Because of this Buddhism was a source of national pride and potential international prestige. Together these arguments formed his strategy for the revival of Buddhism by attracting support among the educated elite under the slogan *gokoku airi*, the defense of the nation through the love of truth.

Gokoku Airi

Gokoku airi united the fundamental sentiments of patriotism, intellectual reverence for the truth, and a Confucian sense of duty. The opening lines of *Bukkyō katsuron joron* asked, "[W]ho has been born that does not care about his country? Who has studied and does not love the truth?" It was the scholar's patriotic duty to study because "when a nation has no scholarship it cannot progress"; it was his obligation to study because a scholar owed his existence to the nation. "When a scholar has no nation he cannot sustain his existence." Because the nation must be independent to produce wisdom and scholarship, Japanese scholars had a duty to work for the preservation of Japan's independence. Because scholars were also citizens and "it is a citizen's duty to defend the nation . . . it is the duty of scholars to carry out, at the same time, both the great principles of defense of the nation and love of the truth."[21]

This apparently secular formulation was transformed into a revitalization of Buddhism by Inoue's Buddhist definition of truth. His term, *shinri no ri*, was emphatically not restricted to a positivist, empiricist truth of Western philosophy, which was, in his view, "appropriate for experiential study of concrete objects but useless for the investigation of the intangible truth."[22] The truth for scholars to pursue was not the truth that forms "the basis of the branches of study and the arts . . . which are allowed to change along with the progress of the world." It was rather "the unchanging and immutable truth," "the truth that forms the basis of religion." It was the truth that is the nature of Buddhism.[23] "The underlying principle of the truth is not bounded by the world nor by the universe, and there is nothing in heaven or the cosmos to which it does not penetrate. It is truly ubiquitous, extensive, unfathomable and profound. It is truly without beginning, without end, immeasurable and innumerable. Therefore, to limit all ideas of it to this earth . . . is . . . the mistaken view of a scholar."[24]

The scholar was called upon to defend the nation through the study of Buddhist philosophy because this was the highest expression of truth. Inoue's formulation of *gokoku airi* also linked patriotism with the more specifically Buddhist concern of reestablishing the relationship between Buddhism and the state, the concern that led Inoue and his colleagues to form the Sonnō hōbutsu daidōdan (Great Society for Revering the Emperor and Worshiping the Buddha). The interdependence between a scholar and his nation that was basic to this scheme can be read as a reformulation of the traditional relationship between the religion and the state familiar in South and Southeast Asia as the reciprocally beneficial interdependence of the *sangha* (community of religious specialists) and the state: the security of the nation is essential for the *sangha* to pursue dharma, and the production of dharma is essential for the prosperity of the state. In Japan the concept was embodied in the expression *ōbō-buppō*, the inseparability of imperial law and the Buddha's law. In Inoue's scheme the *sangha* and its pursuit of dharma was replaced by the lay community pursuing philosophic truth. Because this truth was equated with Buddhist truth, the lay community was in effect to take on the duty of the *sangha*. *Gokoku airi* was a reformulation of Buddhist polity adapted to a modern democratic and secular state, a polity based on the interdependence of the scholar and the nation rather than of the state and the community of religious specialists.

Deploying Western Philosophy

The study of Western philosophy was not excluded by *gokoku airi* but seen as essential, if preliminary, training. As Hōsui, the authorial subject of *Bukkyō katsuron joron* confessed, he had initially failed to recognize the truth in Buddhism because "my scholarly abilities were meager then and I was incapable of making that discovery."[25] He was only able to recognize the truth that had always existed in Buddhism after the study of Western philosophy had increased his intellectual capability. For Inoue, Western philosophy, unlike Christianity, was a source of truth, but its truth was not as complete or profound as the truth of Japanese Buddhism. It occupied a position similar to the preliminary teachings of the Buddha (*hōben*), the teachings that provided the mental development that is a necessary prerequisite to understanding the more profound truth.[26] Inoue left no doubt that Buddhist thought surpassed Western philosophy. "The only thing in which present day Western philosophy excels is providing theories as a foundation of scientific experimentation."[27] Proving this was one function of the survey of Western thought and its comparison with the various teachings of the Buddha which constitute the body of the work.[28]

In *Bukkyō katsuron joron* Inoue summarized the history of Western philosophy, showing how it developed through the dialectical resolution of oppositions. Locke's empiricism, followed by Leibnitz's naturalism, had been integrated by Kant; the materialism of Hume and the idealism of Burke had produced Reid's dualism; Fichte's subjectivity and Schelling's objectivity had been harmonized by Hegel's idealism. Post-Kantian German idealism and Scottish common sense were reconciled by the Frenchman Cousins. Spencer reconciled intellectual and nonintellectual extremes. Inoue's point was that the development was not yet complete: "[A]ll these theories contain some sort of excess which would in turn require resolution. Although the scholars have striven to maintain impartiality they have not been able to do so." The teaching of Sakyamuni, on the other hand, embraced and reconciled these oppositions in the teaching of the Middle Way. "Unlike modern philosophers, Sakyamuni lived three thousand years ago, and yet was aware of the dangers of leaning toward extremes."[29] Because it resolved this excess, the Middle Way is greater than any Western philosophy, "unparalleled in all the world and throughout the ages."[30] The point of the survey of Western philosophy was to prove Buddhist superiority. The various sects of Buddhism contained all the knowledge of Western philosophy, but Western philosophy had not yet reached the stage of evolution of Japanese Mahayana.

Inoue validated this claim by conditionally identifying each of the theories of Western philosophy with the teaching of sects within Buddhism. This "identification" of Western philosophy and Buddhism is exemplified by his discussion of the Hinayana sect, Kusha. Inoue began by equating Kusha with Western materialism on the grounds that it is also based on the constant existence of elements of matter. These are the Five Aggregates (*goun* in Japanese; *panca skandha* in Sanskrit), which Inoue explained at some length.[31] The explanation then led to the qualification that Kusha was essentially different from materialism because among these five Buddhist elements, only one was matter in the Western sense of the word. The other four were perception, conception, volition, and consciousness, which are classified in the West as mind. Hence, Inoue concluded, Kusha differed widely from materialism. "Seen in this light, it [Kusha] is a philosophical theory of dualism."[32] In the space of a few paragraphs he had overturned his original equation, but the tentative identification had served its purpose by providing an opportunity to expound Buddhist doctrine. He had introduced the reader to a fundamental Buddhist concept. By a similarly qualified and partial identification of the Buddhist concept of "storehouse consciousness" (Japanese *araya shiki*, Sanskrit *ālaya vijñāna*) with the absolute subjectivity of Kant and Fichte, Inoue equated the Hossō sect with Western idealism, and the Tendai concept of *ri* with Hegel's absolute reason.

Inoue's scheme was to present Buddhist thought as both encompassing all of Western philosophy and, following the dialectical pattern of the West, having preceded it to its final development. Unlike Western philosophy, however, Buddhist teaching did not gradually evolve through the trials and error of men. It had all been taught by the Buddha Sakyamuni during his lifetime. According to the Tendai doctrine of *goji* (Five Periods) the apparently diverse sects of Buddhism are related as graded and partial revelations of the one truth of the Mahayana Middle Way.

The Buddha's teachings are divided into five periods. In the first, immediately after his Awakening, the Buddha revealed the Middle Way of the Avatamsaka Sutra.[33] However, he realized that this was beyond the comprehension of those in his audience. "They simply could not hear what was being explained to them" because they were "clinging to the belief in the distinction of self and non-self."[34] So he then explained the superficial doctrines of the Hinayana, "simply explaining the vanity of believing in the self." This accomplished, he was then able to teach the Vaipulya sutras and then, by these degrees of the truth adapted to the audience's ability to comprehend, to progress toward the Mahayana sutras. The message was that the Mahayana teaching of the Middle Way had been his original teaching, his last teaching, and the only complete teaching of his truth. The other teachings were expedients. As such, they were not false but incomplete. They were stepping-stones to the truth. The Middle Way of Japanese Tendai

Buddhism was, Inoue explained, a more perfect expression of the conclusions reached thousands of years later by Hegel. By this scheme Inoue not only established Sakyamuni's priority over Hegel but also answered the charge that the Mahayana was not the Buddha's teaching.

Throughout the argument, Inoue's identification of Buddhist concepts with Western philosophical terms was always qualified and, as in the claim of the identity of the teachings of Hegel and Tendai, was always drawn from isolated examples, the coincidence of isolated principles rather than of coherent systems. Nowhere does he give an explication of any Western philosophy. Western names and categories appear rather as signposts within an introductory explication of Buddhist thought—guides to familiarize the territory to his Western-educated audience. Inoue used the prestige of Western philosophy to draw attention to, create interest in, and then expound Japanese Buddhism.

Buddhism and Patriotism

The strong patriotic concern for the welfare and independence of the nation embodied in *gokoku airi* pervaded *Bukkyō katsuron joron*. The first step for scholars was to become better equipped to serve the nation through the study of philosophy.[35] Next, Inoue called upon them to revive Buddhism because it was the highest form of philosophy. "The doctrines of Buddhism are truly unparalleled in the world and peerless throughout eternity. Should we not offer our strength for this truth? Should we not offer our hearts for the sake of this truth?"[36] The intellectual passion for truth was to be justification enough for its preservation. There were, however, more explicitly patriotic reasons for reviving Buddhism, and in 1887, the time of the publication, treaty revision and its implications of Western imperialism were the focus of patriotic concern.

In *Bukkyō katsuron joron* Inoue introduced the basic Seikyōsha premise that defense against Western imperialism depended on developing a strong national spirit. This would win the respect of foreign powers as well as assist in building a strong nation, one that was capable of making a distinctive contribution to international welfare and progress. It was only by maintaining a distinctive national identity that Japan could expect to deal with the world as an equal, and this was the basic aim of treaty revision.

Inoue challenged the belief that adopting Christianity would assist revision with a pragmatic statement of the reality of international relations. Japan's present inability to establish relations of equality with Westerners was not because of any difference in religion or language but a matter of strength: "If a nation creates both financial solvency and strong military power, the people of that nation will have the necessary strength for instantly forming equal friendships with the West and revising unequal treaties, no matter what religion they are practicing."[37]

The role of religion in strengthening the nation lay in its direct relationship with the spirit of man. The advantage of Buddhism was its long connection with Japanese culture. For more than a thousand years, he wrote, it had permeated the hearts and minds of the Japanese. Adopting Christianity would harm the spirit of the country and forfeit the independence of Japan. Progress, he continued, depended on maintaining a balance between heredity and adaptation. Therefore, adapting Japanese Buddhism to modern requirements would be more conducive to progress than following the early Meiji trend of adopting the completely foreign Christianity. "To unseat Buddhism and replace it with Christianity would surely have a negative influence on the spirit of independence." It would result in "the loss of Japan's inherited nature, and would unquestionably impair its development."[38] He simply could not explain "why anyone believes that by abandoning Buddhism and accepting Christianity we will be obtaining a more satisfactory means for establishing international relations, promoting a national constitution, or realizing the goal of treaty revision."[39]

The intimate connection between religion and the spirit of man was also an argument against conversion to assist modernization. Because "the West has a nature peculiar to the West," there was no reason to believe that any benefits that Christianity did bestow on the West would be transferred to Japan.[40] Inoue also confronted the assumed association between Western progress and Christianity, arguing that, even within the West, Christianity obstructed progress, it "oppressed men's spirits and impeded the development of scholarship."[41] Western progress had been achieved in spite of Christianity. Nevertheless, he observed, in Japan Christianity had attracted young men of talent. In a passage of *Bukkyō katsuron joron* that may well have been addressed to the Doshisha Christians, typical of the talented and ambitious men who converted to Christianity, Inoue wrote: "It is said that the talented men, who should have ambitions for the future, are converted early in life to Christianity. . . . When I hear about this, I am deeply grieved. . . . If they have the intention of loving the country how can they not promote their country's traditional religion? If they know that the clergy's ignorance and lack of intelligence make it unfit to map out the revival of Buddhism, why do they not plan for the revival of the religion without the clergy?"[42]

A Secular *Sangha*

The question Inoue posed was particularly pertinent because these converts rejected all traditional religion equally. The Christianity they had originally adopted was a liberal theology, elaborated upon by their own reading of contemporary criticism. By the late 1880s, the time of Inoue's publication, they had distanced themselves from missionaries and were developing their own rationalized, demythologized interpretation of the Christian doctrine. Why, Inoue suggested, invoking the reform ideal of *koji* Buddhism, did they not carry out a similar exercise on Japanese religion? Why not redirect their considerable intellectual effort to making the Japanese religion meet their ideals rather than the foreign one?

Inoue did not attempt to deny that Buddhism as it could be observed in contemporary Japan was in a degraded state and in dire need of reform. Rather, in the mode of all rhetoricians attempting to stir outrage and action, the picture he painted was exaggerated. "Present-day Buddhism is practiced among foolish laymen, it is handed down by foolish clergy, and it is full of depravities; in short it is not free of becoming a barbaric doctrine."[43] This was "nothing intrinsic to Buddhism"; Buddhism simply reflected the "corrupt customs of society."[44] Inoue's own efforts to effect change included promoting Buddhist philanthropy and campaigning against non-Buddhist superstition, folk belief in ghosts and the supernatural.[45]

Another passage of *Bukkyō katsuron joron* that might have been directed at the Doshisha converts confronted the belief of the Min'yusha (Friends of the Nation) that social evolution justified their assiduous Westernization. As they saw it, because social evolution was universally applicable, all societies must pass through the same stages. Therefore, for Japan to outstrip the West it must therefore follow the same path. They believed Japan would be able to overtake the West because of the superiority of the Japanese spirit. Inoue recognized that the intention of "our countrymen in accepting the West and studying English and German is not to make Japan an imitator and follower of other countries, but to make it a competitor and rival that will someday surpass the West."[46] Nevertheless, he warned, Japan would never overtake the West by following in its footsteps, or by discarding its strong points and adopting the shortcomings of the West. This could only be achieved by building a strong national identity, which, as he had already argued, depended on reviving and preserving Buddhism. Buddhism, in spite of its present state, was one of the strengths of Japan.

In an argument that paralleled that of his Seikyōsha colleague Shiga Shigetaka, Inoue argued that imitation was poor political strategy. It would lead the West to despise the Japanese as lacking energy, strength, and an independent spirit. Imitation was the behavior of slaves and flatterers: "[T]hey may regard us as a vassal state . . . but never, by any stretch of the imagination, look upon us as equals."[47] In the *Nihonjin* a year later he would be even more explicit. "The best way Japanese can be made Japanese and Japan can remain independent was to preserve and propagate Buddhism."[48]

Buddhism and International Prestige

Inoue believed in the necessity of projecting Japanese achievement in indigenous terms, not as an imitation of the West. For him Buddhism was the means by which Japan could gain the respect of the world and contribute to international welfare. Buddhism is Japan's "special product," its "strong point," a source of national identity and international recognition and prestige. The proposal carried the nationalistic appeal of Japanese superiority and offered hope for the practical result of gaining recognition as a "civilized" nation and thereby effecting treaty revision. On top of all this, Inoue offered the altruistic appeal of contributing to the benefit of the world as a whole.

First, he argued Japan's responsibility to Asia. Buddhism is the basis of Eastern civilization and has greatly influenced its scholarship, language, customs, and even the sentiments of its people.[49] However, "the good strain" of Buddhism, the Mahayana, had died out elsewhere; it was virtually extinct in its country of origin and the little that did remain "is only the shallow doctrine of the Hinayana."[50] Japan, therefore, as the sole repository of the Buddha's highest teaching, had a particular duty to preserve and propagate it. "Only in our country, Japan, do we have these sacred sects and texts, as well as people who know the profundities of the one vehicle [Mahayana]. If this is not maintained in Japan today, and if the people leave, the writings perish, and the sects are destroyed, in what land will Buddhism rise again? This is why the support of Buddhism is our most pressing urgent need today."[51]

Inoue did not miss the opportunity to suggest that the survival of the Mahayana teachings in Japan was also evidence of the racial superiority of the Japanese. Mahayana Buddhism had died out elsewhere because of the deterioration of the races. His botanical metaphor of the "strains" of a plant emphasized that, though deriving from a common ancestral seed, the Mahayana Buddhism of India and China was not the same as the Mahayana Buddhism of Japan. The "good strain" was "the special product of the country that nurtured it." There was, however, "absolutely no reason why it cannot be transplanted to other lands."[52]

The next step was a pragmatic recognition of the superiority of Western achievement: that there was very little that Japan could produce that was not already available in the West, that the West was also ahead in its social and public institutions, the model for "government, law, the military system, education, the physical sciences and technology." The one advantage that Japan had, he argued, was religion, and because "this fine product of ours excels those of other countries"[53] it was "the one thing that Japan might transmit to foreign countries and thereby win fame."[54]

Inoue then appealed to the sense of duty of his Confucian-educated readers. Just as it is the duty of Japan's farmers to make agriculture flourish and to export food to foreign countries, and the duty of merchants to increase trade and to compete with the foreigners, it is the scholars' duty to their country to make learning and religion prosper and to propagate them abroad.[55] He assured his readers that the West would welcome Japanese Buddhism. "Western scholars have come to hate Christianity bitterly, and day and night, they are eagerly looking for a religion based upon philosophy."[56] Japanese Buddhism offered the evolutionary completion of Western philosophy, as well as philosophical Buddhism, a religion that accommodated the spiritual needs of the modern world. As a religion based on philosophical truth, far from being in conflict with philosophy as Christianity appeared to be, it offered an introduction to it. The fact that Western scholars studied Buddhism indicated an existing interest in Buddhism in the West, but this interest was not as great as it could be because the West only had very limited and biased access to its truth. Their scholars only investigated the Hinayana, "the most shallow of all Buddhism," and Western understanding was further hindered by the fact that "the books about Buddhism sent to the West were all written by Christians."[57] Inoue's message was clear. If the West was to realize the worth of Japanese Buddhism, able Japanese scholars must present it to them.

Fundamental to the whole argument was the evolutionary imperative for competition between species. Not only was Buddhism the most perfect expression of the truth that the Western world had been seeking for centuries, but it would provide the competition with Christianity that was essential if the West was to reach its full evolutionary development. The progress of man depended on competition between different cultures. Japan had a mission—a moral obligation—to develop its distinctive national characteristics to advance world civilization. History demonstrated the need for diversity. The prosperity of the West was a consequence of "competition among all the branches of learning and the arts," but "when any kind of scholarship or religion is implemented as the sole ideology of that nation, progress is impeded."[58] The West had no religion except Christianity, which carried the additional burden of being "often guilty of obstructing the development of science and philosophy." Introducing Buddhism would provide the competition essential to stimulate progress without which Christian civilization could not reach its full potential. "This is one more reason why the promotion of Buddhism in Japan is one of the most pressing needs of the day."[59]

Though this may seem a particularly beneficent concern, Inoue, like Hirai at the World's Parliament of Religions, believed that Christianity at its full development—when it had overcome its reliance on myth, mental props such as its concept of Deity, and unscientific doctrines—would not be different from Mahayana Buddhism. It was an expression of generosity not unlike that of the Christian missionaries who came to the East "not to destroy but to fulfill." Summarizing his argument for the revitalization of Buddhism, Inoue concluded rhetorically, "[I]s it not Buddhism alone that can make our country's scholarship independent in the East, and supersede that of the West? Is it not Buddhism alone that will make our country's doctrines overwhelm the world and swallow the globe? Is it not Buddhism alone that can make Japan's prestige shine throughout the world, and make Japan's fame resound throughout eternity? Should we not defend this teaching for the sake of the nation? Should we not love this religion for the sake of truth?"[60]

Taking Buddhism to the West

Whether in response to Inoue's plea or not, toward the end of the 1880s Japanese Buddhists, led by the Honganji institutions (both Nishi Honganji and Higashi Honganji), developed international contacts. Although there had been contact from earlier times the initiative was formalized with the founding of the Society for Communication with Western Buddhists (Ōbei bukkyō tsushinkai) in 1887 under the leadership of Akamatsu Renjō. Akamatsu, an associate of Inoue, had been one of the first Buddhists to travel to Europe and the first to write on

Japanese Buddhism in English. A branch office was opened in London in 1890, and a journal, *Bijou of Asia*, was published.[61] The arguments of *Bukkyō katsuron joron* explain the essential connection between the propagation of Buddhism overseas and the contest of religions within Meiji Japan. It was at least as much a strategy in the discourse determining the religious future of Japan as a missionary drive for expansion. In this context the invitation to the World's Parliament of Religions was an outstanding opportunity. The Parliament provided a chance to speak directly to a select audience of religious specialists, to introduce them to Japanese Mahayana, and, moreover, offered the opportunity, through the publication of the proceedings, for the reform representation of Buddhism to enter into Western discourse.

Conclusion

The apparent paradox in Inoue Enryō's career is that he broke his formal ties with Buddhism in order to promote it. Such was the authority of the West in Japan in the 1880s that even in a time of reaction against excessive Westernization, a time when many Japanese were looking to their indigenous heritage in search of a distinctive national identity, Japanese Buddhism had to be validated in the international currency of Western standards. To do this, Inoue adopted the title of philosopher—a distinctively Western title at that time—and, with it, the claim to speak on behalf of Buddhism with the voice of unbiased reason.

He used this claim to rational, objective authority to establish the superiority of Buddhist thought by comparison with the standards of universal reason. He used Western philosophical theory to present an analysis of Buddhism. He used the names of Western philosophy to attract the attention of the Western-educated elite and the terms of Western philosophy to signpost the less familiar concepts of Buddhist teaching. But Inoue's identity as a philosopher offered more than this. Just as Fenollosa's authority on Western art and aesthetics had been crucial in launching the revival of Japanese art, Inoue's credentials in Western philosophy validated his promotion of Japanese Buddhism. This recourse to Western authority was also a factor in taking Japanese Buddhism to Chicago. Acceptance of Japanese Buddhism in the international, Western, and Christian event—or at least the appearance of acceptance—validated the revivalist project. However, regardless of the importance of Western philosophy in Inoue's work, there is no question that what he taught in *Bukkyō katsuron joron* was Buddhism.

I suggest that Inoue's use of Western philosophy is best understood as a deployment of Western authority. What was important in this exercise was the authority that Western philosophy commanded among Inoue's target audience. The term "deployment" points to a strategic purpose—in this case, Inoue's related projects of recreating a role for Buddhism in modern Japanese society and establishing a relationship between Buddhism and the new Japanese state.

CHAPTER

DEPLOYING WESTERN AUTHORITY I

Henry Steel Olcott in Japan

Colonel Henry Steel Olcott, founder and president of the Theosophical Society, toured Japan from February 9 to May 28, 1889, at the invitation of a committee of young Buddhists led by Hirai Kinzō, "to do for the religion of [Japan] what he and his colleagues have done for the religion of India."[1] The tour is significant in this discussion as one in a series of events linking the Buddhist revival of Inoue Enryō and his associates, Seikyōsha nationalism, and the delegation to Chicago, and in demonstrating their shared concern with the value of the West in authorizing local initiatives. There is, for a start, a continuity of personnel. Lay delegates Hirai Kinzō and Noguchi Zenshirō were prominent in the organization, and there is a constant background presence of Shimaji Mokurai, Akamatsu Renjō, and Nanjō Bun'yū in both the tour and the delegation.[2] More significant, though, is the organization of the performance itself. In a gesture not unlike Inoue's use of the names and labels of Western philosophy to attract an audience and signpost his introduction to Buddhist thought, Olcott was paraded about the nation as a sign of Western approval of Buddhism. His speeches extolling Buddhism, attacking Christianity, urging the preservation of Japanese heritage, warning of the inadequacies of Western culture, and advocating Buddhist missions to the West reinforced and verified the arguments of the reform movement typified by the writings of Inoue. The timing, too, was ideal. Olcott arrived on February 9, 1889, just two days before the promulgation of the Meiji Constitution. His tour was part of the surge of activity in Buddhist reform in the Meiji Twenties. The political concerns of Buddhist reform were symbolized by the union of nationalist and Buddhist flags flying over the processions of priests and waved by the vast crowds that gathered to welcome Olcott to provincial centers.[3]

The importance of his Western identity is underlined by the discrepancy between the public feting of Olcott by his hosts—among whom are many familiar as supporters of the political Buddhist organizations already mentioned and the delegation to Chicago—and their awareness of the inadequacy of his understanding of Buddhism. Like Ernest Fenollosa, who had fronted the revival of Japanese art, Olcott was a Western authority speaking on behalf of Buddhism. As the "White Buddhist," a title bestowed on him by the press in Ceylon and repeated by the Japanese press, he was living testimony to Western interest in the Buddhist religion, a testimony that was enhanced by his position as founder and president of a Western religious organization.[4] He was a religious specialist. Most significant, however, he embodied many of the ideals of Buddhist modernity. He was a practical man of action, a colonel in the American army (a military rank no doubt added to his standing in a society where the ex-samurai still constituted an elite); a man of science, since he had achieved initial prominence through his research and publications on scientific agriculture; an experienced lawyer and journalist; an ambassador for Buddhism with firsthand knowledge of bureaucratic government.[5] Olcott's credentials, widely reported in newspapers, preceded him on tour, countering the accusation that Buddhism was incompatible with modern Western life. By the time of his tour of Japan his achievements on behalf of Buddhism in Ceylon were added to his authority. He was a proven champion of Buddhism. Noguchi spoke of him as "Jamashaka, 'Bodhisat of the nineteenth century.' "[6]

Olcott's fame did not depend solely on his exploits in Asia. His reputation as founder of the Theosophical Society also aroused interest—particularly among the European community in Japan—and the fact that discussion of Olcott and his Theosophy in Christian circles was often critical did not detract from his prestige among Japanese Buddhists. Rather, the very existence of Theosophy and its growing following confirmed the Buddhist claim that Christianity was failing in the West and that Christians were seeking an alternative religion. Moreover, in the atmosphere of confrontation in Japan, Christian hostility reinforced Olcott's alliance with Buddhists. The discussion within the European community, as well as the publicity of the extensive press coverage of his tour, also served to bring the issues of the revitalization of Buddhism to the attention of the Western-educated elite who previously had little to do with religion. Consequently, Olcott's tour was an extension of previous initiatives such as Inoue Enryō's Philosophical Society, and of the work of Seikyōsha Buddhists like Ōuchi Seiran and Inoue in attempting to engage the secular elite in the preservation and defense of Buddhism.[7] It publicized and lent Western authority to the existing movement.

The importance of Olcott's "Western-ness" is underlined by the lack of media interest in Olcott's traveling companion, the young Ceylonese lay Buddhist David Hevaviratne (Anagārika Dharmapāla), who was rapidly becoming a leader of Buddhist revival in Ceylon. Dharmapāla was unwell and spent almost the entire visit in the hospital in Kyoto, where he was befriended by Japanese Buddhist activists. The Japanese formed a local branch of Dharmapāla's Mahābodhi Society (Indō busseki kofuku) to assist in the project of restoring the sites of Buddhist pilgrimage. Later, at the World's Parliament of Religions, the Mahābodhi link and cooperation between Dharmapāla and the Japanese would be displayed as symbols of Buddhist universality.

Colonel Olcott's Theosophical interpretation of Buddhism was apparently also of little concern to his Japanese hosts.[8] First, the large majority of Olcott's audiences spoke no English and consequently depended on the Japanese translation, which, Olcott "was pained beyond expression" to discover, did not necessarily adhere to his ideas.[9] Second, Japanese would not expect a non-Japanese to have grasped the profundities of Japanese Buddhist doctrine. Olcott, after all, had taken his Buddhist vows in Ceylon, and the superiority of Japanese Buddhism over Theravada was not questioned in Japan. He spoke of the value of Buddhism in general, of its superiority over Christianity, of the need for Western-educated Asians to preserve their distinctive heritage, of the flaws in the Western way of life. His presence on tour attested to his commitment. Although, as we will see, it would become so later, Olcott's actual understanding of Buddhist teaching was beside the point to the tour organizers.[10]

The organizing committee—headed by Hirai Kinzō and the Reverend Sano, "an influential priest," evidence of cooperation between lay Buddhists and clergy in Japan—was clearly aware of events within the international Buddhist community. Its expectations were specific. As Noguchi, who had been dispatched to escort Olcott to Japan, explained to an Indian audience: "We, Japanese Buddhists, now ask you to lend us this worker of social miracles, this defender of religion, this teacher of tolerance, for a little time, so that he may do for the religion of my country what he and his colleagues have done for the religion of India. We are praying that Colonel Olcott will come and help us; to come and revive the hopes of the old men, to put courage into the hearts of our young men, to prove to the graduates of our colleges and universities, and to those who have been sent to America and Europe for education, that Western science is not infallible, and not a substitute, but the natural sister of Religion."[11]

Olcott was to bring hope and encouragement, revive pride in Japanese religion, and counter the tendency toward Western materialism. The committee expected that the commitment to Buddhism of this Western authority would restore Japanese confidence in Buddhism as a religion for the modern world. Noguchi also spoke of the tasks Japan faced: the unification of Buddhist sects, the education of both priests and laymen, the reconversion of Japanese to Buddhism, discrimination in the adoption of things Western.[12] These aims had long been on the reform agenda, and although he would make greater claims, Olcott was invited to Japan to act as a catalyst for developments that had been put in place some time earlier. He was to be a European spokesman for a revival movement that was already well defined and had made substantial progress. His role was to attract the interest of a wider community to the Buddhist cause through his authority as a Western sympathizer of Buddhism.[13] This had been his achievement in Ceylon, which he was invited to repeat in Japan.

Because of this it is necessary to give a brief account of Olcott's career in Buddhist revival in Ceylon before discussing his tour of Japan. The Ceylon experience was important to Olcott's Japanese hosts because it established his reputation as white champion of Buddhism. It is important in this discussion because it characterizes Olcott's interest in and knowledge of Buddhism, and also because it establishes that Olcott was invited to Japan after, and in spite of, Ceylonese disillusionment with Olcott and accusations that he propagated false doctrine.

Olcott and Buddhist Revival in Ceylon

In 1879 R. S. Copleston, Anglican bishop of Colombo, wrote of the "impetus" Buddhism was receiving from displays of European interest.[14] His letter was prompted by a Buddhist pamphlet that reprinted and publicized a letter Olcott had sent to Mohottivatte Gunananda and Hikkaduvē Sumangala, high priest of Adam's Peak, both leaders of the Buddhist revival, congratulating them on their success in debate against Christian missionaries.[15] The letter was accompanied by extracts from Madame Blavatsky's *Isis Unveiled*, described rather loosely by the bishop as "an English book on Buddhism." Copleston expressed his concern for the effect this "nonsense" had on both the common people and on the educated Sinhalese who used it to "justify their adherence to the national religion" and stressed the potency of Western approval in attracting the educated elite to Buddhism. "All that comes out here is made much of," he warned.

The impact of the pamphlet may well have inspired Mohottivatte and Sumangala to organize Olcott's first triumphant visit to Ceylon in May 1880. The tour, as it began, was essentially a parade of Western interest in Buddhism. Although he arrived in Colombo on May 16 and met Mohottivatte there, Olcott and Blavatsky continued on board the ship until the southern port of Galle. Olcott's reception took place in Galle—the area of greatest Buddhist support—and unfolded as a continuous series of processions, welcoming ceremonies, and speaking engagements organized by the monks and reported in the press. The tour was thus preceded into British strongholds by descriptions of its success and the news that a "pukka sahib" and a Russian princess (Madame Blavatsky) had embraced Buddhism. "We were the first white champions of their religion speaking of its excellence . . . in the face of the missionaries, its enemies and its slanderers."[16]

However it might have been originally envisaged, the significance of Olcott's work in Ceylon was not restricted to this legitimation and publicizing of Buddhism. Once involved, Olcott enthusiastically embraced and advanced the Buddhist cause. The Ceylonese Buddhist monks had a clear perception of their needs and aims but were hampered in their ability to achieve them, first by the restrictions Theravada Buddhism imposed on the association between monks and the lay community, and second by Ceylon's colonial status, which placed the monks at a severe disadvantage in dealings with the foreign, English-speaking and Christian-supporting administration. Olcott's anomalous position as a foreign sympathizer allowed the waiving of the rules of the Vinaya forbidding a monk to associate on equal terms with a layman,[17] and from this position he was able to apply his considerable organizational skills liaising between the laity and the priesthood,[18] a major factor in the success of the program to establish Buddhist schools.

His bureaucratic experience was put to use in 1884 when he traveled to London to intercede with the Colonial Office on behalf of Ceylonese Buddhists. The concessions he gained included official recognition of Buddhism's position as the religion of the majority of the people, an achievement symbolized by the instigation of the national holiday for Wesak, the commemoration of the Buddha's birthday. Buddhists of Ceylon were also granted permission to hold religious processions, and Buddhist registrars of births, deaths, and marriages were to be established so that Buddhists would no longer be "forced as hitherto to depend for these services upon their bitter enemies of other faiths."[19] Olcott attributed the success of his mission to his "long familiarity with the methods of public business."[20] His experience in law is also apparent in the drafting of his submissions.[21] In these instances his value to Buddhism depended on his personal skill and experience and on the particular problems faced by Theravada Buddhists under colonial administration. The Japanese situation, however, did not allow Olcott the opportunity for similar achievements on their behalf. Consequently, the tour of Japan was planned along the lines of the original Ceylonese demonstration of Western support, with a similarly tight schedule of orchestrated parades, welcoming crowds, photographic sessions, an exhausting lecture program, and extensive press coverage.

Buddhism as Theosophy

Olcott had originally accepted the invitation to Ceylon as an opportunity to establish branches of the Theosophical Society. Once he became involved in local issues, however, the promotion of Buddhist reform took priority and he declared that the Theosophical Society in Ceylon would be "devoted to all matters concerning Buddhism and would be the means of spreading Buddhist propaganda."[22] The non-Theosophical nature of the society in Ceylon was underlined by the formation of a small and entirely separate "Lanka Theosophical Society composed of Freethinkers and amateurs of occult research."[23]

Similarly, although the invitation to tour Japan included the inducement of forming Japanese branches of the Theosophical Society, the one local branch of the society created with "Hongwanji officials for officers" was, as even Olcott observed, a mere formality; it "never did any practical work as such."[24] By the time of his visit to Japan Olcott had become occupied with the idea of uniting the various Buddhists of the world, creating a united front against Christianity, and a common platform from which to proselytize. This was to be achieved through the Buddhist Division of the Theosophical Society, led by Olcott himself, "for it goes without saying that it can never be effected by any existing organization known as a Buddhistic agency."[25] By the end of his first tour of Japan, Olcott was so enthusiastic about the plan that he considered resigning from the Theosophical movement to devote himself entirely to building up "an International Buddhistic League that might send the Dharma like a tidal wave around the world." Nothing eventuated from this idea because it was opposed by both Madame Blavatsky and "a far higher personage than she."[26]

Olcott's personal ambition for his visit to Japan was to initiate this movement by uniting Southern and Northern Buddhists, and to this end he carried a letter in Sanskrit from Sumangala, representing Theravada Buddhists, to the chief priests of Japanese Buddhism expressing the hope that the Buddhists of Asia would unite for the good of the whole Eastern world.[27] As Olcott informed the gathering of the heads of the Eight Buddhist Sects of Japan: "My mission is not to propagate the peculiar doctrines of any one sect but to unite you in one sacred undertaking."[28] While Meiji Buddhist reformers were similarly committed to a united, nonsectarian platform, their goal was a union of Japanese Buddhist sects. Any vision they might have held of union between Mahayana and Theravada Buddhists was not to be achieved by reduction to a lowest common denominator, as Olcott proposed, but by encompassing the Theravada within the ultimate truth of Japanese Mahayana.

Why did Olcott wish to promote Buddhist unity? One reason was that he was opposed to the Christian missionary effort in Asia and believed that only by banding together could Buddhists be strong enough to compete with the Christians and counter the immense strength and wealth of the Christians with their Bible, tract, Sunday school, and missionary societies.[29] Another reason was his Theosophical interpretation of Buddhism, which saw the Buddha as one of the Adepts and equated his teaching with Theosophy, the occult science that lay at the root of all true knowledge.[30] Olcott's own account of taking Buddhist vows in Ceylon shows that he rejected all existing Buddhist practice: "[T]o be a regular Buddhist is one thing, and to be a debased modern Buddhist sectarian is quite another." He also claimed the greatest possible freedom for personal interpretation: "[I]f Buddhism contained a single dogma that we were compelled to accept, we would not have taken the *pansil* nor remained Buddhists ten minutes."[31] Olcott's public avowal of "Buddhism" was for him simply a statement of his commitment to Theosophy.[32] "Our Buddhism was that of the Master-Adept Gautama Buddha, which was identically the Wisdom Religion of the Aryan Upanishads, and the soul of all the ancient world-faiths."[33]

Consequently, although Olcott's interpretation of Buddhism, like that of Pali scholars, denied the legitimacy of contemporary Buddhists whose practices he regarded as degenerations from the original teachings of the Master-Adept, it diverged significantly in other respects. It did not privilege Theravada Buddhism over the later Mahayana Buddhism, for it was here that he most readily found the "Mahātmas" and the "*siddhis*" of Theosophy. He also accepted the doctrine of the succession of Buddhas, the teaching that Sakyamuni was one in a line of Buddhas that are born in this world to revive the perennial dharma. This doctrine, though found in the earliest Pali sutras, was typically dismissed as "priestly elaboration" because it conflicted with the historical view that Buddhism was founded by Sakyamuni. It did, however, conform to the Theosophical account of the Adepts, conveniently providing Madame Blavatsky's "pre-Vedic Buddhism."

Olcott's Buddhist publications borrowed freely from the sources of both Northern and Southern Buddhism to support his Theosophical mission. *The Golden Rules of Buddhism* (1887) contained a chapter called "Adeptship a Fact"—an overt appropriation of Buddhism to the cause of Theosophy—that depended on selected passages from Chinese Buddhist texts.[34] These liberties did not go unnoticed. Olcott's first publication on the subject was *The Buddhist Catechism* (1881), a Buddhist version of those "elementary handbooks so effectively used among Western Christian sects."[35] It was intended for use in Buddhist schools and Sunday schools, to protest against and substitute for the Christian Bible tracts used to teach English in Sinhalese schools. *The Buddhist Catechism* incorporated Buddhist "legitimation" of concepts of Theosophical interest such as auras, hypnotism and mesmerism, the capacity for occult powers, and displays of phenomena.[36] Apart from such dubious additions, it was a gross simplification of the doctrine and caused considerable uneasiness among the monks who supervised its production. Olcott commented that it would not have been published if he were Asian, but "knowing something of the bull-dog pertinacity of the Anglo-Saxon character, and holding me in real personal affection, they finally succumbed to my importunity."[37] Even with these concessions, an impasse over the definition of nirvana almost aborted the project. Olcott attempted to suggest the "survival of some sort of 'subjective entity' in that state of existence," claiming that this was the view of Northern Buddhists, but "the two erudite critics caught me up at the first glance at the paragraph."[38] On this occasion Olcott reluctantly modified his entry. He did nevertheless manage to produce in the *Catechism* a version of Buddhism that supported and propagated his Theosophical beliefs, and this anecdote—suggesting as it does that the work was produced under the strict supervision of specialists—claimed authentication for it as an accurate interpretation of Buddhism.

Although the *Catechism* served its immediate political purpose and survived through multiple editions in several languages, Olcott's erstwhile patron Mohottivatte began composing his own catechism in 1887, explaining specifically the need to reassert the true doctrines of Buddhism against the false teachings many Western sympathizers had begun to incorporate into the religion.[39] Since this incident occurred before Olcott's trip to Japan, the invitation was presumably offered in the knowledge of the shortcomings of Olcott's mastery of Buddhism.

Because he perceived a relation between Northern Buddhism and Theosophy, Olcott was predisposed to discovering Theosophy in Japanese sects. "It is averred . . . that the Shingons are the esoteric Buddhists of the country. They know of the Mahātmas, the Siddhis (spiritual powers in man), and quite readily admit that there were priests in their order who exercised them."[40] "Esoteric" here refers not to the Japanese Buddhist technical term *mikkyō* but to the Theosophical use of the word as it appeared in Sinnett's *Esoteric Buddhism*, published in 1883, a sense specifically denied by Japanese Buddhist priests.[41] Olcott's comment that Fenollosa and Bigelow's "Guru," presumably the Tendai master from Miidera, was "a mystic and partial adept (they say)"[42] reveals both his expectations of Mahayana Buddhism and his skepticism that a Japanese Buddhist priest could have such powers. His skepticism was also apparent in his disparagement of Japanese paintings of Rakan (Sanskrit *arhat*, Buddhist sages). To Olcott they were mere "caricatures . . . of Mahātmas."[43] Japanese Buddhism was, after all, "debased modern sectarian Buddhism" and was to be measured against Theosophy, which was for him "regular Buddhism."

Japanese disdain for Olcott's understanding of Buddhism became apparent in 1891 when he returned to Japan with the draft of the pamphlet *Fundamental Buddhistic Beliefs*. This was a grossly simplistic reduction of Buddhism to a mere fourteen points "upon which all Buddhists could agree," which Olcott intended to use as the platform for the proposed International Buddhistic League. Like the *Catechism*, it presented Buddhism at the level of sophistication of a Sunday school tract. Olcott, misinterpreting the courtesy shown him on his previous tour, had expected his document to be signed by all the leading abbots, the promoters and supporters of his first visit. To his disappointment, the Japanese refused to sign "these condensed bits of doctrine," complaining that "there was infinitely more than that in the Mahayana."[44] He persuaded one member of the committee to sign by arguing the vital necessity of the Northern and Southern churches offering a united front to a hostile world. However, even this endorsement appears with the qualification that the fourteen points are "accepted as included *within* the body of Northern Buddhism" as "a basket of soil is to Mt.

Fuji," an attempt to avoid the implication that the extract represented the essence of Buddhism.[45] A partial understanding of Buddhism was acceptable, even commendable, coming from a sympathetic Westerner. It could not, however, be endorsed as institutionally accepted truth, even as a political expedient.

Olcott did eventually manage to obtain signatures from representatives of most of the sects, if not at the level of authority he had expected. Among the Japanese names are those of Kōzen Gunaratna and Tokuzawa Chiezō, for example, two young priests sent to Ceylon to study Pali. They had no institutional authority and were guests at Adyar at the time. One sect that is not represented is the Jōdoshinshū, from which came the principal benefactors of his earlier tour and, incidentally, the official, if inactive, representatives of the local branch of the Buddhist Theosophical Society formed in 1889. Olcott, upset at this rejection, fell back behind the defense of Western scholarship and its model of Original Buddhism as the ascetic, world-rejecting, and egalitarian teaching of the historical Sakyamuni. On his first visit he had favorably characterized the Jōdoshinshū as "the Lutherans of Japan."[46] After the rejection, he wrote that they occupied "an entirely anomalous position in Buddhism, as their priests marry—in direct violation of the rule established by the Buddha for his Sangha" (that is, they were not ascetic). They were "the cleverest sectarian managers in all Japan" (not otherworldly), and "the most aristocratic religious body in the empire" (not egalitarian).[47] Olcott, the "champion of Buddhism," exploited the versatility of the Orientalist stereotype against modern Buddhists. Those who conformed to it were criticized for not meeting the needs of the modern world. Those who did meet the needs of the world were simply not real Buddhists and could be criticized for failing to uphold the ideals.

Olcott and the Revival of Buddhism in Japan

I have argued that Olcott's tour of Japan was inspired by the success of his tour of Ceylon and had much in common with it. In both cases Olcott was invited as a European spokesman for a revival movement that was already well defined and had made substantial progress. His role in both countries was to attract the interest of a wider community in the Buddhist cause through his authority as a Western sympathizer of Buddhism. Most important in both countries, the binding factor as well as the reason for the initial contact between Olcott and Buddhist revival was his strong anti-missionary position. His Theosophy was of no interest to Buddhists in either country, except insofar as it signified his authority as a man of religion, and the growing membership of the society signified a Western dissatisfaction with Christianity.

By his own account, Olcott's tour of Japan was both more extensive and more spectacular than his famous welcome to Ceylon, progressing through the major cities and provincial centers from Sendai in the North to Kumamoto in the South, bringing him "before all classes and conditions of men."[48] During his 107-day tour Olcott delivered seventy-six formal lectures, "with an average audience of 2,500 from first to last." He was everywhere welcomed by a retinue of priests in ceremonial robes accompanied by large crowds waving Buddhist and national flags. On top of this heavy speaking engagement, he was introduced and entertained at the highest social levels, regularly dining with high-ranking officials, politicians, and even members of the imperial household. The head priest of the Nishi Honganji, Ōtani Kōsan, himself publicly honored Olcott by pausing to bow to him during a ceremonial procession.[49] He was showered with gifts of valuable Buddhist artifacts and books for the Adyar Library. The tour was, as it is recorded in *Old Diary Leaves*, "one of the most significant events in the Society's history,"[50] progressing from "The Visit to Japan," to "Successful Crusade in Japan" and "Further Triumphs in Japan."[51] In contrast to this retrospective vision of heroic progress, the diary written during the tour, though equally impressed with the fanfare, shows signs of stress (fig. 10).

The grueling schedule arranged for him belied the public show of esteem. He was regularly required to lecture in the evening after traveling all day, or to lecture in several different towns in a day. On March 27, after a full day he "was dragged out to visit a temple and make a ten minute speech." Olcott was also called upon to speak at his dinner engagements, to visit factories and institutions, to receive visitors at all hours. No alteration was made to the schedule to accommodate his regular bouts of illness. On April 29, with still a month to go, he recorded in his diary that he was "almost dead with fatigue."

The consistently vast size of the audiences, frequently made up of members of a school or an institutional body, attests to the organization and activity in Buddhist circles more than to Olcott's personal fame in rural Japan. So does the distribution of flags to the crowds, especially if the "Buddhist flag" mentioned was not a traditional Japanese version, but the flag designed by Olcott himself as the international emblem of Buddhist unity. Buddhist reformers planned Olcott's tour through provincial areas not only to bring the issues of Buddhist revival to wide, public attention, but to demonstrate the strength of support for Buddhism among the people across the nation.

Figure 10. Olcott in Japan (*Theosophist* [August 1932]: 628; courtesy of the Theosophical Publishing House, Adyar, Chennai, India)

As in Ceylon, Olcott was also an ardent spokesman for Buddhist revival. His speeches reinforced and verified the arguments of the reform movement. By his own account, he called for Buddhist unity, "revival, purification, the preparation of elementary and advanced books for the education of the young and the information of adults, and expose[d] the falsehoods circulated against it by its opponents."[52] Although what Olcott intended with his call for unity differed from the intentions of his Japanese hosts, the call itself was familiar. All of these recommendations were major features of the reform agenda promoted in Inoue Enryō's *Bukkyō katsuron joron* just a year or two earlier.

Olcott also repeated the earlier message of Inoue when he urged that the Japanese Buddhists send missionaries to Europe and America "to tell the millions now disbelieving Christianity and looking about for some religion to replace it, that they will find what will convince their reason, and satisfy their heart, in Buddhism." On another occasion he spoke to a large audience of students and Buddhist priests on the necessity of a religious basis in education and, in an echo of Seikyōsha appeals, warned against accepting Western values too quickly and throwing away their own traditions.[53] Olcott, internationally renowned Western orator, speaking with unquestionable personal conviction, confirmed and extended the Buddhist reform message.

Olcott also supported the Seikyōsha call for greater self-confidence among Japanese and stressed, as they did, "the advisability of not prostrating themselves completely before the shrine of foreign civilization."[54] Olcott was impressed that the Japanese "bore themselves as free men" and, unlike the people of India, mixed with Westerners as social equals. He emphasized that the Japanese should preserve their own institutions and systems because "[w]ithout pride, without patriotism, there could be no real prosperity, no sound progress." Modern civilization, he warned, was a two-sided picture; the comfort, refinement, and culture were accompanied by self-seeking greed: "Let the Japanese beware of accepting this civilization in its entirety." Olcott, himself a representative of the modern scientific West, spoke in agreement with Seikyōsha and progressive Buddhists, arguing not for conservative preservation of the past but for progress through the selective adoption of positive and appropriate aspects of Western culture from a base of pride in a distinctive national identity.

Olcott criticized Christianity, declaring, just as Inoue Enryō had some years earlier, that, in spite of missionary claims to the contrary, Christianity impeded progress.[55] Echoing the Japanese sense of insult at the presence of foreign missions in Japan, he deplored the inconsistency of Christians subscribing money to "despatch propagandists to distant lands" while millions in England never entered a church "from year's end to year's end." Moreover, Olcott continued, "Japan had already an excellent creed. She had Buddhism," a religion he believed to be superior to Christianity because it was not in conflict with science. He confirmed the growing Western interest in Buddhism: there were, he said, twice as many Buddhists in America as there were Christians in Japan.[56] The convergence with the Buddhist reform position is again evident. Although Olcott saw himself bringing "the pure light of Buddhism to the benighted land of the rising sun,"[57] the importance of his lectures in the revival of Buddhism was that he, as a Western authority, repeated and confirmed a number of the Buddhist reform arguments. Most significantly, he—the Western celebrity—was able to draw an immense and diverse audience to hear them.

This statement, however, raises the question of what was communicated to his audiences. Predominant though the messages discussed here may have been, they were not the sole content of Olcott's speeches. His address at Maebashi, one of the few attended by members of the foreign community in Japan, was criticized for being essentially an attack on Christianity rather than an address on Buddhism.[58] The same complaint appeared a month later.[59] A Westerner who had attended a lecture near Kyoto complained that the speech there was nothing more than a rehash of the tired old ideas of spiritualism. The *Missionary Herald* reported that Japanese Buddhists did not think highly of Olcott and did not recognize his teachings as good Buddhism.[60] Such are the reports from the rare members of the audience who understood English.

Most of Olcott's lectures were delivered to Japanese-speaking audiences in rural centers. The only time he spoke without the aid of an interpreter was at Tokyo University. His diary attests to the stress suffered by his interpreters. Noguchi became ill shortly after Olcott arrived in Japan (February 9) and was replaced by a Mr. Kimura. By March 29 Kimura was "tired and surly," and on April 6 he "broke down" under the strain of a three-lecture day. Nanjō Bun'yū stepped in to interpret during this emergency, and when his replacement, Sakuma, became unwell, two men took over the task, "one telling the other what I said and he rendering it into Japanese!" Even with the best of intentions it would have been most surprising if Olcott's speeches were communicated anywhere near literally, and Olcott himself seems to have been aware of at least a tendency in his interpreters to be selective. "I cannot say how much of this was translated to them, but at least those present who knew English had the benefit of my opinions."[61] He was distressed when a bilingual member of the audience in Tokyo noticed considerable discrepancies in translation. As the *Mail* reported:

> Colonel Olcott spoke in English which was rendered into Japanese by an interpreter. Considering that the lecture had not been written, and that the interpreter was wholly unprepared, it cannot be denied that the rendering deserved much credit. But, on the other hand, it often erred, and erred very seriously, sometimes by sins of omission, sometimes by sins of commission. Perhaps this was inevitable. One point, however, we deem it advisable to note. To his Japanese audience it must have seemed that Colonel Olcott intended to criticize adversely the tendencies of this empire's leading statesmen towards Western civilization. The impression was entirely due to incorrect interpretation. Colonel Olcott used no words capable of being construed by English hearers in that sense.[62]

The audience on this occasion included a large number of influential people, and the incident becomes even more significant in Olcott's account of it because, he was led to believe, the emperor himself had attended the lecture incognito.[63] How many members of the audience outside of the capital would have sufficient control of both languages to monitor the translations? To what extent was the freedom of translation used to enhance Olcott's delivery of the reform message? Olcott was the perfect puppet, his full-bearded, physical presence the image of a man of substance. He was a forceful rhetorician, self-motivated, committed, and unquestionably sincere in his delivery, exuding enthusiasm while "speaking" the message of his translators.

Olcott's Tour as Performance

Delivering ideas was, however, not his only function. His tour was also a performance, an event creating the opportunity for advertisement, review, and interpretation, publicizing and endorsing Buddhist reform. The tour was orchestrated so that the greatest part of his direct audience comprised provincial Japanese. The success of the lectures, measured in the size of the attendant crowds, was reported in the press, which naturally emphasized those aspects of his speeches most relevant to the current concerns of Japanese readers. The *Dandokai*, for example, reported that "since Colonel Olcott's arrival in Japan Buddhism has wonderfully revived. . . . He has everywhere been received with remarkable enthusiasm. . . . He has taught the people to appreciate Buddhism, and to see that it is our duty to impart it to all nations."[64] In the *Japan Weekly Mail*, March 16, 1889, a letter signed "A Buddhist" commented on the warm welcome Olcott had received in Japan and ventured to "prophesy a revival of our national religion as the certain consequence of Colonel Olcott's visit," but only if, the letter continued with a plea strongly reminiscent of Inoue Enryō's opening to *Bukkyō katsuron joron*, "a number of earnest, unselfish, persevering, and courageous men . . . unite without distinction of sect, for the vigorous promotion of the pure religion taught by Shakyamuni." Significantly, this same issue of the *Mail* expressed regret that no notice of Olcott's Tokyo lectures was posted and that consequently the general public had no chance to hear him.[65] Was this an oversight, or did the organizers decide that the revival movement was better served among the English-speaking community by processing Olcott's lectures through the press? His speech then remained under control.

Olcott's schedule in Tokyo was filled with social engagements rather than lectures. He was introduced into the highest, and politically most influential, levels of society. On one occasion he was introduced to "an Imperial Prince and Princess, a Marquis of high rank, Vicomte, Master of Ceremonies at the Imperial Palace and other men of influence."[66] The governor of Tokyo entertained him at the Nobles' Club. The prime minister, also in attendance, invited him to present his views "about the system of education which I thought most likely to advance the interests of the nation."[67] He also addressed the Japan Agricultural Society on Practical Scientific Agriculture.[68] In Tokyo, the metropolitan center of the modern nation, the Western champion of Buddhism was shown to be a man of public position, someone to be taken seriously, a man of science who saw Buddhism as the religion of the modern world.

Conclusion

The tour of Japan was recorded in *Old Diary Leaves* as a triumph for Olcott, attributing to his three-month tour the achievements of a decade of Buddhist revival. The "visible results of the Colonel's mission" included the institution of "three Buddhist universities and various colleges, and the establishment of about 300 periodicals advocating and defending Buddhism." Moreover, by Olcott's visit "the spread of materialism and scepticism was checked; the insufficiency of Christianity was shown, and the truth of Buddhism vindicated. . . . Imperial princes and princesses have begun to take a prominent part in Buddhistic education and propaganda."[69] As we have seen in a previous chapter, the establishment of Buddhist universities and periodicals had begun well before Olcott's tour. Nor should he be credited with inspiring the imperial family's interest in Buddhism. In 1884, five years before Olcott's visit, the Shingon priest Toki Hōryū—later a delegate at Chicago—twice performed the seven-day Shingon initiation ceremony (*shichinichi gōshūhō*) at the imperial court.[70]

When the fanfare of this first visit to Japan is compared with the cool reception of the second, it is difficult to escape the conclusion that Olcott was used, deployed to the advantage of Buddhist revival in the Meiji discourse on religion. Japanese Buddhists had little respect for his understanding of doctrine and were scornful of his *Catechism* and of Theosophy. Olcott's real contribution was as spokesman for their cause. He lent their arguments the authority of Western science, attracting the attention of the pro-Western elite, and consolidating support for Buddhist revival among the population at large. As an educated man of science, a convert to Buddhism from Christianity, he was living testimony of Buddhist revival claims of Buddhist superiority, Christian inadequacy, and the compatibility of Buddhism with science. He also spoke of the importance of Buddhist education to the prosperity and independence of the nation. As in Ceylon his endorsement of Buddhism allowed the educated elite "to justify their adherence to the national religion." Olcott's tour of Japan was another carefully orchestrated move in the program of Meiji Buddhist revival.

CHAPTER

BUDDHISM AND TREATY REVISION

The Chicago Project

The invitation to participate in the World's Parliament of Religions came as the perfect answer to the recurrent reform cry to take Japanese Buddhism to the West. Reform rhetoric associated the revitalization of Buddhism with issues of modernity and maintaining the nation's sovereignty against Western aggression. Buddhist nationalists, as we have seen, argued that preserving Japan's independence—revising international treaties was an important aspect of this—depended on demonstrating a strong and distinctive national spirit, on identifying and developing something uniquely Japanese that would contribute to the general welfare of the modern international world. Like Inoue Enryō, they argued that Buddhism was the basis of Japanese civilization; more important, religion was the one area of endeavor in which Japan excelled all other nations. It held the truth that the West was now seeking. Taking Buddhism to the West would establish Japan's intellectual and spiritual credentials and thereby win the respect of Western nations—and presenting it at Chicago was a first step in this process. These aims meshed closely with Japan's more general exposition project outlined in Chapter 1: modifying existing perceptions of Japan to establish its right to acceptance among the "civilized" nations of the world and thereby secure favorable revision of its treaties with a number of Western nations.

The nature of Japanese religion was itself central to the question of treaty revision. As Chicago delegate Hirai Kinzō explained, Western powers used the claims that Japan was uncivilized and that the Japanese were heathen idolaters as excuses for not revising the treaties. In particular, they refused Japan's request to abolish the extraterritoriality clause on the grounds that this would expose their nationals to Japanese laws. The definition of "heathenism" and "idolatry" was not simply a religious debate but a pivotal contest in this contentious issue. The delegation challenged these charges through its explication of Buddhism and its place in Japanese society. This chapter considers how the imperatives of treaty revision shaped the presentation of Japanese Buddhism.

Organizing the Delegation

Although the delegates as a group represented the main sects of Japanese Buddhism, as late as April 1893, mere months before the opening of the World's Parliament of Religions, the Japanese Buddhist community was still debating the value of sending official representatives to Chicago. Initial response had been enthusiastic. The *Japan Weekly Mail* reported in July 1892 that "a large representation is promised from Japan." Plans had been disrupted, however, when Japanese newspapers carried a report of a sermon in which the Reverend John Henry Barrows, chairman of the World's Parliament of Religions, had expanded on "the possibilities for Christianity" of the event.[1] The fears of the conservative Buddhist community appeared to be confirmed: the event was a Christian conspiracy, organized by Western Christians to undermine and discredit the claims of other religions. Official endorsement of the delegation was withheld. Even progressive Buddhist leaders who supported the initiative conceded that "there are some aspects of attending this meeting which has been proposed by Christians and in which the Chairman is a Christian which are not entirely satisfactory."[2] They were equally wary of the Christian aggression of the organizers of the Parliament but did not believe that this reason was sufficient to pass up an opportunity that promised such "far reaching benefits for Buddhism," the chance to "expound the truth and attack wrong belief." They were prepared not only to confront Christian aggression but to counter it, even in Christian territory.[3] They argued that this was, "quite simply, not the time to be conservative"; rather than offer "passive resistance to the invasion of the foreign religion . . . why shouldn't we make the great effort and attempt the surprising strategy of expansion?"

The document arguing this position, here referred to as the *Manifesto*, was an open letter from "Concerned Buddhists" to the Buddhist All Sects Council

(Bukkyō kakushū kyōkai) asking its members to reconsider their earlier decision not to endorse the delegation. It was published simultaneously in a number of journals, signed by twenty-five supporters described by the *Japan Weekly Mail* as "leaders of the community and eminent priests." Among them were such prominent leaders of the Buddhist community as Ōuchi Seiran, Shimaji Mokurai, Nanjō Bun'yū, and the Chicago delegates Shaku Sōen, Toki Hōryū, and Ashitsu Jitsuzen. Inoue Enryō is elsewhere listed as a supporter.[4] The *Manifesto* stressed what might be achieved by sending official delegates to this great international gathering where "in one action we can convey the teachings of the Buddha and the truth that is special to Buddhism to the scholars and religious specialists of the world." Its aims, and the list of signatories to the document, link the delegation with the Buddhist nationalism of the Seikyōsha.[5]

The *Manifesto*

The *Manifesto*, the papers presented by the delegates at Chicago, and the papers they published on their return demonstrate the relationship between Buddhist revival and the political developments in Meiji Japan. The *Manifesto* echoed Inoue Enryō's call of *gokoku airi* (defense of the nation through the love of truth), the strongly patriotic association of the promotion of Buddhism and the preservation of national independence. It argued, as Inoue had, that the propagation of Buddhism in the West would benefit not only Japan but the world as a whole. The benefits to Japan, the prestige and respect it would win, depended on the conviction, encouraged by Western Orientalist scholarship, that Japanese Buddhism already held solutions to intellectual and spiritual problems the West was now facing. An official publication prepared for distribution at the Parliament also echoed Inoue: the advancement of science appeared to have induced an interest in Buddhism among the Christian people of the West, and "even the Hinayana doctrine of Southern India was highly admired by them. How much more then must they glorify the wonderful doctrine of Mahayana!"[6] It was the duty of Japanese scholars to bring Japanese Buddhism to international attention. This required positive action, such as making the effort to attend this international conference as the *Manifesto* urged. "The sound of a large bell reaches far and wide, but *the bell must be rung*; the doctrines of a great sage are by no means restricted to a small district, but *opportunities for their propagation must be utilized*."[7] The Parliament "offers Buddhism the opportunity of external expansion and provides the means to achieve it."[8]

The first argument of the need to propagate Buddhism in the West in "active resistance against the invasion of the foreign religion" was a matter of national honor. For Japanese nationalists Christian missions in Japan were not only a threat to Japanese sovereignty through their connection with Western aggression but also another humiliating indication of Japan's inequality with Western nations, a perpetual reminder of their "uncivilized" status. The Japanese perceived and challenged the implied moral superiority of missionary effort. As a correspondent to the *Choya shimbun* wrote, European and American missionaries were sent to Japan in the belief that "Japan is a miserable, uncivilized region, still under the baneful influence of paganism. . . . If any one doubts that the sending of missionaries to this country is a flagrant insult to it, let him imagine the result if the German people were to send missionaries to England, France or the United States. . . . In the very nature of things, missionaries are essentially dispatched by civilized to uncivilized nations."[9] The logical converse of this was that to claim moral superiority, and the power status it legitimated, Japan needed to dispatch missionaries itself. From this time, as the *Japan Weekly Mail* reported, Buddhist missions were established in Korea, Siberia, Tibet, Honolulu, and India.[10] Preparations for missions to China accompanied the Sino-Japanese War.

The second argument for the external propagation of Buddhism engaged directly with the racist lessons of the Columbian Exposition. Japanese Buddhism was proof of Japanese superiority among nations of the East and challenged the assumptions of white supremacy. The *Manifesto* observed how society rises and declines under this general trend of survival of the fittest, how "the whole world is thrown into a hurricane of racial contest." The ultimate contest of the "racial war will be between the white and the yellow," it argued; consequently, "now is the time to decide the success or failure of European nations." Within this war, it continued, religion is the "battlefield of truth" and, again following Inoue, the principal contestants are Buddhism and Christianity. Buddhism's value to the world was its difference from Christianity, because it was competition between different species that stimulated evolutionary progress. The argument was most forcefully articulated by Yatsubuchi in his report on the Parliament,[11] and in his post-Parliament article, "The Conflict between the Yellow Races and the White Races and between Buddhism and Christianity," which presented a rather more aggressive restatement of Inoue's argument that it was Japan's obligation to introduce Buddhism to the West because, without the competition of a strong rival, Christianity would not reach its full development. Yatsubuchi's argument also embraced the idea, more particularly expounded at the Parliament by the Indian delegates, that Eastern spirituality was a necessary antidote to Western obsession with the material world. "Only Buddhism can save the white race. . . . If Europe could receive Buddhism its evils would be healed, spiritual as well as physical progress would be gained, and the perfect civilization would be realized."[12]

The Delegates

These nationalist sentiments were shared by other members of the Japanese contingent. In all, there were fourteen Japanese speakers contributing a total of seventeen papers. Apart from the six Buddhist reform delegates, there were seven Japanese Christians and a representative of Shintō. Papers were also submitted by a member of the Nichirenshū and Mr. Horiuchi, president of the Japanese branch of the Mahābodhi Society. Although one of the principal determinants of the representation was the competition among Buddhists and Christians in the contemporary domestic discourse on religion, in the international forum of Chicago they were united by shared patriotic concerns for the future of Japan, for countering Western incursion and foreign interference in Japan's sovereignty, and for dispelling the humiliating accusation that Japan was "heathen." All saw Japan as the leader of Asia, defending Asia against imperialism and leading Asia into the modern world. They differed only on the means of achieving these aims. The relationship between the Christian and Buddhist delegates and their shared concern for the future of the nation are mapped by Kenneth Pyle's opposition of the Min'yusha (Friends of the Nation) and the Seikyōsha (Association of Politics and Education). Although neither of these associations had specific religious affiliations, they correspond to the Christian and Buddhist delegates respectively.[13]

In spite of the force of its arguments, the *Manifesto* failed to convince the All Sects Council to reverse its decision, and the delegation to Chicago participated without official endorsement. However, even if the delegates could not claim to represent Japanese Buddhism as such, they were representatives of Meiji Buddhist reform rather than simply independents. The Buddhist contingent was a strong group of six speakers: four scholarly priests—in the order in which they appear in the photograph (fig. 11), Toki Hōryū, Yatsubuchi Banryū, Shaku Sōen, and Ashitsu Jitsuzen—and two politically active Buddhist laymen, Hirai Kinzō and Noguchi Zenshirō (on the right). The Buddhist priests of the delegation were well qualified for their task by their rank and education and, among them, represented the major sects. Shaku Sōen (1856–1919) was chief abbot of the

Figure 11. The Japanese delegation (Houghton, *Neely's History*, 37)

prestigious Rinzai Zen complex, Engakuji. Toki Hōryū (1854–1923) was superintendent priest of the Koyasan branch of the Shingon sect.[14] Ashitsu Jitsuzen (1841–1921) was a Tendai scholar, editor of the progressive journal *Meidō*,[15] and a founding member of both the Seikyōsha and the Sonno hōbutsu daidōdan. By the time of the Parliament he had also published two books, *Notes on the Future Religion of Japan* (*Nihon shūkyō miraiki*, 1889) and *The Aim of the Constitution: The New Buddhist Law of the East* (*Kenpō seigan: tōyō no shin buppō*, 1890). His involvement in Buddhist social work and the promotion of lay Buddhism has been mentioned earlier.[16] In 1890 Shaku Sōen, Toki Hōryū, Ashitsu Jitsuzen, and Shimaji Mokurai had been chosen to coedit a five-volume work intended to promote Buddhist unity as part of the reform platform (*The Essentials of Buddhist Teachings*) and therefore already held some claim to be spokesmen for the movement. The fourth priest, Yatsubuchi Banryū, was a Jōdoshinshū abbot from Kumamoto. His journey to Chicago was funded solely by the support of the Kyūshū Buddhist Alliance (Kyūshū bukkyō dō mei kai), a society consisting of his local clergy and parishioners.[17] He emphatically declared that he could in no way be considered a representative of the sect (*ha*) or the head temple (*honzan*) but was a representative of the local people. This is less an admission of failure to obtain official support than a claim to the *zaike bukkyō* ideal.

Although official endorsement may have made funding the delegation much easier, even in this the delegation was not entirely independent. There was a rumor that Shaku Sōen sold a set of paintings from Engakuji to pay for his trip. Though endorsed by Shaku Sōen's biographers as an example of his independent spirit and determination,[18] the Buddhist journal *Hansei zasshi* doubted it was true.[19] The delegation was funded by contributions from forty-two hundred priests[20] and received assistance from institutions in the preparation and publication of books and pamphlets, if nothing else. The Jōdoshinshū, the largest of the sects in Japan, reportedly distributed more than thirty thousand volumes of five different Buddhists publications. Titles mentioned by Noguchi in his introductory paper include *A Brief Account of Shinshu*, *A Shinshu Catechism*, *The Sutra of the Forty-Two Sections and Two Other Short Sutras*, *A Skeleton of a Philosophy of Religion*, and *Outlines of the Mahāyāna as Taught by Buddha*. This last volume achieved greater permanence than others because it was reprinted and further distributed through the Theosophical Society in 1894.[21] *The Skeleton of a Philosophy of Religion* was written by Higashi Honganji scholar Kiyozawa Manshi—at that time known as Professor Tokunaga—and translated by Noguchi, who was a student of his. Noguchi distributed copies as gifts as he traveled to Chicago and passed out the last ten copies to people sitting close by during his speech. The publications indicate strong Jōdoshinshū support for the delegation, even though it was not official. This is not surprising given the problems of overcoming conservative forces described by Kiyozawa Manshi in his *December Fan*.[22] Even projects supported by the chief abbot Ōtani Kōson were vetoed. Ōtani had been responsible for sending scholars to the West and for promoting the study of Western philosophy by priests. Honganji support for Buddhist reform and propagation to the West was considerable. In June 1893 the *Japan Weekly Mail* had reported that although there was as yet no official decision to support the delegation, there was "much moral approval."

The lack of official endorsement in no way affected the reception of the delegation. Barrows introduced them as leaders of the Buddhist Church of Japan. As the *Manifesto* had warned, the Parliament would welcome as a representative whatever Japanese Buddhist priest attended, and a delegate's protests of independence, they predicted, would be interpreted "as simple modesty," "and in so far as he is actually a Japanese Buddhist, whatever he says and does would be taken as fact, recorded as the principles of Buddhism, published in magazines and spread all over the world. If this happens, even if it is found that there are points in what this individual said that are not in accord with the beliefs of some of the schools or sects of Japan, it will not be able to be withdrawn or corrected."[23]

The *Manifesto*'s point was that not sending official representatives could have severe repercussions for the Western understanding of Buddhism. Could the Buddhist Council afford, they pleaded, not to have control over what will be said at Chicago? The council nevertheless voted to allay the fears of the conservatives by officially avoiding the Christian challenge. Can we read the council's lack of response to this argument as confidence in the delegates whose views and scholarly achievements were well known to them? These were, after all, with the exception of Yatsubuchi, the scholars chosen to edit the multivolume *Essentials of Buddhist Teachings*. Could they have chosen official representatives who would have been better qualified than these independents?

The Buddhist delegation also included two laymen, Noguchi and Hirai,[24] both of whom acted as translators but also spoke as delegates representing the new, increasingly influential lay arm of Meiji Buddhism, the *koji* Buddhists.[25] Both had a long history of commitment to Buddhist revival. Their lack of clerical rank was no handicap. Noguchi spoke as a "simple layman" uncommitted to any sect of Buddhism. Hirai's first paper, eloquently delivered in English, was a forceful plea for the West to display the principles of "real" Christianity in their dealings with Japan, specifically by removing the unfair conditions of the treaties. It had more public impact than those of any other of the Japanese representatives. Hirai typified the educated elite of this time, turning to Buddhism, as he told the Parliament, in protest against Christian aggression. He had been one of the first to speak out against Christianity and had attempted to establish a Buddhist school in opposition to the Christian Doshisha, which was attracting many who sought Western education.[26] At least as early as 1887 he had initiated contact with Henry Steel Olcott, the founder of the Theosophical Society,[27] and in December 1888 Noguchi arrived in India to escort Olcott to Japan. Both Hirai and Noguchi were committed to the promotion of a nonsectarian, lay Buddhist practice specifically as a defense of the nation against Christian incursion.

Buddhism in the Campaign for Treaty Revision

Noguchi's opening address for the Japanese delegation explicitly linked the representation of Japanese Buddhism at the World's Parliament of Religions with

American imperialism in Japan and the issue of Japan's treaties with the United States. With a teasing appearance of Japanese collusion in the American vision of the Westward progression of civilization, he compared Commodore Perry, "who led us to open our eyes to the condition of other civilized countries,"[28] with Columbus. The message was, however, an inversion of this dream. The Japanese erected a statue to Perry, as the Americans had done to Columbus, but beside it they placed a statue of Ii Naosuke, the chancellor of the Tokugawa *bakufu* who had been assassinated as a traitor, Noguchi explained, because "he opened the door to a stranger without waiting for the permission of the emperor."[29] The juxtaposition of the statues was a subtle allusion to the invalidity of the treaties forced upon Japan by the United States. Maintaining his ironical message of gratitude, Noguchi thanked America for sending Perry and presented Japanese Buddhism as the most precious gift that Japan could offer, the only fitting exchange for the boon of opening Japan to the modern world and the "wonderful changes and progress" that had taken place in Japan since that time.

His gift consisted of "four Buddhist sorios"[30] (the priests who were the principal Buddhist speakers), "many thousands of copies of English translations of Buddhist works," which had been specifically prepared for this occasion, and "four hundred volumes of the complete Buddha Shaka's Sutras imported for the first time into this country."[31] Noguchi apologized for the fact that the sutras were in Chinese, but "I regret to say that there is probably no Mahayana doctrine, which is the highest order of Buddhist teaching, translated into English."[32] Although the teachings these books contained were incomprehensible to his audience, their bulk and presence carried the important message that there was a great deal of Mahayana Buddhism yet unexplored by Western scholars. Translation would be no easy task, Noguchi conceded, but he was nevertheless confident that it would be the "shortest way" to the one truth that all religions must eventually reach in their full development, the pinnacle of religious evolution where "there will be no more any distinction between [religions] or any difference between faith and reason, religion and science."[33]

Noguchi's paper was short and appears inconsequential as a representation of Japanese Buddhism. It nevertheless outlined the project of the Buddhist delegation, which was developed by the later speakers. As well as the themes of Western aggression and the fundamental illegality of the treaties, he repeated the message of the Hōōden, Japan's vision of itself as a civilized country before the arrival of Perry, and the idea that Buddhism was the source of this civilization. True to the ideals of the Seikyōsha, he recognized and accepted Western contributions to Japan's modernization but remained convinced of the international superiority of Japanese Buddhism. It was Japan's gift to the world.

"Heathenism" and Treaty Revision

Hirai Kinzō was the second speaker for the Buddhist delegation. Under the disarming title of "The Real Position of Japan toward Christianity"[34] he mounted a blistering attack on Christian imperialism in Japan, the main thrust of which was to undermine the unquestioned equation of Christianity and civilization. Citing examples of American injustice toward Japan and the Japanese, typified by the U.S. refusal to correct the glaring injustice of the unequal treaties, Hirai argued that Christians were more barbaric than the so-called heathen Japanese.[35]

Hirai disguised his attack as an explanation of the lack of missionary success in Japan. The first reason Japanese could not accept Christianity, he explained, was its historical alliance with imperial aggression, its "record of foreign devastation under the guise of religion." Japan's experience in the sixteenth and seventeenth centuries had impressed upon the Japanese mind that Christianity is "the instrument of depredation." This "hereditary horror" of Christianity was daily revived by the reality of the "powerful nations of Christendom gradually encroaching on the Orient," by the injustice of the treaties that "deprive us of our rights and advantages," particularly through the extraterritoriality clause and the loss of tariff control: "Would not the people of America and Europe think that they were being trampled upon and their rights ignored, if they were denied the application of their judicial power over those cases which occur at home? Would not Western nations be indignant and consider that they were deprived of independence, if they were compelled to renounce their rightful custom duty?"[36]

The discrepancy between Christian principles and Christian behavior was, he explained, another reason Japanese found it difficult to accept Christianity. This was evident in the refusal to rectify these injustices, but also in innumerable incidents of American abuse of power against Japanese: illegal seal fishing; abuse of consular judicial powers; acts of blatant racism, such as had been recently displayed in San Francisco when Japanese were barred from schools and employment; racist treatment of Japanese in treaty ports of Japan; depriving Japanese in Hawaii of their suffrage.[37]

Hirai's two papers at the Parliament were supplemented by three articles that appeared in the journal *Arena*, suggesting that he, with the aid of sympathetic Americans, used the journal as part of the Japanese campaign in public relations at the Columbian Exposition, this time specifically targeting a liberal intellectual readership.[38] Hirai's article "Religious Thought of Japan" appeared just a few months before the Parliament and foreshadowed the issues he would raise in his two papers, unhindered by the format of the Parliament itself. Unlike the formal papers, the *Arena* article was able to take space to develop and explain ideas and cross the boundaries of the set themes of the Parliamentary agenda. Hirai, who, according to Barrows, had been living in California for some years, apparently wrote the article in English because it appeared in the Japanese religious journal *Bukkyō* with the note that it had been translated into Japanese by Noguchi Fukudō.[39] The second article, "Japan and Her Relation to Foreign Powers," written by an American, Annie Elizabeth Cheney, described by B. O. Flower, an editor of the journal, as "intimately acquainted with" Hirai and other Japanese scholars, appeared in the September edition of the journal immediately before the opening of the Parliament.[40] The third article, written by Flower, a direct call for "Justice for Japan," was strategically timed to revive the issue during the period of final negotiations. All three articles stressed the injustice of the treaties in principle, Japan's legitimate right to demand revision within the terms of the treaties themselves, and the hypocritical contradiction between Christian and American ideals and the behavior of treaty nations toward Japan so eloquently pleaded in the final lines of Hirai's address: "We, the forty million souls of Japan, standing firmly and persistently upon the basis of international justice, await still further manifestations as to the morality of Christianity." The question beneath all three papers was the definition of "barbarian." Was Buddhism "barbaric" simply because it was not Christianity?[41] Were not the Western powers barbaric in their behavior toward Japan? The constant message of the repetition of instances of injustices is "If such be the Christian ethics, well, we are perfectly satisfied to be heathen."[42]

The definition of the term "heathen" was pivotal. Hirai was convinced that the denigrating label was being used by the Western powers as an excuse to avoid giving Japan the simple justice of law: the Japanese "are being called heathen; and this is one of the reasons why our rightful claim to revise the treaty, stipulated forty years ago between the Western powers and Japan on an unequal and disadvantageous footing, is still ignored."[43] The justification for the extraterritoriality clause of the treaty, the sticking point of negotiations, was the perceived need to protect Western nationals from the harsh penalties of law in non-Christian countries. Consequently, Western misunderstanding of Japanese religion was used as an excuse for not granting Japan's request for abolition of extraterritoriality and favorable revision of the existing treaties. Hirai's article therefore concentrated on correcting the "misunderstandings," that is, on explaining that contrary to the assumptions based on superficial observations of Western travelers and missionaries, Japanese religions were not heathen, barbaric, or idolatrous.

Figure 12. Hirai Kinzō (Houghton, *Neely's History*, 169)

Hirai not only spoke English well but was a skilled public speaker.[44] In his contentious and celebrated address to the Parliament, he played to American disapproval of aggressive "European imperialism" and appealed to "the sympathy and integrity" the American people had demonstrated by "their emancipation of the coloured people from slavery" and "the patriotic spirit which established the independence of the United States of America."[45] The *Chicago Herald*, September 14, 1893, reported that "[l]oud applause followed many of his declarations, and a thousand cries of 'Shame' were heard when he pointed to the wrongs which his countrymen had suffered through the practices of false Christianity." He concluded by reciting the Declaration of Independence and then made a direct plea to American conscience:

> You citizens of this glorious free United States, who, when the right time came, struck for "Liberty or Death"; you, who waded through blood that you might fasten to the mast your banner of the stripes and stars upon the land and sea; you, who enjoy the fruition of liberty

> through your struggle for it; you, I say, may understand somewhat our position, and as you asked for justice from your mother country, we, too, ask justice from these foreign powers. . . . We, the forty million souls of Japan, standing firmly and persistently upon the basis of international justice, await still further manifestations as to the morality of Christianity.[46]

Was Hirai's reference to the American battle for independence simply a rhetorical appeal to the hearts and minds of America or a suggestion that Japan may also be willing to fight to the end? Unilateral denunciation of the treaties and the contingent risk of retaliatory war was discussed by some Japanese at this time.[47] Hirai's speech brought the house to its feet in cheering sympathy. Even Barrows, who had tried to suppress the paper,[48] grasped his hand, and "the Rev. Jenkin Lloyd-Jones threw his arm around his neck, while the audience cheered vociferously and waved hats and handkerchiefs in the excess of enthusiasm."[49]

Hirai had discreetly avoided being too specific about Western crimes against Japan on the excuse that "it is not desirable to injure the feeling of good friendship which now exists between Japan and the West." He ventured only that "among many kinds of wrongs, there are some which were utterly unknown before and entirely unknown to us heathen."[50] It was left to Cheney to give a heart-wrenching and detailed account of the impact of the treaty on Japanese society, from the broad economic consequences and financial restrictions on development, to the description of specific cases of injustice such as the crime against a Japanese woman "before the enormity of which the healthy imagination sickens."[51] Her description of the injustices suffered by Japanese citizens through the consular courts system was a pointed inversion of the American argument of the need to retain extraterritorial rights for the protection of its nationals from "barbaric" law.

Flower's article reiterated and elaborated Cheney's principal arguments, declaring the revision of the treaties to be a matter of concern for "every American who loves justice and values the honor of the republic." To ignore Japan's claims, he wrote, "is to dishonour our flag."[52] Treaty revision was "as all absorbing with the Japanese as was the slavery question with us in the closing days of the fifties,"[53] a rhetorical gesture that recalled Hirai's wildly successful recitation of the Declaration of Independence.

The focus of both papers was the fundamental injustice of the treaties. From the time the treaties were originally drafted the terms imposed upon Japan reflected its classification among the "uncivilized." Both quoted the U.S. secretary of state at the time admitting the injustice of interfering with the internal law of a foreign country but regretting that it could not be otherwise. Such were necessarily the terms "when we stipulate a treaty with an oriental country," as with "Turkey, Persia and all other barbarous races."[54] The terms "oriental" and "barbarous" are here used interchangeably. On the other hand, for those who had some knowledge of Japan, including Townsend Harris, the American consul general who had negotiated the Treaty of 1858, the injustice of the inappropriate treaty conditions had been apparent for some years. In 1875 he had regretted that he could not revoke "these unjust articles" before he died.[55] Harris's hope that "others in the future would witness the change" remained unfulfilled nineteen years later, in 1893, and Japan was still attempting to distance itself from association with the "orientals" and the "barbarous."

Japanese Religion, Buddhism, and Heathenism

For Hirai, to counter what he declared to be the widespread misrepresentation of Japanese religion involved extolling the virtues not simply of Buddhism but of Japanese religiosity as a whole, establishing that the apparent diversity of religious practice in Japan, along with what mistakenly appeared to Westerners as idolatry, was only a manifestation—adapted to the varying needs of the people—of the one encompassing Truth. The failure of Westerners to comprehend this, coupled with the absence of any serious scholarship on Japanese religion, which allowed undue weight to be given to the casual observations of travelers and missionaries,[56] was the reason that Japan was so badly misunderstood "and the whole nation is condemned as heathen . . . ignorant, unthinking and superstitious idolaters."[57] Western misconceptions of Japan, Hirai explained, were based in the failure of monotheists to understand the tolerant syncretism of Japanese religion, which saw no conflict in simultaneously being "a Buddhist, a Shintōist, a follower of Confucius and possibly a warm admirer of Christ." He argued that the national understanding and search for truth that encompassed Shintō, Buddhism, Confucianism, and even "real" Christianity was without conflict, without idolatry, and without inconsistency.

This eclecticism was made possible, Hirai explained, by the Japanese realization that "though there are many roads at the foot of the mountain, yet if the top is reached the same moon is seen."[58] This, and metaphors of the same import, occurred frequently in his various presentations. It was the basis of his concept of

"Synthetic Religion," the subject of his second paper.[59] He also called it "entitism," in reference to the essential a priori belief in an entity that is the basis of all religions, and "Japanism" because "it is the inherent spirit of Japan."[60] It was synthetic not in the sense of being artificially constructed but in being the synthesis of all religious activities in Japan and, potentially at least, in the world. Unlike the Christian claim to universality, however, it demanded no changes or conversion. Each religion could continue to exist as before, enriched by its understanding of its place in the hierarchy of expressions of the truth. Hirai left no doubt, however, about where he saw the center of this synthetic religion: "The one and the same center" of the "one synthesized religion . . . is called satori or hotoke in Japanese."[61] *Satori* is the Japanese term for Buddhist awakening or "enlightenment"; *hotoke* is the term commonly used to refer to the Buddha. Clearly, for Hirai, as for Noguchi, "Synthetic Religion," the fundamental religion, culminated in Japanese Buddhism.

Atheism Disrupted

In Hirai's vision, all religions "properly understood" are nothing other than the pursuit of truth, and God, who cannot be limited or "personalized into the form of man, image or picture," is the "real essence of universal reason, the connecting link between cause and effect—truth is God." Consequently, Hirai explained, the word "atheist," a term constantly used by Christians to denigrate Buddhism, is meaningless. Both terms, "theist" and "atheist," he argued, depend upon a concept of deity that is a limiting of the limitless, and this is a logical absurdity. The concept of deity is merely a device whereby the human mind can handle the abstract concept of the unknowable, which is ultimate truth. As each of the world's religions evolves, it will realize this, as Mahayana Buddhism does.

The two main implications of this argument are, first, that all religions, even Christianity, when fully realized will not be different from Mahayana Buddhism; and, second, that since "no-one can deny the existence of truth, those who call themselves atheists are true theists." Hirai pointed out that those presently called atheists—Buddhists and philosophers—are actually, by this reasoning, theists of a higher order, pursuing truth in its most abstract form.[62] The highest stage of religious evolution is "non-ceremonious belief in the unknowable," as espoused by "unbelievers of religion," "non-religionists."[63] For Hirai, in contrast with the prevailing nineteenth-century Western view, philosophy is not in opposition to religion but is its third and highest state.[64] As well as identifying Buddhist truth with the latest concepts in Western philosophy, he had distanced Japanese Buddhism from the nihilistic associations of the atheist label.

Idolatry Dismissed

But what of the external and observable attributes of Japanese religiosity, the temples, images, and ceremonials that have led foreigners to misunderstandings? In a discussion bristling with references to science, the touchstone of truth, he explained the Japanese attitude to images, which are not idols to be worshiped, but aids to the comprehension of abstract and complex ideas.[65] Turning to specific examples he explained that the white paper *gohei* or *nusa* found in Shintō shrines represents "the purity and immutability of universal truth or reason"; the folded shape of the single strips of paper "represent[s] the perpetual changes and revolutions of the phenomena of the universe." The mirror, the other object commonly found in shrines, suggests, he said, that "worshippers should clear their minds." Shintō, the indigenous Japanese religion, is, by Hirai's account, essentially the worship of rational truth. Hirai explained away one of the obvious contradictions of this scheme, the association of certain Shintō shrines with deified historical figures such as Hachiman, God of War, or Tenjin, patron deity of scholarship, by comparing this with the "the American and European notion of naming universities, public buildings and churches after distinguished individuals, and dedicating the buildings as monuments to their greatness."[66] It was, as he put it, conveniently overlooking the common practice of praying to and asking favors of these *kami*, no more than the honoring of great men and women as models of morality. Japanese were no more idolaters than Americans.

Marshaling the forces of nineteenth-century scholarship in his aid, Hirai offered philological evidence that *kami*, the word commonly translated by the English word "God," carries no sense of image or idol in the Japanese but is "an abbreviation of the word *kangami* which literally means to think or perceive the truth." Moreover, Hirai argued, claiming the prestige of Aryan origins for the "pure Japanese language," *koto*, the Japanese word that should be used to represent the supreme deity, "has the same origin as the English word 'God.' "[67]

Hirai's purification of Shintō was aided by the fact that many Shintō shrines had been stripped of images, paintings, and sculptures immediately after the Meiji Restoration as part of the enforced separation of Shintō from Buddhism described in Chapter 5. All that was left for missionaries and visitors to observe in shrines by this time—if one overlooks votive tablets, foxes, and such things that were attributed to "folk superstitions"—were the mirror and the *gohei*, both easily explained by Hirai.[68]

The material evidence of "idolatry" in Buddhism was less easily dismissed. There are images in some Buddhist temples, Hirai conceded, "but they are not regarded as sacred." They are, once again, symbolizations of the truth. This argument depended on understanding the meaning of the term "Buddha." Hirai explained that, contrary to Western understanding, "Buddh" does not simply mean Gautama. "It has a triple meaning: first, truth or reason, or cause and effect; second, the human consciousness of it; third, the one who is conscious or has the potential consciousness of it."[69] That is, Hirai explained at some length, "Buddh" is the universal truth or reason that governs the universe. It applies to any person who understands universal reason, hence its use for Gautama. It refers also to all beings because they all have this potential, even if they are unaware of it. Once this is accepted, the various Buddha images are seen to be nothing other than representations of aspects of the unlimited and unknowable. "The image of Amida-butsu is only the symbol of this eternal universal truth." Hirai conceded that such symbolizations must seem ridiculous to those whose mental capacity was developed enough to comprehend the truth without a symbol, but he justified their existence by comparison with the use of numerals by mathematicians, of formulae by chemists, and the reformed Christian church's resort to verbal imagery to facilitate the comprehension of the average mind.[70] Japanese Buddhism was no more idolatrous than Protestant Christianity or science itself.

Nirvana and Social Engagement

Hirai identified nirvana as the other Buddhist concept misunderstood by Westerners. It was not, as commonly understood, the annihilation of passions, sensations, or desires, but the "eternal and unchangeable principle that governs all things," the principle without which passion would not exist. "It is not the aim of philosophers, including Gautama, to make human beings idiotic or senseless, but to teach them the unchangeable principle which may be utilized and deduced for the changeable daily life of human society."[71]

Hirai's arguments addressed the most prominent issues of Buddhist apologetics—idolatry, atheism, and nihilism—not as a justification of Buddhism per se, but to question the exclusive Western equation of Christianity and civilization. His point was that Japanese are not idolaters but people who have long held an attitude of nonsectarianism and progressive tolerance such as was now being demonstrated in the convening of the World's Parliament of Religions.[72] The followers of Buddhism and Shintō are not atheists but philosophers with a more developed sense of deity such as was only now being approached by the West. Nirvana, as understood by the Japanese Buddhists, is not annihilation, not even annihilation of the passions, which implied a detachment from the concerns of the material world, but a clear-minded and active realization of the nature of truth, an insight to the principles of law that could be used for the benefit of society at large.[73] Japanese Buddhism, he explained, is neither world-denying nor archaic.

Imperialism and the Moral High Ground

Hirai's paper "The Real Position of Japan toward Christianity" was not the description of contemporary Japanese interest in Christianity that his title may have led the audience to expect, but a plea for imperial powers to behave according to the ideals they espoused. In an inversion of the familiar missionary ploy, Hirai compared the observed behavior of so-called Christians with the "real" Christianity of the Bible and found them wanting. They lacked the spirit of charity, compassion for the weak, the spirit of brotherhood, and the sense of justice which were supposedly the foundations of their civilization. Hirai claimed for Japanese religion the moral high ground and demanded that treaty powers behave as "real" Christians, showing the virtues of Christian brotherhood and compassion, the "real" Christianity of the Bible. At the same time he undermined the fundamental justification for colonial enterprise. In the words of a French advocate of colonialism, "[T]he basic legitimation of conquest over native peoples is the conviction of our superiority, not merely our mechanical, economic and military superiority, but our moral superiority. Our dignity rests on that quality and it underlies our right to direct the rest of humanity."[74]

The Japanese delegates were not alone in their attack. Hirai's paper was only one manifestation of the conflict between the Asian delegates and imperialist Christians that seethed beneath the protestations of universal brotherhood and the polite formalities of the occasion. The letter from the Sinhalese high priest Sumangala was more forthright in its criticism of Christianity, claiming the superiority of Buddhist methods of propagation. The teachings of the Buddha had spread because of "their intrinsic excellence and never, as we rejoice to know, by the aid of force, or appeal to the superstitious weakness of the uneducated masses. No blood stains our temples, no profitable harvest have we reaped from human oppression."[75] Dharmapāla continued the crusade, his first paper claiming priority for Buddhism in solving the religious problems of the day. His second, less frequently cited paper, "Buddhism and Christianity,"[76] was even more audacious. It claimed a Buddhist origin for Christian virtue. Dharmapāla introduced the idea by listing biblical quotations as "Buddhist teachings as given in the words of Jesus and claimed for Christianity,"[77] quoting from Western scholars to establish that "the Christian religion has sprung directly from Buddhism."[78] Buddhism not only was superior to Christianity but had bequeathed to the later religion all that was admirable in it. It is no surprise that this last contentious sentence does not appear in Barrows's official history.

Buddhist representatives confidently claimed priority in religious tolerance, the great pride of the Parliament organizers, in their complimentary comparison of Barrows with Asoka.[79] Hirai's distinction between "real" Christianity and the behavior of Westerners preserved Japan's claim to complete religious tolerance. Their apparent rejection of Christianity was explained by the distrust engendered by this observed discrepancy between principle and practice. Consequently, although the Japanese "well know what abstract truth is in Christianity," they could not take Christianity seriously "unless the inconsistency which we observe is removed, and especially the unjust treaty by which we are curtailed is revised upon an equitable basis."[80]

Responses: A Christian Gaze

Hirai's address was clearly aimed at enlisting public sympathy for Japan as the unjustly oppressed, calling on the American people to stand by their ideals. Nevertheless, to the evangelical missionary contingent of his audience, including Chairman Barrows, his paper seemed also to hold the tempting offer that if the treaties were favorably renewed, the Japanese public might convert to Christianity.[81] In spite of Hirai's stress on the injustice of the West and his plea for assistance in removing the particular injustice of the treaties, and in the face of his very strong Buddhist stance, his audience was apparently convinced that he—if not Japan as a nation—was on the point of conversion.

Hirai's paper also found approval among liberal Christians who welcomed his observations on the reasons for the disappointing results of the missionary venture. They saw it as "a stinging rebuke" against "the false Christians who had done so much to impede the spreading of the gospel in Japan."[82] Hirai had touched on an important issue in the American establishment, the discrepancy between the beliefs of the intellectual liberal Christians at home and the often poorly trained missionaries in the field. His paper, reinforced as it was by similar criticisms from Asian delegates to the later Congress of Missions,[83] generated considerable discussion among Christians, and inspired a Mrs. Haskell to establish an overseas lectureship to send Christian intellectuals to speak directly to educated Asians.[84]

Barrows had read and rejected Hirai's paper and, according to Yatsubuchi's account of the incident, had been quite distressed and attempted to stop Hirai when he enforced his right to be heard.[85] He apparently recovered when he saw the audience's enthusiastic reception, and what he heard from Hirai's paper, at least in retrospect when he compiled the official record, was a confirmation of his missionary dream that Japan was ready for conversion. He apparently did not notice Hirai's call to throw out Jesus and tear up the Bible, or at least had edited it from memory as he had from his record.[86] He apparently also failed to notice that what Hirai was offering was that Japanese would accept Christianity *along with* the other religions they were perfectly capable of holding simultaneously, because each of them, including the "real Christianity," was nothing other than the reverence for the ultimate truth most fully expressed in Mahayana Buddhism. According to Hirai, "[W]hether Buddhism is called Christianity or Christianity is named Buddhism, whether we are called Confucianists or Shintōists we are not particular; but we are very particular about the truth taught and its consistent application."[87] Barrows apparently heard only that Hirai was happy to be called a Christian, but there was a crucial difference between Barrows's dream of a universal Christianity and Hirai's synthetic religion. Could Barrows accept Hirai's abstraction of deity? Could he, like Hirai, look forward to a time when there would be no difference between theism and atheism?

Japanese Christians in Defense of National Character

Hirai and the Buddhist delegates were supported in the defense of Japan against the charge of heathenism by the Japanese Christian delegates. These men had been educated in a strongly anti-Buddhist Confucian tradition and in their Japanese publications spoke of Buddhism as an anachronistic link with the feudal past. In the international context of the Chicago fair, however, national unity prevailed. All Japanese religions were allied with Christianity against the destructive forces of materialism, atheism, and pessimism.[88] As Kishimoto Nobuta explained, not only were the Japanese not heathen, but their tolerant religious eclecticism was fundamentally compatible with Christianity. The essence of Shintō was the doctrine of divine immanence. The universal teaching of Buddhism, the law of cause and effect, was not different from the Christian idea that "one reaps what one sows."[89]

The fundamental compatibility of Japanese religions with Christianity was also the subject of papers by the Japanese Christians Matsugama Takayoshi and Kaburagi Peter Goro.[90] Matsugama pointed out that Shintō "was not the original religion" of Japan; that the word itself was of comparatively recent origin when used with its current meaning; that Shintō grew out of "Shingonese Buddhism"; and that "pure" Shintō (his quotation marks) was created in the eighteenth century and early nineteenth century.[91] His project was to establish that the pre-Shintō religion of Japan, that is, the real indigenous religion of Japan, was remarkably similar in principle to the teachings of Christianity. It recognized a trinity—"persons of one supreme creator, the object of worship, a spirit and invisable"—a God who demanded that his followers purify themselves from sin, revere him, and serve him gladly. It further taught that man consisted of body and spirit, that there is life after death, and the existence of hell. The original religion had been "limited to one supreme god."[92] It was essentially monotheistic and "does not oppose [Christianity]."[93] Kaburagi reinforced this by speaking of Shintō as the Way of God, singular and capitalized, as in Matsugama's paper.[94] In Shintō as in Christianity, he pointed out, "[c]onfession of sin is made and the wrath of the Highest being averted"; punishment of evildoers and reward of the just are strictly observed. He specifically dissociated Shintō from two of the common attributes of heathenism: it is not idolatrous and does not involve animal sacrifice. Together the papers assured the Christian audience that there was nothing in the *real* Japanese religion incompatible with the teachings of Christianity.

The second aspect of their defense of Japanese religiosity, however, was more specifically nationalistic and anti-imperialist. Though themselves anti-Buddhist, at the Parliament they presented *Japanese* Buddhism as the highest development of the Buddha's teaching, proof of the intellectual and spiritual superiority of the Japanese people. The Japanese development of Buddhism offered the promise that Christianity—introduced from abroad as Buddhism had been—would similarly reach its highest development under the Japanese genius. The Christianity Japanese Christians envisaged as the religion of their nation was not American Protestantism. It was, as their papers explained, distinctly Japanese, rational and liberal. Although grateful to American missionaries for reminding them of the

Bible, they argued that America had no particular claim to Christian authority. Christ was an Oriental. Christianity was originally an Oriental religion and had been a Japanese religion since the sixteenth century. Christianity, like Buddhism, may have been introduced from abroad but would similarly reach its culmination under the Japanese spirit.

The three distinctive features of Japanese Christianity were, as Kozaki Hiromichi, president of Doshisha College and leader of the delegation, explained, the nature of its converts, its total lack of sectarian spirit, and its liberal spirit in doctrinal matters. These characteristics set it apart from Christianity elsewhere in Asia, distanced it from the various Christianities of the West, and argued its suitability as the religion of the modern scientific world. Through the nature of its converts, Japanese Christianity was a virile (Kozaki's term) religion, with all that word's connotations of energy and power. The Japanese congregation was predominantly made up of young males from the *shizoku* (military) class, a well-educated moral elite, and was consequently quite distinct from congregations in countries like China and India, where missionary success had been predominantly among the least educated.[95] It was, at least in ideal, emphatically nonsectarian, an all-Japan Christianity. In naming it they had deliberately chosen the word *kumiai* (associated) over the word *kaishū* (congregational) to avoid any implied association with English and American churches. It was liberal because the Kumamoto Christians had wanted a new theology of Western scientific scholarship, not the theology of orthodox evangelists. Japanese Christianity was to be totally free from myth and superstition, compatible with the scientific world view. It was, in short, Christianity brought to its modern culmination.

Kumiai theologians had found "large room for improvement and progress" in orthodox Christianity, presumably the teachings of the American Board of Missions who had helped establish Doshisha, and had therefore "done away with some of the Christian doctrines which were regarded as essential in Western countries."[96] They found "the divinity of Christ and the efficacy for us of the death of Christ on the cross" and the miracles of the Bible "stumbling blocks to acceptance."[97] The result was an interpretation of Christianity that was not easily recognized by the orthodox audience at the Parliament. God in this scheme was not unlike Spencer's incommensurable, unknowable supreme existence, which Buddhists such as Hirai identified with the Buddhist truth. Kishimoto summarized their position: "We want the truth of Christianity; nay, we want the truth pure and simple. We want the spirit of the Bible and not its letter. . . . But we

Japanese Christians . . . are ambitious to present to the world the one new and unique interpretation of Christianity as it is presented in the Bible, which knows no sectarian controversy and knows no heresy hunting."[98]

The Kumiai rejected all Western interpretations of Christianity and most particularly rejected American missionaries. They had recently been embroiled in a dispute severing the Doshisha curriculum from missionary control, insisting on the distinction that it was a Christian school but not a mission school.[99] Kozaki told the Parliament that "Japanese will never be contented to work under missionary auspices. To be really useful to our country the missionaries must either cooperate or join the native churches and become like one of the native workers."[100] Kozaki concluded his paper with the Christian formula of submission. In the context of his paper, however, it read less like his personal submission to the Deity than a reminder to the American Board of its Christian duty: "Christianity is from God, and so it will be in all times. We must plan many things, but all will be executed by the divine will. As the saying goes 'Man proposes and God disposes.' Then our prayer is and always must be 'Thy Kingdom come, Thy will be done, as in Heaven, so on earth.' " America had been God's agent in reawakening Christianity in Japan, but Japan had also been given a mission: "I believe there is a grand mission for Japanese Christians. I believe that it is our mission to solve all these problems which have been and are still stumbling blocks in all lands; and it is also our mission to give to all the oriental nations and the rest of the world a guide to true progress and a realization of the glorious gospel which is in Jesus Christ."[101] Japanese Christians no more wanted American Protestantism than their Buddhist compatriots. The future world religion would be Japanese. The contest for them was which of the Japanese religions.

Conservative Buddhist Opposition

There can be no doubt from the *Manifesto* that the reasons for taking Buddhism to the West were, at one level at least, strategies for the defense of Buddhism against Christianity and of Japan against the Western imperialism this signified. The *Manifesto* summarized Buddhist initiatives but, unlike Inoue Enryō's writings on similar themes, it nowhere explicitly mentioned the issues of treaty renewal that are elsewhere so closely related to increasing Japanese prestige in the international context. One explanation for this may be that the purpose of the *Manifesto* was to enlist support for the delegation among Buddhist conservatives. The problem was that by 1893 it was widely accepted that revision of the treaties would involve granting foreign access to the interior of Japan, the concession demanded by Western powers for lifting the hated extraterritoriality clause. Many conservative Buddhists were fearful that the first Westerners to benefit from this would be the Christian missionaries. An article in *Bukkyō koron* warned in mid-1892: "It is probable that when the country is thrown open to foreigners, the first to take advantage of the privilege will be not merchants but missionaries and their zeal will lead to the further spread of Christian schools, this time taught by themselves. Thus Christianity will become stronger and stronger, and the result to Buddhism is plain to be seen."[102]

This fear did not bear rational scrutiny. Christian missionaries had circumvented restrictions and were already established outside the treaty ports, and, moreover, a large body of Japanese Christians—Christians in full possession of the Japanese language—actively proselytized throughout the country.[103] The article as a whole urged progressive reforms, and it seems that this evocation of an old fear may have been intended to stir a complacent clergy to action, espousing conservative views to win support for its proposals to build Buddhist schools and youth camps. The effect of such rhetoric, however, was to reinforce uncertainty among the conservative majority about the consequences of treaty revision.

More generally, progressive Buddhist leaders argued for increased self-confidence. The teachings of Buddhism were more than the equal of Christianity, and if after all these years of close association with the Japanese people Buddhist institutions could be so easily replaced, then they did not deserve to be protected. The following article, which appeared at the same time as the other, is more typical of the reform position:

> It is said that we must give mixed residence in exchange for Extraterritoriality. This means that the contact with new ideas is sure to affect more or less the old customs of the country. Now this would not be an unmixed evil. There are some good customs of the West which we should not be sorry to see supplant some of our unworthy ones. On the other hand, we must hold fast to all that is good in our existing practices, and resist the innovations of Western Customs. For this no support is better or surer than Buddhism. The revival of Buddhism is the only means of preserving our national individuality.[104]

This may be essentially the same message, but it carried a significantly different impact.

One problem in raising support for reform initiatives such as the delegation to Chicago was that the Buddhist community stretched across the whole social spectrum, and the well-educated, internationally oriented elite was vastly outnumbered. At a meeting of the All Japan Convocation of Buddhists (Zenkoku bukkyōsha daikonwakai) in April 1891, 160 representatives passed a resolution to form an alliance against mixed residence.[105] It is apparent from reports in the *Japan Weekly Mail* at this time that treaty revision was a contentious issue among the wide Buddhist community, and for this reason the connection between treaty revision and taking Buddhism to the West—never more than one issue among many—was perhaps better left out of the *Manifesto*. We can note, however, that the list of twenty-six patrons at the end of the document included Ōuchi Seiran, Shimaji Mokurai, and Ashitsu Jitsuzen. For these, at least, it was an issue, as it unquestionably was for the Buddhist delegates themselves.

Conclusion

The delegation to the World's Parliament of Religions was no less a part of Japan's demonstration of its equality with Europe than its display of industrial and material progress in the exhibition halls of the Columbian Exposition, the textbooks on education, or the display of architecture, art, and gardens in the Hōōden. Japanese Buddhism was the embodiment of Japanese culture, evidence of the antiquity and endurance of a sophisticated and intellectual civilization in Japan, a civilization worthy of recognition among world powers. But more than this, it was also the rational, scientific religion of the future, the shortest route to the pinnacle of religious evolution. Because spiritual development was assumed to accompany social evolution in general, this claim to religious superiority supplemented the bid for world status. The delegates also engaged in the debates on racial hierarchy that pervaded the Columbian Exposition. Their claim that Japanese Buddhism was the universal religion for the modern world challenged assumptions of white, Christian supremacy.

The connection between the representation of Buddhism and treaty revision was most particularly addressed by the two Buddhist laymen, Noguchi and Hirai, but the themes they introduced were elaborated and given authority by the Buddhist specialists, the four priests of Noguchi's gift to the West. Their presentations protested against American imperialism and Christianity's complicity in it, and their rejection of the Western religion was reinforced by Japanese Christian delegates who argued for the superiority and universality of a Japanese interpretation of Christianity. Japan may have been grateful to the United States for its contribution to the modernization of Japan but emphatically rejected the foreign religion. Not only was it inferior to the local product, but it epitomized the designation of inferiority Japan was striving to shed: the civilized send missions to the uncivilized.

CHAPTER

DEFINING EASTERN BUDDHISM

Prior to the World's Parliament of Religions, all manifestations of Buddhism were classified as either Southern Buddhism or Northern Buddhism. At Chicago, the Japanese delegates introduced a third category, Eastern Buddhism. This was the *Ekayāna*,[1] the all-encompassing teaching of the Buddha, equated by them with the Buddhism of Japan. It was universal Buddhism, but not simply in the sense of being the underlying essence from which other forms of Buddhism had developed. This was the narrow role that Western scholars had assigned to Theravada. It was universal in an expansive sense, encompassing all other forms of Buddhism and developing these regional variations to their fulfillment. Eastern Buddhism was the full exposition of the Buddha's wisdom, and it was preserved in Japan alone, the one Asian nation, the Japanese claimed, intellectually and spiritually capable of comprehending its profundity. On the basis of the demonstrated flexibility of the component elements of Eastern Buddhism in meeting the spiritual, intellectual, and moral needs of diverse peoples throughout the ages, and its compatibility with Western scientific thought, the Japanese delegates argued that it was the religion best suited to become the universal world religion. Eastern Buddhism was *shin bukkyō*, the product of Meiji reform, rearticulated for Western, international consumption.

Defining Eastern Buddhism was possible because Western academics, pursuing the truth in Pali texts, had totally neglected it. Individuals like Ernest Fenollosa and William Sturgis Bigelow living in Japan had been drawn to personal study, but, as already noted, their knowledge had not been disseminated,[2] so that up to the time of the Parliament in 1893 almost nothing was known about Japanese Buddhism beyond the general assumption that as a form of Mahayana it was necessarily a later and therefore aberrant form of the original teachings of the historical Buddha. The reason for the neglect complicated the task. While even followers of the Theravada had to contend with the problem of establishing their right to speak on Buddhism, for the Japanese delegation this involved the additional obstacle of proving that the Mahayana was taught by the Buddha Sakyamuni, that it did spring from the original source. Their evidence for this was the Mahayana doctrine of the unfolding of the Buddha's teachings over five decades, which inverted Western assumptions by presenting the various Mahayana sutras as the fullest and the earliest expression of the Buddha Sakyamuni's wisdom.

By creating the new category of *Eastern* Buddhism, the delegates opened a space within the existing Western discourse, but not an entirely uncontested one. They first needed to distance Eastern Buddhism from the perceived defects of Northern Buddhism, the Mahayana of China and Tibet, as it was known at the time. Then, because Western approval was directed exclusively to Southern Buddhism (Theravada), they needed to position their religion in relation to it. They argued that Eastern Buddhism not only preserved all that the West approved of in the Pali manifestation but developed and extended it. Eastern Buddhism was not only compatible with the latest findings of Western science and philosophy, but superior to them in offering a more sophisticated philosophical development. In particular, the Mahayana conception of nirvana as preserved in Eastern Buddhism was neither nihilistic nor world-denying but, by means of its distinctive conception of the bodhisattva, provided an ideal of active participation in social welfare and humanitarian activity.

Eastern Buddhism also had the advantage of transcending the dichotomy of religion and philosophy, which had been used to criticize the Theravada. As we have seen in Chapter 4, Western scholars agreed that "Original" Buddhism was a philosophy, but Buddhism as they observed it clearly operated in Asian societies as a religion. They accounted for this discrepancy in terms of the failure of Buddhism to meet the needs of the people, or alternately, the failure of the people to meet the demands of the teaching. Consequently, even supporters criticized Southern Buddhism for being demandingly austere, leaving lesser mortals (inferior races) to turn to atheistic ritual and idolatry. Theravada was ideally an ethical philosophy. Eastern Buddhism, while in no way sacrificing the philosophic ideal, also offered a religion for those who needed such solace. Unlike Christianity, however, the religion of Eastern Buddhism was *based on* philosophy and consequently was not only not in conflict with it, but it assisted the evolutionary development of mankind toward philosophic ideals. It was a religion that answered the questions of existence and morality without recourse to an interventionist God—a religion compatible with science.

The Chicago Presentation

The representation of Japanese Buddhism at the Parliament was based on the rationalized interpretations of Meiji revival, which had been formed out of a need to meet charges of irrationality, otherworldliness, irrelevance to the modern world. It presented Buddhism reinterpreted in accord with the rules of Western scholarship, directed to fulfilling the religious needs of a modern society in a manner acceptable to the Western-educated elite of the new Japan. The Buddhism of Meiji reform had accommodated both Orientalist scholarship and Christian criticism and was ideally suited to meet the challenges of the Christian Parliament of Religions. Eastern Buddhism, the Buddhism of the presentation, was consciously directed to a Western audience with the explicit aim of winning its esteem. The delegates knew of the role Buddhism was playing in contemporary Western religious debates and spoke to these issues. As they saw it, their success depended on establishing the compatibility of Buddhism with the latest developments in science and Western philosophy, presenting Buddhism as a nontheistic ethical system, a humanist alternative to orthodox Christianity.

The Japanese delegation was supported in this project by the delegates of Ceylon and Siam. A certain unity of Asian Buddhist purpose and doctrine was essential for the claim of Buddhist universality as well as of the encompassing nature of Japanese Mahayana. The major difference they promoted was that Japanese Buddhism alone preserved the most advanced philosophical teachings of the Buddha. Western scholars had recognized that Theravada Buddhism *foreshadowed* trends in "the latest speculation among ourselves." Japanese Buddhism, the full disclosure of the Sakyamuni's wisdom, embodied all of Western philosophy and, moreover, resolved its current conflicts. Eastern Buddhism was the fulfillment both of Theravada and of Western religious and philosophical thought.

The evolutionary implications were that Eastern Buddhism was the answer to the religious and philosophical needs of mankind at all degrees of development, in all times and in all places. Inoue Enryō—writing in Japanese and therefore unconcerned by the possibility of offending other Asian delegates—had bluntly stated that Mahayana had died out in India because of the decline in culture there and for similar reasons was virtually nonexistent in China.[3] The delegates at Chicago were more circumspect but frequently reiterated the message that both Mahayana and Hinayana Buddhism "were taught by one Buddha" and "are nothing but different aspects of the same principle, *adapted to the capacity of converts*."[4] The racism of this argument was in keeping with the pervading evolutionary ethnology of the exposition in general and also with Japan's projection of itself as the leader of Asia.

Eastern Buddhism was bound to concepts of Japanese racial superiority and Japan's late nineteenth-century bid for world-power status, and to the project for treaty revision and establishing Japan's place in the comity of nations. It must, however, be stressed that the speakers were all Buddhist priests well versed in Buddhist scholarship. There is no question that they misrepresented their religion, or that their claims for it were unjustified. Nevertheless, the aspects of Buddhism they selected from the vast array of possibilities they might have spoken of and the language they used in their translations reveal political imperatives.

A Note on Sources

Principal primary sources for this chapter are the English and Japanese published records of the papers presented at Chicago. There are, however, problems in trying to establish just what was said there. As I have already discussed, the papers in Barrows's official copyright record have been heavily edited to conform to his agenda. Houghton's edition, though generally presenting longer papers, also shows signs of cuts. There are Japanese-language reports of the event because the delegates published their accounts of it. The two I have referred to are by Yatsubuchi Banryū and Shaku Sōen.[5] While their accounts of the proceedings are frequently valuable in supporting one English-language authority over the other, they are not necessarily more reliable, as their publication was equally politically determined. Most evident is their desire to convince the Japanese audience of the welcome Buddhism received in the West—of the success of their mission.

Among the English-language sources is the considerable body of material written by the Japanese delegation and their supporters who were aware of the power of publication in diffusing and consolidating knowledge. As we have seen, they argued the need to present an officially approved version of Japanese Buddhism because whatever was published would be spread all over the world as the truth of Buddhism and would then be very difficult to alter.[6] Because of this, perhaps the most reliable record of what the delegation as a whole intended to convey to the Parliament is the small book *Outlines of the Mahāyāna as Taught by Buddha*. The title page attributes the book to Kuroda Shintō, superintendent of education of the Jōdo-Sect, under the editorship of the *Bukkyō Gakkukwai*. It was written specifically for circulation at the Parliament and had been "carefully examined by the scholars of the Tendai, Shingon, Rinzai, Sōtō and Shin sects." Because the draft had also been circulated in Buddhist journals for general comment and approval, it represents a transsectarian consensus of knowledge.

The content of *Outlines* corresponds exactly with the priorities specified in the *Manifesto* as "items it is especially important to represent." These were (a) the principles of Buddhism. Buddhist idealism and philosophic idealism; (b) the differences and similarities between Buddhist idealism and philosophic idealism and the extent of each. (c) The generally accepted explanation and evidences concerning the immortality of the spirit. (d) The flow of birth and death (*rinne*). (e) The law of cause and effect (*inga no rihō*). (f) Nirvana (*nehan*). (g) The two approaches to awakening (*shōjō nimon*).[7] The *Manifesto* list continued with the history of Buddhism, the influence of Buddhism, the present state and future prospects of Buddhism. According to the *Japan Weekly Mail* (April 1, 1893), *Outlines* was to deal with all these topics. The papers of the delegates taken together cover the same agenda, each elaborating on key points. However, because the book was prepared in advance and translated into competent English, it avoided many of the obstacles to communication of the spoken presentations. Most particularly, it circumvented Barrows's editorial hand. For this reason, too, the papers Hirai and Ashitsu published in American journals are valuable indications of what these delegates wished to present to the West.

Because, by definition, Eastern Buddhism encompassed all other forms of Buddhism, the papers of the Theravada delegates also contributed to its presentation; here again, it is necessary to work closely with the various edited texts. Dharmapāla's paper in Barrows is long, too long to have been read in the short time allocated to speakers. Houghton presents it in two parts, the paper presented, plus a longer paper Dharmapāla gave to the editor. Here again the paper in Barrows shows considerable editing, omitting the opening quotation of Max

Muller, cutting references in praise of the Theosophical Society and H. G. Blavatsky, and reducing a long paragraph on the universal admiration for the life of the Buddha among Western scholars. On the other hand, the paper in Houghton's edition omits material that appears in Barrows. Going to Guruge, *Return to Righteousness*, does not bring us any closer to a Ceylonese archive since it simply reproduces Barrows, confirming its official status if not its accuracy as a true record of the proceedings.

Reclaiming Buddhism: Orientalism and Asian Modernity

The first step in an Asian representation of Buddhism was to establish that Western approval was for *their* religion, not, as Max Muller and Rhys Davids believed, for an ancient abstraction Asian Buddhists had neglected, smothered under ritual, idolatry, and other practices. Max Muller and Rhys Davids had little but contempt for the contemporary manifestations of the doctrine. Past greatness did not reflect glory on contemporary society but became a measure against which to gauge present "degradation." The ideals of the past became weapons available for use against colonial dependents, justifying colonial domination. By the late nineteenth century Asians responded, and Buddhist nationalists, exemplified by the delegates to the Parliament, attempted to reappropriate their own Orientalist past.

For the delegates from Ceylon who had been in contest with Christian imperialism in colonial Ceylon since midcentury, the Parliament was an extension of earlier contacts with Western Buddhist scholarship. Both Ceylon and Siam shared with Japan the problem of presenting the indigenous religion in terms that would be attractive to their Western-educated elite. In Ceylon this produced Protestant Buddhism; in Siam, new, rationalized accounts of the life of the Buddha.[8] Both showed an active engagement with Western Buddhist scholarship, particularly that of Rhys Davids's Pali Text Society. From the time of its inauguration in 1881 fully 50 percent of the individual subscribers were Ceylonese *bhikkhus*.[9] Early issues of the society's journal reproduced letters of benediction, showing support from more than seventy of the most prominent members of the *sangha* offering manuscripts, help in translation, and advice. The king of Siam, who headed the subscription list, sponsored a number of publications in the Pali Text Society series. *Sangha* support indicated a desire to participate in the propagation of Buddhism to the West, employing the authority of the society and its access to an interested, specialist, international audience.

The Pali Text Society served the interests of Asian Buddhists in a number of ways but particularly in making the indigenous religion attractive to the Western-educated Asian elite, a class most important in the development of modern Asian nations. It offered a rationalized interpretation of Theravada Buddhism that reconciled the indigenous religion with the changes that had accompanied modernity in Asia. It achieved for Buddhism what Rammohan Roy, Dayananda Sarasvati, and others set out to do in Hindu reform, with the added authority that the work emanated from respected Western scholars, validated by their scrupulous concern for the techniques and procedures of scientific scholarship. The authority of the society and its international readership contributed to establishing this interpretation as no local Asian initiative could.[10] The texts, produced in the high tradition of Orientalism, nevertheless provided what indigenous Buddhist movements were trying to establish, a recognition of the value and validity of their religion in Western terms. When Rhys Davids died, letters from India, Ceylon, Burma, and Japan paid tribute to his promotion of Buddhism in the West. "He appeared at a time when missionary prejudice was misrepresenting Buddhism and undermining their faith and beckoned them back to the glories of Buddhism." The problem was to claim these glories for the living practitioners.

The Buddha in Southern Buddhism

The Theravada Buddhist challenge at Chicago began with a paper read by Dhamapāla from the Sinhalese high priest Hikkaduvē Sumangala (1826–1911). Entitled very pointedly "Buddhism: Southern Orthodox," it opened with "greetings, salutations of peace and tolerance" from "the Singhalese followers of the arya dharma, miscalled Buddhism by Western scholars."[11] Although Sumangala's paper demanded the right to define Buddhist orthodoxy, the religion of modern Ceylon, he claimed, was not different from the Buddhism of Pali scholarship. The Theravada argument was rather that there was still more to its wisdom than the West had yet realized. In Sumangala's words, Dharmapāla's task was to give "a summary of what Southern Buddhists believe it necessary for the world to know, in the interest of human progress and human happiness." Rather than attempt a comprehensive explanation of their religion, the Theravada speakers essentially reiterated the Western vision of Buddhism as a system of humanist ethics. The purpose it served for Eastern Buddhism was to confirm for the Parliamentary audience those aspects of Buddhism already admired in the West.

Dharmapāla's paper "The World's Debt to Buddha" strung together quotations from prominent Western scholars to establish that the Buddha's teachings prefigured all the achievements of Western philosophy. He quoted profusely, constructing his argument in the voices of Western authorities—each of whom recognized some aspect of Western thought in Buddhism—as if to convince the audience that what he claimed must be true because their own scholars had said so.[12] Dharmapāla's second paper rather audaciously claimed Buddhist precedents for Christianity itself. The result was that the Dhamma—Dharmapāla followed Sumangala in avoiding the Western term "Buddhism"—as he defined it at Chicago was nothing less than the object ostensibly sought by the Parliamentary gathering, the universal religion of the modern world—a synthetic religion composed of the best that each religion had to offer.

"The World's Debt to Buddha" began with a quotation from Max Muller extolling the virtues of the religions of India and continued on the theme, showing that "history was repeating itself." Twenty-five hundred years earlier India had "witnessed an intellectual and religious revolution" culminating in Sakyamuni's "synthetic religion," which embodied "all the good . . . collected from every source." As he saw it, the World's Parliament of Religions was proof that "the Christian world is going through the same process" and "the thinking minds of Europe have offered a tribute to his divine memory." "The crude conceptions of anthropomorphic deism are being relegated into the limbo of oblivion," and the "thoughtful are accepting evolution and monism."[13] Even Western scholars had noticed the similarities between the conclusions of Sakyamuni and the general trends of Western thought as it groped in its evolutionary development toward resolution. The problem was, Dharmapāla explained, that Western scholars had glimpsed only a part of the wisdom of the Buddha. The result was a variety of conflicting partial identifications rather than an understanding of the full philosophic synthesis:

> The notion that it is a system of materialism has been exploded. The positivists of France found it a positivism; Buckner and his school of materialists thought it was a materialist system; agnostics found in Buddha an agnostic, and Dr. Rhys Davids, the eminent Pali scholar, used to call him the "agnostic philosopher of India"; some scholars have found an expressed monotheism therein; Arthur Lillie, another student of Buddhism, thinks it is a theistic system; pessimists identify it with Schopenhauer's pessimism; the late Mr. Buckle identified it with the pantheism of

> Fichte; some have found it a monism; and the latest dictum of Professor Huxley is that it is an idealism supplying "the wanting half of Bishop Berkeley's well known idealist argument."[14]

The Buddha Sakyamuni, the hero philosopher, was the basis of Southern Buddhism's claim to "have seen deeper than the greatest modern idealists."[15] Upon his existence and his exemplary life rested all that was admired. The space that Barrows granted to Dharmapāla's speech and the care with which he edited it point to the crucial role of Southern Buddhism in Christian discussions of the time, and hence the imperative of articulating Eastern Buddhism in relation to it.

The Buddha in Eastern Buddhism

Sumangala's rejection of the term "Buddhism" obliquely challenged Western assumptions that the dharma originated from the historical Buddha, but Dharmapāla's overall argument of priority was well served by the historicity of Sakyamuni. The issue was more complicated for the Japanese. All Buddhists accepted that Sakyamuni existed in human history, but he was not considered the founder of the religion or to be the only Buddha. From the earliest known records, the Pali sutras and the stone sculptures at Bharhut and Sanchi, Buddhism taught that Sakyamuni was but the latest in a series of Buddhas who were born into the world to revive the eternal dharma. As Yatsubuchi assured the audience at the Parliament, there were innumerable Buddhas, both before the Buddha Sakyamuni had taught and after him. The historical evidence of Sakyamuni's existence, though a product of European preoccupations and Orientalist scholarship, did not contradict Buddhist doctrine but rather gave scientific credence to an already unquestioned, if not particularly central, belief. While a lineage tracing back eventually to Sakyamuni is important, precise dates in a secular world history are not. Dates given for Sakyamuni's life varied widely across Asian traditions, but adopting the dates ascertained by Western scholarship presented no particular problem, precisely because they were of no particular consequence.[16]

Outlines of the Mahāyāna as Taught by Buddha addressed the problem even in its title. It opened with a brief, historical resume of the life of Sakyamuni and referred to the Mahayana canon, *Daizōkyō*, as the "complete works of Buddha Shaka."[17] For Japanese Buddhists to limit the conception of Buddha to identification with Sakyamuni would have required compromise with the Mahayana use of the term, preventing access to more profound aspects of Mahayana doctrine, its conception of self, the world, awakening, and nirvana, which all depended on understanding the nature of "Buddha." In Eastern Buddhism, as Hirai and other delegates explained, Buddha is the universal principle, truth, reason, the law of cause and effect; it is the nature of all beings; it is a name applied to one who understands this.[18] The mission of establishing the similarities between Mahayana Buddhism and philosophic idealism depended on conveying this extended meaning of "Buddha." The dilemma, then, was to confirm that the Mahayana was taught by the Buddha (Sakyamuni) while unsettling the exclusive Western identification of this term with him.

Toki, the first priest to speak, opened with a strong statement grounding the Mahayana in history. "Bhagavat Sakyamuni . . . born 2,020 years ago, according to the chronicle handed down to us . . . died on the bank of a river in the city of Kushi at the age of seventy-nine."[19] He continued, explaining how "[t]he doctrines of Buddha, taught during his lifetime, are divided into two—Mahayana and Hinayana"—and that this distinction was part of the Buddha's plan to provide teaching "according to the plane of intellect of his disciples." The form is dense and cryptic and consequently probably conveyed little to the audience, but these brief sentences encapsulate several crucial arguments: the Mahayana *is* the Buddha's teaching; the Mahayana is superior to the Hinayana (Theravada), which is a preliminary introduction to the truth; there are different levels of the teaching because there are different planes of intellect; the Japanese, who alone have preserved the true Mahayana, occupy the highest. These ideas were reiterated by each of the Japanese delegates.

Eastern Buddhism: Sakyamuni's Highest Teaching

A fundamental concept in the definition of Eastern Buddhism was the Mahayana belief in the five periods of the Buddha's teaching (*goji*), which was outlined most completely by Ashitsu in his paper "Buddha." Ashitsu's summary is rather incoherent as it stands, a schematic outline of the Buddha's systematic revelation of the truth given without explanation of the technical terms, little more than a list of the period names. The five periods in Japanese are *kegonji*, *agonji*, *hōdōji*, *hannyaji*, and *hokke-nehanji*.[20] As Ashitsu explained it, "Right after Buddha attained his perfect enlightenment," he preached the Kegon. This was followed by the teaching of the Hinayana (including Theravada), then the Hōdō which led disciples from Hinayana to Mahayana, the fourth level, and finally he "brought his disciples to the highest summit of his doctrine," by teaching the Hokke.[21]

While this account is intelligible if one is already familiar with the teaching and the way the Japanese names would appear in English, it probably would have meant little to the Parliament audience. It is a vague indication of the doctrine explained in detail in, for example, Inoue Enryō's *Bukkyō katsuron joron*, where it was used to establish that not only was the Mahayana indisputably the Buddha's teaching, directly transmitted to the world by Sakyamuni himself, but it was his first teaching, his last teaching, and the only complete teaching of his truth.[22] The Hinayana sutras are not only secondary, but preliminary and—the racial message—associated with less intellectually developed societies, peoples of less ability to comprehend the higher truths.

The importance of the doctrine in the Chicago presentation is indicated by the repeated references to it and to the closely related messages of the Buddha's skill in teaching "according to the capacity of mankind." Toki explained that Sakyamuni taught the three *yānas* (the three great divisions of Buddhism) over the fifty years of his life. Although they are different, the truth of the *yānas* is the same. The difference in appearance is in the minds of the disciples who receive it because Sakyamuni taught "according to the capacity of mankind."[23] Yatsubuchi reinforced this with his lecture on *shitsu tan*, the four teachings by which the Buddha gave teachings according to the needs of the listeners. The theme is repeated by all the delegates and by each of them more than once. Yatsubuchi used the poetic metaphor of the sun illuminating the world. The Kegon Sutra, the Mahayana doctrine first taught by the Buddha, was like "the first beam of morning light" striking the "highest peak of the mountain." The Hinayana sutras were like the sun of "noon-day [which] shines on every lower object of the earth." The Hokke-Nehan, the "most sublime" teaching, "superior to all," was like "the purple streams of twilight" reflecting off the highest peaks and onto the clouds above.[24] Toki emphasized that the differences between Hinayana and Mahayana were not arbitrary or man-made but emanated from the Buddha himself: Sakyamuni "intended to make this distinction" to provide teaching "according to the plane of intellect of his disciples."[25] This directly confronted Western belief in the later origin of the Mahayana and consequent accusations that it is necessarily a degradation of the Buddha's teaching. The implications of Mahayana superiority were clear, explicit, and no doubt heartfelt.

The evolutionary implications of this doctrine—arising from the nineteenth-century assumptions of the parallel progress of material and intellectual development—were that as Hinayana countries progressed in Darwinian terms, they would also move through the progression of the Buddha's teaching: "We believe the two [Mahayana and Hinayana] will come together without any contest according to the development of the human intellect and the progress of science." The recent formation of the Mahābodhi Society and its Japanese branch, the Indo busseki kofukukai, was proof, claimed Toki, that this union was imminent.[26] Contact with Mahayana through the society would elevate Hinayana toward the greater truth, and Buddhist universalism would culminate in Japanese Buddhism. Note how this differs from Colonel Olcott's vision of Buddhist Union, based on his reductionist pamphlets *The Buddhist Catechism* (1881) and *The Golden Rules of Buddhism* (1887), as the essence of all sects. Olcott's scheme proposed union on a lowest common denominator; Toki's vision was to elevate Hinayana, advancing it toward Mahayana in the progression toward greater truth mapped by the Buddha Sakyamuni himself.

From Pan-Asian Buddhism to Universal Religion

Ashitsu also spoke of the Mahābodhi Society, of cooperation between Japan, Ceylon, India, and the British in bringing it about, and of its potential for promoting pan-Asian ties: "[O]ur Buddha Gaya movement will bring people of all Buddhist countries into closer connection, and will be instrumental in promoting brotherhood among the people of the world."[27] Under the bland heading of "The Present State of Buddhism," the *Manifesto* had listed the Mahābodhi Society as a priority topic. Along with the present state of Buddhism in Northern and Southern Buddhism, initiatives in overseas missionary work, the state of Buddhism in the West ("England, America, Germany and other countries"), and "statistics on Buddhists in the various countries of the world; a chart of research on things like race, occupation, and culture," it was evidence of Buddhist universality and Japan's leading place in it.[28] Eastern Buddhism alone possessed the full disclosure of the universal truth, a truth that transcended boundaries of race, nation, and time. Its universal applicability was manifest in its global spread, its ability to accommodate social and racial differences evident in regional varieties of Buddhism, its diverse but compatible sects. The delegates gave long lists of the various countries professing forms of Buddhism and frequently mentioned the vast number of adherents. Dharmapāla offered the Parliament "the good wishes of four hundred and seventy five millions of Buddhists."[29] Toki spoke of the five hundred million human beings on earth at the present age who pay respect to Bhagavat Sakyamuni.[30] Because these numbers greatly exceed the population of either Ceylon or Japan, both spoke as members of a greater Buddhist community.

Buddhism for the West

Another *Manifesto* priority, the history of Buddhism and its sects, similarly unpacked with strategic significance. Toki's paper under this title not only legitimated the Japanese transmission but also exemplified the versatility of the doctrine, its proven ability to adapt to "the special conditions" of changing historical societies. Japanese history showed that new regimes and new social forms had always given rise to new interpretations of Buddhism.[31] At one level this was a justification and legitimation of the Meiji interpretation as the logical and natural consequence of the new Japanese regime, but it also carried wider implications of the universal applicability of Japanese Buddhism. It was a declaration of the relevance of Eastern Buddhism to America and its problems. Dharmapāla had pointedly addressed questions of social welfare, temperance, benefits to women, patriotism and law, religion and science, showing that the Buddha's teachings answered the needs of the modern world. Conveying this was also part of Toki's plan: "Japanese Buddhists . . . can not but feel rejoiced when we think of the probable result of this new change by which the Buddhism of great Japan will rise and spread its wings under all heaven as the grand Buddhism of the whole world."[32]

In the context of the Parliament, the various expressions of the rich variety of the Buddha's teachings, the Buddha's skill in presenting the truth in forms appropriate to his audience, of "giving medicine according to the disease"[33] transcended the varieties of Buddhism to claim that "[i]t is a Buddhistic idea that 'the truth is but one while its dress may be different.'"[34] Hirai's concept of "Japanism," the "inherent spirit of Japan," which was the recognition that truth is the basis of all religions, reiterated the concept. The implication of this, Hirai explained, was that if Christianity were purified of its irrationalities, it could be encompassed within Japanese religion. Toki made the same point when he explained that "Buddhism regards [the truth of other religions] as the truth of Buddhism disguised under the garment of other religion."[35] In a total inversion of Barrows's vision of the Christian conquest of the world, Japanese Buddhists spoke of Christianity reaching its fulfillment in Eastern Buddhism.

Eastern Buddhism Is Scientific

A principal reason for Western interest in Buddhism, as well as the basis of claims that it was better suited than Christianity to be the future world religion, was its perceived lack of conflict with a scientific world view. Promoting Buddhism's compatibility with science was therefore a major feature of the presentation at Chicago. Buddhism did not depend on a belief in the supernatural and was essentially empirical: the Buddha "earnestly enjoins that nothing whatever be accepted on faith" and that his followers promote education and foster scientific inquiry.[36] The "true nature" of the Buddha's teaching was its lack of dogma and fixed doctrine.[37] It was also perceived to be in sympathy with science in a number of incidental ways. As Toki mentioned, for example, the Nirvana Sutra (*Nehankyō*), which teaches that all beings have the Buddha nature, is consistent with the ideas of "mental science and biology."[38] Edwin Arnold, reading the doctrine of karma as a rather simplistic account of the transformation of species, had spoken of Buddhism as "anticipatory Asiatic Darwinism."[39] Western scholars such as Arnold had pointed out that in Buddhism, as in evolutionary theory, the difference between humans and the higher animals was one of degree rather than kind as all life belonged within the interdependent continuum of samsara. Given these Western models and the desire of the delegates to capture Western approval for Buddhism, it is no surprise that Buddhist delegates scattered their papers with scientific terms, referring to "the law of cause and effect" and "evolution," appropriating the kudos of this "identification." Prince Chudhadharn, for example, working from a definition of dharma as the "essence of nature," developed the idea that dharma is "the accomplishment of eternal evolution." "Dharma represents the universe, and varies according to the degree of evolution accomplished within it. . . . The difference between all material things, as seen outwardly, depends upon the degree of evolution that is inherent to matter," and by extension "the difference between all spirits depends on the degree of will, which is the evolution of the spirit."[40] Buddhism also complied with the scientific principle of the conservation of energy, he argued, as all beings are "destroyed and recreated again and again by an eternal evolution." But these issues were peripheral to the fundamental clash between orthodox Christianity and the scientific world view that had initiated Western interest in Buddhist thought. Buddhism's great advantage was that it offered a moral explanation of the manifest world that was not dependent on the concepts of God as first cause, divine wrath, or Providence. These are the issues that Shaku Sōen addressed in his paper, "The Law of Cause and Effect as Taught by the Buddha," arguably the most influential paper on Buddhism at the Parliament. The title is a translation of the Japanese term *inga no rihō*,[41] listed among the highest priorities of the *Manifesto* and, like other key points, was spoken of by other delegates as well.

Shaku Sōen's argument followed patterns familiar to Western philosophical proofs of the existence of God but arrived at diametrically opposed conclusions. He began by explaining that the law of cause and effect, as the Buddha taught it, was a complex system of interdependence where all the necessary causes may be difficult to identify but were, for all that, in "an endless progression." His second point arose from this. Because "a cause must be preceded by another cause," the search for an origin was an infinite regression. This is, of course, precisely the point reached by Western theologians who therefore posited the need for God, an external force, a first mover, the first cause, "an original principle of all transition from mere potency into act, a being self-existing, whose essence is pure act and the source of all actuality."[42] This speaker used the metaphor of a long train of cars requiring a locomotive to make his point. The Buddha's response, as Shaku Sōen explained, was to argue instead that the universe must therefore be eternal, without beginning and therefore without need of Creator. "Since even if we trace back to eternity, absolute cause cannot be found, so we come to the conclusion that there is no end in the universe. The assertion that there is a first cause is contrary to the fundamental principle of nature." Buddhism here was again consistent with science, offering a view of the universe in a continual, but ultimately conservative, change of state, following the pattern of evaporation and condensation of water as it shifted from rivers, to clouds, to rain.[43]

Although Shaku Sōen's paper impressed monist Paul Carus, for more orthodox Christians such ideas were simply unthinkable, as one delegate to the Parliament explained: if we admit that "there may be a world of dependent beings each of whom depends on another, and no one of them nor all of them depend on an independent being . . . philosophy is made impossible and theology deprived of its subject matter." It was literally unthinkable because "such an admission would destroy thought itself."[44]

Shaku Sōen spoke of the "self-formation of cause and effect" and its implications for the ability of individuals to influence their own existence by their own actions—how the action of cause and effect over the interdependent three worlds of the past, present, and future explained the inequalities and apparent injustices among individuals. The Buddhist virtue of self-reliance, so much a part of Western regard for Buddhism, depended on the doctrine of cause and effect because it taught that "the pleasure or pain of the future depends on our present actions." "There is no-one in the universe but one's self who rewards or punishes." Rewards and punishments, Shaku Sōen explained, are determined according to the doctrine of "self-deed and self-gain" and "self-make and self-receive."[45] "Heaven and hell are self-made. God did not provide you with a hell, but you yourself."[46] Conversely, glorious happiness is the effect of present virtue. What Shaku Sōen explained was the concept of karma, which is literally "action." However, even by the time of the Parliament it was regularly translated as "rebirth" or "transmigration." By avoiding these words he shifted the focus away from the Theosophical interest in reincarnation and questions of the soul that it more usually connoted to the humanist concerns of individual morality and theodicy. Human morality did not depend on the external authority of divine wrath but on self-discipline against the inevitability of self-induced retribution.

Shaku Sōen finished his presentation by explaining how the immutable law governed the progress of the universe. "Things grow and decay, and this is caused not by an external power but by an internal force which is in things themselves as an innate attitude." He invoked the familiar Western metaphor of the clock "which moves by itself without external intervention" to illustrate the Buddhist view of the world that eschewed the concept of Providence. The law of cause and effect was an immutable law that not even the Buddha himself can contradict;[47] that is, it was an entirely consistent system dependent on the conception of the Buddha nature of all things and the inexorable workings of the consequences of actions. As he put it, "[T]he Buddha was not the creator of this law of nature, but . . . the first discoverer . . . who led thus his followers to the height of moral perfection."[48] The Buddha was not God, Buddhism was compatible with science, and Eastern Buddhism was the Buddha's teaching.

Eastern Buddhism and Philosophical Idealism

Prominent on the *Manifesto* list of important points to convey to the audience at Chicago was showing the "differences and similarities and extent of . . . Buddhist idealism and philosophic idealism,"[49] the basis of the Japanese claim that Eastern Buddhism concurred with the latest intellectual developments in the West. Dharmapāla's paper had listed the "identifications" already made by Western scholars.[50] His aim was to claim Buddhist priority, that "it is a remarkable indication of the subtlety of Indian speculation that Gautama should have seen deeper than the greatest of modern idealists."[51] Although this message was also of great importance to the Japanese, they did not rely on the discoveries of Western scholars. Inoue Enryō had gone further, claiming that Japanese Buddhism contained all the truth of Kant and Hegel, without the "excess" that left these philosophies unresolved.[52] The Middle Way, the Buddha's highest teaching, "is not being nor is it emptiness; it is both being and emptiness and materialism and idealism are reconciled within it. . . . it simultaneously embraces subjectivity and objectivity. . . . As a theory it lacks nothing, and as an explanation there is nothing in it that is insufficient. All the other theories and explanations of the past and present, East and West, are no more than a trickle or a molecule of it."[53]

As we have seen, in *Bukkyō katsuron joron*, Inoue used the labels of Western philosophy to attract the attention of Western-educated Japanese intellectuals (Chapter 6). While not identifying Eastern Buddhism with Western idealism, he argued that Eastern Buddhism had dealt with the same issues and with greater success. His initial provisional identifications were quickly qualified in his discussion to demonstrate Buddhist superiority. The Chicago delegates, all of whom had studied Western philosophy, were similarly conscious of the fundamental differences that accompanied the similarities between Western philosophy and Buddhism. They simply held up Mahayana ideas in the expectation that Western scholars would make the identifications as they had done with Pali Buddhism, and regularly drew their audience's attention to the vast oceans of Buddhist thought that Western scholars had not yet discovered.[54]

Kuroda's *Outlines of the Mahāyāna* culminates in its chapter 5, "All Things Are Nothing but Mind," in which he translates Buddhist technical terms into the English of contemporary philosophy to explain, with reference to the Mahayana sutras, the Buddhist view that the apparent phenomena around us have no constant nature of their own and are produced by mental operations within us. Their difference in appearance is caused only by differences in mental phenomena.[55] The pivotal concept of this idealist position, Kuroda explains, is "Bhūtathatā (permanent reality)," which he translates as "essence of mind." This is the Japanese term *shinnyo*, translated as "[t]husness, suchness, the true form of reality." It is regarded as identical with *hosshin*, the *dharmakāya*, which, Kuroda explains, "cannot be expressed in words or contemplated by the unenlightened man."[56] This is the absolute reality that transcends the multitude of forms in the phenomenal world, the underlying reality upon which all phenomenal existence depends. The entire phenomenal world is produced of it by the action of ignorance (the minds of unenlightened sentient beings).

> Underlying the phenomena of mind, there is an unchanging principle which we call essence of mind; the fire caused by fagots dies when fagots are gone, but the essence of fire is never destroyed. The essence of mind is the entity without ideas and without phenomena, and is always the same. It pervades all things, and is pure and unchanging. It is not untrue or changeable, so it is called "Bhūtathatā" (permanent reality). The essence and the phenomena of mind are inseparable; and as the former is all pervading and ever-existing, so the phenomena occur everywhere and continually, wherever suitable conditions accompany it. Thus the perceptible and imperceptible phenomena are manifestations of the essence of mind, that according to the number and nature of conditions develop without restraint. All things in the universe, therefore, are mind itself.[57]

Interdependence and Karma

The law of cause and effect was also pivotal in presenting Japanese Buddhism as philosophical idealism since it established the interdependence of all things. Realizing it was to realize the true nature of the world; it was the law one must understand to attain nirvana. All things have essentially the same nature, variously described as dharma, truth, mind, Buddha nature (*busshō*), the *tathatā* inherent in all things. The perceived differences are the result of causes, motion, actions, karma, or evolution. As Toki explained it: "The action of the law of cause and effect is the operation of truth, and truth and the law of cause and effect are respectively appellations of the substance and action of the one thing, but not of two things. The truth is the substance and absolute, and cause and effect is the action and relative. By the surface of the sea and the motion of its waves, the truth and the cause and effect can be understood."[58]

Like so much of the Japanese speeches at the Parliament—at least as recorded in the official publications—Toki's explanation is a cryptic condensation that is decipherable only by those who already know. This last sentence, crucial to the claim that all is mind, was explained in more detail by Prince Chudhadharn: "The waves of the ocean are formed but of water, and the various shapes they take are dependent upon the degree of motion in the water; in a similar manner the Dharma represents the universe, and varies according to the degree of evolution accomplished within it. . . . The difference between all material things, as seen outwardly, depends on the degree of evolution that is inherent to matter. . . . These differences, however, are only apparent; in reality, all is one and the same essence, merely a modification of the one great eternal truth, Dharma."[59]

Ashitsu and Yatsubuchi elaborated the idealist nature of Kuroda's *Bhūtathatā* (*shinnyo*, *dharmakāya*, *hosshin*). "The fundamental principle of Buddha is the mind, which may be compared to a boundless sea." It was described as colorless, formless, omnipresent, and eternal. "Every form or figure such as heaven, earth, mountains, rivers, trees, grasses, even a man, or what else it may be, is nothing but the grand personality of absolute unity . . . so it is clear that the principle of the Buddha is the mind. . . . There is nothing but the grand personality of absolute unity."[60]

The relationship between essence of mind and phenomena was developed through their explication of the doctrine of the three bodies of the Buddha.[61] As Yatsubuchi explained, the first body of the Buddha is the absolute unity of "Hosshin" (*dharmakāya*), which is "colourless, formless omnipresent and eternal," hence the "Buddha makes the truth or original body of universe his own body."[62] This body is identical with the *shinnyo*, translated by Kuroda as "essence of mind." The second body is "Hoshin" (*sambhogakāya*), the body that resulted "as an effect by the cause, proving that even the Buddha is not beyond this great and immutable law of causation." This he identified with the Buddha Amida as seen in his Pure Land. The third body, "Oshin" (*nirmanakāya*), he identified with "the Lord Buddha Shaka, the earthly manifestation of the Buddha." Yatsubuchi, confirming and elaborating Toki's paper, stressed that the three states differ only in response to cause and are essentially the same. The world as we know it is a consequence of the law of cause and effect acting within the essence of mind.

Buddha Nature and the Nature of Buddhas

Each of the delegates spoke of the Buddha nature inherent in all beings, explaining that there is no difference between the Buddha and other people except in his achievement, his realization of his Buddha nature.[63] It followed logically then that "as every object of the universe is one part of the truth, of course it may become Buddha"[64] and that "the only difference between Buddha and all other beings is in point of complete enlightenment." The subject was dealt with most fully by Ashitsu, who related the doctrine of the bodies of the Buddha to the concern of Western philosophy, the individual human intellect. The three bodies of the Buddha are "attributes of the Buddha's intellectual activity," and are also possessed by humans. The only difference between ordinary beings and the Buddha is that "he is developed, by his self culture, to the highest state, while we ordinary beings are buried in the dust of passions. If we cultivate our minds, we can, of course, clear off the clouds of ignorance and reach the same enlightened place with the Buddha." There is nothing but the absolute mind-unity throughout the universe.[65]

Apart from establishing Buddhist idealism, these discussions by Yatsubuchi and Ashitsu on the nature and various meanings of the terms translated into English as "Buddha" attacked the exclusive association by Western scholars of the term with the historical Sakyamuni. As Hirai had previously explained, though with less concern for validation by reference to sutras and technical terms than these professors of Buddhism, "Buddha" means truth and is the basis of the law; it also means one who has realized the truth (hence its application to the sage Sakyamuni), and it is the real nature of all beings and all things. "Buddha" is the substance of the universe and Buddhism corresponded with the latest developments in Western philosophy.[66]

Nirvana in Eastern Buddhism: Compassion and Social Action

Western interpretations of nirvana, as the term was encountered in Pali Buddhism, had led to accusations that Buddhism was nihilistic and world-denying or, at best, self-centered and selfish since its highest objective was personal enlightenment. The delegates aimed to distance Eastern Buddhism from these critical features, and to achieve this they explained the different conceptions of nirvana available in Mahayana thought. They expressed dismay that European scholars still thought that Hinayana nirvana is the ideal of "our Buddhism."[67] Kuroda was adamant that the true nature of nirvana could not be understood from the Hinayana alone. The Japanese delegates repeatedly explained that in Mahayana teaching *moksha* (attainment of nirvana) meant "mastering the mind, abiding in truth . . . even among worldly relations," and that only Hinayana *moksha* was equivalent to extinction.[68] Explaining the difference was a function of Ashitsu's paper, "Buddha." The centrality of the term to the project becomes evident when we look at the post-Parliament exchange between Shaku Sōen, Ellinwood, and Barrows.[69]

Ashitsu explained that Eastern Buddhist texts described four kinds of *nehan* (nirvana), *honrai jishōshōjo nehan*, *uyoe nehan*, *muyoe nehan*, and *mujūsho nehan*.[70] The first and fourth are specifically Mahayana forms of nirvana since they both depend on the realization that there is no distinction between the realms of samsara and nirvana. The first, *honrai jishōshōjo nehan*, refers to the essential Buddha nature of all phenomena, equivalent to the *hosshin* (*dharmakāya*), explained above as the colorless, formless, eternal, omnipresent, and unchangeable nature of the universe. The other specifically Mahayana form of nirvana is *mujūsho nehan*, the state when one who has attained complete awareness of reality does not elect to dwell in tranquillity, but actively works in the worlds of transmigration for the benefit of sentient beings.[71] This is the basis of the Mahayana conception of Bodhisattva personified in Avalokitesvara, the bodhisattva of compassion—or, following Ashitsu, "humanity"—who attained a state of perfect enlightenment and vowed not to leave the world until all beings had attained a similar state. The Meiji interpretation of this ideal, as explained by Hirai, was most important in the Japanese projection of their religion as a positive social force. It was evidence of Buddhism's power to solve the problems of the modern world, the Eastern Buddhist ideal of a life of service to humanitarian ideals that was characteristic of Meiji Buddhism, and in keeping with the *koji* Buddhist movement. Nirvana as presented by Japanese Buddhists at Chicago is not annihilation—not even annihilation of the passions, which implies a detachment from the concerns of the material world—but a clear-minded and active realization of the nature of truth, and insight into the principles of law, which could be used for the benefit of society at large. As Shaku Sōen explained to Barrows, "The positive side of nirvana consists in the recognition of truth. The destruction of desires, of envy, hatred, extinction of selfishness implies charity, compassion with all suffering, and a love that is unbounded and infinite. . . . The eradication of all that is evil in man's heart will set all his energies free for good deeds, and he is no genuine Buddhist who would not devote his life to active work, and a usefulness which would refuse neither his friends nor strangers nor even his enemies."[72]

The nirvana of Eastern Buddhism, unlike that of Southern Buddhism, was not nihilistic and, far from demanding renunciation of worldly affairs in the pursuit of personal spiritual attainment, it enjoined its followers to devote themselves and the knowledge they attained to selfless work for society as a whole. As Hirai, quoted earlier in Chapter 8, put it, attaining nirvana was realizing "the unchangeable principle which may be utilized and deduced for the changeable daily life of human society."[73] The relevance of nirvana to this life was also emphasized by Toki, who took care to distinguish "transmigration"—the effect of actions of body and mind on future life—from "absorption," the attainment of nirvana. This was the point when "those who go along the Mahayana road" aspire "to engage in active exertion for humanity."[74] He dissociated nirvana from death and rebirth, and from connotations of personal extinction or annihilation. Far from being nihilistic, the nirvana of Eastern Buddhism produced the highest and most constant engagement in the promotion of human welfare. Unlike the nirvana Western scholars understood from Southern Buddhism, it was not selfish, self-centered, otherworldly, or nihilistic.

Eastern Buddhism Is a Philosophical Religion

The *Manifesto* priorities included the doctrine of *shōjōnimon*, the Japanese Buddhist doctrine of the two approaches to awakening, the "Holy Path" (awakening through one's own efforts) and the way of the Pure Land schools (dependence on the compassionate vows of Amida).[75] The doctrine of *shōjōnimon* extended the case for the infinite adaptability and universal applicability of Buddhism. It also resolved the conflict between the intellectual pursuit of philosophy and the human need for an emotional response to religion. Buddhism answered both needs. As Inoue Enryō had argued in *Bukkyō katsuron joron*, "Buddhism is a complete religion of both the intellect and the emotions."[76] In Buddhism, religion, science, and philosophy were not simply compatible. The religious practices were based on the same principles as the philosophy and acted to introduce people to the higher modes of truth. Eastern Buddhism therefore stimulated the evolution of mankind and progress of civilization. It offered a religion that could be held without compromise of progress.

Of God and Soul

What of the problems of theism and the soul? As already discussed, the delegates did address the question of Buddhism's attitude to God, but simultaneously denied the designation of atheism and argued that the Christian concept of God was both unnecessary and illogical. Toki made it clear that Buddhism had no strong objection to the concept of creator, that it spoke of Vairocana as "the first origin of all . . . the base of the universe," but this was "a relative concept," "a one-sided view," stressing the "differentiality," which in reality was merely an aspect of the essential unity of the universe.[77] Buddhism was not atheistic as such, but as Hirai had explained, the question was simply beside the point, a limiting of the unlimitable. Alternately, by defining religion as "a priori belief in an unknown entity," Eastern Buddhism offered "the perfect union between theism and atheism." God is truth, "the connecting link of cause and effect, the essence of phenomena."[78]

The related question of personal immortality, the nature of soul, was addressed on the first page of Kuroda's *Outlines of the Mahāyāna*. He conceded that *anātman*, which he translated as "non-individuality" rather than the more familiar but nihilistic "absence of soul," was a general principle of Buddhism, but explained that it was less a denial of individuality than a device to "destroy man's erroneous attachment to ego."[79] This was hedged still further by his reassurance that the Buddha "never set forth unchanging doctrine by establishing fixed dogmas." Toki went so far as to describe a soul concept. It was "not an incorporeal substance of reason . . . but it has a fine phantasmal form."[80] His main point was that transmigration did not depend on an external power. The existence of an immortal soul that transmigrated from one life to the next was also implied by Shaku Sōen's account of the moral aspects of the law of cause and effect. No doubt it would have detracted from his argument, which as it stands was praised for its clarity and intelligibility, to have introduced the radically un-Christian concepts of *anātman* and *sūnyatā*, but there was also another reason. As Shaku Sōen said some years later in his lectures to Americans, "Most people are exceedingly alarmed when they are told that the self or the soul, which they cherished so fondly is void in its nature, and will overwhelm us with a multitude of questions."[81] The "destruction of the popular belief relating to the nature of the ego . . . tends to emphasize the negative aspect of Buddhism," and "we must have something positive when this erroneous belief is removed." That is, Shaku Sōen practiced the Buddhist principle of teaching according to the preparedness of the audience. In 1907 he was also willing to relate the *dharmakāya* (Japanese *hosshin*) to the "Johannean view of God."[82] At the World's Parliament of Religions the delegates avoided confronting the question of the nature of personal existence in order to convey an understanding of the Buddhist system of morality to the Christian audience and thereby win acceptance of Eastern Buddhism among world religions, an initial step in establishing its preeminence.

Conclusion

In his memorial diary, Shaku Sōen recorded with satisfaction what he saw as the achievements of the delegation. Chief among them were convincing the audience, both foreign and Japanese (*naigaijin*), that Buddhism is a universal religion; showing that "our Buddhism" closely corresponds with the teachings of modern science and philosophy; and overthrowing "the deluded notion that the Mahayana is not the Buddha's teaching."[83] These are, at first glance, modest claims, but they were significant statements in the context of the Japanese discourse on religion of the Meiji Twenties, claiming Western validation for Eastern Buddhism's challenge to Christian universality and for its claim to possess the highest truth. Establishing that the Mahayana was the Buddha's teaching was pivotal. Upon this rested the claim that Japanese Buddhism was "real" Buddhism, defined in the Western discourse as the teaching of the Buddha Sakyamuni, and the right of Japanese delegates to speak with authority on Buddhism as such, not simply on their regional beliefs. Establishing the authenticity of Mahayana Buddhism was also fundamental to their claim that Eastern Buddhism both encompassed all that was admired in the West of Theravada and contained none of those aspects of Theravada open to criticism. The superiority of Eastern Buddhism as the repository of the first, the last, and the highest of the Buddha's teaching also implied Japanese racial superiority and underpinned Japanese claims to be the preservers of Asian tradition and the future leaders of Asia.

Shaku Sōen's diary also mentioned as an achievement of the delegation the conversion of a "Mr. Straw, a wealthy New York merchant."[84] Although the conversion of an American was in itself important, indicating success at Chicago in winning Western approval for Japanese Buddhism, Shaku Sōen's mention that Mr. Straw was a man of commerce was also significant. This was evidence of the suitability of Eastern Buddhism as a religion of the modern world, a challenge to the image of Buddhism as "otherworldly." Eastern Buddhism was the future world religion, and as Shaku Sōen recorded in his diary, this had already been recognized by at least one American. Most significant, however, is his awareness that the delegation spoke simultaneously to two audiences. Taking Eastern Buddhism to Chicago was not simply an exercise in bringing Mahayana Buddhism to the West. It was also a statement in the Japanese discourse on religion.

CHAPTER

PAUL CARUS

Buddhism and Monist Mission

To the extent that the aim of the delegation was to gain respect from Western scholars and men of religion for the profundity of Mahayana thought, the representation of Eastern Buddhism at Chicago was a failure, at least in the short term. Japanese Buddhism remained marginalized, and authority on Buddhism remained in the possession of Pali philologists. Eastern Buddhism did, however, make an impact on publisher and philosopher Paul Carus (1852–1919), who is now remembered less for his contribution to American philosophy than for the consequences of his contact with Buddhist delegates: his role in the transmission of Zen to the West and his book *The Gospel of Buddha*.[1] The *Gospel* was an archetypical example of Orientalism, the appropriation of the Orient—in this case Buddhism and the life of the Buddha—to support a decidedly Western and Christian project. Carus was quite explicit about this, declaring in his preface that "[i]f this *Gospel of Buddha* helps people to comprehend Buddhism better, and if its simple style impresses the reader with the poetic grandeur of the Buddha's personality, these effects must be counted as incidental. Its main purpose lies deeper still. The present book has been written to set the reader a-thinking on the religious problems of today. It presents a picture of a religious leader of the remote past with the view of making it bear upon the living present and become a factor in the formation of the future."[2]

Whatever the title might suggest, *The Gospel of Buddha* was written to propagate Carus's post-Kantian Christian religion of science. Carus believed that it was the duty of all true believers to proselytize. There were two reasons for this, both characteristically scientific. The first was his conviction that universal truth would be revealed by comparison. The second was based on evolutionary theory. Because evolution depended on the struggle for existence and the survival of the fittest, Carus believed that progress toward the ultimate universal religion would be hastened by bringing protagonists into greater proximity through active missionary work. He was particularly interested in Buddhism because he genuinely admired it and had no doubt that it was the only possible contender against Christianity for the role of the religion of the future. Comparison and competition with Buddhism in the minds of a Christian audience would force the evolution of Christianity to its inevitable and ultimate perfection.

It is no surprise that the book is an extremely idiosyncratic interpretation of Buddhism. It does, however, remain in print more than a century later. *The Gospel of Buddha* took on greater importance than it would normally have attained because of Carus's personal connection with the Asian delegates to the World's Parliament of Religions, which led to its publication in a number of Asian languages. It went into three editions within nine months and was eventually translated into Japanese, Chinese, Thai, Malay, Urdu, and Tamil, as well as German, French, Dutch, and Spanish. An English-language edition was used in schools in Ceylon, an alternative to the Bible—as Olcott's *Catechism* was—in language instruction.[3] Because of these Asian editions, Carus has rather misleadingly been described as "one to whom Buddhists throughout the world looked for source material and instruction in their own religion."[4] His Buddhist writings are considered here both as a consequence of the Japanese delegation to Chicago and as an illustration of the processes of the formation, presentation, and validation of knowledge of Buddhism in the West.

This chapter first looks at the Western response to the Japanese representation immediately after the Parliament, examining in particular Carus's interpretation and deployment of Buddhism. It points to the tension between his dependence on characteristically Mahayana Buddhist concepts of Eastern Buddhism and the regime of truth within which he wrote that continued to refuse to accept anything but the "original" Buddhism of the Pali canon. Carus's text also bears the signs of an inherent tension between a genuine overlap of certain monist and Buddhist concepts—at least in their superficial expression—and the distortion required to bring Buddhism within the bounds of what was accepted as Christian. How convincing was Carus's proposition that Christ was a Buddha? It then analyzes *The Gospel of Buddha* showing Carus's impeccable control of his text, the care and attention with which every aspect of it is ordered toward fulfilling his mission; the care with which he attempted—unsuccessfully—to provide the work with academic validation. Carus failed to popularize monism, but the *Gospel* was nevertheless installed as a source of popular knowledge of Buddhism. It is still in print in at least two editions. The 1973 paperback edition boasts that it had by then already sold more than 3 million copies.

Eastern Buddhism Dismissed

The reception of Eastern Buddhism by Western academics and religious specialists was summarized in a public exchange between Shaku Sōen, Barrows, and the Reverend Dr. F. F. Ellinwood reproduced in *Open Court*.[5] What so "greatly disappointed" Shaku Sōen and initiated the exchange was that after the Parliament, Barrows still persisted in repeating "those errors which were common in the various Western books on Buddhism."[6] He continued to discredit Buddhism on the basis of a nihilistic definition of nirvana, which was, for him, "the goal which made Buddha's teachings a dubious gospel . . . the extinction of love and life."[7] As Shaku Sōen protested to Barrows, his show of "friendly and sympathetic treatment" of non-Christians at the Parliament had endowed him with a certain authority on the subject. Consequently, "your utterances are of importance because they will be received as an impartial representation of our religion, since you, having been Chairman of the Religious Parliament, are commonly considered to have the best information about those religions that were represented at this famous assemblage."[8]

Shaku Sōen's concern was well founded. As a direct consequence of the Parliament, a wealthy widow, Mrs. Caroline Haskell, made several bequests to extend the work of the Parliament in the Christian conquest of Asia. One was to found the chair of comparative religion at the newly established University of Chicago, and another was for an external lectureship on "the Relationship of Christianity and the Other Religions" to be delivered to the English-speaking native intelligentsia of Indian cities.[9] Barrows, America's authority on Asian religions presumably because of his personal contact with its representatives, filled both positions. Consequently, although the Parliament did not alter Barrows's attitude to non-Christian religions, it greatly enhanced the authority with which he spoke on them. Mrs. Haskell funded Barrows's dream of the Christian conquest of Asia, and he devoted the rest of his life to this mission.[10]

In his letter, Shaku Sōen carefully, patiently, and politely explained, as he had at the Parliament, that even in its negative aspect "nirvāna means extinction of lust, not of love; extinction of evil, not of existence; of egotistic craving, not of life" and that its positive aspect set the energies of man free for good deeds, to devote his life to active work for general good. Barrows's reply was short and dismissive, not only placing Western philological authority above that of the Japanese Buddhist abbot but dismissing Mahayana entirely. For him there was no question that Buddhism—and its true definitions—resided in the texts of the South. "My interpretation of *nirvāna* is that of some of the most friendly students of Buddhism who have gained their views from reading Buddhist scriptures."

This exchange did not end the matter. Ellinwood, responding to Shaku Sōen on Barrows's behalf, elaborated on Barrows's theme, again citing Western Buddhist scholarship to convince Shaku Sōen of his error in understanding his own religion and to dismiss Eastern Buddhism as heretical. "If, then, we are to decide upon the meaning of *nirvāna*, or *parinirvāna* as taught by Buddha, we must turn back from all these northern developments to the older canonical teaching."[11]

The delegation had failed in its attempt to distance Eastern Buddhism from the Buddhism of the South and North. Ellinwood quoted Pali scholar T. W. Rhys Davids in his support. Rhys Davids, as the authority on Buddhism, dismissed Ashitsu's account of the four kinds of nirvana as the misconceptions of "popular beliefs." He simply stated that the "two forms of nirvana which Ashitsu ascribed to the Southern literature cannot be found there." He was bemused at the idea of ascribing Mahayana concepts to the immediate disciples of Buddha[12] and totally unconvinced by the delegation's claim that the Mahayana sutras were the Buddha Sakyamuni's teaching. For him, the claim indicated only how much in error contemporary "so-called Buddhists" could be, how astounding "the gulf on all sides between popular beliefs and the conclusions of science." Eastern Buddhism remained a regional variation, a later falling away from the true word.

Ellinwood appeared to be impressed by the Mahayana development of the Bodhisattva concept but commented that it "comes nearer to the doctrine of the Apostle Paul than those of Sakyamuni." The curious inconsistency embedded in this admiration is that the positive features of Japanese Buddhism made it a "heresy" against the Buddha's teachings, but Japanese, as Buddhists of sorts, remained stigmatized as believers in nihilism, "the meaning of nirvāna *as taught by the Buddha.*" Alterity had to be preserved. In 1899, six years after the Parliament, Barrows still repeated the message of Hardy and Saint-Hilaire: "In no religion are we so constantly reminded of our own as in Buddhism, and yet in no religion has man been drawn so far from the truth as in the religion of the Buddha."[13] What appeared to be admirable in the presentations of Buddhism, Barrows warned, was due to the contact these Westernized Buddhists had had with Christianity. In his letter to Shaku Sōen, Barrows commented that "if modern Japanese Buddhism teaches conscious personal life after death and believes in a personal Heavenly Father, full of love, its divergence is not so marked as we had supposed."[14] To the extent that Eastern Buddhism became acceptable by Christian standards, it ceased to be Buddhism at all. The rules of Western academic scholarship provided the means of excluding Eastern Buddhist voices from definitions of Buddhism.

Neither Rhys Davids nor Max Muller, the two leading Orientalists, had attended the Parliament.[15] Muller later expressed his regret that he had not attended but clearly he had not expected anything more than a Christian theological event, "a part of the great show of industry and art."[16] In retrospect he admired the spirit of brotherhood displayed but was critical of the absence of textual authority, which "interfered with the usefulness" of the event. The very idea of accepting statements put forward by "those who professed to speak in the name of Buddhism, Brahmanism, Christianity and Zoroastrianism—by followers of these religions who happened to be present"—was simply unacceptable. Muller doubted that these speakers would have been able to substantiate their claims with references to "chapter and verse from their own canonical books."[17] This comment seems to have been particularly leveled at the representatives of Eastern Buddhism, since he further observed that "it might have seemed hardly courteous to call upon a Buddhist archbishop to produce his authority from the Tripitake or from the nine Dharmas." The more useful Parliament of Religions was, for him, the "forty silent volumes" of his series, Sacred Books of the East. In spite of his claim to the belief that "true religion" is "practical, active, living religion,"[18] the authority of the edited and selected texts overrode living authority. Like Ellinwood, Muller apparently admired much of what was said by the delegates, but "enthusiastic descriptions of the supreme excellence" of religions cannot be accepted as true accounts of the religion without textual reference. The evidence for Eastern Buddhism was inadmissible. If it had actually been taught by the Buddha, it could not be accepted because it had not been preserved in the early texts. If it was the result of twenty-five hundred years of development in

Buddhist thought, it was equally unacceptable because Buddhism was defined as the original teachings of the Buddha. Western academic Orientalists were simply not interested. Living Buddhism—for this is what the Parliament offered—was the concern of missionaries, not scholars.

Buddhism Appropriated: Paul Carus and Monist Mission

Paul Carus was not an Orientalist but a post-Kantian philosopher (Ph.D. Tübingen, 1876) and dedicated missionary of the religion of science. For Carus "missionarizing is the inevitable outcome of a serious conviction"[19] and, moreover, provides the competition that promotes religious health, broadens minds, and promotes constructive thought. "Every religious man should study other religions in order to understand his own." For him the Parliament had been an opportunity to share his conviction of the harmony of science, philosophy, and religion.[20]

Carus was the editor of two journals devoted to "earnest and thoroughgoing reformation of religion under the influence of science" through the publication of an eclectic mixture of articles on scientific developments, psychology, philosophy, archaeology, biblical research, and non-Christian religions, "all of which directly or indirectly throw light on the origin of our own religion today."[21] *Open Court*, founded 1886, was followed in 1890 by the *Monist*, which published articles on similar topics but of a more technical and philosophical nature.[22] Through the Open Court Publishing Company Carus published more than a thousand articles and fifty-odd book-length monographs. Only a small proportion of these writings were concerned with Asian topics and the popularization of Oriental religion in America he is now remembered for. Everything he wrote, including these, was directed to the same end, propagating his Western philosophy, and it was through this that he expected to win fame. Carus believed his mission was the fulfillment of Kant's ideas. "If Kant compared his work to that of Copernicus," he wrote in his first American publication, "I may fairly liken mine to that of Kepler who filled out the Copernican system and reduced the law of motion of the planets to simple mathematical formulae."[23]

It is not surprising that Carus's philosophy seemed to have so much in common with Eastern Buddhism as it was presented at the Parliament. The delegates had particularly focused on those areas of religion of interest to Carus: Buddhism's compatibility with science and philosophy—especially philosophic idealism—and their resolution with religion. As well as this, certain Buddhist concepts did overlap with ideas in Carus's own post-Kantian philosophy published some years before the Parliament.[24] Most important, the delegates had emphasized the life-affirming and social aspects of Buddhism. After his contacts with Japanese delegates at Chicago, Carus read Buddhism as a version of his own Christian monism and, driven by a strong belief in the positive good of missionary activity, propagated it as such.[25]

There is no doubt that the Japanese presentation was a major revelation for Carus. In spite of his commitment to comparative religion, his writing before the time of the Parliament indicated a surprisingly vague acquaintance with Buddhism. His 1890 note on "The Religion of Resignation" suggests that he found nothing of interest in the nihilistic image of Buddhism current at the time.[26] His first article on Buddhism, "Karma and Nirvana,"[27] was published within months of the Parliament and covered most of the doctrinal information that formed his future publications. His dramatic change of attitude is clear.

The article opens with a statement of the negative assumptions of the nature of Buddhism as he had previously understood it. "Buddhism is generally characterized as a religion without a belief in God and the human soul, without hope of a future existence, pessimistic and desolate, looking upon life as an ocean of suffering, quietistic in its ethics, and finding comfort only in the final extinction into nothingness."[28] The body of the article overturns these assumptions point by point. Quoting from major Orientalists, it shows that Buddhism does have a concept of deity, does not deny the existence of the human soul, does teach of life after death, is not pessimistic, and is not quietistic but teaches active self-improvement.[29] This realization that Buddhism was not nihilistic was pivotal to his project. Carus had recognized similarities between his own previously formulated monist ideas and several of the Buddhist concepts presented by the Japanese delegates. His problem was that orthodox Christians dismissed monism, as they did Buddhism, as nihilistic. As he later put it, "[N]ot only are the similarities that obtain between modern psychology and Buddhism striking, but we must meet with the same misconceptions and objections."[30] In distancing Eastern Buddhism from these charges, the Japanese delegates had provided Carus with a model and a precedent for the defense of monism.

The Japanese delegation's assurance that Eastern Buddhism offered not only a philosophical system but also a religion answered another of Carus's difficulties. He shared with more orthodox Christians an abhorrence for any conception of the world that denied notions of the soul or God.[31] In his Parliament paper "Science a Religious Revelation," he had argued that while a conception of religion that rejects science is inevitably doomed, humanity must have a religion because belief in God was "the innermost conviction of man which regulates his conduct." The resolution as he saw it was that religion would undergo changes, would "free itself from paganism, evolve and grow"[32] in keeping with scientific developments. A new conception of the soul such as he had described in *The Soul of Man* was fundamental to this transition. In 1890 he had written: "The new view is monistic: it regards the soul as identical with its activity; the human soul consists of man's feelings and thoughts, his fears and hopes, his wishes and ideals."[33] After his introduction to Eastern Buddhism he wrote that the Buddhists "anticipated the modern conception of the soul as it is now taught by the most advanced scientists of Europe"[34] and restated this view in Buddhist terminology. "Buddhism is monistic. It claims that man's soul does not consist of two things, of an *ātman* (self) and a *manas* (mind and thoughts), but that it is made up of thoughts alone. The thoughts of a man constitute his soul; they, if anything, are his self, and there is no *ātman*, no additional and separate 'self' besides."[35]

The point is that Buddhism did not alter Carus's philosophy but provided him with the words to express it. He was not unique in using Eastern religions in this way. Ralph Waldo Emerson wanted "not the metaphysics [of Hinduism], only the literature of them,"[36] and wrote that "should another's words describe the fact, use them as freely as the language of the alphabet."[37] Emerson had recognized Oriental precursors of his ideas and "like some other preachers, I have added my texts—derived from the Chinese and Hindoo scriptures—long after my discourse was written." Eastern Buddhism, Buddhism presented in its modern, Japanese guise, provided this resource for Carus.

Buddhism also rendered Carus a service in providing a relatively neutral ground for discussing these ideas. As he expressed it, it was easier to explain the "natural difficulties of the Western mind" in understanding the concepts of a foreign religion than to directly confront these same problems in understanding monism. In his first article on Buddhism he wrote that "the difficulty to a Western mind in the comprehension of the term nirvana lies mainly in our habit of conceiving of the nature of the soul in the old Brahmanical sense of an ego-entity, the doer of our acts, the perceiver of our sensations, and the thinker of our thoughts."[38] Although here he disparagingly refers to the dualistic conception of the soul as "old Brahmanic," this is precisely how he described the orthodox Christian concept of soul he argued against in *The Soul of Man*. My point is that he used the label "Brahmanic" to cloak his attack on the Christian dualistic soul conception. Carus's conception of God, the "Soul of the Universe,"[39] was correspondingly unorthodox, and, by putting forward a case for Western understanding of Buddhism, he simultaneously commended monism. Ostensibly defending Buddhism, Carus wrote that "our popular conceptions of a Creator-God and an ego-soul are so deeply rooted in the minds of our people, that, as a rule, they still consider these two ideas as the indispensable foundations of all religion."[40] Unsettling these assumptions was as essential to the acceptance of Carus's monism as it was to Buddhism.

Christ Is a Buddha

Carus's ideal had much in common with Eastern Buddhism. One problem, however, was that his vision was unquestionably Christian. He attempted to overcome this by arguing that Buddhism and Christianity were essentially the same religion. They were both allegorical expressions of the one universal truth, their apparent differences nothing more than culturally determined "modes of expression." Christianity had "assumed a less abstract and more concrete shape, so as to appeal to the energetic races of the North."[41] The Christian conceptions of an anthropomorphic God, God the Creator, and of a personal, immortal ego-soul are allegorical vestiges of the religion suited to an earlier period.[42] One implication of this argument was that neither Buddhism nor monism was nihilistic as such. What they denied were merely these outmoded allegorical expressions.

As Carus saw it, one advantage of Buddhism over Christianity was that its followers were aware of the allegorical nature of their belief. He referred to Buddhist and Christian iconographic sculpture to make this point, juxtaposing a Roman Catholic representation of Madonna and child with a Chinese porcelain figure of "Kouan-yin," the bodhisattva Avalokitesvara, depicted in this case in a seated, feminine form, holding a child. The external similarity of form demonstrated the "palpable affinity," "the unmistakable coincidence of aspiration," between Christian and Buddhist conceptions of deity in their iconographic art. The important difference, however, was in their focus: unlike Jesus in the arms of Mary, "Buddha [that is, the bodhisattva figure] is conceived not as the object of motherly love, not as the infant, but as Love itself." Both icons were attempts to express the same truth, but, he argued, the Buddhist concept of deity was more obviously the anthropomorphization of an abstraction. Orthodox Christians had simply forgotten the allegorical nature of these images.

The identity of Buddhism and Christianity was essential to Carus's project.[43] He rejected suggestions that the similarities between the two great religions might be explained in terms of cultural influence imposed on different bases. The identity had to be fundamental. Buddhism and Christianity had to be expressions of the same truth. His most radical declaration of their essential identity was his hypothesis that Christ was the Buddha Maitreya, a claim he "validated" by a rather dubious use of Buddhist texts. The entry for "Maitrēya [*sic*]" in Eitel's *Handbook of Chinese Buddhism* mentioned a legend in which Sakyamuni appointed Maitreya to "issue thence as his successor after a lapse of 5,000 years."[44] By slipping a zero, Carus quoted the text predicting Maitreya's appearance in the world five hundred years after the death of Sakyamuni, a date approximating the birth of Christ. Hence he could write that "Buddha prophesied that the next Buddha after him would be Maitrēya, the Buddha of kindness, and without doing any violence to Buddha's words, this prophecy may be said to be fulfilled in Jesus of Nazareth. Thus the Christians may be said to be Buddhists that worship Maitrēya under the name of Christ."[45]

Although this extreme claim no doubt stretched Carus's credibility among his Christian audience, it does indicate the significance of his constant stress on the "extraordinary similarities" between the two religions. By equating the essence of Buddhism with the spirit of Christianity, Carus claimed that Buddhism's insights—those areas where he saw Buddhism to be more compatible with the evidence of science—were common to both religions and only more readily apparent in Buddhism. That is, monism, though at odds with current orthodox assumptions, was in fact within the spirit of Christianity. Carus marshaled Christian witnesses for this claim: "[T]hough the great majority of Christians believe in a soul entity . . . the great representatives of Christianity, St Paul, Thomas Aquinas . . . show strong tendencies towards the doctrine of anatman."[46]

Trinity and *Trikāya*

Perhaps the greatest doctrinal debt Carus owed to Eastern Buddhism was the Mahayana doctrine of the *trikāya*, the Three Bodies of the Buddha.[47] Eliding this with the Christian Trinity provided him with an acceptable alternative to the Christian anthropomorphic conception of God. Carus argued that although they do not believe in a personal God, "Buddhists believe not only in the Sambhōga Kāya which is an equivalent of the Christian God-idea, but even in a Trinity of Sambhōga Kāya, Nirmāna Kāya, and Dharma Kāya, bearing a close resemblance to the Christian conception of Father, Son and Holy Ghost."[48] This is a peculiar arrangement of the three terms that are usually presented in Buddhist literature in the order of increasing manifestation: *dharmakāya*, *sambhōgakāya*, and *nirmānakāya*, or in Carus's equation, Holy Ghost, Father, and Son, an arrangement less obviously parallel. He compared this Buddhist conception of deity to the attitude of "many faithful Christians . . . who look upon the theist dogma merely as the symbolical expression of a deeper truth." Carus devoted a whole chapter of the *Gospel* to suggesting this parallel but the implications of it are most explicitly stated in "Buddhism and Christianity," where he concluded that "Buddhist atheism, apparently, is not wholly unlike Christian theism."[49]

Although Carus rejected an atheistic world view, he was satisfied with the abstract Buddhist conception. An immortal soul was similarly so important to Carus that he would rather accept "the erroneous conception" of the "immortality of the disembodied ghost," as he characterized the orthodox Christian belief, than deny the possibility altogether.[50] The problem was not adequately resolved in *The Soul of Man*,[51] but Carus discovered a solution in Buddhism, "the transfer of the Samskaras according to the law of Karma."[52] This doctrine, as Shaku Sōen had explained at the Parliament, supplied the "ultimate authority of conduct" lacking in Carus's monist system. The Buddhist conception of the self constituted by the *samskaras* provided not only a scheme for both rebirth and immortality[53] but a system for "the elevation and sanctification of every one's self,"[54] because by the law of karma, as Shaku Sōen's paper had explained, there will be retribution for actions, the unfailing justice of moral law. One problem for those used to the Christian conception of immortality was that the system depended on recognizing the connection between the individual formed from the *samskaras* after death and the individual of before. "The 'I' of today has to take all the consequences of the actions which the 'I' of yesterday performed . . . the individualized Karma of future times will reap all that which the individualizing Karma of the present time sows."[55] To accommodate this, Carus's vision of the self constituted by the *samskaras* was a cohesive entity persisting beyond death. It was a soul.

Carus's interpretation of Buddhism owed a great deal to the Japanese delegates, but he gave them credit only in the most indirect way. Their positive attitude inspired him to turn to the books, that is, to the translations of Buddhist texts by Western authorities and, consequently, to the Southern Buddhism and Northern Buddhism from which they had hoped to distinguish themselves. Like Eastern Buddhism, however, the Buddhism Carus promoted stressed compatibility with science, particularly in the nature of the soul, the nonduality of the world, and the impossibility of creation out of nothing. Also, although it was compatible with idealist philosophy, it was not the purely philosophical construct of the hypothetical original Buddhism, but a religion. This change in perspective was also a consequence of Carus's contact with the Japanese delegation. A footnote in "Karma and Nirvana"[56] explained that the Hinayana or Southern school "prefers to some extent negative and philosophically strict definitions," whereas the Mahayana or Northern school of Buddhist thought "aims at positive and religious definitions." In the preface to the *Gospel* we see: "The Mahāyāna is a step forward in so far as it changed a philosophy into a religion and attempts to preach doctrines that were negatively expressed in positive propositions."

Carus nevertheless remained ambivalent in his attitude toward the Mahayana, if only to avoid being associated too closely with criticism directed at it. "Although the Mahāyāna unquestionably has its shortcomings, it must not be condemned offhand, for it serves its purpose," which was, as he saw it, changing the intellectually and morally demanding philosophy of original Buddhism—a philosophy "which enabled a thinker, but not the masses, to understand the dispensation of the moral law that pervades the world"—into a religion that rendered the Buddha's teachings "accessible to the multitudes." This was most important to Carus. His monism was not just a philosophy but a religion to replace orthodox Christianity in the scientific age.

The Gospel of Buddha: Popularizing the Construct

Carus's encounter with the Japanese delegation at Chicago gave him a Buddhist vocabulary to rearticulate his philosophical vision. However, the articles in *Open Court* and *Monist* reached only a small audience, mainly liberal intellectuals.[57] The evolutionary struggle from which, Carus believed, the religion of the modern world would emerge, would have to take place at the level of the body of the Church. The ideas had to reach a wide general readership. This popularization was the function of *The Gospel of Buddha*, which appeared a year after the Parliament. The ideas it contained were those of the earlier articles. The genius of the book was Carus's control of their presentation.

The title, *The Gospel of Buddha, Compiled from Old Records, as Told by Paul Carus*, presented the book as nothing more than a short version of the Buddhist canon. It was the truth of the life of the Buddha, the Gospel truth with all the colloquial connotations of the term, in the same way that the Christian Gospels, upon which the text was modeled, was the truth of the life of Christ. The religious nature of the work was signaled to his Christian audience by the familiar form of chapter and verse, and the King James style of language he purposefully adopted. Buddhism was a religion, if a philosophical one. The preface, like the title, attempted to efface the presence of the author, stressing the book's reliance on the canon, claiming that many passages, indeed the most important ones, were literally copied. It admitted to modifications such as trimming needless repetitions and adornments, but reassured the reader that there was nothing in the book for which prototypes could not be found in the traditions of Buddhism. For Carus, unlike his Orientalist contemporaries, this included the traditions of all Buddhist societies in all times, not just the Pali canon.

The claim that the book was merely a compilation, however, hardly does justice to what is in fact a most ingenious original composition. Carus's claim that the most important passages are copied is not exactly incorrect but is misleading. He used Buddhist texts in a number of ways. Some chapters he copied extensively from Buddhist sources, but often with a revised ending that attached a new lesson to a familiar story. He developed whole chapters from a short quotation—typically a two-line verse from the *Dhammapada*—but the lesson of the chapter was monist rather than Buddhist. In contrast, one very short chapter in the *Gospel* (ch. XXIV) carries the reference to a very long section of text, verses 1496–1521 of Asvaghosha's life of the Buddha.[58] Following the example of all Orientalists of the time, he trimmed texts of "apocryphal adornment." Chapter 6, not an atypical example, gives an idea of how extensive this trimming could be. Verses 191 to 322 (131 verses) of the *Fo-Sho-Hing-Tsan-King* were reduced to 23 verses in the *Gospel*. Elsewhere he strung together various passages from assorted Buddhist works, using them like words in a vocabulary to create totally new statements. He nevertheless succeeded in stitching together this incredible patchwork in a highly readable continuous narrative, creating a work in prose that deliberately rivaled Edwin Arnold's epic poem *Light of Asia*.[59]

Carus's own late discovery of Buddhism indicated how little academic knowledge of Buddhism had diffused beyond specialist circles. Rhys Davids had argued against the nihilistic interpretation of the doctrines of *anātman*, karma, and nirvana in his *Buddhism* (1878) and in the Hibbert Lectures in 1881. That the prevailing characterization of Buddhism should still be nihilistic, as Carus testified in "Karma and Nirvana" (1894), suggests that the message of missionaries and the influence of Western philosophers such as Schopenhauer had a greater impact on the general knowledge of Buddhism than the Pali scholars. Clearly, if Carus wished to modify this general perception, his work had to reach a wider audience than the Orientalists did. Sir Edwin Arnold's *Light of Asia* provided an alternative model. It had been spectacularly popular, but because it was a work of literature rather than scholarship, it lacked the claim to authority that Carus wanted for his work. Carus's *Gospel* aimed at a compromise, a narrative account of the life of the Buddha, but with the academic validation that Arnold's work lacked—hence his stress on the *Gospel*'s reliance on the canon and the pseudo-academic trappings of a "table of reference," "where the reader can find the sources and the parallelisms of the Buddhistic doctrines with Christianity, a full glossary of names and terms, and an exhaustive index."[60]

Appending Authority

The table of reference appended by Carus compensated for the absence of footnotes in the biblical format. In this the sources for each chapter are indicated by an abbreviation, which the reader must decode in a further table several pages over. A casual glance reassures that each chapter has a textual reference, that its truth is pinned to a Buddhist text. "M.V." one discovers refers to the *Mahāvagga*, "D.P." to the *Dhammapada*. But how many readers would have been sufficiently diligent in tracing the sources to discover, for example, that "E.A.," the reference for the first three chapters and for some of the most outstanding passages, stands not for a Buddhist text but for "Explanatory Addition," and designates Carus's own original contribution? "E.A." indicates material for which Carus could find no textual reference, and it is in these passages that he expounded his principal themes. One other imaginative passage carries the reference "E.H.," which decodes to Eitel's *Handbook of Chinese Buddhism*. Few readers would recognize that this is actually a dictionary and that consequently this reference—the meaning of one term—is used to suggest that a whole chapter of Carus's work has a canonical basis. Given the author's unidentified intrusions in most other chapters, the function of this attribution seems less to confess to his own creation than to conceal the absence of a Buddhist reference. The dubious nature of the source has been buried in the bibliography. The table of reference not only claimed academic legitimation; it concealed the author's considerable personal contribution to the work.

Not even the glossary is free of the author's presence. Amid the list of Sanskrit and Pali technical terms the entry "Mahāse'tu" sits unobtrusively. This is not, however, a Buddhist term but a pseudo-Sanskritic neologism that confirms the author's commitment to Christian superiority: "Mahāse'tu. The great bridge. A name invented by the author of the present book to designate the importance of Christianity compared to the Hīnayāna and Mahāyāna of Buddhism."

A survey of sources for chapter XCVI, "Maitrēya" (Metteyya, in Pali, in later editions), illustrates Carus's control of texts. The function of this key chapter is to allow the Buddha to predict the advent of a Messiah to continue his teaching. It presents the basis of Carus's argument that Jesus is a Buddha, the Buddha Maitreya, and his conviction that Buddhism and Christianity are the same religion. Since the substance of Carus's chapter is a dialogue between the Buddha, Sakyamuni, and his principal disciple, Ananda, on the eve of the Buddha's *parinirvāna*, the principal reference is Rhys Davids's translation of the *Mahāparinibbāna Suttanta*.[61] Carus opened the chapter by following the text very closely, exemplifying his claim that "[m]any passages, and indeed the most important ones, are literally copied from the translations of original texts."[62] He made editorial changes to avoid repetitions, and substituted the more biblical "thou art" for "you are" in keeping with the style of the Christian Gospel. In this way, verses 1–3 of the *Gospel* correspond to verses 3–6 of the *Mahāparinibbāna Suttanta*, though not to the more substantial fourteen-verse block indicated. Carus cut out the "apocryphal adornments," verses 7–14 of the sutra, which concern the presence of gods and spirits as witnesses to the Great Decease.[63] The omission itself is characteristic of his rational approach, but why did he include these eleven rejected verses in his reference if not to make it seem more substantial?

Carus's text then leaps forward, beyond his reference, to verse 32 of the *Mahāparinibbāna Suttanta*, which finds Ananda weeping at the thought of the Buddha's passing. After a brief reiteration of the real nature of the self in Carus's own words (since this is not indicated as an "Explanatory Addition," is it an example of the adaptation of the passage for modern readers?), Carus then has Ananda ask the question "Who shall teach us when thou art gone?" (96:12), which allows the Blessed One of Carus's *Gospel* to predict the coming of Carus's Buddhist Christ.

In this chapter, Carus has used three verses of the *Mahāparinibbāna Suttanta* (3–6) to establish the scene and its characters. The lesson of this chapter in the Buddhist sutras is, however, quite different, concerned not with future teachers but with the conduct of the brethren after the Buddha's death; the four places of pilgrimage (16–22); the correct deportment toward women (23); the correct forms of treating the remains of a Tathāgata (24–31). There is no mention of

Maitreya in this sutra, and these issues—the substance of the reference—are not mentioned in the *Gospel.*

Here we find the prediction that Maitreya will appear five hundred years after Sakyamuni's decease, once again inaccurately quoting Eitel's dictionary.[64] Careless transcription seems highly unlikely as an explanation because Carus's other references for this section, Rhys Davids's *Buddhism* (pp. 180, 200), also confirm Eitel's prediction that Maitreya Buddha is expected to appear five thousand years after Sakyamuni.

This pivotal equation was enhanced by illustrations in the second edition (fig. 13). That the scene is the Buddha's *parinirvāna* is signaled by the twin *sala* trees in bloom behind the figure and the grieving disciples before him. In Buddhist art the dying Buddha is more commonly depicted lying on one side and never with a beard. The garment, hand gestures, hairstyle, and small earlobes all owe more to depictions of Christ than to Buddhist iconography. Such artistic liberties would be inconsequential except that the book includes a five-page testimony by the illustrator, Olga Kopetzky, claiming years of research on Asian art and her assurance that "historical fidelity has been preserved in my work."[65] The Buddha even looked like Christ.[66]

Carus's use of texts in this chapter is typical of the work as a whole. The references provided are an unreliable guide to the extent of Carus's marshaling of the texts to his purpose. Some do indicate his sources, but rarely do the verses, or the lessons, actually match. Although it may well have functioned as a general indication of directions for further reading, "for those who wish to trace the Buddhism of this book to its fountainhead," the table of reference was in no way a substitute for the footnotes and references of academia. Its advantage, at least for the author, was that unless one actually attempted to use it, it did create the impression of textual scholarship. The *Critic* praised the table of reference for "showing at an eye glance the sources of his extracts and parallelisms in the Gospels."[67] At a glance, if not on closer inspection, the reader could be reassured of the "authenticity" of the work.

Carus made full use of the preface, the one area of a book—even a philologically correct translation of the canon—that allows the author the prerogative of interpreting his work.[68] He defended Buddhism against the Christian charges that the doctrine of *anātman* denied the existence of a soul,[69] denied that Buddhism is "negativism," and pointed out Buddhism's "many striking agreements" with Christianity, and in general established the features of Buddhism basic to his monist project. In the preface Carus declared that his purpose was not to

Figure 13. Christ is a Buddha (Carus, *Gospel*, 243; courtesy of Open Court Publishing Company, Peru, Ill.)

popularize Buddhism but to aid in the formation of the religion of the future and expressed the hope that the book would "bring out a nobler faith which aspires to the cosmic religion of truth."[70] He was quite explicit that his intention was not to explain Buddhism but to stimulate the evolutionary development of religion. The *Gospel* concluded with a poem, "In Praise of All the Buddhas," composed by Carus himself but presented as a Buddhist hymn. It was a song of Carus's universal religion of truth: all the Buddhas are one in essence, all teach the same truth. Carus's Christ was a Buddha.

The Content of the Form: The Bible as Model

Carus used the form of the work to reinforce his message of the similarity between Buddhism and Christianity. The name, *The Gospel of Buddha*, immediately signaled to his Christian readership the essential comparison between the Buddha Sakyamuni and Jesus Christ. Dropping the article before the title "Buddha" personalized the voice with which the author purported to speak.[71] The Christian Gospels, the source of information on the life of Christ, have become, in colloquial speech, a synonym for truth itself. Hence the title implied that this was a true account of the life of the Buddha and that this was the truth that Buddha, the historical man, taught. Because "gospel" means the glad tidings of the teaching, the title also signaled Carus's intention of reversing negative perceptions of Buddhism. "Rejoice at the glad tidings. . . . The Buddha our Lord has revealed the Truth" is the refrain and lesson of the opening chapter. The three opening chapters, referenced to "E.A.," were entitled "Rejoice," "Samsara and Nirvāna," "Truth the Saviour."

Carus also appealed to the Bible as a model to justify his free use of diverse Buddhist sources. He informed his readers in the preface to the *Gospel* that he had chosen to follow the model of the Fourth Gospel of the New Testament,[72] presenting the "data of the Buddha's life in the light of their religio-philosophic significance." For Carus this meant "not shrinking from the marvellous . . . whenever its moral seemed to justify its mention."[73] This gave him the freedom to range over the existing versions of the Buddha's life, introducing material outside that recognized by previous chroniclers who had been attempting to establish the historical presence behind the mythology. Just as the Gospel of Saint John apparently derived from a wider range of sources than the Synoptic Gospels, Carus's *Gospel of Buddha* included material from Pali, Sanskrit, Chinese, and Japanese Buddhist works. His constant reference for the narrative was, curiously, not the Pali material used by Oldenberg, the logical contender for the title "original contents of Buddhism" he claimed to have marshaled, but the fifth-century Chinese translation of *Asvaghosha*, a text from Northern Buddhism.

In defense of his use of Mahayana sources, Carus declared that his intention was not to present "Buddhism in its cradle" but "Buddhism up to date."[74] This position not only allowed him to break away from adherence to the Buddhism of the Pali texts but to incorporate the modern views of Dharmapāla and the Japanese Buddhists who stressed the compatibility of Buddhism with science and the modern world, the Buddhism presented at the World's Parliament of Religions. The problem Carus faced was of legitimating contemporary Buddhist ideas in an academic regime where truth was tied to the interpretation of canonical texts. Given that the *Gospel* was the culmination of inspiration on Buddhism Carus received at the Parliament, it is curious that his bibliography and references do not include the papers on Buddhism presented there, which had been published by both Houghton and Barrows.

Carus's *Gospel*, in common with all Western scholarship at the time, claimed to pursue the essence of Buddhism, "the universal in the particular," the "non-sectarian . . . ideal position upon which all true Buddhists may stand as upon common ground,"[75] that is, a transnational and textual Buddhism, the "real" Buddhism compared with which each Asian practice was a distortion or aberration. In spite of his dependence on characteristically Mahayana thought, he conformed to the prejudice toward Theravada texts where possible, and his life of the Buddha was as purged of "adornment" and "accretions" as any Pali scholar's. As a result, Carus's Buddha was the archetypal nineteenth-century intellectual: "the first positivist, the first humanitarian, the first radical freethinker, the first iconoclast and the first prophet of the Religion of Science."[76]

Reception

The Gospel of Buddha was a great success as a popular work. Carus had "made a very agreeable and instructive book of it. . . . Dr. Carus deserved the thanks of all readers for his painstaking in the preparation of a work so instructive, so practically helpful."[77] Others appreciated "the simplicity of this presentation, the freedom of the text from notes or uncouth and outlandish diacritical points."[78] In Carus's *Gospel* "[t]he best thoughts of the great Oriental faith [are] put into readable and understandable shape by a clever, learned and a sympathetic scholar."[79]

The book naturally attracted criticism from less tolerant sections of the Christian community. Some refused to be impressed: "Compared with the Gospel of Christ, this story is as water unto wine, as a dim candle by the full orbed sun." Others were affronted: "The book is misnamed. Buddha was a noble character; but he taught no Gospel. There is one Gospel, and one only, the Gospel of our Lord Jesus Christ." Many commented on Carus's demonstration of the similarity between the careers of the Buddha and the Christ, but some refused to concede the point: "A useful book to all who are curious to know how little Buddhism resembles Christianity and how superficial and pretentious the tenets of its Gospel."[80]

Carus was particularly offended by the charge that he was attempting to convert Christians to Buddhism and protested that this was definitely not his purpose. The preface to *Gospel* showed particular concern not to antagonize its targeted Christian audience, speaking of the advantages of Christianity over Buddhism, and concluding with a statement of the religious hierarchy as Carus understood it: "Above any Hīnayāna, Mahāyāna, and Mahāse'tu is the Religion of Truth." Carus's image, which appropriated the Buddhist metaphor of the doctrine as a vehicle to transport followers to awakening, likened Christianity to a great bridge, "still more adapted to the needs of the multitude" than the large vessel of the Mahayana for crossing "the stream of self-hood and worldly vanity."[81] "While the schools of Buddhism may be compared to ships that cross the stream, Christianity is a large and solid bridge. Christianity is a Mahāse'tu. A child may walk over in perfect safety."[82] Whatever Carus's personal path to salvation may have been, his publications were intended to bring general enlightenment within the existing Christian society of his readers, to "bear upon the living present and become a factor in the formation of the future," the formation of a "non-pagan Christianity," a religion for the present generation.

The *Gospel* was not well received by scholars. Professor J. Estlin Carpenter, for example, wrote that it was "worthless stuff" because the compiler showed no concern for historical development, indiscriminately using texts from different countries and different periods; ignored the differences in "metaphysical and ontological speculation" among the sects; placed "side by side extracts from books separated by hundreds of years in date and by still wider intervals of philosophic thought as though they all alike represented the teachings of the founder of Buddhism." For Carpenter it was as unacceptable as "a Gospel of Christ compiled from writings of the first, fourth and thirteenth centuries." In all, the work was neither philological nor historical, the only academically acceptable approaches to Oriental religions. Of Carus's use of his sources, he wrote, "[H]is spirit is excellent, but his method is execrable."[83]

Carus took the opportunity to reiterate and clarify his position by addressing Estlin Carpenter's criticisms in the *Open Court*.[84] Under the title "Scholarmania" he dismissed the Orientalists who translated the ancient texts as the laborers, those who gathered the material for intellectuals such as himself to work with. He accused Carpenter, "the hodcarrier," of "hooting at the mason," and explained again that his purpose was different. He was not attempting to represent "Buddhism in its cradle, but . . . BUDDHISM UP TO DATE, in its nobler possibilities."[85] His final argument of the worth of the book, however, was that it had been translated into Japanese, and that a group of Japanese were undertaking to translate it into Chinese. There was "[n]o better evidence, that I have succeeded at least to some extent, in my aspiration" than that contemporary Asian Buddhists appeared to accept his book as representative of their religion.

This was not the only occasion on which Carus used this apparent Asian approval of Buddhism to counter Western academic criticism. Soon after this, *Open Court* also carried a favorable review from a Ceylonese journal, and again Carus quoted their appreciation of his work to deflect academic criticism. The review was proof that "our interpretation of the Buddhistic doctrine is in harmony with representative thinkers of Southern Buddhism." Elsewhere in the same issue he wrote, "Whether or not [*The Gospel*] faithfully represents the Buddhistic doctrine, it is for Buddhists to say."[86] Although he flaunted news of the Japanese publication of *Gospel*, the approval of Southern Buddhists was particularly important to him because "they have preserved the tradition most faithfully and are very punctilious in the statement of doctrinal points." Here again we see the tension between Carus's debt to Mahayana Buddhism, particularly the Eastern Buddhism of the Japanese delegation, and the need to defer to Hinayana—the older, the original, and therefore the more doctrinally punctilious—for legitimation within the dominant regime of academic Orientalism.

Conclusion

Paul Carus's writings on Buddhism were a direct consequence of the representation of Buddhism at the World's Parliament of Religions and, in particular, of the emphasis the Japanese delegation placed on Eastern Buddhism's resolution of religion with science and philosophy through Mahayana doctrine. Carus's monism, though essentially quite different, did overlap some Buddhist concepts, and Carus's work in promoting Buddhism as a religion of science and in denying its association with nihilism did reinforce the Buddhist project at the Parliament. Consequently, the king of Siam could sincerely thank Carus "for the very hard and difficult task of compilation you have considerately undertaken in the interests of our religion."[87] Prince Chandradat Chudhadharn could be exceedingly generous with his praise: "[A]s far as I could see, it is one of the best Buddhist scriptures ever published." D. B. Jayatilaka, headmaster, Buddhist High School, Kandy, Ceylon, could declare it to be "undoubtedly the best popular work on Buddhism in the English language." The criticisms they had can only be inferred from the polite qualifications: "as far as I could see"; "it comprises *almost* all knowledge of Buddhism itself."

The Gospel of Buddha was a success in that it made Buddhism familiar to a new and wider audience. It was undoubtedly a Westernization—even, as Verhoeven writes, an Americanization—of Buddhist ideas, emphasizing the empirical, psychological, and "positivist" aspects of Buddhism, and perhaps because of this, it succeeded in presenting a nonthreatening Buddhism that Westerners could accept. Carus's achievement, summarized in Suzuki's tribute, was as "a pioneer in introducing Oriental ways of thought and feeling to the English-reading public. In that respect all Oriental scholars, Eastern as well as Western, are deeply indebted to Dr. Paul Carus."[88] Carus should rightly share in the credit Seager gives the Asian delegates to the World's Parliament of Religions for helping to usher in the era of religious plurality to North America. As Verhoeven and Tweed demonstrate, with the possible exception of Henry Steel Olcott, Carus was probably the most influential person in stimulating discussion and interest in Buddhism in the United States.[89]

The *Gospel* was less successful in promoting monism. Meyer, speaking of Carus's attempt to establish a religion of science, says bluntly, "He failed. The public to which he spoke was deaf to his voice: his ideas were too abstract for the average man and too simple for the intellectual."[90] The role of the *Gospel* in the propagation of the religion of science presented the additional problem that the ideas explicitly expressed in Carus's other works were here embedded, unsuspected in their Buddhist guise, suggested rather than argued. Although Carus considered his Buddhist writings integral to his philosophy, his audience typically separated them. Philosophers read and dismissed the philosophy. Orientalists read and rejected his writings on Buddhism. He conformed to the rules of neither discipline.[91] His success with *The Gospel of Buddha* was among a general readership. The cover of the paperback edition currently available carries the boast "More than three million copies sold."[92]

Reasons for the success of *The Gospel of Buddha* include the appeal of the book itself. It is a skillful compilation, and Carus succeeded in giving it something of the literary attraction of Arnold's epic poem. Access to his own press and journals to promote the publication to a targeted audience no doubt also contributed, and, as noted earlier, it offered a nonconfronting alternative to orthodox religions. The success of the *Gospel*, however, was to a great extent dependent on the acceptance of the book by Japanese and Sinhalese Buddhists. Apparent Asian approval validated the work, provided a guarantee of its truth in the absence of the more usually accepted academic criteria. A promotion for the 1895 edition of the *Gospel* announced in boldface type, "A Japanese translation for the use of Buddhists of Japan has already appeared and is now in its second edition."[93] The edition currently available still carries the message: "The best evidence that this book characterizes the spirit of Buddhism correctly can be found in the welcome it received throughout the entire Buddhist world. It has even been officially introduced in Buddhist schools and temples of Japan and Ceylon."[94] Carus's representation of Buddhism had apparently been endorsed by practicing Buddhists. Carus shared in their authority, at least in the popular arena. The work has never been considered academically acceptable in the West.[95]

CHAPTER

DEPLOYING WESTERN AUTHORITY II

Carus in Translation

Within months of its American release, Paul Carus's *The Gospel of Buddha* had been translated by D. T. Suzuki and published in Japan with a preface and endorsement by Shaku Sōen and a biography of Carus by Suzuki. This book, *Budda no fukuin*, a conscientiously literal translation of the original text, was imbued with the political concerns of Meiji Japan.[1] Its value was in attracting the attention of the Western-educated elite of the nation—Inoue Enryō's "young men of talent and education"—introducing them to Buddhist ideas, presented in an accessible form acceptable by Western standards, and reassuring them of Western intellectual interest in and approval of their indigenous religion. *Budda no fukuin* was both a consequence of the Japanese delegation to the World's Parliament of Religions, validating the mission abroad, and an extension of its project, presenting Eastern Buddhism as the religion of modern Japan through its claim to be the universal religion of the modern world. It was an event in sequence with the Meiji Buddhist revival project outlined in Inoue Enryō's *Bukkyō katsuron joron*—another example of the deployment of Western authority demonstrated by the highly orchestrated Japanese tour of Henry Steel Olcott and by the performance at the Chicago Parliament. A most important feature of the book was the Western status of its author. As Suzuki's biography presented him, he was a German philosopher who rejected Christianity in favor of Buddhism as the modern scientific religion. As such he illustrated reform claims that Western intellectuals were finding Christianity inadequate.

Contrary to the assumption of Carus's biographers, the reason for the publication was not that Shaku Sōen saw him as a source of Buddhist wisdom. He and Suzuki were well aware of the shortcomings of Carus's representation of Buddhist thought, but in the context of Buddhist revival the content of the book was of secondary importance. The Asian publication of the work was, however, a major factor in the enduring reputation of the book and its author, and the principal reason it still circulates as a source of knowledge of Buddhism to this day. This chapter describes its function in the Meiji Buddhist revival and its apparent endorsement by Japanese Buddhists.

The Gospel of Buddha in Japan

The preface to *Budda no fukuin* lists three reasons for its publication: "First, to make our readers know how much our Buddhism is understood by Western scholars; second, to point out a short road for studying Buddhism for the younger generation; third, through the life of Sakyamuni, to sow widely the seeds of the great teaching of Buddhism."[2] The first of these reasons is the most compelling: it is a statement uncommitted to the quality of the work, suggesting "Let the book speak for itself," and carrying the dual implication that this is evidence of the strength of Western interest in Buddhism and of the limit of Western understanding on the subject. The second and third reasons indicate the audience targeted by the publication, the young Western-educated elite, namely, Japanese seeking a religion compatible with modern science, with modern Western thought, precisely those who had been interested in Christianity but who were now looking for an indigenous answer to their spiritual needs. The Western authorship of *Gospel* was essential to the force of its communication, testimony to the truth of Shaku Sōen's claims that "there are signs that the West might welcome Buddhism," even if "there is doubt attached" to whether Western scholars have fully understood the "essential principles of Buddhism."

The importance of Western interest in Buddhism in the Meiji context of rivalry between Japanese Christians and Buddhists is shown in the address made by the delegates Shaku Sōen, Yatsubuchi, and others to the Young Men's Buddhist Association (YMBA) of Yokohama shortly after their return from Chicago: "The Parliament was called because the Western nations have come to realise the weakness and folly of Christianity, and they really wished to hear from us of our religions and to learn what the best religion is. The meeting showed the great superiority of Buddhism over Christianity, and the mere fact of calling the meetings showed that the Americans and other Western peoples had lost their faith in Christianity and were ready to accept the teachings of our superior religion."[3]

The existence of *The Gospel of Buddha* was further evidence of these claims, which were repeated, though rather more subtly, in Shaku Sōen's preface, where he connected the achievements of modern science, which had "made the truth more and more clear," with the fact that "there are many signs in the Western civilization that it will welcome Buddhism."[4] Scientific developments were preparing the West to receive the truth of Buddhism. Shaku Sōen mentioned the current interest in Oriental literature, history, and fine arts and the "new and powerful interest in comparative religion" as indications that "the time is at hand in which Western scholars begin to see how brilliantly our Buddhism shines in all its glory."[5] "The World's Parliament of Religions held in America the previous year was a great achievement that was proof of the westward advance of Buddhism."[6]

As the delegates' address to the YMBA shows, Western interest in Buddhism was not only claimed as proof of the worth of Buddhism but was also construed by the Buddhists to imply the failure of Christianity to meet the needs of the modern world. Suzuki's biography of Carus presented him as a case study of this process. It related how Carus, born in Germany, the son of a prominent Christian clergyman, a scholar who had taken a doctoral degree in philosophy from a prominent German university, had rejected Christianity in favor of Buddhism. The existence of the *Gospel* was material evidence of the claim. Suzuki's emphasis on Carus's German background and training reflected the high esteem for German philosophy in Japan. That Carus, a German philosopher and man of science, rejected Christianity because he perceived it to be incompatible with the scientific world view was a specific challenge to Japanese converts, many of whom had turned to Christianity as the natural concomitant of modernization and Westernization.[7]

Carus's book, concerned as it was with the religion of science, was particularly valuable in Meiji religious debate because, in an inversion of its function in Carus's monist project, it actually argued the case for the Buddhists, defending Buddhism against the common charges of nihilism, skepticism, and atheism. Its emphasis on present concerns, future developments, and the religious basis of modernity supported the Buddhist reform project because it presented Buddhism as a religion suited to the modern scientific world view represented in Japan by the West. Most important, its Western authorship verified these claims, claims that had been made by Japanese scholars such as Inoue Enryō for some years.

Shaku Sōen remarked on Carus's use of Mahayana sources as a particular feature of the work.[8] The relationship of Mahayana Buddhism to the historical existence of the Buddha was a contentious issue in Meiji Buddhism. That the Mahayana was taught by the Buddha was central to the reform position. In his summary of the achievements of the delegation, Shaku Sōen mentioned his sense of satisfaction that "the mistaken idea that Mahayana Buddhism was not actually the Buddha's teaching had been put to rest."[9] The book's acceptance and inclusion of the Mahayana sutras in this Buddhist "gospel" gave it additional value.

Though these features provided evidence of a Western interest in and sympathy for Buddhism, the value of this went just so far. In his introduction to the second edition of *Fukuin*, Suzuki expressed misgivings about the quality of the work. "The book, which was not intended for Japanese hands, was unsatisfactory." One problem was its simplicity. It had been written in simple language that made it accessible to "anyone with a junior high school education," but as a consequence there were "many immature words," which, Suzuki was concerned, might hinder understanding.[10] This was not his only complaint. "In the translator's view, there are not a few passages where there are omissions or where there are revisions. This is the work of a Westerner and, from my personal view, it has the odour of a Westerner about it."[11]

Shaku Sōen, referring to the works of major Orientalists, explained how each produced an incomplete and idiosyncratic interpretation: "Swedenborg came to Buddhism through his interest in mysticism; [Edwin] Arnold through his elegant poetic vision; Olcott through his interest in superior intellect; Max Muller through his interest in the refined Sanskrit language."[12] Although each of them is excellent in his own field, he concluded, "as for attaining the essential meaning of the noble truths of Buddhism, there is reason to doubt whether these scholars had penetrated the secret."[13] If these great leaders of Oriental scholarship had failed in the task, what was Shaku Sōen suggesting his readers should expect of Carus?

In spite of whatever shortcomings he may have seen in the work, Shaku Sōen compared the arrival of Carus's book to "the rainbow and clouds after a serious drought."[14] This was because "an eager demand for a concisely compiled work on Buddhism has arisen throughout the country which it is our duty to satisfy."

Shaku Sōen was explicit that it was neither absence of information on Buddhism nor a falling off in Buddhist scholarship that led to the publication of the book. As his preface explained, "[H]ere [in Japan] the tradition is not disappearing; the writings are accumulating at a vast rate, and there is an exceedingly great superabundance of books"; "the Buddhist tradition which had existed in Japan for more than a thousand years was not disappearing; we have the complete Tripitaka, specialist teachers of the sutras, and the commentaries." The problems were rather that the literature, already so vast, continued to accumulate, and that canonical texts required a profound skill to master. "The characters are difficult and the sentences scholarly and intricate."[15] Hence the scholars of today "are at a loss how to begin the study of the Tripitaka, the 'perfection of the ancients.'" These "scholars of today," "the up-and-coming young Buddhists" to whom *Fukuin* was directed, were the growing class of Western-educated young moderns who had not the classical training needed to cope with the special difficulties of Buddhist texts, which are not only written in Chinese but are further removed from even the educated general reader by specialist technical terms. For the benefit of this audience the *Gospel* was translated by Suzuki into "a very easy style."

There were already some introductory books in modern language available in Japan. Inoue Enryō's works, written specifically to meet the needs of this audience, have already been mentioned, as have those of Nakanishi Goro. There was the five-volume work intended to promote Buddhist unity that Shaku Sōen, Toki Hōryū, Ashitsu Jitsuzen, and Shimaji Mokurai had begun to compile in 1891.[16] Although this work was probably not suitable for the general distribution that Shaku Sōen envisaged for *Budda no fukuin*, it does contradict the assumption that Japanese Buddhists went to Carus for knowledge of their religion. There were as well at least three short introductions to Buddhism that had been written in Japanese before being translated into English for distribution at the Chicago fair, and there had also been books on the life of Sakyamuni.[17] The fact that Shaku Sōen also saw a use for *Fukuin* as a primer of Buddhism does not detract from its primary function as a sign of Western recognition of the superiority of Buddhism as a religion for the future.

One advantage of Carus's *Gospel* was that a book on Buddhism by a Western scholar could be expected to reach a wider audience than these previous works. The Buddhist content of Carus's *Gospel* was not new to Japan. The audience for a book by a Western author, however, would presumably consist of the already pro-Buddhist audience of Inoue, Nakanishi, et al., extended to include the pro-

Western Japanese as well as that element of society which in any country is curious to find out what outsiders have to say about it. Just as Carus had used the book to extend his message to the general public, beyond the elite readership of his journals, Shaku Sōen's *Fukuin* could popularize and extend the audience for Buddhist reform arguments. Shaku Sōen has been described by Furuta Shokin as the founder of lay Zen in Japan, but his work was only part of the more general movement of *koji* Buddhism, bringing Buddhism out of the institutions and into the lives of the lay community. Carus's book, which was intended to introduce Buddhism-monism to the general public in America, was put to a similar task in Japan.

Validating the Chicago Mission

The Gospel of Buddha was also a sign of the success of the Japanese delegation to Chicago, a reply to conservative critics who had withheld official endorsement. That the book had been the consequence of the meeting between the Japanese Buddhist delegation and this German philosopher was spelled out in both the preface and the biography of Carus that Suzuki appended to *Fukuin*. The existence of the *Gospel*—the fact that exposure to Eastern Buddhism had inspired Carus to write it—justified the initiative taken by the delegates; it was proof that they had advanced Buddhist understanding by their attendance in Chicago. The content of the *Gospel* validated Shaku Sōen's specific claim that the delegation had shown "that Buddhism closely corresponds to modern science and philosophy."[18]

In his *Bankoku shūkyō taikai ichiran* (Outline of the World's Parliament of Religions), where Shaku Sōen listed the achievements of the delegation, he concluded modestly that "we have simply fulfilled our mission in spreading the wisdom of the Buddha and we will not make an announcement of this to the public." This "private memento" was nevertheless published through a number of editions. These, as well as addresses such as that to the YMBA, the Buddhist journals, and local newspapers, made much of the success and achievements of the delegation. The delegates became the Champions of Buddhism[19] and *Fukuin* became evidence for the Japanese public of the success of the delegation. Shaku Sōen's communication of the success of the delegation should not be read as a sign of personal pride unbecoming in a Zen abbot. The message is rather proof of the argument in the *Manifesto* quoted previously: the times call for action, not passive resistance to the Christian invasion. The future of Buddhism in Japan depended on it, and the Parliament offered an excellent opportunity to take Eastern Buddhism to the West—to "attempt the surprising strategy of expansion."[20]

The delegation to Chicago had been a strategy in the defense of Buddhism against Western encroachment in Japan, and it had achieved its initial, modest, purpose: "It is beyond our expectations to achieve an immediate positive result from sending one or two delegates to the Conference. . . . what is important is simply to make a step in the grand design for future progress." Christian investment in Japan was inefficient, the *Manifesto* argued, in that their immense effort had not been compensated. Nevertheless, it was undeniable that "Christianity had built up a great latent force in our society" through its activity, and, the argument ran, Buddhists should also be willing to take action. Reviewing the achievements of the delegation, which dealt less with transmission of doctrine than with the conversion of a New York businessman, and the cooperation of an expatriate Japanese businessman in funding extra lectures at the exposition, Shaku Sōen mused on the possibilities for Buddhism if the wider Buddhist community could be moved to such action: "It would be a marvelous event which would change the face of the country."[21] The *Gospel* was an indication of the possibilities.

Creating Space for Discussion

Shaku Sōen's endorsement of the book lent it authority among Buddhist readers, because he was not only chief abbot of an important Rinzai Zen temple complex but also a well-known Buddhist scholar, but his disclaimer on the accuracy of Western understanding of Buddhism suggests that the book could have created a space for the discussion of the place of Buddhism in the modern world. Because it was written by a non-Japanese, a Buddhist sympathizer but not an educated Buddhist priest, the ideas it presented were open to freer discussion in Japan than if it had been written by Shaku Sōen himself, for example, with the responsibility his position within institutional Buddhism demanded.

The careers of the two extremely influential Meiji Buddhist scholars, Inoue Enryō and Murakami Senshō, show some of the difficulties. Inoue, though a graduate of the Ōtani Buddhist university, resigned from the Honganji institution to remain in the intellectually less restricted climate of the academic world. Murakami Senshō, whose writings also contributed to a deeper understanding among non-Buddhists, particularly intellectuals and statesmen, remained a priest, but controversy caused by his scholarship forced him to resign from the Ōtani sect in 1901.[22] Although he always maintained his belief in the doctrinal superiority of the Mahayana, Murakami's study of Buddhism using Western academic methods led him to question whether it had actually been taught by the historical Buddha, Sakyamuni. Some issues of importance if Buddhism was to conform to Western criteria for acceptance as truth were not open for discussion by institutional clergy.

In Japan Carus was respected as an authority on the West and on Western philosophy. The title page identified him as a German doctor of philosophy (in Japanese the distinction is made that his doctorate was in the discipline of philosophy, *Tetsugaku hakushi*), claiming for him a share in the high esteem in which German philosophy was held among Japanese intellectuals. Shaku Sōen could enthusiastically endorse him for his goodwill in wishing to promote Buddhism and for his achievement in avoiding some of the errors of other Western scholars, but his opinions on Japan and Buddhism could be questioned without upsetting orthodoxy. They could be easily dismissed as yet another example of the inadequacy of foreign understanding. The foreign origin of the book was signaled by the title, *Budda no fukuin*, where *fukuin* was the word coined by Christian missionaries in Japan to designate the Christian Gospels. The Japanese rendering of the characters is "glad tidings," corresponding to the etymology of the English "gospel," and current Japanese-English dictionaries indicate its close association with Christian evangelism.[23]

Shaku Sōen apparently chose not to transmit Carus's emphasis on the similarities between Christianity and Buddhism; *Fukuin* does not include the "Table of Reference" which showed these parallels. The "List of Abbreviations" was transformed into a bibliography, effectively a statement of the extent of Western scholarship on Buddhism, again an endorsement of the claims of the reformers, presented in both English and in Japanese. Non-English readers could see the extent and nature of Western scholarship in the Japanese. The English version of the bibliography provided a source of reference and further study for the Western-educated.

Budda no fukuin in Buddhist Nationalism

Paul Carus's *The Gospel of Buddha* was deployed in Japan as a sign of Western recognition that Buddhism was the most appropriate religion for the modern, scientific world. This idea was fundamental to Meiji Buddhist reform but by no means the total issue. It is no surprise that Shaku Sōen's preface also spoke on other issues in the discourse: the reinstatement of Buddhism as a state religion and the benefits that Buddhist teaching bestows upon the nation.

The preface opened with a message of hope for Buddhism in overcoming its present problems, of Buddhism's strength in adversity, its adaptability. "The strength of Buddhism is like fire . . . the more you beat it, the more it burns . . . if attacked it becomes more and more aroused."[24] Arguing from history, it described how in ancient India Buddhism survived the dissension of ninety-six heretical sects; in China, it survived the opposition it faced from the two competing religions and oppressive rulers; over the hundreds, thousands of years of its eastward advance, Buddhism had survived crushing attacks, but its real character had not been decreased in the least.[25] The state of Buddhism in Meiji Japan, stripped of its power, suffering attack from Christians, was nothing new, the preface suggested. Buddhism had survived greater adversity, and not only survived but had emerged stronger for the purification. "Now, once again, although we met the crushing attack of *hai ki*[26] Buddhism's real character had not been decreased in the least."

The preface then retold the story of an interview between an ancient Chinese emperor and a Buddhist sage that argued the virtues of Buddhism, its benefits for beings of all ranks, and its benefits to the state. The emperor asked the sage to teach him what benefits Buddhism offers living beings. The emperor, convinced by the sage of Buddhism's superiority, converted to Buddhism and established it within his kingdom. The lesson of this sermonlike section of the preface was that "the Buddha is truly the Sage of complete wisdom and virtue, and the dharma which he preached is the true principle of *all ages and all countries, East and West*" (emphasis added). The unspoken conclusion is clearly that the Buddha dharma, the future universal religion, must also be the true principle to guide Meiji Japan.

In summary, as well as its messages of Western interest in Buddhism as the religion of the future, the preface argued that Buddhism was the solution to the questions of Meiji religion, the problem of the ideological base for modern Japan, a religion to assure the welfare of the nation. It also continued the campaign to reestablish the relationship between Buddhism and the state. *Budda no fukuin*, Carus's text as it was deployed in Japan, was imbued with the political concerns of the Meiji period and owed its publication to its strategic value in the discourse of Meiji religion.

The Two Prefaces: The Extension of the Parliament Project

My concern so far has been the significance of *The Gospel of Buddha* in the discourse of Meiji religion in Japan. But Shaku Sōen's preface to *Budda no fukuin* appeared in two versions. The second, which purported to be the English translation of the original, was published in Carus's journal, *Open Court*.[27] This "translation" shared a few paragraphs with the original but was essentially rewritten for the American journal, suggesting that Shaku Sōen also realized the opportunity offered by the publication of *Budda no fukuin* to intervene in the Western discourse on Buddhism. In effect it was an extension of the project of the Chicago delegation: an attempt to gain Western respect and appreciation for Buddhism, on the one hand to satisfy the Buddhist missionary ideal but, more important, as the *Manifesto* indicated, to strengthen the position of Buddhism in Japan.

Shaku Sōen's summary of the achievements of the delegation began with the statement that "we drew the attention of both foreigners and Japanese to the following points at least," indicating his awareness that by speaking in Chicago he was also addressing a certain local audience. The Japanese and American discourses intersected for a Japanese elite which was typified by people such as Hirai and the Christian delegates to the Parliament—that is, progressives, both Buddhist and Christian—many of whom contributed to the *Monist* and *Open Court*.[28] Articles by Japanese also appeared in liberal magazines such as *Arena* and *Forum*. Even non-English-speaking Japanese were brought into contact with articles of particular interest in English journals, which were translated and republished in Japan. In *Open Court* 9 (1895), for example, a letter from Mr. K. Ohara of Japan reported that he had published a translation of the "Triangular Debate on Christian Missions," an article from the *Monist*, in his journal the *Shi-Do-Kwai-Ko-Koku*.[29] Hirai's article from *Arena* was translated and republished in Japan. The *Monist* regularly noted the contents of Japanese journals received. It was not unreasonable to assume that an article on Japanese Buddhism in *Open Court* or the *Monist* would reach members of this particular elite, either directly or by report. Indeed, certain parts of the preface seem directed more particularly to this elite than to a Christian readership. The "translation" of the preface to *Fukuin*, therefore, like the delegation to Chicago before it, was a strategic intervention in both discourses. Shaku Sōen not only appropriated Carus's text for deployment in the discourse on the religious future of Meiji Japan; he took the opportunity of the Japanese publication to continue his intervention in the Western discourse on Buddhism.

The Preface in *Open Court*: The Message to the West

The version of Shaku Sōen's preface to *Budda no fukuin* reproduced in *Open Court* differed from the original in both omissions and additions. The initial historical paragraph illustrating the resilience and adaptability of Buddhism in the face of adversity, and the discussion between the emperor and the sage were omitted, perhaps a consequence of Carus's editorial hand. The sections dealing with the westward advance of Buddhism, Orientalist scholarship, and the reasons for the Japanese publication were reproduced more or less completely. There were, however, significant additions that had no parallel in the original. These we must attribute to Japanese authorship and an extension of the delegation's mission to the West.

The opening paragraph stressed the Buddhist belief that the dharma predates the historical Sakyamuni, challenging the Western assumption that Buddhism was originally a secular philosophy, the creation of a historical man, an assumption that underlies Carus's vision of the Buddha as the first humanist, first positivist, and so on. The preface stated emphatically that "Sakyamuni was born in India about three thousand years ago, but Buddhism existed long before his birth. . . . Buddhism is not an invention of Sakyamuni, but the Truth of the world."[30]

Although equating Buddhism with the truth of the world has a superficial coincidence with Carus's representation of Buddhism as the religion of truth presented in the *Gospel*, Shaku Sōen's claim is fundamentally different. In Carus's vision, Buddhism and Christianity shared equally in the truth. They were the result of parallel evolution, the result of the same truth adapted to two different cultural and historical environments. For Shaku Sōen, Buddhism, the truth of the world, was the fulfillment of all world religions. He described Buddhism as the center of the solar system of religion, and relegated Christianity to a position among all other religions, one of "the larger or smaller planets revolving around this brilliant sun of the Truth."[31]

The difference here is profound. The friendship between Carus and Shaku Sōen was apparently based on their shared commitment to the principles of the Parliament, universal religious tolerance and dedication to the search for truth. Carus wrote to Shaku Sōen that "[a]ll religions contain more or less truth, and all Bibles and sacred books more or less error. What we want is the best of them, the truth without the error, the good without the evil."[32] This statement seems in remarkable accord with Shaku Sōen's lecture to a meeting of Japanese religious leaders, Christian and Buddhist: "In both Buddhism and in Christianity, truth and untruth are, without doubt, mingled. . . . We are a people with a strong belief in truth, therefore we must search for whatever glimmer of truth there is, even amongst the rubbish, even amongst the excrement, we are willing to bow before it and rejoice."[33]

The coincidence of aim between Carus and Shaku Sōen was not as close as it first appeared. Shaku Sōen advocated religious tolerance and coexistence, but he had no doubts about the relative status of the ultimate rewards of Buddhism and Christianity. In the religious crisis of Meiji Japan, he called upon both the Christian and Buddhist communities to drop their rivalry and prejudice and cooperate for the good of the nation. There were, for him, undeniable differences in belief: "The doctrinal arguments of philosophers cannot be reconciled . . . but men of religion should disregard this and adopt the basic position of nondiscriminating, impartial benevolence. . . . Christians and Buddhists both together must meet the urgent task of today through carrying out philanthropic work."[34] Both believed in the imperative of the search for truth and both believed it was present in all religions, but for Shaku Sōen the unity of Buddhism and Christianity was not to be found at the level of the highest Truth, which Buddhism alone possessed, but in the common belief in charity, benevolence, and compassion. "Those who have the aptitude to believe in Christianity can follow Christianity and obtain consolation. Those who are born to follow Buddhism can accept Buddhism and attain liberation."[35]

But let us return to the preface. From this firm conviction of the superiority of Buddhism in the hierarchy of world religions, Shaku Sōen described his vision of their interrelationship. Confucius is, he wrote, "a Bodhisattva that appeared in China; and Jesus and Mohammed are Arhats in the West." (Here again Shaku Sōen differed from Carus. He granted Jesus a high spiritual status but not that of a Buddha.) The function of each of these great teachers was to prepare their followers to receive Buddhism, and although "some religious doctrines are inferior to and less deep than others . . . as far as they are consistent with the Truth, they may freely find their place within our Buddhist doctrines." This is more than a restatement of the encompassing tolerance of Buddhism. In this scheme the preexistence of an established religion is a necessary condition for the entry of Buddhism into a nation: "If Brahmanism had not arisen in India, Buddhism would never have come into existence"; similarly, the existence of Confucianism in China and Shintō in Japan made it possible for Buddhism to be introduced into those countries. Without the Arhats of the West, Jesus and Mohammed, there would be no Buddhism in the countries where those religious teachers are worshiped. "For all these religions, I make bold to say, are nothing but so many conductors through which the 'White Light' of Buddha is passing into the whole universe."

Kitagawa sees the use of this typically Christian formula of fulfillment by Asian religious reformers as a legacy of the Parliament, a lesson learned from Christians.[36] Although this may be the case for the Indian delegates he quotes, the idea has a much earlier origin in Japan. Edward J. Reed recorded an interview with Akamatsu Renjō, a Honganji priest who had accompanied Shimaji Mokurai to England for two and a half years from 1873. Akamatsu believed, said Reed, that his sect of Buddhism contained all that was good and true in the Christian religion and that the people of England were ripe for the reception of Buddhism.[37]

How did Shaku Sōen expect a Western audience to respond to this Buddhist appropriation of Carus's concept of the religion of truth and its claim of Asian priority? I do not believe that his argument was intended to attract converts to Buddhism. On the one hand, the preface attempted to dispute Carus's representation of Buddhism; it also challenged the Christian and Western assumption of natural superiority. On the other hand, it assured Japan's pro-Western generation that Buddhism already has all that the modern West was striving for. The publication of this statement in *Open Court* was a form of Western endorsement.

Shaku Sōen's preface, recomposed for American publication, was a minor strategy in Western discourse, but as Foucault points out, the overall effect of a strategy escapes the author's intentions. "People know what they do; they frequently know why they do what they do; but what they don't know is what what they do does."[38] Carus and his American readers gave no sign of noticing Shaku Sōen's vision of Buddhism as the fulfillment of Christianity, his opposition to Carus's position on truth and the relationship of Buddhism and Christianity, or his doubts on the success of Orientalists in understanding Buddhism. What was communicated to the Western reader, what did enter the Western discourse, was that Shaku Sōen, a high-ranking Buddhist, propagated Carus's work in Japan. Whatever the reason for the deployment of this Western text in the Japanese discourse, and regardless of any reservations Asian Buddhists may have held about the accuracy of its representation of Buddhism, Japanese acceptance of the *Gospel* validated the text in the West.

Budda no fukuin was the first of more than thirteen different editions that appeared in Carus's lifetime.[39] Japanese Reform Buddhists started on a Chinese translation in 1895 as part of their mission into the Chinese mainland, and this was reportedly tested out on prisoners of the Sino-Japanese War. The *Gospel* was republished in Ceylon but was not translated into Sinhalese because it was of greater use to the anticolonial Buddhist movement there as a Buddhist reader to replace the Bible used in government schools to teach the English language, the key to obtaining positions within the bureaucracy. It continued to be used for this purpose until the middle of the twentieth century.[40] In Ceylon, as in Japan, the book was endorsed not because it was a source of knowledge on Buddhism as such, but because it was of strategic value in the Buddhist nationalist movement. However, the constant reiteration of this Asian acceptance in Carus's publications and in promoting the book was, in the absence of its conformity to the rules of a historical or scientific presentation of the subject, the guarantee of the *Gospel*'s truth as a representation of Buddhism. As Carus himself put it, "Whether or not it faithfully represents the Buddhist doctrine, it is for Buddhists to say."[41] As recently as 1973 the work was republished with the reassurance that "[t]he best evidence that this book characterizes the spirit of Buddhism correctly can be found in the welcome it has received throughout the entire Buddhist world."

CHAPTER

FROM EASTERN BUDDHISM TO ZEN

A Postscript

On March 10, 1895, Daisetsu Teitarō Suzuki wrote to Paul Carus introducing himself as the translator of *The Gospel of Buddha*, a student of philosophy, and an avid reader of *Open Court* and the *Monist*. In December of the same year, a letter from Shaku Sōen to Carus (in Suzuki's handwriting) commended Suzuki to Carus as a diligent student of philosophy, "greatly inspired by your sound faith" and earnestly desiring to study under Carus's personal guidance. He offered the inducement that Suzuki would be able to introduce Carus's ideas to Japan and suggested that he start work early next spring.[1] So began Suzuki's twelve-year apprenticeship in La Salle (March 1897 to February 1909), which was to have profound consequences for Western knowledge of Japanese Buddhism. When Suzuki died at the age of ninety-five, his publications in English included seven major translations of Mahayana texts, twenty-two books, and well over a hundred articles, essays, reviews, and miscellaneous writings.[2] His Japanese-language corpus is many times greater: the Suzuki *Collected Works* runs to more than forty volumes and is still in progress.[3] His work provided the basis of what the West knows of Japanese Buddhism at both popular and scholarly levels, and contributed substantially to the by now popularly accepted equation of Zen with Eastern Buddhism, and the attribution to it of the culture and civilization of Japan.

Although a direct consequence of the delegation to Chicago, and perhaps the culmination of its mission, the story of the formation of Zen as the essence of Eastern Buddhism and its acceptance in the West belongs to a later period of history and to other studies.[4] Suzuki's career spans periods of massive change in Japan's relations with the West and with Asian countries; his writings participate in an even wider set of discursive formations, republished, recirculated at different times and in different languages and to different purposes. It is not my intention in this concluding chapter to take on a survey of Suzuki's long and productive career but to look at one or two aspects of his work at La Salle to demonstrate continuities with the Chicago mission, signpost changes, and foreground the work already done on the subject. Suzuki's journey to the West was both a continuation and a point of change.

Learning from the West

It is clear from the letters just mentioned that Suzuki (with Shaku Sōen's encouragement) instigated his apprenticeship with Carus.[5] His journey to the West followed the pattern of early Meiji Buddhists who studied at Oxford, seeking the methods of academic scholarship to produce a modern canon, the basis of modern Buddhist studies.[6] Suzuki went to Carus to learn from him the various skills required to disseminate knowledge of Buddhism to the West. The need for this had been brought home to him very sharply in the year before he arrived in America by the controversy between Barrows, Ellinwood, and Shaku Sōen.[7] Suzuki, as Shaku Sōen's translator, would have been at the center of the exchange, reminded of the ignorance of and prejudice toward Mahayana in the West, even among Buddhist scholars, and directly encountering the arrogance and power of the Western Buddhist establishment to exclude Asian authority. At La Salle he acquired both the authority to be heard and the means to win sympathy and understanding for Mahayana Buddhism.[8]

Although assisting Carus in translating Chinese may or may not have instigated his trip to America, it was an important part of Suzuki's work. Their joint translation of *Lao-Tze's Tao Teh King* was published in 1898; two other cotranslated Taoist texts appeared in 1906.[9] Suzuki's translation of *Asvaghosha's Discourse on the Awakening of Faith* was published in 1900, and it is clear from this immaculately documented display of erudition that he had by this time mastered the rules of scientific Buddhology. With this publication and the related scholarly articles in professional journals, he made the shift from "popular believer" and claimed his authority to contribute to academic discourse.

Studying Carus's philosophy of science was another central aspect of the program, providing both the framework and the vocabulary of Suzuki's Buddhist writings. Carus himself observed the striking similarities between the "very terms of Asvaghosha's system and expressions which I have used in my own philosophical writings," and was delighted that Suzuki's work "fully justified" his own interpretations of Buddhism.[10] The similarities with Carus's monism are even more striking in *Outlines of the Mahāyāna*.[11] As Verhoeven observes, "[L]ike Carus, or perhaps because of Carus Suzuki presents a Buddhism to Americans that recapitulates the German doctor's."[12] In these early writings promoting Buddhism to American audiences, Suzuki took considerable license with central Buddhist concepts, some that Verhoeven traces directly to Carus's writings, which make Buddhism appear "eminently compatible with approved values."[13] Although there are undoubtedly strong similarities, as Carus himself notes, "the coincidence of some salient points need of course not exclude disagreements in other important matters."[14] Suzuki's unquestionable admiration for Carus and their mutual friendship did not preclude an agreement to disagree on the relative merits of Buddhism and monism, as we saw in the relationship between Carus and Shaku Sōen. It was in 1901—shortly after the publication of *Asvaghosha's Discourse* and well into his American sojourn—that Suzuki expressed his concern that *Buddha no fukuin* had "the odour of a Westerner about it," seriously qualifying his endorsement of it as a vehicle for teaching Buddhism to Japanese. I suggest it may be more useful to consider Suzuki inverting the process Carus had used in *The Gospel of Buddha*, deploying monism in the cause of Buddhism.

Suzuki's period at La Salle offers further parallels with the Oxford experience of Nanjō Bun'yu and Takakusu Junjirō. He too combined academic study with networking, establishing his credentials, studying the state of religion abroad. Where better than the Open Court editorial office to keep abreast of currents in Western thought? Carus's journals attracted papers on psychology, archaeology, science, and religion. Who better than Carus himself to teach the arts of reaching audiences? His achievements in promoting and maintaining interest in Buddhism in America cannot be denied. He made the unfamiliar less confronting, "less alien and worrisome," through his Christianizing and even Americanizing of Buddhism.[15] His writings, disseminated through his journals and publishing company, facilitated acceptance of Buddhism among his predominantly Protestant North American readers. By the end of his apprenticeship with Carus, Suzuki had acquired an appropriate philosophical vocabulary and intellectual framework for presenting Japanese Buddhism to Western audiences. He had published books and papers to establish his credentials within the Western Buddhist discourse. He had also learned the basic skills of editing and publishing, which were to be used in establishing, first, the Japanese-language journal *Zendō*[16] and, later, *Eastern Buddhist*.

Suzuki at La Salle

Suzuki's stay at La Salle was extremely productive. He began the translation of *Asvaghosha's Discourse* not long after he arrived.[17] While working on this he also published book reviews and articles for the *Monist*, *Open Court*, and other journals.[18] *Sermons of a Buddhist Abbot* appeared in 1906 and *Outlines of the Mahāyāna* in 1907. The first book was based on lectures given by Shaku Sōen on his second trip to America in 1905[19] but was substantially Suzuki's work. He not only translated the lectures, but edited them, "condensing several articles into one," and made substantial additions—"making a special essay out of subjects only cursorily referred to," and, where necessary, "put the thoughts in a form more comprehensible to the American public." *Sermons* also contained his translation of the *Sutra of the Forty-Two Sections*.[20] While at La Salle Suzuki also wrote articles for the Japanese journals *Rikugo zasshi* and *Shin bukkyō*[21] and, most significant, published his first English-language article on Zen, "The Zen Sect of Buddhism" (1906–7).

It is not difficult to trace a continuation of the *Manifesto* agenda in these early writings. The Buddhism they present is the familiar deinstitutionalized, deritualized, scientific and philosophical expression of *shin bukkyō* as a universal religion. They reiterate the familiar themes: the Mahayana *is* the teaching of the Buddha; Eastern Buddhism is not pessimistic or nihilistic; although it is a religion of self-reliance, people are not left unaided; Mahayana offers a noninterventionist system of moral retribution, is rational, and is compatible with science; "philosophical thought in this twentieth century runs parallel to Mahayana Buddhism."[22] Each work laments Western ignorance and misunderstanding of the Mahayana. The trajectory is particularly clear in *Outlines*, in which Suzuki presents Eastern Buddhism to the West as the delegates to Chicago no doubt would have liked to have done. It addresses all of the priorities identified in the *Mani-*

festo and presents Eastern Buddhism—the need for this third discursive space is clearly articulated—unconstrained by time or language, equipped with knowledge of the interests of the audience and mastery of the vocabulary to make the ideas relevant to them.[23] There are, however, significant differences, new strategies in a changing discursive environment, that contributed to the formation of the well-documented features of popular Western perceptions of Zen. The differences speak of the lessons of Suzuki's journey to the West as well as of changing strategies in the promotion of Eastern Buddhism.

Decentering Original Buddhism

The publication of *Asvaghosha's Discourse* made a key Mahayana text available to Western scholars. The introductory essay on the dating of Asvaghosha is an immaculately scholarly comparison of all the evidence available in Chinese sources on the dating of the lost Sanskrit original, challenging Western assumptions of the priority of Theravada. In this book Suzuki established the development and systematization of key Mahayana concepts several centuries earlier than previously believed, significantly closer to the time of the life of Sakyamuni. With this work Suzuki located the articulation of concepts of Suchness, of the three bodies of the Buddha (and therefore *dharmakāya*), and of the idea of salvation at a time not much later than the Pali sutras.[24] From this it followed that the Mahayana and Hinayana both emerged out of a period of development soon after the Buddha's death when the various schools that had formed during the Buddha's life were formalized. They were more or less contemporary; Theravada had no more claim to originality than Mahayana.[25] Working within the textual parameters of the Western paradigm, Suzuki challenged the priority of Pali Buddhism. There were "Hindu types," not just one Indian Buddhism.

In his next book, *Outlines of the Mahāyāna*, he takes a bolder step, inverting focus on the older canonical teachings and speaking instead to late nineteenth-century confidence in progress and evolution, of development. "Is Mahāyāna Buddhism the Genuine Teaching of the Buddha?" he asks in the introduction. Unquestionably yes, but "the role of an originator is necessarily indefinite and comprehensive." The concern to show that Mahayana and Japanese Buddhism are the teachings of the historical Buddha remains, but rather than pursue the tradition of the five periods of teaching, which he no doubt realized had little chance of being accepted against the evidence of Western scholarship, he approached the problem differently. Eastern Buddhism is a living religion, the culmination of thousands of years of development, a living force. "Just as Kant's philosophy instigated the diverse philosophical systems of Jacobi, Fitche, Hegel, and Schopenhauer," the followers of the Buddha developed his teachings "as required by their needs and circumstances, finally giving birth to the distinction of Mahāyānism and Hīnayānism."[26]

In this scheme Mahayana is progressive; Hinayana, conservative. Both came from the one source, but one tended to preserve the monastic rules and traditions, the other drew nourishment where available and unfolded the germs of concepts presented in the original system.[27] Eastern Buddhism then is the Buddha's teaching, not in the fundamentalist sense of return to origins but as a thoughtful development of the ideas presented. Development gives rise to the Mahayana and, in time, to Eastern Buddhism. Eastern Buddhism deserves a separate space because, Suzuki argues, its sects have differentiated so distinctly from their original Hindu types (note the plural) in the twenty centuries of its development under the East Asian genius.[28] The scheme, introduced in Suzuki's first essay on Zen and repeated in each of his writings, is spelled out completely in a lecture he gave soon after his return to Japan in 1911. "We know that the acorn is different from the oak, but as long as there is a continuation of growth their identity is a logical conclusion. To see really into the nature of the acorn is to trace an uninterrupted development through its historical stages. When the seed remains a seed and means nothing more, there is no life in it; it is a finished piece of work and, except as an object of historical curiosity, it has no value whatever in our religious experience."[29] Following Carus, Suzuki is not concerned with "Buddhism in its cradle" but with "Buddhism up to date," the living spiritual experience rather than the ancient texts.

Decentering the Canon

Suzuki's boldest challenge to Western assumptions appears in "The Zen Sect of Buddhism" (1906–7), provocatively placed in the *Journal of the Pali Text Society*, the flagship journal of Orientalist Theravada scholarship. By introducing Zen, Suzuki challenges the heart of Orientalist scholarship, circumventing the texts and the words of the Buddha entirely. In this article he presents an alternative system of legitimation through direct, face-to-face transmission from master to disciple, an unbroken lineage originating with Sakyamuni himself. Zen is the quintessential teaching of the Buddha, but for Zen, texts are beside the point. A detailed history of the transmission of Zen from Sakyamuni onward, patriarch by patriarch (pp. 9–18), establishes authenticity. A footnote on page 13 explains the importance of the lineage to anyone who might have missed the point.

Suzuki's stress on development, together with a guarantee of authenticity through the unbroken lineage of direct transmission, decentered the importance of the Founder and his very words that so obsessed Western scholars at the time and was used by them to dismiss Mahayana. Under the heading "Principles of Zen" are the subsections "Facts and Not Words" (p. 19) and "No Sūtras, No Books" (p. 20). Zen "does not find any intrinsic importance in the sacred sutras, or their exposition by the wise and learned" (p. 9), but insists "most emphatically" on inner spiritual development. Zen discourages "blind acceptance of an outside authority and a meek submission to conventionality"; Zen teaches life, individuality, and inspiration. It gives "perfect freedom to the self-unfolding of the mind within one's self, which was not to be obstructed by any artificial instruments of torture, such as worshiping the Buddha as a savior, a blind belief in the sacred books, or an unconditioned reliance upon an outside authority" (p. 21). The article concludes with a list of traditional texts that may be consulted for further information. Although "it is an avowed enemy of literature," Zen has produced many learned scholars (pp. 42–43). Textuality is repositioned rather than abandoned.

Positive, Energetic, Practical

Throughout the article Suzuki emphasizes the positive and energetic aspects of Zen ("Not Asceticism," "Zen and General Culture"); its adaptability and appeal to the practical mind; its "simplicity, directness, and efficiency." It flourished in Japan, we are told, because it was introduced at a time "noted for its able, military administration."[30] Zen is practical, active, and energetic, "the very antithesis of Oriental 'fatalism.' "[31] The section "Zen Discipline" describes *zazen* and offers meditation and mental discipline, speaking of their benefits beyond Buddhism, especially in "these days of industrial and commercial civilization" when many people have little time to devote themselves to spiritual culture.[32] As Tweed has shown, many Americans came to Buddhism in the late nineteenth and early twentieth centuries because—thanks largely to Paul Carus—they saw it as a positive, optimistic, active, and energetic alternative. Others came seeking spiritualism and mysticism, and still others came to it through an interest in Japanese art and culture. Suzuki's Zen offered much to attract interest in the West at that time.

Zen: The Essence of Eastern Buddhism

Although Eastern Buddhism is the result of twenty centuries of development of the Buddha's idea, Zen is unique within Eastern Buddhism, Suzuki argues, as the one sect peculiarly suited to the Far Eastern mind. Unlike the T'ien T'ai, Avatamsaka, the Mādkyamika, or the Yoga, which reflect the "elaborately speculative genius of the Hindus" (p. 32), Zen offers a simple and practical spirituality, suited to the down-to-earth Chinese mind.[33]

> When we come to Zen, after a survey of the general field of Buddhism, we are compelled to acknowledge that its simplicity, its directness, its pragmatic tendency, and its close connection with everyday life stand in remarkable contrast to the other Buddhist sects. Undoubtedly the main ideas of Zen are derived from Buddhism, and we cannot but consider it a legitimate development of the latter; but this development has been achieved in order to meet the requirements peculiarly characteristic of the psychology of the Far-Eastern people. Therefore I make bold to say that in Zen are found systematized, or rather crystallised, all the philosophy, religion, and life itself of the Far-Eastern people, especially of the Japanese.[34]

The ease with which Zen accommodated Confucianism and Taoism in China was also to its advantage, Suzuki argues. It is a sect so elastic, so comprehensive it could readily reconcile itself to the Chinese environment and, by extension, into any other environment. The idea that Zen is suited to the East Asian mind in general and the Japanese in particular, is repeated and elaborated in later works. Buddhism is the quickening spiritual force of the Far East (p. 32), but Zen is unique; it is Buddhism in a form particular to the needs of the Far Eastern mind. It is the basis of the life and culture of Japan. Paradoxically, however, the argument of East Asian particularity, based on Zen's simplicity, practicality, and flexibility, is also the seed of its universality.

In Suzuki's 1907 essay on Zen, it is uniquely Japanese, the basis of Japanese culture, and as the essence of Buddhism, both of it and beyond it. This decontextualized essence then, paradoxically, can develop into a transreligious, universal spirituality. In a continuity with the Chicago position, it is uniquely Japanese and hence a source of national pride, but of universal applicability, and therefore available to be Japan's contribution to the world. The delegation repackaged *shin bukkyō* as Eastern Buddhism and offered it as the universal religion of the future;

Suzuki—after an apprenticeship with Carus and years of engagement with the Western discourse on religion and science—made the further transition from Eastern Buddhism to Zen. Although they did not circulate widely at this time, the core ideas which were later to obtain popular currency were apparent at La Salle.

Buddhism, Zen, and Japanese Culture: The Hōōden Revisited

The idea that Buddhism (and even Zen) was the basis of Japanese civilization was neither new nor unique to Suzuki. It had been an essential part of *shin bukkyō*'s call for popular support. The delegation to Chicago emphasized the point, and it was given material form in the Hōōden, the Japanese Pavilion at the exposition (Chapter 1). When Suzuki wrote in 1907, the connection had been eloquently articulated and disseminated in Europe and America by Okakura Kakuzō—director of the art exhibition at Chicago—in his *Ideals of the East* (1903), *The Awakening of Japan* (1903–4), and *The Book of Tea* (1906), and in Nitobe Inazō's *Bushido: The Soul of Japan* (1906 in English, 1899 in Japanese). The enthusiastic reception of these books in the West extended the discursive context within which Suzuki's writings circulated.[35]

The first two of Okakura's books had been written while he was in India visiting Buddhist archaeological sites and staying at the house of the Tagore family, leaders of Hindu Renaissance and Indian cultural nationalism, where he had been introduced by the Irish-born disciple of Vivekananda, Sister Nivedita. The books were written with the explicit intent of stirring the youth of India to follow Japan's example in throwing off the "White Disaster," waking from "the colonial night of Asia." The "ideals" of the title are the shared Hindu-Buddhist ideals of Indian origin, which, when subjected to the Japanese genius, provided the basis of Japan's success.[36] The Kamakura, a time of military rule and bureaucratic achievement during which Zen took hold among the samurai, is central to the scheme of the book. It is the time when a distinctive *Japanese* form of Buddhism emerged. Okakura compares it with the European age of chivalry (p. 154), and likens the stories of its hero, Yoshitsune, to the tales of the Round Table, and his death to that of King Arthur (p. 157). But Japan's age of chivalry is merely preparation for the Ashikaga period, the Age of Bushidō, the way of the warrior, an age of chivalry and also of great artistic achievement, a time when the influence of Zen has brought Japanese culture to a point of even higher development. The result is a restatement of the message of the Hōōden: Japan was exquisitely civilized while Europe was still in the Dark Ages.[37] In this section of the book we find all the elements of the now familiar equation of Zen Buddhism with the essence of Japan, and the attribution of all the accomplishments of Japanese culture to the union of Zen and the warrior class (pp. 172–84 especially).

The point here is the way in which Okakura's contacts in Calcutta circulated the texts of Japanese Buddhist nationalism into new arenas. Nivedita had introduced Okakura to the Tagores as the "William Morris of Japan," linking him with Western critics of the Industrial Revolution and the materialistic society of the late nineteenth and early twentieth centuries. His books, written for an Indian audience, were popular in the West because of the mutually supportive concerns of Asian cultural nationalism and the ideas of Ruskin, Carlyle, and William Morris. He gave them the spiritual East, an idealized Age of Chivalry and refined aestheticism. Okakura's pan-Asian anti-imperialist writings served in this Western cause and in doing so bound Buddhism, particularly Zen, to warrior culture and to artistic achievement.[38]

As we have seen, when Suzuki wrote of Zen and Japanese culture in 1907, he wrote of the appeal of Zen to the samurai rulers to illustrate the positive, life-affirming aspects of Zen. It was a religion that appealed to men of action, to efficient administrators; it was life-affirming, the opposite of "Oriental fatalism." It appealed not just to the elites but to all levels of society. "Not only emperors, statesmen and generals came to see Zen masters, but also men of letters, artists, singers, actors, wrestlers, merchants, masters of tea ceremony, and swordsmen" (p. 34). The list is of practitioners, again emphasizing that Zen is active and practical. It is clear that Suzuki is aware that he is engaging with other writers here. He writes that, while Bushidō, "much talked of since the conclusion of the Russo-Japanese War," is "in fact, a production of . . . Shintōism, Confucianism and Buddhism," "no fair observer will deny that Zen had a great deal to do with the religious and spiritual aspects of Bushidō. For the *Lebensanschauung* of Bushidō is no more nor less than that of Zen."

The Changing Contexts of Buddhist Nationalism

When Inoue Enryō spoke of Japan as the repository of Asian culture, of Japan as leader of Asia, of Japan's duty to lead the battle of the yellow races against the white, his focus was essentially domestic; his project, the formation of a sense of national belonging based on allegiance to and pride in Buddhism. Hence the delegation to Chicago could be seen to be very largely an event for reinterpretation within the Japanese discourse. In contrast, by the early years of the twentieth century when Suzuki began his career, the discourse of nation was a matter of international projection, of negotiating the definition of the nation in relation to Asia and to the West. Japan's military successes, as well as its growing imperial presence and increased status in Asia, gave potential reality to rhetoric such as Inoue's. Aspiring Asian nationalists looking to emulate Japan's success came to study in Japan. Indians thrilled to Okakura's vision of "Buddhaland" in opposition to "Christendom." Filipinos saw Japan as what they sought to become, free from colonial rule, sovereign in their capacity to determine their own history.[39] In colonial domains as remote as Egypt Mustafa Kamil's book *The Rising Sun* (al-Shams al-mushriqua, 1904) stirred anti-imperial passion with the Meiji model.[40] Decades before the military appropriation of the idea, Japan was seen by some Asians at least as model and leader.

Military success also won Western esteem at this time. "As a gentle, peaceful, honest and honourable nation, Christians would have none of her except as a semi-contemptuous field for mission work," observed a writer in *Arena* (1894) soon after Japan's victory in the Sino-Japanese War, but "as a slayer, as a fighter, she has brought all Christian nations to her side with hats off, and a surprised: 'By Jove, she's great. She has won our respect. She must henceforth be reckoned with as a nation.' "[41] Respect increased when Japan protected Western interests in China during the Boxer uprising (1900–1901) leading to the signing of the Anglo-Japanese alliance (1902) and recognition of Japan's status as a major power.[42] Japan's new status was demonstrated most spectacularly in the defeat of Russia in 1905. For the first time an Asian nation had defeated a Western power.

There can be little surprise that writings of this period show a pride in Japan's military heritage.[43] Military success and Buddhist culture were explicitly, and proudly, linked by Shaku Sōen, who wrote that "it was impossible to explain Japan's string of military victories in terms of military equipment or logistics. This was not something that took place because of military prowess built up in Japan over a few decades . . . but was due to the samurai spirit, the Spirit of Japan, nurtured by the country over the past two thousand years."[44] *Sermons of a Buddhist Abbot* contained three short essays defending Japanese aggression in Manchuria,[45] as well as "Buddhism and Oriental Culture," which explained Buddhist equanimity in the face of death and sacrifice, the Bushidō spirit shown by the heroes in the recent war.

The pervasiveness of Bushidō at this time prompted Basil Hall Chamberlain, contemporary observer and longtime resident of Japan, to produce a pamphlet,

The Invention of a New Religion (1905), explaining to Westerners that this "high minded chivalry" was an entirely new phenomenon "fabricated out of whole cloth, chiefly for *foreign consumption*." There was no end of people ready to spread the "new religion of loyalty and patriotism," readily swallowed by Europeans and Americans in their enthusiasm for the marvelous and for Japan, "a land of fabulous antiquity and incredible virtues." Although Japan did have its valiant heroes as all nations have, he wrote, "*the very word [*"Bushidō"*] appears in no dictionary, native or foreign, before the year 1900*."[46] In terms of creating Western understanding of modern Japan, Chamberlain's concern was well founded.

The connection between Zen, art, and Bushidō is elaborated in *The Book of Tea*, the one book that Okakura specifically directed to the West. Written after the Russo-Japanese War to foster international respect based on cultural achievement rather than success at war, the preface tells us, it introduced Zen and its influence on Japanese aesthetics as displayed through various aspects of tea-related arts. It concludes with a romanticized account of the final tea and death by *seppuku* of the sixteenth-century tea master Sen no Rikyū, the point of which is to show the composure and awareness of beauty of a *chajin* even in moments of extremity. "The last moments of the great tea-masters were as full of exquisite refinement as had been their lives." *The Book of Tea* remains in print to the present and has had enormous influence on Western understanding of Japan, leading many to an appreciation of Japanese aesthetics and serious study of tea and Zen. It was, nevertheless, self-Orientalizing, projecting an image of Japanese cultural practice long past as the essence of the present. When General Nogi Maresuke followed the emperor Meiji in death by committing ritual suicide on September 13, 1912, Japanese were shocked by what was to them such an archaic, anachronistic act. In the West, remote from the reality of Japan, it merely confirmed what people had so recently read.[47]

The transition from Eastern Buddhism to Zen as the repackaged version of *shin bukkyō* for Western consumption occurred with Nukariya Kaiten's *Religion of the Samurai* in 1913. It developed ideas such as those expressed in Suzuki's 1907 essay and appropriated for Zen—the religion of the samurai—Eastern Buddhism's claims to universality and its uniqueness to Japan.[48] Nukariya equated Zen with *shin bukkyō* and, in an echo of Inoue Enryō's plea, offered it as the ideal doctrine for "the rising generation." He advocated Bushidō as the code of conduct for all citizens in their struggle for existence. Zen was the essence of Eastern Buddhism, "the very heart of Asian spirituality, the essence of Japanese culture, and key to the unique features of the Japanese race." Japan remained the exclusive repository of this transnational truth. Zen was both universal and uniquely Japanese.

Suzuki offers similar ideas in his extremely influential book *Zen and Japanese Culture*, but this belongs to later times, and other stages of Japan's relations with Asia and the West.[49] In *Eastern Buddhist* (1921) we see the more cautious statement that Buddhism in general is the basis of the arts in Japan, the basis of Japanese intellectuality. Echoing Inoue Enryō, Suzuki suggested that the training in Buddhist thought over the centuries was "one of the chief reasons the Japanese were readily able to assimilate the highest flights of Western intellect."[50]

The Eastern Buddhist Society

Suzuki's English-language writings on Zen did not have wide circulation until *Essays in Zen Buddhism* appeared in 1927, and the reprint of the essays written for *New East* as *Introduction to Zen Buddhism* in 1934. Meanwhile, his work of promoting knowledge of Mahayana, including Zen, continued with the founding of the Eastern Buddhist Society, an emphatically nonsectarian Mahayana counterpart to the Pali Text Society. It fostered study of Buddhism and translations of primary sources into Japanese and European languages. It would support and propagate and legitimate scholarship on Mahayana in the way that the Pali Text Society had so admirably done for Theravada. Its aim was to bring knowledge of Japanese Buddhism to the West; to address Western ignorance and misunderstanding of the Mahayana; to publish in both English and Japanese, "raising the beacon of Buddhism in the West"; and to make knowledge of Buddhism accessible to the Japanese general public.[51] The subscription rates for England, France, India, and the United States on the cover of the society's journal signal its transnational vision.

Eastern Buddhist stressed the fact that Buddhism is a living religion in Japan and that Buddhist scholarship in Japan remains active. It reported on scholarly activities and reviewed (in English) recent Japanese publications. *Eastern Buddhist* exemplified the Chicago message: only in Japan do we still have the texts and the people who understand them and write new ones.[52] It chronicled the public vitality of Buddhism in Japan, noting major public celebrations, events, and debates. A regular frontispiece introduced a major artwork illustrating Buddhism's long, active, and culturally rich history in Japan. Much of the work that circulated in later publications first appeared in the pages of the journal.

Throughout his career Suzuki wrote prolifically on Mahayana Buddhism, particularly on Pure Land schools and on Zen, the sect of his own practice. It was Zen, however, that caught popular attention, accepted, as the Western Theravada construct had been, because of its perceived relevance to Western concerns. As Sharf observes, the single most attractive feature of Zen was the idea of "direct experience," which he sees as a Japanese appropriation of the idea of "religious experience" emphasized in the work of scholars such as Friedrich Schleirmacher, Rudolf Otto, Joachim Wach, and William James.[53] This "direct experience," touted as characteristic of Eastern spirituality in general and Zen in particular, appealed to Westerners seeking alternatives to their own seemingly moribund religious institutions.[54] Robert King sees Suzuki's Zen as an ideal Asian export to the spiritually inclined Westerner searching for an exotic alternative to institutional Christianity, a "classic example of the universality of 'mysticism,' increasingly conceived of as the common core of the various 'world religions.' Suzuki's Zen thus functioned as the archetypal Japanese example of the perennial philosophy for Theosophists and scholars of mysticism alike."[55] Decontextualized from Buddhism, Zen could also be seen as a spiritual technology, something that could be adopted as an adjunct to Christian practice. In his preface to the 1963 reprint of Suzuki's *Outlines of Mahāyāna Buddhism*, Alan Watts would write: "Although Dr. Suzuki speaks here of Buddhism as a religion, this is only in the most vague and general sense of the term. . . . The real concerns of Buddhism are closer to psychology, or even to something such as ophthalmology, than to the differing systems of belief which we recognize in the west as adopting a religion. . . . It is so thoroughly experimental and empirical that the subject-matter of Buddhism must be said to be an immediate, non-verbal experience rather than a set of beliefs or ideas or rules of behaviour."[56] Buddhism here (not even Zen in particular) is scientific, transreligious, universal. The impact of Suzuki's Zen owes much to interpreters like Watts and Hugo Munsterberg,[57] whose own works depend on it, and its diffusion through the literary works of Jack Kerouac, Allen Ginsberg, Gary Snyder, and others of their generation.[58]

As I wrote at the start of the chapter, my aim was to foreground the work that has been done on Japanese Buddhism in the West. I mention Sharf and King here because their work shows a persistence of certain patterns discussed already. The most important of these are the political dimensions of the discourse, interaction between East and West, the deployment of Western scholarship for intrinsically Japanese purposes, and the Western Orientalist gaze that continued to see only those aspects of the representations of Japanese Buddhism that were relevant to its present preoccupations. The result has been that Zen, represented in Japanese nationalist strategies as the essence of Japaneseness, has been accepted in the West as the "full and unmediated experience of life itself untainted by cultural accretions . . . the ultimate source of all religious teaching, both Eastern and Western . . . no more Buddhist than it is Christian, Jewish or Muslim."[59] Eastern Buddhism, essentialized in Zen, is now respected, accepted, and practiced around the world. Japan has over time derived cultural kudos by taking Eastern Buddhism to the West, but with little consequence for general Western knowledge of the nature and variety of Buddhism in Japan.

Orientalism, Occidentalism, and Eastern Buddhism

I have argued that the Buddhist delegation to Chicago was a nationalist initiative, promoting *shin bukkyō* as the basis of Japan's modern identity by attaining apparent Western validation for its claim to be the universal religion of the future. The delegation did not succeed in winning Western regard for Japanese Buddhism at that time. Mahayana Buddhism remained excluded from academic consideration. This, however, did not detract from the importance of the event as a strategy in the Japanese discourse. The delegation itself, Japanese inclusion and participation in the international conference at Chicago, was an event that could be interpreted to the Japanese audience to support Buddhist revival.

The Japanese Buddhists were not alone in using the Parliament this way. Histories of nationalist movements in nineteenth-century India show the successful deployment of the Western reception of Vivekananda's Hinduism. Less apparent, probably because it was the continuation of a long-established tradition and challenged none of the presuppositions of readers, was the deployment of Christian success at the Parliament in Barrows's books, the two-volume official history as well as his later works, *The Christian Conquest of Asia* and *Christianity: The World Religion*. The Japanese, Hindus of India, and Barrows all demonstrated the familiar process of "Orientalism," of defining themselves by reference to a construct of remote reality. In the case of Japan and India, a more appropriate term might perhaps be "Occidentalism," since the West, rather than the East, was the external resource.

The parallel between Orientalism and Occidentalism was, however, not complete. The "West," as the Japanese used the term, was as amorphous as the "East" is in English and operated in precisely the same way to signify an alterity. *Seiyō* or *ōbei* defined by contrast the Japanese *wa* (us) and was used within the Japanese discourse of this time with equal lack of concern for the reality of this other. The important difference, however, was the reality of Western dominance in the relationship and the function of the West in Meiji Japan as both model and judge of achievement. Consequently, even in the 1890s, at a time of intense reaction against Westernization, Western authority was deployed to promote Buddhism as a source of intrinsically Japanese identity. The development and promotion of *shin bukkyō* illustrated some of the various functions the West was put to in Meiji discourse.

Shin bukkyō owed a great deal to the West. Buddhist scholars adopted the methods of Western academic scholarship, using them to define modern Japanese Buddhism and to present it in a form acceptable to Western-educated Japanese. The West also provided models for the function of religion in society. The YMBA must be recognized as the domestication of the Protestant Christian institution. A similar influence is evident in the formation of lay Buddhist organizations; in the movement to provide direct personal access to the teachings of Buddhism through specially prepared introductory tracts; and in the emphasis on philanthropic works, such as the foundation of hospitals and pastoral work in prisons. However, the delegation to Chicago shows the West put to a different function. The West was neither a source of knowledge nor an example, but a source of legitimation.

From this point of view, taking Eastern Buddhism to Chicago was one in a series of events in the revitalization of Buddhism, linked by their reference to Western authority. The first was the Japanese tour of Colonel Olcott. In spite of the fact that his Japanese hosts were fully aware of the deficiencies of his understanding of Buddhism, they presented him as living evidence of reform claims that Western intellectuals and men of science were dissatisfied with Christianity and turning to Buddhism. Reform Buddhists paraded Olcott around rural Japan, having him speak the messages of Buddhist reform through his translators, creating opportunities for press coverage that diffused the message further still. Similar processes can be seen at work in Shaku Sōen's Japanese publication of Carus's *Gospel*. What links these events is their recourse to a Western authority—even a dubious one—to validate things Japanese. In these cases, the West was not copied, borrowed from, or domesticated. The West was neither exemplar nor source of inspiration. Its only function was to appear to endorse Japanese Buddhism, and even the reality of this was beside the point.

One problem in this "Occidentalist" process, however, was the lack of separation between the Japanese nationalist and the Western Orientalist discourse on

Buddhism. Discursive statements, once put into circulation, are subject to interpretation, available to be put to other uses. Hence, in Olcott's Western publications, his tour of Japan became a personal triumph, and he became one who brought the light of the East back to the benighted Japanese. Carus similarly reinterpreted his Japanese exposure to his own credit. The apparent approval of Japanese Buddhists in promoting these men as champions of Buddhism in Japan was used to give their enunciations on Buddhism an authority they would not otherwise have been granted. Because both these authors referred their readings of Buddhism to the Pali texts, the net effect of the Japanese Buddhist strategy was to reinforce the existing Western Orientalist construct of Buddhism. A statement made to Buddhist reform advantage in the Japanese discourse was turned against it in the West.

The attempt by Buddhist delegates at the World's Parliament of Religions to appropriate and deploy the Western construct of Buddhism had a similar result. The Buddhist delegates were excluded by the prevailing rules of truth, which gave priority to the written texts of "original" Buddhism over the voices of contemporary practitioners. What they said was only "true" when it endorsed what was already accepted. It was otherwise rejected as the modern, popular practice of "so-called Buddhists."

This does not, however, imply that there was unanimity of Western opinion on the nature of Buddhism. Theosophists, missionaries, transcendentalists, positivists, and others each continued to see Buddhism differently. The reception of Buddhism here followed the pattern evident in the American representation of material culture in the Hōōden. In a continuation of the basic principle of Orientalism, the representation of Japanese Buddhism at Chicago—like the representation of Japanese art and architecture—was appreciated to the extent that it fitted with a current American vogue. Carus's appropriation of Buddhism in the cause of his post-Kantian, Christian monism was only the most clearly articulated exercise of this kind. Missionaries clung to their vision of the nihilist foe. Others admired Buddhism, as Lafcadio Hearn observed, because of the delight of discovering it contained "the very thoughts of Emerson."[60] How significant is it that Ashitsu's paper that had suggested the links between Japanese Buddhism and philosophic idealism was translated into German, and that Catholic France—where Toki Hōryū spent some time on his return from Chicago—published the first account of Shingon ritual?[61] This selective acceptance was no doubt encouraged by the Japanese attempt to present those aspects of Eastern Buddhism they expected would meet European interests, making Eastern Buddhism accessible to Western readers. Suzuki's success as interpreter of Mahayana Buddhism to the West supports this.

Although Japanese Buddhism has been a strong and growing presence in America since the 1950s, the most significant immediate impact of the delegation on its Western audience may not have been in conveying knowledge of the Mahayana teachings but in its contribution to the wider Japanese project at the exposition, the campaign to establish that Japan was a civilized nation, so closely tied to the concurrent diplomatic campaign for treaty revision. Seager writes that the Parliament provided the first contact that many Americans had had with educated Asians. They were impressed by the obvious intelligence, erudition, commitment, and sincerity of the delegates. Seager's point is that their civilized demeanor undermined preexisting assumptions about the "heathen" and made it possible to take non-Christian religions seriously. For all its deficiencies as a source of knowledge of Buddhism, Carus's *Gospel of Buddha* must also be credited for contributing to this process of making Buddhism approachable. Although the delegation had expected to achieve this through Buddhist philosophy, one of its aims was realized. As Seager argues, this also had profound repercussions for the United States. The favorable impression created by the Asian delegates was important in effecting the transition from the nineteenth-century American ideal of religious assimilation to the pluralism of the twentieth century. The Parliament, Seager continues, "marked the formal debut of Asian religions into the mainstream of American religious life."[62] Dharmapāla, Shaku Sōen, and Vivekananda all made subsequent lecture tours of the United States. This had repercussions not just for American religious awareness but for the continuing projection of the various Asian nationalist projects, most apparent in the Indian nationalist deployment of Vivekananda's Vedānta Societies in America.[63]

The delegates had been realistic in their expectations. As the *Manifesto* explained, they did not expect immediate benefits from sending a few people to a conference but hoped only to lay foundations for future progress, and from this perspective they were successful. The term "Eastern Buddhism" is now in general use, and if Mircea Eliade's work *From Primitives to Zen* can be taken as representative of comparative studies in religion, Zen, if not Japanese Buddhism as such, had, by the mid-1960s, won a place at the pinnacle of religious evolution. Interest in Mahayana Buddhism now far outstrips that in the Theravada at both popular and scholarly levels. Although it may not be anything the delegates would recognize, Eastern Buddhism—as Zen—is now sufficiently well established in the West to have produced new cultural forms[64] and transmitted its lineages abroad.[65] By the time of the centenary of the World's Parliament of Religions, Shingon, Tendai, and Pure Land schools had a growing presence.

NOTES

ABBREVIATIONS

BKJ	Inoue Enryō. *Bukkyō katsuron joron* (Introduction to revitalizing Buddhism). Tokyo: Tetsugaku shoin, 1887. Reproduced in *Meiji bunka zenshū*, vol. 9, *Shūkyō*, 377–416. Tokyo: Tōyō University, 1954. Translated in Kathleen M. Staggs, "In Defence of Japanese Buddhism: Essays from the Meiji Period by Inoue Enryō and Murakami Senshō," 350–458. Ph.D. diss., Princeton University, 1979. Page references are to this version.
Fukuin	*Budda no fukuin*. Translated by D. T. Suzuki. Preface by Shaku Sōen. Tokyo, January 1895. 2d ed., 1901. Translated from Paul Carus, *The Gospel of Buddha*. Chicago: Open Court, 1894. The 1901 edition is reprinted in *Suzuki Daisetsu zenshū* (The complete works of Suzuki Daisetsu), vol. 25. Tokyo: Iwanami Shoten, 1970. Page references are to this version.
JEBD	*Japanese-English Buddhist Dictionary*. Tokyo: Daitō shuppansha, 1965.
Manifesto	"*Bankoku shūkyō dai kai gi ni tsuite kaku shū kyō kai ni nozomu*. A Request to the All Sects Council concerning the World's Parliament of Religions." *Shūkyō*, April 5, 1893, 297. This document was an open letter from "Concerned Buddhists" calling for support of the delegation.
ODL	Henry Steel Olcott. *Old Diary Leaves*. 6 vols. Adyar: Theosophical Publishing House, 1972.
WPR	John Henry Barrows, ed. *The World's Parliament of Religions*. 2 vols. Chicago: Parliament Publishing, 1893.

INTRODUCTION

1. Rydell, *All the World's a Fair*.

2. *Manifesto*, 297.

3. The published record includes a paper by a Nichiren representative, Kawai Yoshigiro, but he was not part of the delegation. His claim that he alone represented the Buddhism of Japan failed to impress the organizers.

4. The one representative of Shintō was Shibata Reiichi, president of the recently founded independent Jikkō sect.

5. Said, *Orientalism*.

6. Clausen, "Victorian Buddhism and the Origins of Comparative Religion"; Brear, "Early Assumptions in Western Buddhist Studies."

7. Wilson, "On Buddha and Buddhism," 235, referring specifically to Spence Hardy's two books, *Manual of Buddhism* (1853) and *Eastern Monachism* (1850). The political implications of Hardy's interpretation are discussed in Chapter 4.

8. Foucault, "Two Lectures," 99.

9. Shaku Sōen's second paper, "Arbitration Instead of War," remains contentious. See Aitken, "Three Lessons from Shaku Sōen." Typical of the narrative histories of Zen in the West are Fields, *How the Swans Came to the Lake*; Bandō, "D. T. Suzuki's Life in La Salle"; Fader, "Zen in the West." A publication with a wider perspective is Kitagawa, *The 1893 World's Parliament of Religions and Its Legacy*. It nevertheless shares the characteristic focus on Shaku Sōen.

10. This tendency persists, no doubt because of the importance of Zen in the West. McRae, "Oriental Verities on the American Frontier," reassesses the event as North America's first serious contact with Eastern religion, with due consideration for the exposition context of the Parliament and the Protestant Christian parameters within which the delegates spoke. His observation on the representation of Japanese Buddhism nevertheless perpetuates the emphasis on Shaku Sōen and the assumption that he was there to transmit Zen.

11. Ketelaar, *Of Heretics and Martyrs*, and "Strategic Occidentalism."

12. See McMullin's cogent criticism of this attitude in "Historical and Historiographical Issues in the Study of Pre-Modern Japanese Religions," 30–31.

13. Ibid., 22.

14. Ibid., quoting Bourdieu, *Outline of a Theory of Practice*, 1.

15. McMullin, *Buddhism and the State in Sixteenth Century Japan*; Ooms, *Tokugawa Ideology*; Collcutt, *Five Mountains*.

16. Grapard, "Japan's Ignored Cultural Revolution," points to previous neglect of Buddhism in history, citing, for example, W. G. Beasley's work on the Meiji Restoration (240). See also Collcutt, "Buddhism: The Threat of Eradication"; Thelle, *Buddhism and Christianity in Japan*; Ketelaar, *Of Heretics and Martyrs*; Jaffe, *Neither Monk nor Layman*.

17. Staggs, "In Defence of Japanese Buddhism." In her introduction Staggs complains of the total neglect of Meiji Buddhism even among Japanese scholars. They found her interest in it curious. See also her article " 'Defend the Nation and Love the Truth.' "

18. Thelle, *Buddhism and Christianity in Japan*, 219–20.

19. I am indebted to Richard Hughes Seager's work on the World's Parliament of Religions for insights into the place of the Parliament in American intellectual and religious history. He describes the problems faced by the Asian delegates in challenging the Christian presuppositions of the Parliament, its pervading racism, and the controversies over whether the fundamental American ideal of the freedom of religion implied the right of non-Christians to persist in error or their right to have free and equal claim to religious truth. The presence of representatives of non-Christian religions at the Parliament played a vital part in this debate. I first read his work in its thesis version, "The World's Parliament of Religions, Chicago, Illinois, 1893: America's Religious Coming of Age." He has since published *The Dawn of Religious Pluralism: Voices from the World's Parliament of Religions* and *The World's Parliament of Religions: The East/West Encounter, Chicago, 1893*.

20. The study began as a doctoral thesis in history at the University of Sydney: "The Representation of Japanese Buddhism at the World's Parliament of Religions, Chicago, 1893" (1994).

CHAPTER 1

1. Rydell, *All the World's a Fair*, discusses this aspect of the Chicago exposition in detail.

2. The complex issue of treaty renewal is discussed in Perez, "Mutsu Munemitsu and the Revision of the 'Unequal' Treaties"; Sandra Davis, "Treaty Revision, National Security and Regional Co-operation." For attitudes to the treaties in the early Meiji period, particularly the realization of the association between "civilization" and revision, see Mayo, "The Iwakura Embassy and the Unequal Treaties." Perez documents the attempts at revision and in particular the determination with which Mutsu Munemitsu, the minister in charge of the Chicago exhibition, pursued the issue, resulting in his eventual success in 1894.

3. Mayo, "The Iwakura Embassy and the Unequal Treaties," 9.

4. Perez, "Mutsu Munemitsu and the Revision of the 'Unequal' Treaties," 161. The groundbreaking ceremony for the Trans-Siberian railway, which would give Russia rapid access to China and Korea, took place in 1891.

5. Ibid., 115. This was the ostensible reason, but comparison with the "white mutiny" in reaction to the Ilbert Bill in India, 1883, which attempted to remove the British exemption from appearing before British-trained Indian judges administering British law, suggests that a racist reluctance of Westerners to be judged by nonwhites may also apply here. See Hirschmann, *White Mutiny*.

6. Mayo, "The Iwakura Embassy and the Unequal Treaties," 10.

7. Perez, "Mutsu Munemitsu and the Revision of the 'Unequal' Treaties," 115–19.

8. Tateno, "Foreign Nations at the World's Fair: Japan," 42.

9. McCabe, *The Centennial Exhibition*, 446, quoted in Neil Harris, "All the World's a Melting Pot?," 30.

10. Ibid., 46.

11. Tateno, "Foreign Nations at the World's Fair: Japan," 34 and 43.

12. Ibid., 43.

13. Perez, "Mutsu Munemitsu and the Revision of the 'Unequal' Treaties," xi.

14. Mutsu Munemitsu, *Kenkenroku*, ch. 9, "The Korean Affair and Treaty Revision in Great Britain." Also Perez, "Mutsu Munemitsu and the Revision of the 'Unequal' Treaties," 135–40. For an interesting account of Japanese Foreign Office manipulation of the foreign press, see Valliant, "The Selling of Japan."

15. Tateno, "Foreign Nations at the World's Fair: Japan," 36.

16. See, for example, "The Educational and Moral Value of the Exposition," in Rossiter Johnson, *A History of the World's Columbian Exposition*, vol. 4, ch. 13.

17. See Rydell, *All the World's a Fair*, for the part played by world fairs, and particularly the Chicago fair, in disseminating and popularizing evolutionary ideas about race and progress.

18. Snider, *World's Fair Studies*, 238, 237, and 255 respectively.

19. Ibid., 256–57.

20. From a newspaper report on the Japanese exhibit at Philadelphia, quoted in Neil Harris, "All the World's a Melting Pot?," 36.

21. The Japanese term *ōbei*, commonly used at this time to designate "the West," literally denotes Europe and America.

22. Originally planned for 1892, the opening was delayed by competition between rivals for the right to host the fair.

23. Gates, "The Significance to Christianity," 39. Gates's book—an exposition of the Protes-

tant doctrine of America's divine mission, its obligation to proselytize, and the unfolding of Providential history—is discussed in the following chapter.

24. Ibid., 40–44.

25. Sanford, *Manifest Destiny and the Imperialism Question*, 5.

26. John L. O'Sullivan, 1839, quoted in ibid., 93. O'Sullivan coined the term "Manifest Destiny" in 1845, but as Sandford points out, the ideology was present from the early colonial period, originally as a justification for continental expansion, but logically extended across the Pacific in later years. O'Sullivan's vision of the hemisphere is more expansive than continental.

27. Theodore Roosevelt, 1902, quoted in ibid., 94.

28. *New York Independent*, quoted in the *Japan Weekly Mail*, July 15, 1893, 67–68.

29. Commodore Mathew Perry, letter to the Secretary of the Navy, December 14, 1852, quoted in Hawks, *Narrative*, 12.

30. Quoted in *WPR*, 1071–72.

31. Sanford, *Manifest Destiny and the Imperialism Question*, 7–8.

32. Commodore Mathew Perry, letter to the Secretary of the Navy, December 14, 1852, quoted in Hawks, *Narrative*, 11.

33. Letter from the Secretary of the Navy to Commodore Perry, February 15, 1853, quoted in ibid., 12.

34. Professor Ephraim D. Adams, 1913, quoted in Sanford, *Manifest Destiny and the Imperialism Question*, 7.

35. Ibid., 2.

36. Seager, "The World's Parliament of Religions, Chicago, Illinois, 1893," 12 and 18. See also ibid., 47–50, and Rydell, *All the World's a Fair*, on the exclusion of nonwhites from the representation of the United States at the Chicago Exposition. Burg, *Chicago's White City of 1893*, discusses the significance of the Columbian Exposition in American history. See Trachtenberg, *The Incorporation of America*, for information on the social unrest of the period.

37. Cutler, *The World's Fair*, 532.

38. Burg, *Chicago's White City of 1893*, 92.

39. Ibid., 97.

40. Snider, *World's Fair Studies*, 37.

41. Ibid., 18.

42. Ibid., 19.

43. Ibid., 16–17.

44. Ibid., 12.

45. Ibid., 30.

46. Ibid., 35.

47. Ibid., 95–97.

48. Ibid.

49. Fenollosa, "Contemporary Japanese Art," 580.

50. Ibid. The modernity of the work is particularly apparent in the paintings reproduced in the catalog of an exhibition held at the Tokyo National Museum, April 3–May 11, 1997: *World's Columbian Exposition of 1893 Revisited*.

51. Okakura Kakuzō, "The Hō-ō-den: An Illustrated Description of the Buildings Erected by the Japanese Government at the World's Columbian Exposition, Jackson Park, Chicago" (Tokyo, 1893), reprinted in *Okakura Kakuzō: Collected English Writings*, 2:5–29.

52. Ibid., 8.

53. Ibid., 1:82 (emphasis in original).

54. Ibid., 12.

55. Ibid., 13.

56. Ibid., 14.

57. Ibid., 8.

58. Ibid., 6.

59. Ibid., 16.

60. Ibid.

61. *Japan Weekly Mail*, January 30, 1892.

62. Lancaster, *The Japanese Influence in America*, 77.

63. Byōdōin was originally a villa of Fujiwara no Michinaga, A.D. 966–1024. It became a monastery in 1052. The main building, the Hōōdō, was built in 1053.

64. Rossiter Johnson, *A History of the World's Columbian Exposition*, 1:42.

65. *Japan Weekly Mail*, January 30, 1892.

66. Ibid. The agreement was honored by the Japanese. The buildings and gardens were completely refurbished in 1935 and survived until 1946. For fifty years they provided inspiration for American architects and designers. See Lancaster, *The Japanese Influence in America*.

67. Rydell, *All the World's a Fair*, 40–71.

68. Rossiter Johnson, *A History of the World's Columbian Exposition*, 1:75.

69. Tateno, "Foreign Nations at the World's Fair: Japan," 41.

70. Rydell, *All the World's a Fair*, 50.

71. Snider, *World's Fair Studies*, 350–56.

72. Ibid., 220–31.

73. *Japan Weekly Mail*, May 6, 1893, 545. This was the fortieth anniversary for Japanese, who count the years from 1 rather than 0.

74. Ibid., 535.

75. Ibid.

76. Snider, *World's Fair Studies*, 229.

77. Ibid., 231.

78. Ibid., 230.

79. Ibid., 229.

80. Ibid.

81. Ibid., 145. This was, of course, precisely the kind of appreciation that the Japanese did not want. It particularly irked those progressive, Western-educated Japanese who wanted to be praised not as "pretty weaklings" but for the country's achievements in transport and industry.

82. Lancaster, *The Japanese Influence in America*, 83.

83. Neil Harris, "All the World's a Melting Pot?," 32–33.

84. *Japan Weekly Mail*, March 4, 1893.

85. *Japan Weekly Mail*, August 26, 1893.

86. Neil Harris, "All the World's a Melting Pot?," 40.

87. See *Japan Weekly Mail*, April 15, 1893. The theme for the design was a justification of Japanese expansion into Korea: Japan in symbolic union with the United States, defending Korea against the swooping eagle of Russia, bringing it out of the chill of China's dying power into the springtime of Japanese protection.

88. See, for example, the reconstruction of Toyotomi Hideyoshi's portable tea room in Varley and Kumakura, *Tea in Japan*. The room itself and all utensils in it are metallic gold. Hideyoshi's great tea master, Sen no Rikyū, credited with the formalization of the *wabi* aesthetic, presumably also performed chanoyu in this environment.

89. For a description of Azuchi castle and its paintings, see Wheelwright, "A Visualization of Eitoku's Lost Paintings at Azuchi Castle."

90. *Pacific Friend* 19:11 (March 1992): 19.

91. Ibid., 21.

92. Ibid.

93. Mutsu, *Kenkenroku*, 74–76.

94. Ibid., 74.

CHAPTER 2

1. Snider, *World's Fair Studies*, 33.

2. Gates was president of Amherst College, and this was the opening address of the Congress of the Evangelical Alliance, held in connection with the Auxiliary Congresses.

3. Gates described this process under headings such as "What Race Shall Rule the Continent?" "French Repression vs. English Self-Reliance," "The Very Best Blood of England," "The Best of England's Ideas," "Liberty Loving Hollanders," etc., in Gates, "The Significance to Christianity," 40–41.

4. Ibid., 41.

5. Houghton, *Neely's History*, 15, quoting Charles C. Bonney. For contemporary records of the Auxiliary Congresses, see also Rossiter Johnson, *A History of the World's Columbian Exposition*; *WPR*; and Bonney, "The World's Parliament of Religions." For a most thorough and comprehensive study of the Parliament and its significance for late nineteenth-century America, see Seager's two books, *The Dawn of Religious Pluralism* and *The World's Parliament of Religions*.

6. Trachtenberg, *The Incorporation of America*, 213. Contemporary records of the exposition contain vast quantities of self-confident and self-congratulatory descriptions of the genius of the concept and the importance of the congresses. Trachtenberg and also Burg, *Chicago's White City of 1893*, analyze their significance in American history.

7. Seager, *The World's Parliament of Religions*, 10.

8. Gates, "The Significance to Christianity," 55.

9. The chairman of the advisory committee responsible for this transformation of scope, and subsequently chairman of the Parliament itself, and editor of its official record, the Reverend John Henry Barrows, published two books on this theme: *Christianity: The World Religion* and *The Christian Conquest of Asia*.

10. Rossiter Johnson, *A History of the World's Columbian Exposition*, 4:2.

11. Ibid.

12. Quoted in Wherry, *Missions at Home and Abroad*, 7. Such sentiments were repeated frequently.

13. *WPR*, 126.

14. Rossiter Johnson, *A History of the World's Columbian Exposition*, 4:12. Bonney's chronological frame conveyed the accelerated pace of evolution and also articulated the idea of the United States rising from the European Renaissance graphically depicted in the Dome of Columbus (fig. 1).

15. Ibid.

16. See particularly "Harmonies and Distinctions in the Theistic Teaching of the Various Historic Faiths" by Professor M. Valentine, in *WPR*, 280–89. Valentine discussed Buddhism precisely as imperfect Christianity. He judged all religions against the ideals of Christianity,

justifying his comparative approach by the need for standards against which to measure. He measured the worth of the various beliefs against their answers to the questions, Is there a monotheistic idea of God? Is it a personal God? Is he the Creator? Is he a moral governor?

17. Seager, "The World's Parliament of Religions, Chicago, Illinois, 1893," iv–v.

18. Bonney, opening the Congress of Women. See also Rossiter Johnson, *A History of the World's Columbian Exposition*, 4:8.

19. Seager, "The World's Parliament of Religions, Chicago, Illinois, 1893," 5.

20. Ibid., 12.

21. Ibid., 39.

22. This particular quotation is from *WPR*, 43, but these images recur frequently.

23. Rev. Alex McKenzie (Puritan), in ibid., 85.

24. In Wherry, *Missions at Home and Abroad*, 81. The publication is subtitled *Papers and Addresses Presented at the World's Congress of Missions, October 2–4, 1893*.

25. Seager, "The World's Parliament of Religions, Chicago, Illinois, 1893," 7.

26. Bonney, "The World's Parliament of Religions," 325–26, gives the list of his proposals. See also Rossiter Johnson, *A History of the World's Columbian Exposition*, vol. 4, which is devoted to the various congresses; *WPR*, 221–337.

27. Bonney, "The World's Parliament of Religions," 326.

28. *Manifesto*, 295.

29. See Chapter 4. Barthélemy Saint-Hilaire's *The Buddha and His Religion* exemplifies this position.

30. The committee members were Rev. John Henry Barrows, D.D., Chairman (Presbyterian); Rev. Prof. David Swing, Vice Chairman (Independent); Archbishop P. A. Feehan (Catholic); Rt. Rev. Bishop William E. McLaren, D.D., D.C.L. (Protestant Episcopal); Rev. Dr. F. A. Noble (Congregationalist); Rev. Dr. William M. Lawrence (Baptist); Rev. Dr. F. M. Bristol (Methodist); Rabbi E. G. Hirsch (Jewish); Rev. Dr. A. J. Canfield (Universalist); Rev. Jenkin Lloyd Jones (Unitarian); Rt. Rev. Bishop C. E. Cheney (Reformed Episcopal); Rev. M. C. Ranseen (Swedish Lutheran); Rev. John Z. Torgersen (Norwegian Lutheran); Rev. J. Berger (German Methodist); Mr. J. W. Plummer (Quaker); Rev. L. P. Mercer (Swedenborgian). Bonney, "The World's Parliament of Religions," 327.

31. As noted elsewhere, his official publication is still taken at face value as a true record of proceedings in spite of its heavy editing and biased selection of material.

32. "Objects of the Parliament" listed in the official invitation, reproduced in Bonney, "The World's Parliament of Religions," 330–31, and in *WPR*, 18.

33. Barrows, *Christianity: The World Religion*, 297.

34. The Anglican archbishop of Canterbury refused to participate, but his letter setting out his objections to the idea was published in the official record complete with a response from an American theologian. He was thereby made a participant in the discussion, focusing attention on the central issues of the relations between the various denominations within Christianity, and the "right to be" of non-Christian religions and their relationship to "the one religion." *WPR*, 21–23. Little seems to have changed. At the 1993 centenary reconvening of the event, the Greek Orthodox delegates withdrew in reaction to "the distinctive participation of certain quasi-religious groups with which orthodox Christians share no religious ground." The article specifically mentions groups that "pray to ancestors and a pantheon of gods," *Washington Post*, September 4, 1993.

35. Bonney, "The World's Parliament of Religions," 331.

36. *WPR*, 1581.

37. *WPR*, 326.

38. *WPR*, 44.

39. Rev. Robert A. Hume, D.D., "Universal Christianity," appendix to Barrows, *Christianity: The World Religion*, 332.

40. Rossiter Johnson, *A History of the World's Columbian Exposition*, ch. 13, "The Educational and Moral Value of the Exposition."

41. Hume, "Universal Christianity," 332.

42. *WPR*, 113. Compare Bonney's scientific metaphor: "[A]s the light is differently received by different objects, so the light of divine revelation is differently received by different minds."

43. Hume, "Universal Christianity," 332. This comment occurs after a long passage describing the technological exhibitions in much the same terms as I have quoted from Johnson, glorying in the fact that the technology of Western countries was vastly superior to that of South American and Pacific Island countries. His expression "in the same way" refers to the comparative method of display.

44. Manilal Mahbubhai D'Vivedi, B.A. (b. 1858), "Member of the highest caste of Brahmans. Justice of the Peace of the town of Nadiad and prominent member of the Philosophical Society of Bombay," in *WPR*, 1585. D'Vivedi's paper was informative, orthodox, and highly critical of Western Orientalist scholarship. This may also have contributed to his lack of popularity.

45. *WPR*, 9.

46. The statistics of the vast number of Buddhists in the world is a common feature of lectures and writings at this time, either to establish that Buddhism must therefore have something to offer or to show that it must be considered a serious threat. Precisely because of its vast number of adherents, Christians recognized that it had to be taken seriously.

47. Quoted in *WPR*, 20–22.

48. *WPR*, 1574.

49. See frontispiece, reproduced from Rossiter Johnson, *A History of the World's Columbian Exposition*. Not all of the non-Christian delegates were present when this photograph was taken.

50. *WPR*, 62–64.

51. Bonney, "The World's Parliament of Religions," 330–31.

52. *WPR*, 19.

53. Ibid.

54. *WPR*, 28.

55. Rev. Dr. W. C. Roberts, in *WPR*, 114–15.

56. *WPR*, 23.

57. *WPR*, 3.

58. Barrows himself refers to this incident: "One of the Chairman's addresses to a Christian convention wherein he showed the Christian possibilities of the Parliament had disturbed some of the Buddhist priests in Japan." *WPR*, 61.

59. *Manifesto*, 297.

60. Ibid.

61. Ibid., 295.

62. Dharmapāla, in *WPR*, 95–96.

63. Shaku Sōen, *Bankoku shūkyō taikai ichiran* (An outline of the World's Parliament of Religions), 57.

64. Rev. George T. Candlin, in *WPR*, 169.

65. Vivekananda, in *WPR*, 170–71.

66. *WPR*, 171.

67. *WPR*, 169.

68. Barrows, *Christianity: The World Religion*, 306. Compare Rev. Dr. George Washburn, quoted approvingly by Bonney: "No missionary ever made a convert by avoiding him, refusing to listen to him, or cursing his religion. If I wish to reveal Christ to a man, I must not only treat him as a brother, but feel that he is a brother, and to find some common ground of sympathy. This was what was attempted on a grand scale at Chicago." Bonney, "The World's Parliament of Religions," 338. Moreover, Bonney believed that one of the achievements of the Parliament was that the "Orientals" showed themselves willing to listen.

69. *WPR*, 61.

70. *WPR*, 66.

71. I am also bearing in mind here that the sources I have aimed to emphasize Japanese success in Chicago and the West's acceptance of Buddhism and would therefore play down antagonism.

CHAPTER 3

1. Bonney, President of the Auxiliary Congresses, "The World's Parliament of Religions," 329–30. The list of objects of the Parliament "reproduced exactly as it was sent to those invited to take part in the convocation" appears on pp. 330–31 and in *WPR*, 18.

2. Bonney, "The World's Parliament of Religions," 331. These are rules 2 and 3.

3. Ibid., 332.

4. Ibid., 333.

5. Japanese reform Buddhists published the list of the aims of the Parliament to reassure conservative opponents to the delegation. *Manifesto*, 294.

6. Rossiter Johnson, *A History of the World's Columbian Exposition*, 4:223. This is a condensation of objects 1, 2, 6, 7, and 9 on Bonney's list.

7. Bonney, "The World's Parliament of Religions," 324.

8. Ibid., 333. This is an elaboration on rule 2.

9. *WPR*, 1561.

10. Bonney, "The World's Parliament of Religions," 330 (emphasis added).

11. Ibid., 349 (emphasis added).

12. Ibid., 332.

13. *WPR*, 746. "[T]he next century will review it." The most notable alternative is Houghton, *Neely's History*, but a survey of the centenary publications shows that Barrows's official history remains the standard reference.

14. Rossiter Johnson, *A History of the World's Columbian Exposition*, 4:7.

15. Ibid. (emphasis added).

16. Trumbull, "The Parliament of Religions," 334. Note the distinction, intended by the author, between theology, Christian scholarship, which was the main focus of the event, and the "others."

17. This incident is described by Barrows in *WPR*, 127. It was not, however, the only incident. See also p. 143 where he mentions an exchange between the Reverend Pentecost and Indian delegate, Virchand Gandhi, on the fourteenth and fifteenth days of the Parliament. Whatever happened in the actual proceedings, in the permanent record harmony was to be seen to have prevailed. Bonney quoted an "oriental delegate" saying that "these sour notes only

served to sweeten the whole." However, neither Bonney nor the official record mentions the clash between Barrows and Hirai described by Yatsubuchi in his *Shūkyō taikai hōdō* (Report on the Parliament of Religions), 39–40. Barrows apparently attempted to prevent Hirai giving his paper, but Hirai "with eyes full of anger" demanded his right to speak, and "they went into a heated argument." Were there other incidents not recorded, or was this one conducted with such decorum that only the Japanese were aware of it?

18. Bonney, "The World's Parliament of Religions," 333.

19. Ibid., 332.

20. Ibid., 333.

21. The exception here is Paul Carus's journals *Monist* and *Open Court*, which carried post-Parliamentary papers by the Asian delegates, proof of their desire to participate in the debate if given the opportunity. The readership of these was select and important but in no way compared with the readership of the Christian journals or public press that carried most of the discussion.

22. Barrows, *Christianity: The World Religion*, 326.

23. Bonney, "The World's Parliament of Religions," 327.

24. Houghton, *Neely's History*, 316.

25. Sunderland, "The Importance of a Serious Study of All Religions," in *WPR*, 627.

26. McFarland, "Buddhism and Christianity," in *WPR*, 1296–97.

27. Doshisha was the Christian college established by Niijima Jō and the American Board of Missions, at this time controlled by the Kumamoto Band, the Christian delegates to the Parliament.

28. Quoted in *WPR*, 53.

29. *WPR*, 152.

30. *Japan Weekly Mail*, July 15, 1893, 68a, gives the missionary's response.

31. Pung Kwan Yu, "Confucianism," 374–439.

32. *WPR*, 118; Kung Hsien Ho, "Confucianism," 596–604.

33. Houghton, *Neely's History*, 267–68, simply noted as Dr. Ernst Faber of Shanghai, presumably a missionary. Barrows placed this paper in the Scientific Section. *WPR*, 1350–53.

34. Bonney, "The World's Parliament of Religions," 332.

35. *WPR*, 1565.

36. Hardy, *Eastern Monachism*, 344. Hardy's writings are discussed in Chapter 4.

37. Barrows, "Results from the Parliament of Religions," 56.

38. See the Reverend George F. Pentecost's response to the Indian appropriation of this technique, in *WPR*, 143. "Some of the brahmans of India have dared to make an attack upon Christianity. They take the slums of New York and Chicago and ask us why we do not cure ourselves. They take what is outside the pale of Christianity and judge Christianity by it." This occurred toward the end of the Congress and created one of the rare opportunities for Asian response taken up by Virchand Gandhi, who similarly explained that the unacceptable aspects of Indian society were "not from religion but in spite of it." *WPR*, 145.

39. Gordon, "Some Characteristics of Buddhism as It Exists in Japan Which Indicate That It Is Not a Final Religion." Note the significant difference between "Japanese Buddhism," the term used by Japanese priests, and his expression "Buddhism in Japan," which reduced Japanese Buddhism to one aspect of the monolithic Western creation, Buddhism.

40. Ibid.

41. See Rev. George F. Pentecost, in *WPR*, 143. Reverend T. E. Slater of Bangalore, India, spoke on Hinduism with special reference to idolatry and sacrifice, in *WPR*, 456–60.

42. Nagarkar, "The Work of Social Reform in India." Nagarkar was described as a "writer and lecturer on Theism," a Christian-educated brahmin, and member of the Brahmo Samaj of Bombay. His paper on social reform discussed the caste system, "infant marriage," and "injustice to women." The Brahmo Samaj was also represented by P. C. Mozoomdar, who spoke on "The World's Religious Debt to Asia," offering Eastern spirituality to balance the overmaterialism of the West, a paper that was "particularly pleasing to his audience of Western admirers." Houghton, *Neely's History*, 596.

43. Rossiter Johnson, *A History of the World's Columbian Exposition*, 4:232.

44. Malalgoda, *Buddhism in Sinhalese Society*.

45. Barrows read the first of Shaku Sōen's papers, "The Law of Cause and Effect as Taught by the Buddha," but the delegates apparently found this unsatisfactory because Hirai read the second as well as Toki's paper. Noguchi read Yatsubuchi's.

46. Barrows wrote to President Alexander Tison of the Imperial Law School of Tokyo asking for his assistance in finding English-speaking Buddhists. Rossiter Johnson, *A History of the World's Columbian Exposition*, 4:223.

47. Barrows, "Results from the Parliament of Religions," 56, and *The Christian Conquest of Asia*, 152.

48. Rossiter Johnson, *A History of the World's Columbian Exposition*, 4:502–5, lists forty-one publications. There were also the various foreign-language sources. Barrows's history was translated into Japanese and no doubt other languages. The Japanese delegates produced their own accounts.

49. Houghton, *Neely's History*, 11.

50. The word he used was *ikyōsha*. *Ikyō* means heathen, pagan, heretic, a believer in a wrong teaching. See Shaku Sōen, *Bankoku shūkyō taikai ichiran*, 65. Houghton, *Neely's History*, softens it to a remark on the joy of having none but Buddhists on the platform.

51. The Very Reverend William Byrne, in Houghton, *Neely's History*, 141.

52. *WPR*, 253n.

53. *WPR*, x.

54. Barrows, *Christianity: The World Religion*, and also *The Christian Conquest of Asia*.

55. Houghton, *Neely's History*, 802.

56. Ashitsu, "Buddha."

57. Houghton, *Neely's History*, 541.

58. Ketelaar, "Strategic Occidentalism," 49, comments on the discrepancy between Ashitsu's clear exposition of Buddhist doctrine in the Japanese text of his paper and the incomprehensible English version. McRae, "Oriental Verities on the American Frontier," 30, is similarly disparaging. Both refer to Barrows's record.

59. See Aitken, "Three Lessons from Shaku Sōen."

60. Hirai, "The Real Position of Japan toward Christianity," in *WPR*, 447.

61. This is consistent with the paper as he wrote it in Japanese under the less contentious title of "Harmony instead of War." Shaku Sōen, *Bankoku shūkyō taikai ichiran*, 65.

62. Some examples are of archbishop of Constantinople, in *WPR*, 69; Most Holy Archbishop and Ecumenical Patriarch Neoplytos VIII, in *WPR*, 77; Mgrditch Khriman, Catholis of All Armenia, in *WPR*, 83.

63. *WPR*, 978.

64. *WPR*, 64.

65. Barrows's later work, *The Christian Conquest of Asia*, a series of "studies and personal observations of oriental religions," barely mentions Japanese Buddhism. Comments on Japan

appear in the chapter on Confucianism and relate mainly to Christianity, the beauty and cleanliness of Japan, and its achievements in modernization.

66. Ibid., 150.

67. Note, for example, Anna Leonowens's shock on meeting the bare-chested prime minister of Siam, recorded in her *The English Governess at the Siamese Court*, 8–9. Miyoshi Masao records reactions of early visitors to Japan in Miyoshi, *As We Saw Them*.

68. Smith, *Fine Art in India and Ceylon*, 182.

69. Barrows, *The Christian Conquest of Asia*, 152.

70. *Manifesto*, 296.

71. Listed in detail elsewhere. One of the most widely distributed was Kuroda Shintō, *Outlines of the Mahāyāna*.

72. Ashitsu, "The Fundamental Teachings of Buddhism." An article by Annie Elizabeth Cheney, "Mahāyāna Buddhism in Japan," appeared in *Arena* 16 (1896). Her account of Mahayana Buddhism, like her 1893 article on treaty revision referred to elsewhere, shows a marked similarity to Hirai's papers, one of which appeared in the same journal. The evidence is purely circumstantial, but it does suggest the possibility of a connection between them.

73. Muller, "The Real Significance of the Parliament of Religions," 1.

74. Ibid., 8.

75. Ibid., 10.

76. Ibid., 11.

CHAPTER 4

1. The papers in defense of Islam by Mohammed Webb confirm that old enmities continued to stir passion among Christians.

2. *WPR*, xvi.

3. *WPR*, 894.

4. Shaku Sōen, Barrows, and Ellinwood, "A Controversy on Buddhism."

5. T. W. Rhys Davids, *Buddhism: Its History and Literature*, 216–17. Ashitsu was not just a practicing Buddhist with a "popular" understanding of his religion but a prominent Meiji Buddhist intellectual and scholar.

6. James D'Alwis, missionary in Ceylon, in a review of Max Muller's *Dhammapada* (1870), quoted in Welbon, *The Buddhist Nirvāṇa*, 133 (emphasis added).

7. This was itself a problem. Conze, "Problems in Buddhist History," discusses the shortcomings of a purely textual approach to Buddhism which is, and always has been, essentially a practice, and the effects of this limitation on the image produced. Neil McMullin also points to the preeminence of ritual and practice in Japanese Buddhism in "Historical and Historiographical Issues in the Study of Pre-Modern Japanese Religions." See also Hallisey, "Roads Taken and Not Taken in the Study of Theravāda Buddhism."

8. For an overview of early writing on Buddhism, see Almond, *The British Discovery of Buddhism*, and De Jong, "A Brief History of Buddhist Studies." Both have details of early accounts of Buddhism in European languages.

9. Elison, *Deus Destroyed*, uses Jesuit reports for his account of Christian incursion in sixteenth-century Japan. See also Cooper, *They Came to Japan*. For a narrative account of Jesuit encounters with Buddhism, see Batchelor, *Awakening of the West*.

10. Mungello, *Curious Land*, 68–70.

11. Kaempfer, *The History of Japan, 1609–1692*, vol. 2.

12. Dumoulin, "Buddhism and Nineteenth-Century German Philosophy." For Hegel on Hinduism, see Inden, *Imagining India*.

13. Dumoulin, "Buddhism and Nineteenth-Century German Philosophy," 464.

14. Oldenberg, *The Buddha: His Life, His Doctrine, His Order*.

15. Ward, *A View of the History, Literature, and Religion of the Hindoos: Including a Minute Description of Their Manners and Customs and Translations from Their Principal Works*, 2 vols. (London: Black Parbury and Allen, 1817), quoted in Almond, *The British Discovery of Buddhism*, 70.

16. Quoted in ibid., 71.

17. Strong, *The Legend of King Asoka*, 11.

18. T. W. Rhys Davids, *Buddhist-Sūtras*, xlv–xlviii, gives a brief summary of his calculation using the Chronicles which link Asoka's dates to the death of the Buddha. His calculations appear in full in his first publication, *Ancient Coins and Measures of Ceylon* (1877), although the identification of Asoka this is based on was not confirmed until the twentieth century.

19. Klostermaier, *Survey of Hinduism*, 37–38, offers an alternative view. D'Vivedi, "Answers of Orthodox Hinduism to Certain Religious Problems," 333–39.

20. The British treaty with Ceylon was signed in 1815. Incursion of Burma occurred later. There was a British resident in Ava, a Burmese court, from 1830. Pegu was annexed in 1852.

21. Charles Grant, quoted in Stokes, *English Utilitarians and India*, 34.

22. Arthur Buller, Queen's Advocate of Ceylon, 1844, quoted in De Silva, *Social Policy and Missionary Organizations in Ceylon, 1840–1855*, 44.

23. Hodgson, "Notices of the Languages, Literature, and Religion of Nepal and Tibet," and "Sketch of Buddhism." These collections of manuscripts eventually provided Burnouf with the material for his translation. Is it pure coincidence that scholars from Catholic cultures were the first to show an interest in the "Romish" Mahayana Buddhism, whereas Protestants devoted themselves to the Pali texts of what they recognized as a fundamentalist Theravada?

24. Hodgson, "Sketch of Buddhism," 35.

25. Ibid., 41–50. See text for the complete list.

26. Ibid., 44–46.

27. This was a question posed by Buddhist reform leaders in Ceylon in 1873. See Peebles, *The Great Debate*, 63 and 82. This not only compromised Christianity but left missionaries open to criticism. In a public debate at Panadure, Ceylon, in 1873, the Buddhist orator Mohotivatte accused the Christians of using Indian names for God and Jesus to "ingratiate themselves into the favour of Hindus" (82).

28. Clausen, "Victorian Buddhism and the Origins of Comparative Religion," 12.

29. T. W. Rhys Davids's work is discussed later.

30. Brear, "Early Assumptions in Western Buddhist Studies," 137.

31. Ibid., 145–46. For an extensive discussion of misrecognized concepts, see Conze, "Buddhist Philosophy and Its European Parallels" and "Spurious Parallels to Buddhist Philosophy."

32. Brear, "Early Assumptions in Western Buddhist Studies," 148, quoting Edkins, *The Religious Condition of the Chinese*, 190. As McMullin points out, the inapplicability of these terms to Buddhist societies is still a problem in understanding premodern Japanese Buddhism. McMullin, *Buddhism and the State in Sixteenth Century Japan*, 15.

33. The *Anguttara Nikāya* addresses this issue: "A brahman asked the Buddha whether he was a god, a demi-god, a demon or a human." The Buddha answers that he is none of these.

"Realise brahman, that I am a Buddha." Gods, demigods, demons, and humans are all inhabitants of the world, *samsara*. A Buddha is one who has transcended the distinctions of this world and, most significantly, has transcended the opposition of man and God.

34. Wilson, "On Buddha and Buddhism."

35. Hardy, *Eastern Monachism*, viii–ix.

36. Hardy, *The British Government and Idolatry*.

37. Ibid. The pamphlet was published in Colombo in 1839 according to Malalgoda, *Buddhism in Sinhalese Society*, and in London in 1841. It appears that Hardy attempted to lobby opinion not only in Ceylon but also in England, where the matter would ultimately be decided.

38. Hardy, *The British Government and Idolatry*, 8. Cf. Charles Grant quoted earlier.

39. Ibid. Hardy reproduces the letter of August 8, 1838, ordering the separation of government from the control of temples on pp. 8–9.

40. Tennent, *Christianity in Ceylon* (1850). Hardy, *Eastern Monachism* (1853). Hardy's *Manual of Budhism [*sic*] in Its Modern Development* appeared shortly after in 1853. In spite of its title, Tennent's book was largely devoted to Buddhism because it dealt with reasons why Christianity had not yet succeeded in Ceylon. It also included a section on devil worship, significantly separated from Buddhism.

41. Hardy, *Eastern Monachism*, 1.

42. Hardy follows the pattern of Western scholarship, referring to the Buddha Sakyamuni by the "personal" name, Gautama, stressing the Buddha's human identity. By contrast, the Buddhist texts on which their works are supposedly based use titles such as Tathāgata, Blessed One, Lord.

43. Wilson, "On Buddha and Buddhism." More recent scholarship on Theravada Buddhism confirms the discrepancy. See, for example, Southwold, *Buddhism in Life: The Anthropological Study of Religion and the Sinhalese Practice of Buddhism*; Gombrich, *Theravāda Buddhism: A Social History*; and most particularly Reynolds and Carbine's significantly titled *The Life of Buddhism*. Late twentieth-century scholarship has shifted the focus from the Buddha to the practice of Buddhism.

44. *Church Missionary Gleaner*, 1878–83, 52–53. Cf. Hardy, *Eastern Monachism*, 344–45.

45. Hardy, *Eastern Monachism*, 345.

46. Ibid., 339.

47. Hardy, *Manual of Budhism*, 506.

48. Hardy, *Eastern Monachism*, 334.

49. Torrington, Minute of October 13, 1847, quoted in De Silva, *Social Policy and Missionary Organizations in Ceylon*, 104.

50. Tennent, *Christianity in Ceylon*, 206.

51. Ibid., 256.

52. Ibid., 207.

53. Ibid., 222.

54. Ibid., 197. Buddhism is equated with Protestant Christianity either as the original teachings of the Founder or as Lutheranism.

55. Ibid., 210.

56. Ibid., 207.

57. Ibid., 210.

58. Ibid., 38.

59. Ibid., 192.

60. Hardy's later publications attempted a more open attack on Buddhism, using the

mythological aspects of the work to discredit the authority of the Buddha. The message was too blatant, and the works remained curiosities. Hardy, *The Sacred Books of the Buddhists Compared with History and Modern Science* (1863), and *The Legends and Theories of the Buddhists Compared with History and Modern Science* (1866).

61. Christy, *The Orient in American Transcendentalism*, 292–94. Christy concluded that *Eastern Monachism* was probably one of the most influential books in disseminating Buddhist lore in Concord.

62. Arnold, *The Light of Asia*; Wright, *Interpreter of Buddhism to the West*, 73. According to Wright (86), other sources used by Arnold were Beal's translation of the *Abhinishkramma Sūtra* (1875), Max Muller's *Dhammapada*, and a Burmese version of the parables of Buddhaghosha. The estimate of U.S. readership is from Tweed, *The American Encounter with Buddhism*, 29.

63. For Saint-Hilaire's indebtedness to Hardy, see Saint-Hilaire, *The Buddha and His Religion*, 20. Saint-Hilaire, a student of Eugène Burnouf, read Sanskrit and Nepalese texts but depended on Hardy for knowledge of Southern Buddhism. This book continues to circulate. Whether a Christian or purely commercial response to the current interest in Buddhism, a new paperback edition appeared in 1996.

64. Ernest Renan, *Vie de Jesus* (Paris, 1974), 46, quoted in Kent, "Religion and Science," 8.

65. Ibid., 7.

66. Saint-Hilaire, *The Buddha and His Religion*, 13–16. Cf. Hardy, *Manual of Budhism*, 506.

67. Saint-Hilaire, *The Buddha and His Religion*, 11. Max Muller praised Saint-Hilaire as the first real historian of Buddhism. Welbon, *The Buddhist Nirvāṇa*, 67. Rhys Davids condemned his book as "a thoroughly erroneous and unreliable view of early Buddhism." T. W. Rhys Davids, *Hibbert Lectures*, 197.

68. Saint-Hilaire, *The Buddha and His Religion*, 14.

69. Ibid., 13.

70. Others include Max Muller's *Dhammapada* (1872), which was less useful for those seeking information on the Buddha himself. Muller, *Dhammapada*.

71. "The Passing of the Founder," *Journal of the Pali Text Society* (1923): 5.

72. Ibid., 2. There are extensive footnotes to Hardy throughout the early edition. Successive editions are updated to refer to his own translations as they appear.

73. Conze, "Recent Progress in Buddhist Studies," 1. Conze continues that it is from its work that the general public still derives its ideas of what Buddhism is. The society was founded as a voluntary cooperative of Pali scholars in Europe and included Herman Oldenberg, Professors Fausboll, Kern, and Lanman, and M. Senart. For a full list of the scholars initiating the society, see T. W. Rhys Davids, *Hibbert Lectures*, 233–34. Charles Hallisey, quoting Edward Said, refers to Rhys Davids as an "inaugural hero" for his phenomenal work in carving out a field of study. Hallisey, "Roads Taken and Not Taken in the Study of Theravāda Buddhism," 34.

74. T. W. Rhys Davids outlines his project in *Hibbert Lectures*, Lecture 1; *Buddhism: A Sketch*; and "What Has Buddhism Derived from Christianity?," 37–53.

75. T. W. Rhys Davids, "What Has Buddhism Derived from Christianity?," 52.

76. Ibid., 44.

77. Ibid., 53.

78. T. W. Rhys Davids, *Hibbert Lectures*, 47.

79. T. W. Rhys Davids, "What Has Buddhism Derived from Christianity?," 52–53.

80. T. W. Rhys Davids, *Hibbert Lectures*, 31.

81. Ibid., 145.

82. "Passing of the Founder," 8, a modified quote from T. W. Rhys Davids, *Hibbert Lectures*,

145, establishing that this was Rhys Davids's aim at the start of his career and remained so at the end. A similar point was made by the publication of his 1877 lecture on the subject in 1923.

83. T. W. Rhys Davids, *Buddhism: A Sketch*, 55.

84. *Pali Text Society Dictionary*, 427b, quoted in Welbon, *The Buddhist Nirvāṇa*, 231.

85. Without doubt the influence of the Pali Text Society and the publication of its dictionary has contributed to this. Childers's dictionary, the only one available when Rhys Davids was working on his early translations, defines *bodhi* as "[t]he knowledge possessed by a Buddha supreme, or infinite knowledge, omniscience, the Truth; Buddhahood." Childers, *A Dictionary of the Pali Language*, 93.

86. *Encyclopedia of Buddhism*, 3:178.

87. Lillie, *The Popular Life of the Buddha* (1883), reprinted as *The Life of the Buddha*, vii.

88. See Hallisey, "Roads Taken and Not Taken in the Study of Theravāda Buddhism," for the most recent discussion of nineteenth-century scholarship. He identifies the study of the production of meaning of texts in living societies as one of the "roads not taken."

89. Muller, *Selected Essays on Language, Mythology and Religion*, 2:300.

90. This quotation is from his student, wife, and colleague, C. A. F. Rhys Davids, *Buddhism*, 16–17.

91. T. W. Rhys Davids, *Hibbert Lectures*, xxv.

92. Quoted in Almond, *The British Discovery of Buddhism*, 102.

93. Ibid.

94. Walpola, *What the Buddha Taught*, ch. 2, "The Four Noble Truths," addresses the question, suggesting the persistence of the pessimistic interpretation to the present time.

95. T. W. Rhys Davids, *Buddhism: A Sketch*, 106–23.

96. *Pali Text Society Dictionary*, 477b, quoted in Welbon, *The Buddhist Nirvāṇa*, 231.

97. Arnold, quoted in Clausen, "Victorian Buddhism and the Origins of Comparative Religion," 5.

98. Rhys Davids's sources here are Burnouf, *Le Lotus de la bonne loi*; Beal, *A Catena of Buddhist Scriptures from the Chinese*; and Csoma's *Tibetan Grammar*. This quotation is from T. W. Rhys Davids, *Buddhism: A Sketch*, 199.

99. T. W. Rhys Davids, *Buddhism: A Sketch*, 207.

100. Takakusu, "The Amitāyur-Dhyāna-Sūtra."

101. Muller, *Buddhist Mahāyāna Texts*, part II, xxi.

102. Nanjio [*sic*], *A Catalogue of the Chinese Translation of the Buddhist Tripitaka*.

103. Muller, "On Sanskrit Texts Discovered in Japan," in *Chips from a German Workshop*, 5:236.

104. Muller, *Lectures on the Origin and Growth of Religion*, 236–37.

105. MacFarlane, *Japan*, vii–viii. McFarlane gave an account of Japan's sixteenth-century encounter with Christianity as a warning to the forthcoming American expedition of Commodore Perry. His advice was that the difference between the Church of Rome and the Reformed churches be made clear and that missionaries be kept out of politics and from every display of military force (230–34).

106. Yokoyama, *Japan in the Victorian Mind*, comments that guidebooks on Japan were similarly content to reproduce old stereotypes, formed before the English had access to Japan, long after they had the opportunity for firsthand observation. Even the academic journal *Transactions and Proceedings of the Japan Society* shows very little interest in religion before 1890. There is one article on phallicism, but it is not related to Buddhism.

107. Griffis, *The Mikado's Empire*. See the section "Buddhism in Japan," 158–75. Griffis was not a missionary.

108. Ibid., 158.

109. Ibid., 161.

110. Ibid., 166.

111. Ibid., 170–74.

112. Ibid., 174. Jesuit documents used by Elison in his study of early Japanese Christianity show that the Jesuit Valignano, in possibly the earliest Western accounts of Japanese Buddhism, also likened "Amidaism" of the Jōdo schools to Lutheran Protestantism, but with different connotations. Elison, *Deus Destroyed*.

113. Reed, *Japan: Its History, Tradition and Religions*. Reed was a naval architect employed in Japan.

114. Ibid., 83–84. The idea apparently appealed to Reed. He commented elsewhere that "[i]t will be gratifying, doubtless, to the many good people at home who look upon Buddhists as eligible for conversion to their particular view of the Christian religion . . . to find their own generous intentions so entirely reciprocated. . . . It may be interesting to some of my readers to learn that [Akamatsu] possessing a knowledge of England and the English [after two and a half years' residence] and also the chief priest who was our host on this occasion find embraced in their sect of the Buddhist faith all that they consider good and true in the Christian religion, and are not without hope of seeing England adopt this view, and with it the tenets and practice of their faith, which they consider most excellent" (214–15). Cf. Kitagawa, *The 1893 World's Parliament of Religions and Its Legacy*, 11–12, attributing Japanese initiatives in these areas to the Christian example of the Parliament. Sumangala, high priest of Southern Buddhism, also expressed a similar expansive ambition at least as early as 1886, reported in the *Times Democrat*, April 19, 1886. Nishizaki, *Lafcadio Hearn*, 83–86.

CHAPTER 5

1. The reasons for attending the Parliament were explained in the *Manifesto*, signed by Concerned Buddhists.

2. Literally "New Buddhism." The term does not refer to a particular sect or specific doctrine, but to a number of Buddhist initiatives of the period that shared these general characteristics.

3. See Ketelaar, *Of Heretics and Martyrs*, for a comprehensive account of the persecution and redefinition of Buddhism in this period.

4. Hirata Atsutane, for example, argued that ideology must be in harmony with the national spirit. Buddhism, a product of the "inferior Indian mind," was a harmful influence on the Japanese. See also Collcutt, "Buddhism: The Threat of Eradication"; Grapard, "Japan's Ignored Cultural Revolution"; Hardacre, *Shintō and the State*. On the doctrine of *honji suijaku*, which assimilates Shintō *kami* as indigenous manifestations of Buddhist deities, see Alicia Matsunaga, *The Buddhist Philosophy of Assimilation*. Kuroda Toshio in his important article "Shintō in the History of Japanese Religion" points out that *Shintō* did not even exist as a word until the modern era. McMullin, "Historical and Historiographical Issues in the Study of Pre-Modern Japanese Religions," gives a concise summary of the interconnectedness of pre-Meiji Japanese religion. Ketelaar, *Of Heretics and Martyrs*, ch. 2, gives a fascinating account of the radical nature of the separation, and the arbitrary—or at least nonobjective—basis for many of

the identifications. Only 1 of 4,500 shrines in Satsuma, for example, was free of Buddhist taint. Ise, the principal Shintō site, was cleared of several hundred Buddhist temples. The distinctive features that make Shintō shrines so readily recognizable today were defined during this period. The *shimenawa* and *torii*, previously part of a common religious lexicon, were from this time associated exclusively with Shintō. Mirrors were installed to replace images in shrines. Ibid., 58–59.

5. Ketelaar, *Of Heretics and Martyrs*, 47–54.

6. Ibid., 56. The impact did not fall evenly across the Buddhist community but varied by both domain and sects. For details, see also Collcutt, "Buddhism: The Threat of Eradication," 163; Kishimoto Hideo, *Japanese Thought in the Meiji Era*, 2:113–24. Census reports show that between 1872 and 1876 the number of Buddhist priests dropped from 75,925 to less than 20,000 (Collcutt, 162). Because the four preceding years, 1868–71, were the most destructive, these figures give only a small indication of the extent of the reduction of the Buddhist institutions in the transition from Tokugawa to the Meiji. Kishimoto gives figures for representative domains. Sadoshima reduced a population of more than five hundred temples to eighty.

7. Ketelaar, *Of Heretics and Martyrs*, 8, identifies prominent nativists in the Ministry of Rites and traces their influence in the drafting of the Separation Edicts.

8. Literally "abolish Buddhism and destroy Sakyamuni." Again, Ketelaar gives a most detailed account of this campaign, describing the disclaimer as a "gesture of disarming ingenuousness" (74), and arguing that the separation, as the government defined it, could only occur through the destruction of Buddhism (222). He also argues that article four of the Meiji Charter Oath that declared that "[e]vil customs of the past shall be broken off and all will be based on the just laws of nature" prefigured the accomplishments of *shinbutsu bunri*.

9. There were earlier pre-Meiji initiatives, but this was the first united effort, the first step in creating a unified "Japanese Buddhism."

10. Kishimoto Hideo, *Japanese Thought in the Meiji Era*, 2:128.

11. Soviak, "On the Nature of Western Progress."

12. Kishimoto Hideo, *Japanese Thought in the Meiji Era*, 2:137–48.

13. Thelle, *Buddhism and Christianity in Japan*, 28–29.

14. From "The Late Kenjū Kasawara," obituary, *Times*, September 22, 1883, reprinted in the *Journal of the Pali Text Society* 1:2 (1883): 69–75.

15. Muller, *Lectures on the Origin and Growth of Religion*, 237.

16. Quoted by Takakusu in the introduction to *I-Tsing*.

17. Nanjio [*sic*], *A Catalogue of the Chinese Translation of the Buddhist Tripitaka*. The Tripitaka held in the India Office library had been donated by Iwakura Tomomi in 1875. The first mission to the West apparently also perceived the value of promoting Buddhism. Nanjō's catalog was a landmark work in Western Buddhist studies because it provided the means to cross-reference Chinese, Sanskrit, and Pali texts.

18. Nanjō Bun'yū and Maeda Eun, *Bukkyō seiten*; Takakusu Junjirō and Watanabe Kaigyoku, *Taishō shinshū daizōkyō*. Both Nanjō and Takakusu had studied with Max Muller. Takakusu published two works in English in Muller's Sacred Books of the East series, "The Amitāyur-Dhyāna-Sūtra," and *I-Tsing: A Record of the Buddhist Religion as Practised in India and the Malay Archipelago (AD 671–695)*. In 1947 he published *The Essentials of Buddhist Philosophy*. See Ketelaar, *Of Heretics and Martyrs*, ch. 5, "The Making of a History," for the importance of these works in creating Japanese Buddhism.

19. Takakusu, "Buddhism as We Find It in Japan."

20. See De Jong's "A Brief History of Buddhist Studies." Japanese Buddhism is the one area where De Jong defers to native scholarship.

21. The subscription list appears in *Journal of the Pali Text Society* 1:3 (1884). Kasawara's obituary also appears in this issue.

22. Active members of the association that it represented included Takakusu Junjirō, Shimaji Mokurai, Akamatsu Renjō, and Inoue Enryō. By 1895 it had a membership of almost twenty thousand. Thelle, *Buddhism and Christianity in Japan*, 200.

23. "Monthly Summary of the Religious Press," *Japan Weekly Mail*, October 3, 1891.

24. For an account of Shaku Sōen's voyage, see his *Seiyū nikki* (Diary of a journey to the West). He was not the first to go to Ceylon, and others followed later. See also Furuta, "Shaku Sōen," 70–74.

25. Kozaki, *Reminiscences*. See also Scheiner, *Christian Converts and Social Protest in Meiji Japan*, 34.

26. Fukuzawa Yukichi, *Jiji shimpō* (1888), reported in the *Japan Weekly Mail*, March 3, 1888, and quoted in Schwantes, "Christianity vs. Science," 128 (emphasis added).

27. Kozaki, "Christianity in Japan: Its Present Condition and Future Prospects," in *WPR*, 1013.

28. Ibid., 1012.

29. Kozaki, *Reminiscences*, 39.

30. Scheiner, *Christian Converts and Social Protest in Meiji Japan*, 6, argues that many of the Christian converts in the early Meiji were former samurai of domains that had not joined the Restoration and found that traditional routes to bureaucratic positions had been cut.

31. Kozaki, *Reminiscences*, 29.

32. Ibid., 20. The text of the oath is in Kōsaka, *Japanese Thought in the Meiji Era*, 9:175–76.

33. Kozaki, *Reminiscences*, 204. This was Ebina Danjō, who was to become a leading theologian in the Japanese interpretation of Christianity. Ebina's nationalist Christianity eventually equated the Christian God and the divinity of the imperial line. See Chapter 8, note 89.

34. Staggs, "In Defence of Japanese Buddhism," 147–48, quoting Niijima Jō.

35. *Kokumin no tomo*, June 15, 1887, quoted in Pyle, *The New Generation in Meiji Japan*, 25. *Kokumin no tomo* (Friend of the nation) was the journal of the Min'yūsha (Society of Friends of the People). The Min'yūsha and the Seikyōsha, nationalist groups that are discussed later in this chapter, represent two poles in the spectrum of opinion concerning the problem of how to be both modern and Japanese. Though Pyle avoids the religious affiliations of these fundamentally political associations, they correspond to the Christian delegates and the Buddhist delegates to the World's Parliament of Religions respectively.

36. Tokutomi Sohō was also known as Tokutomi Ichirō. Although he would have been only thirteen years old at the time, he was among the Kumamoto Band who participated in the mass conversion on Hanaoka Hill. He described himself as a follower of Niijima rather than a follower of Christ. Quoted in Pyle, *The New Generation in Meiji Japan*, 107.

37. Ibid., 51.

38. Kozaki, *Reminiscences*, 358.

39. Ibid.

40. *Japan Weekly Mail*, October 3, 1891, 412. Yokoi, son of the influential Confucian scholar Yokoi Shōnan, contributed a paper on "Christianity in Japan" at the World's Parliament of Religions.

41. Quoted in Schwantes, "Christianity vs. Science," 124.

42. Quoted in Pyle, *The New Generation in Meiji Japan*, 70, from the manifesto of the founding of the Seikyōsha.

43. Inoue and his project in *Bukkyō katsuron joron* are the subject of the following chapter. His work was followed by that of Nakanishi Goro. A summary of the aims of *shin bukkyō* appeared in *Japan Weekly Mail*, March 5, 1892, under the title "The New Buddhism," 450–52.

44. *BKJ*. An English translation is available in Staggs, "In Defence of Japanese Buddhism."

45. Tamamuro, *Nihon bukkyōshi*, 3:340.

46. Ibid.

47. See, for example, *Manifesto*, 294–99. Christianity was not the only model for this. The value of community support had been demonstrated by the events of early Meiji. Jōdoshinshū temples had survived the devastation of *haibutsu kishaku*, and later financial crises, because of their broad community support.

48. Tamamuro, *Nihon bukkyōshi*, 352. A number of youth organizations developed before this. The *Japan Weekly Mail* reported that Shaku Sōen addressed the Yokohama chapter of the YMBA on his return from Chicago in 1893.

49. Jaffe, *Neither Monk nor Layman*, 169, mentions Tanaka Kōho writing a wedding ceremony in 1886 for Rengekai, the lay association for the promotion of the Lotus Sutra and Nichiren Buddhism. Tanaka also devised a ceremony for conferring the Lotus Sutra on newborn children. Ibid.

50. Ketelaar, *Of Heretics and Martyrs*, 60, discusses the funeral issue as an attempt to break community links with Buddhism. The first Shintō wedding was performed in 1901.

51. Tsunemitsu, *Meiji no bukkyōsha* (Meiji Buddhists), 182–92; Tamamuro, *Nihon bukkyōshi*, 340.

52. Collcutt, "The Zen Monastery in Kamakura Society," and *Five Mountains*.

53. Ooms, *Tokugawa Ideology*. The most recent book on the subject is Adolphson, *Gates of Power*.

54. McMullin, "Historical and Historiographical Issues in the Study of Pre-Modern Japanese Religions," 14. McMullin here relates *ōbō-buppō* to the Buddhist polity familiar to scholars of South and Southeast Asia as the principle of the interdependence of the *sangha*, the community of religious specialists, and the state.

55. The association was formed in 1869. Its topics for discussion are quoted in Kishimoto Hideo, *Japanese Thought in the Meiji Era*, 2:128.

56. Ibid., 125.

57. Ketelaar, *Of Heretics and Martyrs*, 72.

58. Hirai, "The Real Position of Japan toward Christianity," in *WPR*, 445.

59. *Japan Weekly Mail*, June 4, 1892.

60. Pyle, *The New Generation in Meiji Japan*, 5. Pyle translates Seikyōsha as Society for Political Education. Thelle, *Buddhism and Christianity in Japan*, 101, gives Society for Politics and Religion. The flexibility in the reading of *kyō* (religion or education) encompassed the variety of opinion among its members. Kishimoto Hideo, *Japanese Thought in the Meiji Era*, 2:151, calls it the National Religio-ethical Society of Japan. The term *shūkyō* was coined in the Meiji period to translate the English "religion." *Bukkyō*, translated as Buddhism, is literally the teaching of awakening, or the teaching of the Buddha; *kirisutokyō* is the teaching of Christ.

61. *BKJ*, 377. Inoue contributed regularly to the Seikyōsha journal *Nihonjin*, first published April 3, 1888. It became a weekly magazine but was banned because of political controversy from June to October 1891 and replaced for this period by a journal called *Ajia*. Nishida, *Meiji*

jidai no shimbun to zasshi, 207–8. In these articles Inoue elaborated on the ideas expressed in *Bukkyō katsuron joron*.

62. *BKJ*, 368. Cf. Buddhist delegate Toki Hōryū's paper at Chicago, "What Buddhism Has Done for Japan," 780: "And now let me tell you that this Buddhism has been the living spirit of our beloved Japan for so many years. . . . But don't too hastily conclude that we are only blinded in imitating others. We have our own nationality; let me assure you that we have our own spirit." The other delegates made similarly strong statements of Buddhism as the spirit of Japan.

63. Inoue Enryō, "Nihon shūkyō ron," 12.

64. *BKJ*, 366.

65. *BKJ*, 370–71.

66. *Japan Weekly Mail*, March 9, 1889. The article was headed "Political Buddhism."

67. The intention to introduce constitutional government with a new political system based on elected representation had been announced in 1881.

68. Thelle, *Buddhism and Christianity in Japan*, 104, quoting the *Daidō shimpō* 1 (March 11, 1889): 17. Thelle, who disapproves of Buddhists engaging in politics, is extremely critical of the organization: "With the establishment of the Sonnō Hōbutsu Daidōdan the potential exclusionism and aggressive anti-Christian character of Buddhist nationalism became manifest and was developed into a concrete strategy. Religious strife was politicized in a fatal way, apparently with the public sanction of prominent Buddhists, and the violent methods of political struggle found a way into the sphere of religion" (103). "Daidōdan intensified the animosity between Buddhists and Christians by combining Buddhist apologetics with political struggle. . . . violence increasingly dominated the political climate of this period" (107). Clearly for Thelle, Buddhism and politics should not be mixed. He did not apply the same critical standards to the political activity of Japanese Christian converts.

69. Yoshida, *Nihon kindai bukkyōshi*, 44–45.

70. A chapter could be devoted to the entanglement of the freedom of religion clause with foreign relations and treaty revision on the one hand—it was a prerequisite for revision—and Buddhists' attempts to reestablish their position in society on the other. See Kitagawa, *Religion in Japanese History*, 212 and 238–39; Kishimoto Hideo, *Japanese Thought in the Meiji Era*, 2:139–44, discusses Shimaji Mokurai's support for religious freedom. Abe Yoshiya, "Religious Freedom under the Meiji Constitution," 79.

71. In 1891 Inoue Tetsujirō's *Chokugo engi* appeared. This was an interpretive commentary on the Imperial Rescript on Education, which attempted to set forth a national morality based on loyalty to the divine emperor, an organic theory of sovereignty and Confucian ethics. Inoue Tetsujirō's work is important in this context because of its strongly anti-Christian stance, which became even more explicit in his *Kyōiku to shūkyō no shōtotsu* (Collision of education and religion) (1893). The press reaction to this brought Buddhist and Christian opposition into focus in the months immediately preceding the delegation to Chicago. See Yamazaki and Miyakawa, "Inoue Tetsujirō: The Man and His Works"; W. Davis, "The Civil Religion of Inoue Tetsujirō"; Gluck, *Japan's Modern Myths*, ch. 5.

72. The term "civil religion" is used by Davis to describe the government-sponsored work of Inoue Tetsujirō. See Hardacre, *Shintō and the State*, for the condition of the Shintō experiment at this time.

73. Kishimoto Nobuta, "Future of Religion in Japan," in Houghton, *Neely's History*, 794.

74. Brinkley, *Japan and China*, 5:90.

75. *Japan Weekly Mail*, December 5, 1891.

76. The Doshisha group were Kumiai Protestants. While *kumiai* might be translated as Congregational, this was explicitly rejected by its leaders, who wanted no part of the sectarianism evident among Western Protestants and even more ardently wished to distance themselves from mission associations of this imported term.

77. Kishimoto Nobuta, "Future of Religion in Japan," 796.

78. The *Mail*'s observation that it was the conservative Buddhist magazines alone that published technical articles supports this.

CHAPTER 6

1. *BKJ* (Introduction to revitalizing Buddhism).

2. The character for *tetsu* had been used in Chinese in association with Confucian thought.

3. *Japan Weekly Mail*, March 1893.

4. This is not surprising considering Inoue's association with delegate Ashitsu Jitsuzen in the formation of the Sonnō hōbutsu daidōdan and the Seikyōsha, and the number of Inoue's close associates and colleagues in Buddhist revival who were signatories to the document.

5. Chisolm, *Fenollosa*, 42.

6. Fenollosa, *Epochs of Chinese and Japanese Art*, 1:xiv.

7. Fukuzawa Yukichi, *Chrysanthemum* (October 1881): 393, translated by Walter Dening.

8. Chisolm, *Fenollosa*, 50, describes the Ryūchikai incident. The introductory essay by Mary Fenollosa in Fenollosa, *Epochs of Chinese and Japanese Art*, xviii, lists his imperial honors.

9. The institute, under Okakura's direction, was responsible for the Hōōden, the Japanese Pavilion at the Chicago Exposition.

10. Staggs, "Defend the Nation," 258. Shimaji Mokurai and Ōuchi Seiran should need no further introduction. Kitabatake Dōryū was a Honganji priest recently returned from study overseas, the first Japanese to visit Bodhgaya. Kiyozawa was also a Honganji student studying philosophy and later wrote on Hegel and Buddhism. His Hegelian-inspired lectures on Buddhism were circulated at the Parliament as the book *Outlines of the Mahāyāna*. He was to become the founding president of Ōtani University. Inoue Tetsujirō studied philosophy in Europe. Miyake, Tanabashi, and Shiga were major Seikyōsha spokesmen. Shiga was the editor of their journal *Nihonjin*.

11. Tsunemitsu, *Meiji no bukkyōsha*, 174.

12. Staggs, "Defend the Nation," 154.

13. Although reform was supported at the highest levels the conservative opposition should not be underestimated. It is apparent in the refusal to endorse officially the delegation to Chicago, and in the absence of Honganji priests in the delegation in spite of the fact that invitations were originally extended to Nanjō, Shimaji, and Akamatsu as the Buddhists most well known overseas. See also Murakami Senshō's resignation from the Honganji over the controversy of his history of Buddhism. Ibid., 295–96. Kiyozawa Manshi mentions the factions in the Honganji, Inoue's institution. See Haneda, *December Fan*.

14. *BKJ*, 350 and 360. Part 2 of *Bukkyō katsuron* was entitled "Destroying Evil."

15. Staggs, "Defend the Nation," 154. The ploy apparently worked. Thelle, *Buddhism and Christianity in Japan*, 100–101, is generous in his praises for Inoue's rational approach. Inoue's earliest publications were anti-Christian: *Haja shinron* (A new refutation of Christianity) (1885); *Shinri kishin* (The guiding principle of Truth) (1886–87). Volumes 1 and 2 were a "point by point refutation of what Inoue deemed the erroneous and irrational tenets of Christianity." Staggs, "In Defence of Japanese Buddhism," 191–202. Inoue's publishing house, Tetsugaku shoin, published

numerous anti-Christian works through the 1890s. Inoue warned, however, against taking Christianity too lightly. "It is much more profound than would be indicated by the foolish chattering of the missionaries we hear" (190).

16. *BKJ*, 350.

17. *BKJ*, 362–64.

18. In reality, Inoue (1858–1919) would have been only ten years old at this time and, contrary to the implication of this "autobiography," remained a priest until 1885.

19. *BKJ*, 363–64.

20. Chisolm, *Fenollosa*, 131. Inoue's Buddhist philosophy was based on Tendai teachings.

21. *BKJ*, 334–35.

22. *BKJ*, 397.

23. *BKJ*, 351 and 361.

24. *BKJ*, 358–59.

25. *BKJ*, 364.

26. The Buddhist term *hōben* (Sanskrit: *upāya*) refers to provisional truth used as a means of leading beings to greater understanding. It relates to the Buddha's skill in teaching according to the ability of the audience to comprehend. See the subsequent account of the Five Periods of the Buddha's teachings.

27. *BKJ*, 397.

28. *BKJ*, 397–98. Staggs's thesis provides a detailed analysis of this, "In Defence of Japanese Buddhism," 248–72.

29. *BKJ*, 398.

30. *BKJ*, 398–99.

31. *BKJ*, 399. See Inagaki, *A Dictionary of Japanese Buddhist Terms*, 83, for a definition of *goun*.

32. *BKJ*, 402.

33. Japanese *Kegonkyō*. This is a Mahayana sutra. For Inoue's account of this, see *BKJ*, 426–28. The five periods are *Kegonji*, when Sakyamuni taught the *Avataṃsaka-sūtra*; the *Agonji*, when he taught the *Agama-sūtras*; the *Hōdōji*, when he taught the *Vaipulya-sūtras*; the *Hannyaji*, when he taught the *Prajñāpāramitā-sūtras*; and *Hokeji* or *nehanji*, when he taught the *Saddharma-puṇḍarīka-sūtra* and *Māhaparinirvāna-sūtra*. The periods take their names from the Japanese names of the sutras.

34. *BKJ*, 427.

35. *BKJ*, 354; Staggs, "Defend the Nation," 274 n. 69.

36. *BKJ*, 365.

37. *BKJ*, 377.

38. *BKJ*, 368.

39. *BKJ*, 377.

40. *BKJ*, 374.

41. *BKJ*, 375.

42. *BKJ*, 386.

43. *BKJ*, 351.

44. *BKJ*, 378.

45. Staggs, "Defend the Nation," 226–28.

46. *BKJ*, 370.

47. Shiga Shigetaka (1863–1927) published his *Nanyō jiji* (Conditions in the South Seas) in 1887, the same year as *BKJ*. His voyages in Australia and New Zealand, among other places, had

convinced him of the danger of "naive and weak-willed association with Westerners and their culture." Pyle, *The New Generation in Meiji Japan*, 56–58.

48. Inoue Enryō, *Nihonjin* 1 (April 1888).

49. *BKJ*, 368.

50. *BKJ*, 365.

51. *BKJ*, 365–66.

52. *BKJ*, 366.

53. *BKJ*, 370–71.

54. *BKJ*, 366.

55. *BKJ*, 371.

56. *BKJ*, 366.

57. *BKJ*, 366–67.

58. *BKJ*, 372.

59. Ibid.

60. *BKJ*, 372–73.

61. Thelle, *Buddhism and Christianity in Japan*, 110.

CHAPTER 7

1. *ODL*, 4:83. *ODL* was first published in 1910 as a narrative expansion of Olcott's diaries. I have also consulted microfilms of the handwritten originals, *Colonel Olcott's Diary*, vol. 4 (1883–91). This quotation is from the text of the invitation reproduced in *ODL*.

2. Hirai's home address in Kyoto appears on the inside cover of Olcott's diary for 1887 and 1888, suggesting that Hirai made the contact. Kasawara Kenjū, the Nishi Honganji priest who had been studying with Max Muller since 1879, appears in the 1883 diary. Kasawara had returned to Japan via Ceylon in 1882. Once Olcott was in Japan, his tour received the endorsement of the combined sects and was backed financially by the Nishi Honganji and the Higashi Honganji. *ODL*.

3. See, for example, *ODL*, 4:153.

4. For the most recent and well balanced account of Olcott and his religious position, and a detailed account of Olcott's mission in Asia, see Prothero's insightful book, *The White Buddhist: The Asian Odyssey of Henry Steel Olcott*.

5. Murphet, *Hammer on the Mountain*, ch. 2, gives account of Olcott's early career. His work on agriculture is generally overlooked in Western sketches of the founder of Theosophy but was most important in Japan. He was asked to lecture on the subject.

6. Quoted in *ODL*, 4:86.

7. Compare Tamamuro, *Nihon bukkyōshi* (History of Japanese Buddhism), 3:340. Olcott receives only passing reference.

8. I expand on Olcott's idiosyncratic interpretation of Buddhism later. Prothero, using a linguistic metaphor, describes Olcott's Buddhism as a "creole." Prothero argues: "What shifted for Olcott was merely the 'lexicon' of his faith. The structural framework out of which he spoke his Buddhist words—what has been described here as his 'grammar'—remained Protestant, and 'his accent' remained decidedly theosophical" (*The White Buddhist*, 96).

9. *ODL*, 2:190.

10. It became an issue later when Olcott asked his former Japanese Buddhist sponsors to endorse his platform for Buddhist unity.

11. *ODL*, 4:83.

12. *ODL*, 4:85.

13. See Malalgoda, *Buddhism in Sinhalese Society*, for a discussion of the Buddhist revival in nineteenth-century Ceylon, including details of Olcott's contribution. *ODL*, vol. 2, presents Olcott's own account. This is elaborated upon in Murphet, *Hammer on the Mountain*, and, most recently, Prothero, *The White Buddhist*.

14. Copleston, bishop of Colombo, letter to the Society for the Propagation of the Gospel, 1879, quoted in Malalgoda, *Buddhism in Sinhalese Society*, 230.

15. This was a famous debate held at Panadure in August 1873, described in detail in Peebles, *The Great Debate*. See also Malalgoda, *Buddhism in Sinhalese Society*, 222–31.

16. *ODL*, 2:165.

17. *ODL*, 2:179.

18. *ODL*, 2:325.

19. Christianity had been installed as the state religion under Dutch administration, and its ceremonies remained the only legal registration of births, deaths, and marriages until civil registration was installed in 1868. Specifically Buddhist registration was a symbolic victory because it placed Buddhism as an equal and valid alternative to Christianity.

20. *ODL*, 3:124.

21. Correspondence with the Colonial Office is reproduced in *ODL*, vol. 3.

22. Wickremeratne, "Religion, Nationalism, and Social Change in Ceylon," 127. There is, however, a slippage here between what "Buddhism" denoted for Olcott and for the *sangha*.

23. *ODL*, 2:189.

24. *ODL*, 4:49.

25. *ODL*, 4:150.

26. Ibid.

27. Sangharakshita, *Flame in Darkness*, 56–57.

28. Olcott, "On the President's Japan Tour," 246.

29. Ibid.

30. Fields, *How the Swans Came to the Lake*, 98.

31. *ODL*, 2:168.

32. Cf. Fields, *How the Swans Came to the Lake*, 97: "As early as 1875, HPB (Madame Blavatsky) had told W. Q. Judge in New York that she considered herself a Buddhist, and that the beliefs of the Masters 'might be designated pre-Vedic Buddhists.' Since, however, as HPB told Judge, 'no one would now admit there was any Buddhism before the Vedas,' it was best to think of the Masters as 'Esoteric Buddhists.' "

33. *ODL*, 2:168–69.

34. Olcott, *The Golden Rules of Buddhism*, 16–17.

35. *ODL*, 2:298.

36. Olcott, "Buddhism and Science," in *The Buddhist Catechism*, 114–21.

37. *ODL*, 2:301–2.

38. *ODL*, 2:300.

39. *ODL*, 2:406–7.

40. Olcott, "On the President's Japan Tour," 243.

41. See, for example, *Japan Weekly Mail*, September 19, 1891: "They disclaimed for Buddhism that esoteric side which is so much talked of in Europe." *Japan Weekly Mail*, September 3, 1892, reports on a conversation between Sir Edwin Arnold—also a Theosophist—and a group of

Zen priests, the thrust of which was the amusement of the Buddhists at Arnold's obsession with supernatural powers and the futility of trying to explain to him that although Buddhists did not deny the existence of extraordinary powers, acquisition of these powers was incidental to Buddhist achievement (27).

42. *Colonel Olcott's Diary*, February 15, 1889.

43. Ibid., March 21, 1889.

44. *ODL*, 4:412.

45. Ibid.

46. Olcott, "On the President's Japan Tour," 244.

47. *ODL*, 4:413.

48. *ODL*, 4:156.

49. *ODL*, 4:148.

50. *ODL*, 4:81.

51. *ODL*, vol. 4, chs. 6, 7, and 8 respectively.

52. Olcott, "On the President's Japan Tour," 247.

53. *Japan Weekly Mail*, March 16, 1889, 249–50.

54. Ibid.

55. Ibid., 249.

56. *Japan Weekly Mail*, April 6, 1889, 333c–334b.

57. Ibid.

58. Ibid.

59. *Japan Weekly Mail*, May 6, 1889, 430.

60. "Editorial Paragraphs," *Missionary Herald*, May 1889, quoted in Prothero, *The White Buddhist*, 126.

61. *ODL*, 4:142.

62. *Colonel Olcott's Diary*, March 16, 1889.

63. *ODL*, 4:127.

64. Quoted in *ODL*, 4:134.

65. *Japan Weekly Mail*, March 16, 1889, 250.

66. *Colonel Olcott's Diary*, March 4, 1889.

67. *ODL*, 4:31.

68. *Colonel Olcott's Diary*, March 18, 1889.

69. *ODL*, 4:164–66. Olcott quotes from a speech made by a Mr. Tokusawa, one of the Buddhists who accompanied Olcott back to Ceylon to study under Sumangala, which was given at the 1890 Theosophical Society Convention in Adyar. Tokusawa's excesses may perhaps be excused in this context: the good guest, speaking far from home.

70. *Mikkyō daijiten*, 5:2036.

CHAPTER 8

1. *Manifesto*, 297. Barrows himself refers to this incident. *WPR*, 61.

2. *Manifesto*, 297.

3. Ibid. See also Yatsubuchi's *Shūkyō taikai hōdō*, 57: "[W]e proceeded on their own actual territory."

4. *Japan Weekly Mail*, May 6, 1893, 542, and June 3, 1893, 650.

5. *Manifesto*, 295. As mentioned in Chapter 6, Ōuchi, Shimaji, Ashitsu, and Inoue were all founding members of the Seikyōsha and of the Sonnō hōbutsu daidōdan.

6. Cf. Kuroda Shintō, *Outlines of the Mahāyāna*, iii. See the following chapter on the status of the book.

7. Ibid. (emphasis added).

8. Early moves in this direction have been discussed previously.

9. *Choya shimbun*, quoted in *Japan Weekly Mail*, February 2, 1889, 97.

10. *Japan Weekly Mail*, December 30, 1893, 790. The mission to India refers to Japanese participation in the Mahābodhi Society. Other than this, the Buddhist missions largely correspond with Japanese territorial expansion at this time, confirming the link between missions and imperialism. One-quarter of the population of Hawaii was Japanese. The "surprising strategy of expansion" does not seem to have extended to sending unsolicited missions to the West. Buddhist priests were sent to minister to expatriates in California but not to actively proselytize among Americans. Shaku Sōen accepted an *invitation* to teach in America.

11. Yatsubuchi, *Shūkyō taikai hōdō*, 3.

12. Yatsubuchi, reported in *Japan Weekly Mail*, April 7, 1894, 413.

13. The Christian delegates, all Kumiai Christians from Doshisha College, contributed regularly to the Min'yusha journal *Kokumin no tomo*. The sentiments they expressed in their own more specifically Christian journals, *Rikugo zasshi* and *Kirisutokyō shimbun*, are consistent with Min'yusha views and are frequently quoted by Pyle to establish his arguments, although he avoids the religious label. The Seikyōsha connections of the Buddhist delegation are discussed in the previous chapter.

14. *Mikkyō daijiten*, 5:2036.

15. *WPR*, 57.

16. See the discussion of *shin bukkyō* in Chapter 5, and Tamamuro, *Nihon bukkyōshi* (History of Japanese Buddhism), 3:354.

17. Yatsubuchi, *Shūkyō taikai hōdō*, 21. On Yatsubuchi's rank, see Ketelaar, *Of Heretics and Martyrs*, 159.

18. Furuta, "Shaku Sōen," 75, records that Engakuji, like other Zen temples that had lost patronage since the Meiji Restoration, was in severe financial distress at this time. The total income the main temple collected from its branch temples in 1890 was seventy yen.

19. Quoted in *Japan Weekly Mail*, November 4, 1893.

20. *Japan Weekly Mail*, February 1894, 146.

21. *Prasnottara*, vol. 2 (Adyar, 1894).

22. Haneda, *December Fan*.

23. *Manifesto*, 297. The prediction turned out to be accurate, but did they expect Barrows's contribution as editor?

24. Referred to throughout Barrows's record of the Parliament as Kinza Riuge M. Hirai. Ryūge is a Buddhist initiatic name. Hirai had taken lay ordination through the Rinzai Zen temple Myōshinji in Kyoto. The triple name compares with the practice of Japanese Christians of including a baptismal name, as, for example, the Doshisha delegate Kaburagi Peter Goro.

25. The development of lay Buddhism was a most significant feature of Meiji Buddhist revival, taking Buddhism out of the confines of institutions and arcane texts and bringing it into the community and the vernacular language. See Tamamuro, *Nihon bukkyōshi*, 340–41, "Koji bukkyō no tenkai" (The development of lay Buddhism).

26. Hirai, "The Real Position of Japan toward Christianity," in *WPR*, 449. An alternative version is in Houghton, *Neely's History*, 157–61. References in this chapter are from Barrows except where otherwise specified. Hirai wrote *Shinyaku zensho danpaku* (Refutation of the New Testament) in 1883. See *Japan Biographical Encyclopedia and Who's Who*, 285.

27. Olcott's personal diaries for 1887 and 1888 list Hirai's name and Kyoto address.

28. Noguchi, "The Religion of the World," 440. Note his inclusion of pre-Meiji Japan in this category of the already civilized.

29. Ibid. The Tokugawa *bakufu* which had held political and military power in Japan since the early seventeenth century was nevertheless nominally subservient to the emperor. Because Perry arrived at a time of waning *bakufu* power, the signing of the treaty against the court's advice became a point of political contention. Hirai, "The Real Position of Japan toward Christianity," 446, elaborates on this point: "It is perfectly right and just that we reject this whole treaty because its term has already passed, and because it is the treaty negotiated and signed by the feudal Shogun and his officers without the ratification of the Emperor."

30. Japanese *sōryo*, priest.

31. Noguchi, "The Religion of the World," 442.

32. Note also the claim here to validate the Mahayana sutras as the actual teachings of Sakyamuni: "Buddha Shaka's sutras."

33. Noguchi, "The Religion of the World," 443.

34. Hirai, "The Real Position of Japan toward Christianity."

35. Ibid., 449.

36. Ibid., 446.

37. Ibid., 448.

38. "Religious Thought in Japan," 257–67. Cf. Tateno, "Foreign Nations at the World's Fair: Japan," quoted in Chapter 1, on the exposition as chance to come into contact with intelligent, thinking people and win their support for treaty revision. The publication of the article is also consistent with Mutsu Munemitsu's deliberate manipulation of public opinion through the press. In 1895 *Arena* also carried an article justifying ("explaining") Japanese aggression in Korea.

39. *Japan Weekly Mail* described Hirai's article as "the best thing yet written on Japanese Buddhism" (August 5, 1893). Fukudō is Noguchi's family name; Zenshirō the name he took after lay initiation (cf. Hirai's second name, "Ryūge"). I am indebted to Professor Higuchi Shoshin of Ōtani University, Kyoto, for this piece of information. The article refers to the author as "Kinza Hirai of Los Angeles, California" (October 14, 1893). He alone of the delegates spoke English fluently.

40. The Parliament opened on September 11. The journal must have appeared earlier since it is reviewed in "Letter from Chicago," *Japan Weekly Mail*, August 26, 1893, 417. Cheney also published an article, "Mahayana Buddhism in Japan," which expressed the ideas of Hirai and Meiji Buddhist revival right down to its conclusion: "And now, as the glow of the dawn of the twentieth century heralds a coming morning, the keen specialists of the West recognize that between the covers of the Tripitaka may be found the duplicate of the key with which modern science unlocks the doors of truth." Was Cheney herself a Buddhist? What was her relationship to Hirai?

41. Shaku Sōen jokingly implied this in the opening of his second paper, in which he expressed satisfaction in having no one but "we heathen" (*ikyōsha*) on the platform. *Bankoku shūkyō taikai ichiran*, 65. Note, however, that the term Shaku Sōen used to translate "heathen" in his report on Hirai's paper is *yaban*, which more specifically denotes "barbaric" or "uncivilized."

42. Hirai, "The Real Position of Japan toward Christianity," 449; in Houghton, *Neely's History*, 160.

43. Hirai, "Religious Thought in Japan," 258. This was mentioned in Chapter 1.

44. Barrows himself commented on this in *WPR*, 115.

45. Hirai, "The Real Position of Japan toward Christianity," 450.

46. Ibid. A Japanese account of the speech in Shaku Sōen's outline of the Parliament intended for circulation among the Japanese public and therefore unconcerned with eliciting American passion, reduced this concluding message to its essence: "Gentlemen, we are inspired to action by the way you escaped the shackles of England and gained independence. . . . lend us a little of your strength in the treaty revision." Shaku Sōen, *Bankoku shūkyō taikai ichiran*, 13.

47. Chang, "The Question of the Unilateral Denunciation and the Meiji Government, 1888–1892."

48. Yatsubuchi, *Shūkyō taikai hōdō*, 39.

49. *Chicago Herald*, September 14, 1893, quoted in *WPR*, 116.

50. Hirai, "The Real Position of Japan toward Christianity," 446.

51. Cheney, "Japan and Her Relation to Foreign Powers."

52. Flower, "Justice for Japan," 235.

53. Ibid., 225.

54. Cheney, "Japan and Her Relation to Foreign Powers," 462; Flower, "Justice for Japan," 227.

55. Townsend Harris, quoted in Flower, "Justice for Japan," 227.

56. Hirai, "Religious Thought in Japan."

57. Hirai, "The Real Position of Japan toward Christianity," 444.

58. Hirai, "Religious Thought in Japan," 267. Cf. the dominant Christian metaphor at the Parliament of degrees of light and darkness. Translated to Hirai's scheme there would be many roads, but only one would reach the place where the moon could be seen clearly. The conditional expression "if the top is reached" carries the same warning that some paths will be misdirected and will fail to reach the top.

59. Hirai, "Synthetic Religion."

60. Hirai, "Synthetic Religion," in Houghton, *Neely's History*, 800. This paper has been edited to an inconsequential fraction of its length in Barrows's record of the Parliament.

61. Ibid., 802. Dharmapāla used the term "synthetic religion" to refer to Buddhism. It is the nature of Buddhism to be encompassing.

62. Cf. *BKJ*, 395: "I have always insisted that Christianity with a scientific explanation would turn into something like Buddhism."

63. Hirai, "Synthetic Religion," in Houghton, *Neely's History*, 800.

64. Cf. Inoue Enryō's claims that Buddhism is the highest form of religion because it offers philosophy for the intellectually advanced and the reassurance of the trappings of religion for "women and common folk." *BKJ*, 392.

65. Hirai, "Religious Thought in Japan," 261–63.

66. Ibid., 260.

67. Ibid., 259. *Japan Biographical Encyclopedia and Who's Who*, 258, records that Hirai was a linguist and that his life's mission was the pursuit of Aryan roots of Japanese language.

68. For details on the arbitrary decisions made defining the material representations of Shintō at this time, see Ketelaar, *Of Heretics and Martyrs*, ch. 2.

69. Hirai, "Religious Thought in Japan," 260. This key concept was the subject of another paper by the Buddhist priest Ashitsu and one touched on by all speakers.

70. Ibid., 261–62. Toki Hōryū also makes this point: "[T]o pray to and worship a symbol is

not the idea. . . . the symbol is an example presenting the grand, uniform and absolute truth." "The prayer and worship of the symbol in Buddhism is very different from the so-called idol worship." Toki, "Buddhism in Japan," 547–48.

71. Hirai, "Religious Thought in Japan," 265.

72. Ibid., 267.

73. Ibid., 263–64.

74. Quoted in Said, *Culture and Imperialism*, 17.

75. Sumangala, "Buddhism: Southern Orthodox," 894.

76. Houghton, *Neely's History*, 803–6.

77. Ibid., 804.

78. Ibid., 806.

79. Asoka, the great Buddhist king of the third century B.C., was known for his edicts on religious toleration and patronage of all religions.

80. Hirai, "The Real Position of Japan toward Christianity," 449; in Houghton, *Neely's History*, 160. (This gives "entailed" for "curtailed.")

81. *WPR*, 1513–16.

82. Houghton, *Neely's History*, 157.

83. Highlights from this congress are found in *WPR*, 1093–1100.

84. Barrows, *Christianity: The World Religion*, 9–17, and "Results from the Parliament of Religions," 60.

85. Yatsubuchi, *Shūkyō taikai hōdō*, 39.

86. Hirai, "Synthetic Religion," in Houghton, *Neely's History*, 802. This part of the paper does not appear in Barrows's heavily edited version.

87. Hirai, "The Real Position of Japan toward Christianity," 449.

88. Kishimoto Nobuta, "Future of Religion in Japan," in *WPR*, 1279. Kishimoto had interrupted his studies in comparative religion at Harvard to speak at the Parliament. He later joined Anesaki Masaharu in founding the study of comparative religion in Japan. Suzuki Norihisa, "Nobuta Kishimoto and the Beginnings of the Scientific Study of Religion in Modern Japan." He wrote a series of articles on Buddhism for Paul Carus's journal *Open Court*, 1894, which illustrate the idea that Japanese Buddhism is the highest development of the teaching: "The Influence of Buddhism on the People," "The Zen and the Shin Sects," "Present Condition," "Sacred Literature," "Northern and Southern Buddhism," and "Buddhism in Japan."

89. Kishimoto Nobuta, "Future of Religion in Japan," in *WPR*, 1280. In the year preceding the Parliament Japanese Christians had suffered attack in the controversy over the Imperial Rescript on Education, which brought up the very relevant issue of whether it was possible to be both Christian and Japanese, because strict monotheism was an obstacle to accepting the divine ancestry of the emperor. The end point was reached by Ebina Danjō, also a Kumiai thinker who equated the Christian God with the supreme deity of the Japanese Imperial House: "Though the encouragement of ancestor worship cannot be regarded as part of the essential teaching of Christianity (!), it is not opposed to the notion that, when the Japanese empire was founded, its early rulers were in communication with the Great Spirit that rules the universe. Christians, according to this theory, without doing violence to their creed, may acknowledge that the Japanese nation has a divine origin. It is only when we realise that the Imperial Ancestors were in close communion with God (or the Gods), that we understand how sacred is the country in which we live." Quoted in Chamberlain, *The Invention of a New Religion*, 16. The exclamation mark is presumably Chamberlain's. The seeds of this idea are apparent in Matsugama's and

Kaburagi's papers. This not only nationalized Christianity but extended Japan's special position as the divine land from the home of the gods, to the home of God.

90. Matsugama, "Origin of Shintō," 1370–73; Kaburagi, "The Shintō Religion," 1373–74. These papers were presented in the Scientific Section.

91. Matsugama, "Origin of Shintō," 1372. He dates it between 1776 and 1843. Matsugama wrote this some eighty years before Kuroda Toshio's influential article, "Shintō in the History of Japanese Religion," brought this to more general attention.

92. Matsugama, "Origin of Shintō," 1372.

93. Ibid., 1373.

94. Shintō in Japanese is usually translated as the "way of the *gods*" because there are innumerable *kami*.

95. Kozaki, "Christianity in Japan: Its Present Condition and Future Prospects," in Houghton, *Neely's History*, 489; in *WPR*, 1012.

96. Kozaki, "Christianity in Japan: Its Present Condition and Future Prospects," in *WPR*, 1013.

97. Kozaki, *Reminiscences*, 36.

98. Kishimoto Nobuta, "Future of Religion in Japan," in *WPR*, 1283.

99. Kozaki, *Reminiscences*, 94.

100. Kozaki, recorded in Houghton, *Neely's History*, 494. This proposition was clearly too radical for Barrows, who modified it to read "take their place side by side with native workers." *WPR*, 1014.

101. Kozaki, quoted by Barrows in the caption to his photograph. *WPR*, 1015.

102. *Japan Weekly Mail*, July 2, 1892, 13. The American Board missionaries ensconced in Kyoto were nominally teachers of Western learning at the Doshisha College. They had paid for the establishment of the college, but it was held in the names of Japanese.

103. Thelle confirms that the introduction of mixed residence after 1899 passed largely without incident. Thelle, *Buddhism and Christianity in Japan*, 10.

104. *Japan Weekly Mail*, July 2, 1892, 13, quoting the progressive Shingon journal *Gokoku*.

105. Thelle, *Buddhism and Christianity in Japan*, 109.

CHAPTER 9

1. "Mahāyāna does not exclude Hīnayāna and together they are called *Ekayāna*." Toki, "Buddhism in Japan," 544. Ekayana (Japanese *ichijō*) is a Sanskrit term meaning the One Vehicle to awakening. Although *JEBD*, 124, describes it as comprising both the Hinayana (Japanese: *shōjō*, Small Vehicle) and the Mahayana (Japanese: *daijō*, Great Vehicle), Toki clearly *equated* it with (Japanese) Mahayana. A synonymous term is *ichiu*, the one rain that falls from the sky that nurtures many diverse plants, just as the one teaching of the Buddha can guide men of different natures. *JEBD*, 124–25. The idea is most particularly stressed in the *Saddharma-pundarīka-sūtra* (Japanese *Hokke-kyō*), repeatedly referred to by the delegates as the culmination of the Buddha's teachings. The Japanese delegates consistently use the term "Hinayana" to designate the Buddhism of the South. Theravada (The Way of the Elders) is the term preferred by its adherents.

2. Bigelow's *Buddhism and Immortality* was published in 1908, but Fenollosa's sophisticated notes on Tendai and Shingon appear only in his personal notebooks. Tweed, *The American Encounter with Buddhism*, 70.

3. *BKJ*, 365.

4. Kuroda Shintō, *Outlines of the Mahāyāna*, ii (emphasis added). For other examples, see Ashitsu, "The Fundamental Teachings of Buddhism," 160; Yatsubuchi, "Buddhism," in *WPR*, 719; Toki, "Buddhism in Japan," 544; Ashitsu, "Buddha," in Houghton, *Neely's History*, 541; *BKJ*, 427.

5. Yatsubuchi, *Shūkyō taikai hōdō*, and Shaku Sōen, *Bankoku shūkyō taikai ichiran*. Barrows's official history was also translated into Japanese.

6. *Manifesto*, 296.

7. *Manifesto*, 299.

8. See Malalgoda, *Buddhism in Sinhalese Society*, on the creation of Protestant Buddhism in Ceylon; Nidhi, "A Preliminary Study of Central Thai Writings on Buddha's Life," and Jory, "Thai and Western Buddhist Scholarship in the Age of Colonialism," on rational interpretations of Buddhism in Siam.

9. Subscription list, *Journal of the Pali Text Society* (1882).

10. *Journal of the Pali Text Society* (1922): 28–31.

11. Sumangala, "Buddhism: Southern Orthodox," 894.

12. Cf. Shaku Sōen's request that the audience "not be so narrow-minded" as to reject his ideas because they came from "one who belonged to a different nation, different creed and different civilization."

13. Dharmapāla, "The World's Debt to Buddha," in Houghton, *Neely's History*, 408. Barrows has edited the comment on anthropomorphic deism, and reference to Europe's respect for Sakyamuni's "divine memory."

14. Dharmapāla, "The World's Debt to Buddha," in *WPR*, 866. The discrepancy and overlap suggest that the paper shown in Barrows is an amalgamation of the speech and a later paper.

15. Houghton, *Neely's History*, 408; Guruge, *Return to Righteousness*, 4.

16. Although some Japanese delegates repeat the Western dates for the birth of the Buddha, Kuroda gives 1027 B.C., Toki 127 B.C. This may be a typographical problem. Ashitsu: 1026 years before Christ.

17. Noguchi first made this statement. It was repeated by Ashitsu, "Buddha," in Houghton, *Neely's History*, 542; Yatsubuchi, "Buddhism," in *WPR*, 716.

18. Hirai, "Religious Thought in Japan." This is discussed in Chapter 8. The nature of the term "Buddha" was also the subject of the papers by Ashitsu and Yatsubuchi.

19. Toki, "History of Buddhism and Its Sects in Japan," in Houghton, *Neely's History*, 222. The paper in Barrows is different but nevertheless begins with the unequivocal statement that "Bhagavat Setyammie [*sic*] taught three yanas or vehicles for the conveyance of the truth"; Toki, "History of Buddhism and Its Sects in Japan," in *WPR*, 543.

20. Cf. *JEBD*, 81.

21. Ashitsu, "Buddha," in Houghton, *Neely's History*, 541.

22. *BKJ*, 399. This is discussed in Chapter 6.

23. Toki, "Buddhism in Japan," 543.

24. Yatsubuchi, "Buddhism," in *WPR*, 719.

25. Toki, "History of Buddhism and Its Sects in Japan," in Houghton, *Neely's History*, 222; in *WPR*, 543.

26. Toki, "History of Buddhism and Its Sects in Japan," in *WPR*, 544.

27. Ashitsu, "Buddha," in Houghton, *Neely's History*, 543. This material, printed in *Neely's*

History as part of Ashitsu's paper, appears in Barrows as a letter from a Mr. Horiuchi, secretary of the Japanese Mahābodhi Society, who had also traveled to Chicago. *WPR*, 130–31. It had been read to the Parliament by the chairman on the eleventh day (September 21). Horiuchi was a signatory to the *Manifesto*.

28. *Manifesto*, 298.

29. Dharmapāla, reported in *WPR*, 95.

30. Houghton, *Neely's History*, 222.

31. Toki, "History of Buddhism and Its Sects in Japan."

32. Toki; see also the caption to his portrait, *WPR*, 544. The sentiment, however, does not appear in Barrows's version of the paper but in Houghton, *Neely's History*, 226.

33. Shaku Sōen, "Shūkyōka kondankai ni tsuite," 174.

34. Ashitsu, quoted in Carus, "The World's Religious Parliament Extension," 348.

35. Toki, "What Buddhism Has Done for Japan," 779.

36. Dharmapāla, "The World's Debt to Buddha," in Guruge, *Return to Righteousness*, 20; Sumangala, "Buddhism: Southern Orthodox," 894.

37. Kuroda Shintō, *Outlines of the Mahāyāna*, ch. 1.

38. Toki, "Buddhism in Japan," 546.

39. Arnold, quoted in Clausen, "Victorian Buddhism and the Origins of Comparative Religion," 5.

40. Prince Chudhadharn, "Buddhism as It Exists in Siam," 645.

41. Pali: *Paticca-samuppāda*; Sanskrit: *pratītya-samutpāda*. Current translations (conditioned genesis, dependent origination, codependent origination) remove the stress from the concept of strict causality. It was also discussed by Dharmapāla, "Points of Resemblance and Difference between Buddhism and Christianity," 1288–90; Prince Chudhadharn, "Buddhism as It Exists in Siam," 645–49; Toki, "Buddhism in Japan," 546–47.

42. Hewitt, "Rational Demonstration of the Being of God," 260. The same arguments were advanced by other speakers, such as T. Harris, "Proofs of the Existence of God."

43. Shaku Sōen, "The Law of Cause and Effect as Taught by the Buddha," in *WPR*, 830. Cf. similar metaphors used by Hirai and Dharmapāla. Toki conceded that Buddhism did have a kind of a creator God in Brahmā, a deity taken over from the Indians, but explained that he did not "make something out of nothing."

44. T. Harris, "Proofs of the Existence of God," 306.

45. Japanese *jichō jido*, in *Bukkyō daijiten*, 1930; Japanese *jigō jitoku*, in *Bukkyō daijiten*, 1772, respectively.

46. Cf. Toki, "Buddhism in Japan," 547. "There is no Buddha or Divinity" who administers pleasure or pain; like the thread of a silkworm, both come from within; "No pleasure or pain will come from without, but they are only the effect felt like the sound or shadow of good or bad action produced by the mind of ourselves."

47. Ibid., 546.

48. Shaku Sōen, "The Law of Cause and Effect as Taught by the Buddha," in *WPR*, 831.

49. *Manifesto*, 299.

50. Dharmapāla, "The World's Debt to Buddha," in *WPR*, 863.

51. Ibid.

52. *BKJ*, 398.

53. Note again the scientific language used. *BKJ*, 398. See Staggs, "In Defence of Japanese Buddhism," 248–60, for an analysis of Inoue's explanation of the evolution of Western philoso-

phy and its parallels in the various sects of Buddhism. It depends on a "simplified dialectics" (her term) in which two extreme and opposing theories are reconciled in a third. There is always, except in the Buddha's teaching, an "excess," an unresolved portion.

54. Shaku Sōen's second paper at the Parliament, "Arbitration Instead of War," called for recognition of differences, as did his lecture in Shaku Sōen, "Report on a Meeting of Religious Leaders."

55. Kuroda, *Outlines of the Mahāyāna*, 16–19.

56. Japanese: *Shinnyo*; Sanskrit: *tathatā*. *JEBD*, 284. Cf. Yatsubuchi, "Buddhism," in *WPR*, 717.

57. Kuroda, *Outlines of the Mahāyāna*, 16.

58. Toki, "History of Buddhism and Its Sects in Japan," in *WPR*, 546–47.

59. Prince Chudhadharn, "Buddhism as It Exists in Siam," 645. Kuroda, *Outlines of the Mahāyāna*: "But though the law of causation extends to all things and is limitless in its dominion, all these things are yet but waves raised on the sea of man's mysterious mind" (iv). Cf. "So the essence of mind is compared to water, and its phenomena to waves" (20). There is nothing that has any reality in the sense of unchanging and permanent existence: "when conditions come, things begin to appear; when conditions cease, things likewise cease to exist."

60. Ashitsu, "Buddha," in *WPR*, 1039, and in Houghton, *Neely's History*, 539. "The innumerable phenomena before our eyes . . . are the shadow or appearance of the absolute unity." The version in Barrows is reduced to about half the length of the paper in Houghton.

61. Japanese: *sanshin*; Sanskrit: *trayah kāyāh*. *JEBD*, 258. Yatsubuchi, "Buddhism," in *WPR*, 718.

62. Yatsubuchi, "Buddhism," in *WPR*, 718–19.

63. Toki, "Buddhism in Japan," 544. All beings have the Buddha nature, "the essential spirit in full completeness," and their apparent differences are due to the "various forms of development on the physical plane." Kuroda, *Outlines of the Mahāyāna*, iv.

64. Yatsubuchi, "Buddhism," in *WPR*, 717.

65. Ashitsu, "Buddha," in Houghton, *Neely's History*, 538–39.

66. Hirai, "Religious Thought in Japan," 260–61.

67. This particular reference is to Yatsubuchi, "Buddhism," in *WPR*, 723. The views of Ashitsu and Toki are clear from their papers, and the definition of the term was the basis of Shaku Sōen's contentious correspondence with Barrows.

68. Kuroda, *Outlines of the Mahāyāna*, 6.

69. Shaku Sōen, Barrows, and Ellinwood, "A Controversy on Buddhism."

70. See *JEBD*, 289. *Shishu-nehan*, the four kinds of *nehan* (nirvana). The spelling here follows the dictionary rather than Barrows, which has some minor differences.

71. Ibid.

72. Shaku Sōen, Barrows, and Ellinwood, "A Controversy on Buddhism," 43–44.

73. Hirai, "Religious Thought in Japan," 264.

74. Toki, "Buddhism in Japan," 549.

75. Ibid., 546.

76. *BKJ*, 394.

77. Toki, "Buddhism in Japan," 544.

78. Hirai, "Synthetic Religion," in Houghton, *Neely's History*, 801–2.

79. Kuroda, *Outlines of the Mahāyāna*, 1.

80. Toki, "Buddhism in Japan," 548.

81. Shaku Sōen, *Sermons of a Buddhist Abbot*, reprinted as *Zen for Americans*, 46–47.

82. Ibid., 48.

83. Shaku Sōen, *Bankoku shūkyō taikai ichiran*, 5.

84. Ibid. Shaku Sōen gives the name in katakana as *sutorō*, hence my spelling. However, Rick Fields, *How the Swans Came to the Lake*, 129, records that a Mr. Strauss took vows after Dharmapāla lectured at the Atheneum Building and was accepted as a member of the Mahābodhi Samaj. Ahir, *Pioneers of Buddhist Revival in India*, 17, also speaks of a "C. T. Strauss of New York, a lifelong student of philosophy and comparative religion." The actual name was of less importance to Shaku Sōen than the fact that he was an American businessman. Note also that the differences between Mahayana and Theravada dissolve before the opportunity to record Western approval of Buddhism.

CHAPTER 10

1. On Carus's contribution to the propagation of Buddhism in America, see Verhoeven, "Americanizing the Buddha," and Tweed, *The American Encounter with Buddhism*. On Carus's impact on philosophy in America, see Meyer, "Paul Carus and the Religion of Science"; Hay, "Paul Carus: A Case Study of Philosophy on the Frontier"; Jackson, "The Meeting of East and West."

2. Carus, *Gospel*, viii.

3. *Monist* 6:1 (October 1895): 142.

4. Fader, "Zen in the West," 141.

5. Shaku Sōen, Barrows, and Ellinwood, "A Controversy on Buddhism," 43–58.

6. Ibid., 43.

7. Barrows, in ibid., quoted by Shaku Sōen from a report of Barrows's second Haskell lecture in the *Chicago Tribune*, Monday, January 13, 1896. Shaku Sōen's letter is dated March 1.

8. Shaku Sōen, in ibid.

9. Barrows, *Christianity: The World Religion*, 9–10.

10. *The Christian Conquest of Asia* was the title of a volume of Barrows's lectures in 1898, recounting the observations of his Asian lecture tour. It is subtitled *Studies and Personal Observations of Oriental Religions*, Morse Lectures of 1898. The earlier work, *Christianity: The World Religion*, contains the lectures delivered in Japan and India.

11. Shaku Sōen, Barrows, and Ellinwood, "A Controversy on Buddhism," 46.

12. T. W. Rhys Davids, *Buddhism: Its History and Literature*, 208, and also quoted by Ellinwood, in Shaku Sōen, Barrows, and Ellinwood, "A Controversy on Buddhism," 50.

13. Barrows, *The Christian Conquest of Asia*, 179.

14. Shaku Sōen, Barrows, and Ellinwood, "A Controversy on Buddhism," 46.

15. Max Muller did contribute a paper but not one that dealt with Asian religion, the field for which he was best known. See "Greek Philosophy and the Christian Religion," 935–36.

16. Muller, "The Real Significance of the Parliament of Religions."

17. Ibid., 10.

18. Ibid., 13.

19. Carus, "Christian Missions: A Triangular Debate," 276.

20. His paper was entitled "Science a Religious Revelation," in *WPR*, 978–81.

21. Carus, "The Work of the Open Court," iii.

22. *Monist* 2:4 (1891–92): 640.

23. Carus, "Monism and Meliorism," 7. First published in New York in 1885.

24. These early publications include *Monism and Meliorism* (1885); *The Soul of Man* (1891); and "The Religion of Science" (1891–92).

25. Carus, *Buddhism and Its Christian Critics*, 5.

26. Editorial note in the *Open Court* 3 (January 1890).

27. *Monist* 4:3 (April 1894).

28. Carus, "Karma and Nirvana," 417.

29. Carus, "Buddhism and Christianity," 98. Cf. "Karma and Nirvana," 428: Whereas the Hinayana "is marked by a certain negativism . . . the Mahayana makes the positive aspect of the Dharma and *nirvāna* more prominent."

30. Carus, "The Philosophy of Buddhism."

31. Tweed, *The American Encounter with Buddhism*, analyzes the "limits of dissent" of those like Carus who turned to Buddhism in the Victorian religious culture.

32. Carus, "Science a Religious Revelation."

33. Carus, *The Soul of Man*, 435.

34. Carus, *Buddhism and Its Christian Critics*, 25. Toki had of course mentioned this in his paper.

35. Carus, *Gospel*, vii, in the 1898 edition, p. ix in the 1973 edition.

36. Ralph Waldo Emerson, *Journals*, 10:248, quoted in Christy, *The Orient in American Transcendentalism*, 269.

37. Emerson, "Quotation and Originality," in ibid.

38. Carus, "Karma and Nirvana," 438.

39. Carus, *The Soul of Man*.

40. Ibid., 419.

41. Carus, *Buddhism and Its Christian Critics*, 310.

42. Carus, "The Religion of Science," *Monist* 3:3 (April 1893): 353.

43. This idea was developed at the Parliament in Hirai's second paper, "Synthetic Religion." Hirai used terms of contemporary Western thought and so his exposition is closer to Carus's, but all the Japanese delegates proposed the idea that if Christianity purified itself of its miracles and illogicalities, it would not be different from Buddhism. Again, Carus's idea appears to coincide with Eastern Buddhism but was rather an extension of the Christian belief that God, their God, had not left himself without witness. This was not the Buddhist position.

44. Eitel, *Handbook of Chinese Buddhism*, 92. This is a reprint of the 1888 edition referred to by Carus. Carus used this spelling, as given by Eitel, in the early editions, but by the 1915 edition he had switched to the Pali "Metteyya," the language of orthodox Buddhology.

45. Carus, "Buddhism and Christianity," 79, and *Buddhism and Its Christian Critics*, 195. The article was reprinted in 1897, slightly modified by placing "may" in italics, but the author maintained his point. The epithet, Buddha of kindness, strengthens the association with the image of Jesus. In *Gospel*, ch. LVI:13, Carus repeated Sakyamuni's prediction that another Buddha would arise and teach the "selfsame eternal truth" after five hundred years.

46. Carus, "Karma and Nirvana," 427.

47. The *Trikāya* doctrine was presented at the Parliament by Ashitsu and Yatsubuchi in particular. See *Gospel*, ch. XCVIII, especially verses 18–21, for Carus's version.

48. Carus, "Karma and Nirvana," 417, and *Gospel*, 252.

49. Carus, "Buddhism and Christianity," 80. See also *Gospel*, ch. XCVIII.

50. Carus, *The Soul of Man*, 389.

51. Meyer, "Paul Carus and the Religion of Science," 603.

52. Carus, *Buddhism and Its Christian Critics*, 138, and "Karma and Nirvana," 424.

53. Carus, "Karma and Nirvana," 421.

54. Ibid., 422.

55. Ibid., 427.

56. Ibid., 428.

57. In 1903 *Open Court* had fewer than 3,700 subscribers; the *Monist*, 1,000. Meyer, "Paul Carus and the Religion of Science," 598.

58. Carus's reference is to "The Fo-Sho-Hing-Tsan-King. A Life of the Buddha by Asvaghosha, translated from Sanskrit into Chinese by Dharmarakhsha, A.D. 420, and from the Chinese into English by Samuel Beal. Vol. XIX of The Sacred Books of the East. Oxford, 1883."

59. This was based on the life of the Buddha described in the *Lalitavistara*.

60. *Monist* 6:1 (October 1895): 142.

61. The references for the chapter are "MPN. V. 1–14, concerning Maitrēya see E. H. s.v. Rh. DB. pp. 180, 200; Old; G. p. 153 etc." This decodes to fourteen verses from T. W. Rhys Davids, *Buddhist-Sūtras*; two pages of T. W. Rhys Davids, *Buddhism*; and one page of Oldenberg, *Buddha, sein Leben, seine Lehre und seine Germeinde* (1890). Is "etc." intended to suggest that such ideas may be widely found? The Christian "parallelism" for this concept is John XIV:26.

62. Carus, *Gospel*, v.

63. Ibid., vi.

64. Eitel, *Handbook of Chinese Buddhism*, 92. Eitel gives five thousand years. Later editions read "In due time," but the Japanese translation, the concern of this study, confirms Carus's original statement of five hundred years, making the prediction roughly coincident with the birth of Christ.

65. Olga Kopetzky, "Remarks on the Illustrations of the Gospel of Buddha," in Carus, *Gospel* (1973 edition), 307–11. This is a reprint of the 1917 edition. She details visits to libraries, art museums, interviews with experts in Europe and Asia, study of "dogma, symbols and religious observances," study of photographs and books on the subject.

66. The second edition appeared in 1907. In late 1899 Carus had written of the need for an image of the Buddha "according to more modern American notions" (Tweed, *The American Encounter with Buddhism*, 111). It was to be "Greek in taste and most noble and elevating," and, as Verhoeven sums it up, "an active socially engaged Buddha like the figure of Christ." Verhoeven, "Americanizing the Buddha," 207.

67. Carus, *Gospel*, v.

68. See, for example, the prefatory introductions to the publications of both the Pali Text Society and the Sacred Books of the East series, where Rhys Davids and Max Muller have used this privilege.

69. Carus, *Gospel*, vi–vii.

70. Ibid., xiv–xv.

71. This was a conscious decision. Carus explained that he did this in the spirit that the article is commonly dropped from "The Christ" when referring to Jesus. The note underlined the parallels so important to his project. However, using "Buddha" as a personal name instead of designation of achievement was a device used by Western scholars to humanize and historicize the Buddha.

72. Carus, *Gospel*, xv.

73. Ibid., viii.

74. *Open Court* 9 (1895): 4435–36.

75. Carus, *Gospel*, iv.

76. Carus, *Buddhism and Its Christian Critics*, 309.

77. *Presbyterian Reformed Review*, quoted in an insert between pages 4546 and 4547 in *Open Court* 9 (1895). This insert contains a collection of reviews and comments of Carus's *Gospel*.

78. *Critic* (New York), in ibid.

79. *Secular Thought* (Toronto), in ibid.

80. An unnamed critic in the same collection of reviews.

81. Carus, *Gospel*, preface.

82. Carus, *Buddhism and Its Christian Critics*, 233.

83. *Open Court* 9 (1895): 4435–36.

84. Since the propagation of monism was the founding mission of the publishing company, Carus naturally used the journals he edited to promote the *Gospel*.

85. *Open Court* 9 (1895): 4436 (emphasis in original).

86. Ibid., 4732 and 4733.

87. This and the following quotes are taken from an appendix to the sixth edition of Carus, *The Gospel of Buddha* (1898), "Commendations and Criticisms," i–ii.

88. D. T. Suzuki, "Introduction: A Glimpse of Paul Carus," xiv. His concerns about the *Gospel* as an interpretation of Buddhism were reserved for his Japanese audience. See Chapter 11.

89. Verhoeven, "Americanizing the Buddha," and Tweed, *The American Encounter with Buddhism*.

90. Meyer, "Paul Carus and the Religion of Science," 606–7.

91. In spite of his doctorate from a reputable German university, Carus was never accepted as a philosopher or taken seriously as an academic. As his biographer, Bates, wrote in Allen Johnson, *Dictionary of American Biography*, 548: "Philosophy still tended to be the exclusive property of the universities." The quality of his work aside, academics were scandalized by his editorial independence. Using the facilities of the Open Court he published at will, without any of the formal institutional controls. He was his own editor; he had no supervision; his articles were not refereed, did not pass peer review, and did not conform to the rules of the discipline. On top of this, his eclectic editorial policy and the vast scope of his own interests were held against him. He lacked consistency and associated with intellectual fools.

92. La Salle, Ill.: Open Court, 1973. The *Gospel* was also recently reprinted in an Indian hardcover version.

93. *Open Court* 9 (1895): insert between 4546 and 4547.

94. Carus, *Gospel*, vi.

95. The *Gospel* was even overlooked by Welbon's extensive survey *The Buddhist Nirvāṇa and Its Western Interpreters*.

CHAPTER 11

1. Published under the direction of Shaku Sōen in January 1895 (2d ed., November 1901), *Budda no fukuin* is reprinted in *Suzuki Daisetsu zenshū* (The complete works of Suzuki Daisetsu), vol. 25.

2. *Fukuin*, 280. Substantial passages from Shaku Sōen's preface to *Budda no fukuin* were translated by D. T. Suzuki and published in *Open Court* 9 (1895): 4405. References to *Fukuin* are my own translations; to *Open Court*, Suzuki's.

3. *Open Court* 9 (1897): 47, quoting a newspaper report from *New York Independent* (1895).

4. *Open Court* 9 (1895): 4405.

5. Ibid.

6. *Fukuin*. Modified in the English version of *Open Court*, which reads, "This was partly shown . . ."

7. See Schwantes, "Christianity vs. Science." His argument is that science was a greater threat to Christianity in Japan than Buddhism.

8. *Fukuin*, 280.

9. Shaku Sōen, *Bankoku shūkyō taikai ichiran*, 6.

10. Translator's preface to the second edition of *Fukuin*, 281.

11. Ibid.

12. Ibid., 279.

13. Ibid.

14. Ibid.

15. "*Kikkutsu gōga*," in ibid., 279.

16. *Bukkyō kakushū kōyō* (Essentials of the Buddhist sects), 5 vols.

17. Inoue Tetsujirō (1889) wrote "the first historical analysis of the life of the Buddha." Kishimoto Hideo, *Japanese Thought in the Meiji Era*, 2:159. His *Shaka shuzoku ron* (The history of the Sakya tribe) was published by Inoue Enryō's Tetsugaku shoin in 1897.

18. Shaku Sōen, *Bankoku shūkyō taikai ichiran*, 5.

19. Ketelaar, *Of Heretics and Martyrs*. For Ketelaar the main function of the trip to Chicago was to provide this opportunity for interpretation.

20. *Manifesto*, 295.

21. Shaku Sōen, *Bankoku shūkyō taikai ichiran*, 5.

22. Kishimoto Hideo, *Japanese Thought in the Meiji Era*, 150 and 164.

23. *Kenkyusha's New Japanese-English Dictionary*, 259; Nelson, *The Modern Reader's Japanese-English Character Dictionary*, 661. Tobita, *Meiji no kotoba jiten*, 498, confirms its evangelical Christian origins.

24. *Fukuin*, 277.

25. Ibid., 2.

26. *Haibutsu kishaku* or calumny?

27. *Open Court* 9 (1895): 4404–5.

28. Kishimoto Nobuta, a Christian delegate to the Parliament, contributed a series of articles on "Buddhism in Japan." The six parts were titled "The Religious Compound in Japan," "Northern and Southern Buddhism," "Sacred Literature," "Present Condition," "The Zen and the Shin Sects," and "The Influence of Buddhism on the People." The scope of these articles prefigured his future work on comparative religion with Buddhist Anesaki Masaharu. See Suzuki Norihisa, "Nobuta Kishimoto and the Beginnings of the Scientific Study of Religion in Modern Japan."

29. *Open Court* 9 (1895): 4542.

30. Ibid., 4404.

31. Ibid., 4405.

32. Quoted in Dornish, "Joshū's Bridge," 23.

33. *Nihon shūkyō* (October 1896): 173–77. This quotation is from 175.

34. Ibid., 175.

35. Shaku Sōen, "Shūkyōka kondankai ni tsuite," 176. The term he used for "liberation"

("enlightenment") is *gedatsu*; and that for "consolation" is *anki*. The distinction is not unlike Inoue Enryō's recognition that "women and stupid folk [*gumin*]" need the consolation of religion, whereas his "young men of spirit and education" should pursue philosophy. *BKJ*, 392.

36. Kitagawa, *The 1893 World's Parliament of Religions and Its Legacy*, 12. Thelle concurs.

37. Reed, *Japan: Its History, Tradition and Religion*, 2:214–15.

38. Michel Foucault, quoted in Dreyfus and Rabinow, *Michel Foucault: Beyond Structuralism and Hermeneutics*, 187.

39. Fader, "Zen in the West," 141.

40. Peiris, *The Western Contribution to Buddhism*, 237.

41. *Open Court* 9 (1895): 4733.

CHAPTER 12

1. The letter is presented in Fader, "Zen in the West," 143. As Sharf points out, this contradicts Suzuki's own retrospective account (D. T. Suzuki, "Introduction: A Glimpse of Paul Carus," xi) of responding to Carus's plea for assistance with the translation of Chinese texts. "Zen of Japanese Nationalism," 17.

2. Dornish, "Joshū's Bridge," provides a comprehensive list.

3. Kirita, "D. T. Suzuki and the State," 52.

4. See Tweed, *The American Encounter with Buddhism*, on early interest; Fields, *How the Swans Came to the Lake*, for a narrative account of the transmission of Buddhism to North America; Sharf, "Zen of Japanese Nationalism," for a more sophisticated analysis of East-West interaction in the introduction of Zen to the West. Dornish, "Joshū's Bridge," is an excellent study of D. T. Suzuki's early career. Seager, *Buddhism in America*; Prebish, *Luminous Passage*; Tworkov, *Zen in America*; Hori, "Japanese Zen in America." The appendices of Williams and Queen, *American Buddhism*, reveal the extent of interest. Appendix A lists dissertations and theses on American Buddhism; appendix B, North American dissertations and theses related to Buddhism. Other works have been referred to previously. The number of books and articles on the topic is itself testimony to the success of the project.

5. See note 8.

6. Masahiro Shimoda, "The Significance of the Publication of the Taisho Tripitaka in Modern Buddhist Studies," paper presented at the Association for Asian Studies conference, Washington, D.C., 2002.

7. Discussed in Chapter 10. Barrows's sermon was published in the *Chicago Tribune*, January 13, 1896. Shaku Sōen's reply is reproduced in *Zen for Americans*. The incident was covered in *Open Court*, January 1897. Reflecting on remarks made by Suzuki in 1958, Sharf observes that "[o]ne is led to suspect that Suzuki's lifelong effort to bring Buddhist enlightenment to the Occident had become inextricably bound to a studied contempt for the West, a West whose own cultural arrogance and imperialist inclinations Suzuki had come to know all too well." "Zen of Japanese Nationalism," 29. Might such an attitude have its origins in 1896?

8. I am interested to know to what extent Carus may have coordinated the program. His support for the promotion of Buddhism continued throughout his life. Wayne Yokoyama, a member of the editing team for the new volumes of the *Suzuki Daisetsu zenshū*, has brought my attention to a letter by Shaku Sōen to Carus offering heartfelt thanks to Carus for writing the letter to Barrows in response to the *Chicago Tribune* report. "The reply you have written for us, just and thoroughly expresses what we wish to utter, and I hope it will remove these important misconceptions concerning Buddhism which are cherished by American preachers and

scholars. I myself examined it repeatedly. Though I was more than once tempted to add my own opinion to that reply, yet I did not dare to do so, thinking that such a beautiful statement as this should not be defiled by touching with any unskilled hands. The only alteration I have made is the adding of the word Vairochana-Buddha next to the word Amitabha-Buddha. I ordered Suzuki to copy the reply and to send it to Dr. Barrows by the same mail with this letter to you. I do not doubt that he will be magnanimous enough to make it public in the Chicago daily papers or in some religious paper." It is dated March 1, 1896. Because this event intervenes between the earlier letters and Suzuki's arrival, is it possible that Carus did respond—saying words to the effect that something must be done, send Suzuki to me and I will teach him the ropes; he can learn by assisting with Chinese translations.

9. *T'ai-Shang Kan-Ying P'ien* (Treatise of the exalted one on response and retribution); *Yin Chih Wen* (The tract of the quiet way).

10. Carus, publisher's preface to D. T. Suzuki, *Asvaghosha's Discourse*, iv. Wayne Yokoyama has also brought to my attention a German article in Suzuki's name, "Die buddhisteische Psychologie bei Asvaghosha. Expose aus Asvaghosha's Mahayanasraddhotpadacastra," *Buddistische Warte* 2 (1908–11): 36–46, 161–64. How do Suzuki's ideas read when translated into German, Carus's language?

11. Dornish, "Joshū's Bridge"; Sharf, "Zen of Japanese Nationalism," comments that there are passages of *Outlines* that could have come from the pen of Carus himself.

12. Verhoeven, "Americanizing the Buddha," 218.

13. Ibid., 219. Cf. Sharf, "Zen of Japanese Nationalism," 19.

14. Carus, publisher's preface to D. T. Suzuki, *Asvaghosha's Discourse*, iv.

15. Tweed, *The American Encounter with Buddhism*; Verhoeven, "Americanizing the Buddha."

16. Suzuki edited *Zendō* with Shaku Sōen from 1910, soon after his return to Japan. The English-language journal, *Eastern Buddhist*, began in 1921. Both Dornish and Sharf comment on its similarity to Carus's journals.

17. A letter to Shaku Sōen dated 1898 mentions that he goes to the editorial office to work on the translation every morning. Quoted in Fader, "Zen in the West," 143.

18. "Notes on the Madhyamika Philosophy" (1898); "The Madhyamika School in China" (1898); "Confucius" (1899); "Asvaghosha, the First Advocate of Mahāyāna Buddhism" (1900); "The Breadth of Buddhism" (1900); "What Is Buddhism?" (1902); "Mahayana Buddhism" (1902); "Individual Mortality" (1903); "A Buddhist View of War" (1904); "Philosophy of the Yogacara: The Madhyamika and the Yogacara" (1904); "The First Buddhist Council" (1904); "The Essence of Buddhism" (1905); "A Religious Book of China" (1905); "Moral Tales of the Treatise on Response and Retribution" (1905); "Is Buddhism Nihilistic?" (1906); "Japanese Conception of Death and Immortality" (1906); "The Zen Sect of Buddhism" (1906–7); "The Seven Gods of Bliss" (1907); "A Brief History of Early Chinese Philosophy" (1907, 1908); "The Development of Mahayana Buddhism" (1909, 1914).

19. The tour was financed by a wealthy American couple, Alexander and Ida Russell, who had come to Engakuji to learn meditation. His disciple Senzaki Nyōgen accompanied him to America, stayed on, and, though he did not begin teaching until 1922, eventually established a Zen mission in San Francisco. See Shaku Sōen, "Reflections on an American Journey."

20. D. T. Suzuki, translator's preface to Shaku Sōen, *Zen for Americans*, iv.

21. Kirita, "D. T. Suzuki and the State," 55, comments that Suzuki wrote a number of articles for *Rikugo zasshi* and *Shin bukkyō* while he was in America. Other papers from this period published in *Suzuki Daisetsu zenshū*: "Zen to Rinri" (Zen and ethics), 31 (1897): 53–

56; "'Zenshū' kisha ni ataete shūkyō to kon'in," 31 (1898): 53–56; "Zakkan roku" (Random thoughts), 31 (1898): 64–70; "Seiza to susume" (Encouragement of sitting still), 18 (1889): 391–404; "'Sammai' toiu koto ni tsukite" (Regarding samādhi), 31 (1899): 53–56; "Bukkyō no hirosa" (The breadth of Buddhism, presumably a translation of the paper with the same name in *Open Court* 14:1 [January 1900]: 51–53), 31 (1900): 75–77; "Zen to Rinri" (Zen and ethics), 31 (1900): 75–77. For a complete list, see Kirita, "Suzuki Daisetsu."

22. D. T. Suzuki, *Outlines of Mahāyāna Buddhism*, xiii.

23. In a further continuity of the Chicago mission, he offered this book to Shaku Sōen with the wish that it might be of help in Japan, an alternative perhaps to *Budda no fukuin* as an easy reader for Western-educated Japanese.

24. D. T. Suzuki, "Asvaghosha, the First Advocate of the Mahāyāna Buddhism." Carus, in his review of *Awakening of Faith*, cuts through Suzuki's academic caution to make the date explicit. See also Suzuki's paper "The First Buddhist Council," which seeks to establish the presence of a large body of alternate opinion at the time of the Buddha's death.

25. D. T. Suzuki, "Asvaghosha, the First Advocate of the Mahāyāna Buddhism."

26. D. T. Suzuki, *Outlines of Mahāyāna Buddhism*, 6. Note again the simultaneous origin of the two forms.

27. Ibid., 3–4. See also D. T. Suzuki, "The First Buddhist Council" (1904), where he goes back to the earliest texts to establish that there were different interpretations of the Buddha's words at his death and therefore even when he lived; there was a large body of opinion alongside the Theravada.

28. D. T. Suzuki, "The Zen Sect of Buddhism," 8.

29. D. T. Suzuki, "Zen as Chinese Interpretation of the Doctrine of Enlightenment." Although this reference is to the 1949 publication in *Essays in Zen Buddhism*, the paper had been published in *Eastern Buddhist* 2:6 (1923) as a translation of the 1911 lecture. The idea appears slightly less elegantly expressed in the opening of *Introduction to Zen Buddhism*, 32. The essays in this book had first appeared in a short-lived journal, *New East* (Tokyo, 1917), edited by Robertson Scott.

30. D. T. Suzuki, "The Zen Sect of Buddhism," 33.

31. Ibid., 34.

32. Ibid., 38. This section offered extracts from *Sermons of a Buddhist Abbot*.

33. Compare this with the 1917 version: the sects other than Zen "bespeak their Indian origin in an unmistakable manner. No Chinese or Japanese mind could have conceived of the complex rituals of the Shingon, or the highly speculative philosophy of the Tendai and Kegon." The racial hierarchy implied in the argument of the Five Periods of the Buddha's teaching has now given way to the concept of different racial genius: each race produces a religion in keeping with its individual genius.

34. D. T. Suzuki, *Introduction to Zen Buddhism*, 37.

35. Okakura's *Awakening of the East*, written 1901–2, was more overtly anti-Western and anticolonial.

36. Buddhism, Okakura explains in this India context, is simply Hinduism for export.

37. Contents page of *The Awakening of Japan*. In ch. 1, "The Night of Asia," there is a subheading that reads, "While Christendom struggled with medievalism the Buddhaland was a garden of culture."

38. While there is a historical connection between the flourishing of Zen in the Kamakura period under the Hōjō regency, Martin Collcutt argues convincingly that although among the followers of Zen, never one of the largest sects, members of the samurai classes might have been

predominant, it cannot be said that most samurai were followers of Zen. See his "The Zen Monastery in Kamakura Society."

39. Rafael, *White Love*, 105–6.

40. Laffan, "Mustafa and the Mikado."

41. Gardener, "Japan: Our Little Neighbor in the East," 176.

42. Iriye, "Japan's Drive to Great-Power Status," 320–21.

43. Chamberlain, *The Invention of a New Religion*, 6.

44. Shaku Sōen, "Reflections on an American Journey," 144.

45. These are "The Buddhist View of War"; "At the Battle of Nan-Shan Hill"; "An Address Delivered at a Service Held in Memory of Those Who Died in the Russo-Japanese War." The papers also appeared in the *Monist* and *Open Court*.

46. Chamberlain, *The Invention of a New Religion*, 19, 13 (emphasis in original).

47. Nogi had practiced Zen with the Zen master Nantembō Tōjū (1839–1925), whose teaching and practice exemplified the sort of energy and eccentricity Suzuki wrote of.

48. Nukariya (1867–1934) was a Sōtō Zen priest and personal friend of Suzuki. This book was published while he was living in America and lecturing at Harvard University. Sharf, working without reference to the 1907 paper, sees Suzuki's writings on Zen beginning much later. Sharf, "Zen of Japanese Nationalism," 10.

49. *Zen Buddhism and Its Influence on Japanese Culture*, published by the Eastern Buddhist Society, Japan, in 1938, was based on lectures given in England and America in 1936. It was published in Japanese as *Zen to Nihon Bunka* in 1940, and revised and issued in America in 1949 as *Zen and Japanese Culture*; it continues as a standard reference to the present. It has been circulating through the time of Japan's invasion of mainland Asia, the war in the Pacific, the postwar flush of American appreciation of Japanese culture, the Zen boom of the 1960s and 1970s—its influence multiplied by the reliance on it of Western authors. For discussion of Zen and nationalism in these later periods, see Heisig and Maraldo, *Rude Awakenings*; Victoria, *Zen at War*.

50. *Eastern Buddhist* 1:1 (May 1921): 84.

51. *Eastern Buddhist* 1:1 (April 1925): 81.

52. Reference to Noguchi's opening address, and to Shaku Sōen's preface to *Fukuin*, both quoted in previous chapters.

53. Sharf, "Zen of Japanese Nationalism," 1–2, summarizes the "woeful misreadings" that have led to Western attitudes to Zen.

54. Ibid.

55. King, *Orientalism and Religion*, 156.

56. Watts, in D. T. Suzuki, *Outlines of Mahāyāna Buddhism*, x–xi.

57. Watts, *The Way of Zen*, "made considerable use of the works of Professor D. T. Suzuki" (xv); Munsterberg's preface to his *Zen and Oriental Art* expresses his debt to "Daisetz Suzuki, the famous Zen abbot, and Alan W. Watts, the Western world's chief interpreter of Zen." As influential as he unquestionably was, Suzuki was not an abbot but a lay Buddhist.

58. See Ziolkowski, "The Literary Bearing of Chicago's 1893 World's Parliament of Religions," 18. Ziolkowski also notes the influence of Suzuki's ideas on such diverse people as composer John Cage, psychoanalysts C. G. Jung and Eric Fromm, religious thinker Thomas Merton, William Butler Yeats, and Reginald Horace Blyth.

59. Sharf, "Zen of Japanese Nationalism," 2.

60. Quoted in Nishizaki, *Lafcadio Hearn*, 103.

61. Ashitsu Jitsuzen, *Die buddhistische Religion in Japan*, cited in Bandō, *A Bibliography on*

Japanese Buddhism, 19. Ashitsu's "Das Wesen des Buddhismus im Lichte der (Japanischen) Tendai-Schule" was also published in Germany; also cited in Bandō, *A Bibliography on Japanese Buddhism*, 76. The French published a translation by Toki Hōryū, of a Shingon manuscript held in the Musee Guimet, *Si-Do-In-Dzou*. France was at this time the center of interest in Mahayana Buddhism.

62. Seager, "The World's Parliament of Religions, Chicago, Illinois, 1893," 13.

63. Ziolkowski confirms Seager's thesis in his analysis of post-Parliamentary poetry in the United States in his "The Literary Bearing of Chicago's 1893 World's Parliament of Religions," 10–25. He also surveys the enduring influence of the representation of Eastern religions on literature in English. The first Vedānta Society was founded by Vivekananda in New York in 1895. Chapters opened in other European and American cities later. Consequently his impact continued after his death in 1902, persisting through the literature of Romain Rolland, Aldous Huxley, and Christopher Isherwood. Ibid., 19.

64. See, for example, Seager, *Buddhism in America*, ch. 7, "Zen and Its Flagship Institutions," 90–112; Tworkov, *Zen in America*; Hori, "Japanese Zen in America"; Prebish, *Luminous Passage*.

65. Spuler, *Developments in Australian Buddhism*, for example, looks at the Diamond Sangha in Australia. Rocha, "Being a Zen Buddhist Brazilian," studies Zen Buddhism in Brazil.

BIBLIOGRAPHY

Abe Masao, ed. *A Zen Life: D. T. Suzuki Remembered*. New York: Weatherhill, 1986.

Abe Yoshiya. "Religious Freedom under the Meiji Constitution." *Contemporary Religions in Japan* 10 (December 1968): 268–338; 10 (March–June 1969): 57–97; 10 (September–December 1969): 181–203; 11 (September–December 1970): 27–79; 11 (March–June 1970): 223–96.

Adolphson, Mikael S. *Gates of Power: Monks, Courtiers, and Warriors in Pre-Modern Japan*. Honolulu: University of Hawai'i Press, 2000.

Ahir, D. C. *Pioneers of Buddhist Revival in India*. Delhi: Sri Satguru Publications, [1989?].

Aitken, Robert. "Three Lessons from Shaku Sōen." In *The Path of Compassion: Contemporary Writings on Engaged Buddhism*, edited by F. Epstein and D. Maloney, 145–49. Berkeley: Parallax Press, 1985.

Almond, Philip C. "The Buddha in the West: From Myth to History." *Religion* 16 (1986): 305–22.

——. "The Medieval West and Buddhism." *Eastern Buddhist*, n.s., 19:2 (Autumn 1986): 85–101.

——. *The British Discovery of Buddhism*. Cambridge: Cambridge University Press, 1988.

Anderson, Ronald Stone. "Nishi Honganji and Japanese Buddhist Nationalism, 1862–1945." Ph.D. diss., University of California, 1956.

Anesaki Masaharu. *History of Japanese Religion*. Tokyo: Tuttle, 1963.

Arac, Jonathan, ed. *After Foucault: Humanistic Knowledge, Postmodern Challenges*. New Brunswick: Rutgers University Press, 1988.

Arnold, Edwin. *The Light of Asia*. London: Kegan Paul, Trench, Trübner, 1879. Reprint, 1906.

——. *Seas and Lands*. London: Longman, 1892.

Ashitsu Jitsuzen. *Die buddhistische Religion in Japan*. Leipzig: Lotusblüten, 1895.

——. *Nihon shūkyō miraiki* (Notes on the future religion of Japan). Kobe: Funai Seitarō, 1889.

——. *Kenpō seigan: tōyō no shin buppō* (The aim of the constitution: The new Buddhist law of the East). Osaka: Kyōgaku Shoin, 1890.

——. "Buddha." In *The World's Parliament of Religions*, edited by John Henry Barrows, 1038–40. Chicago: Parliament Publishing, 1893.

——. "Buddha." In *Neely's History of the Parliament of Religions*, edited by W. R. Houghton, 537–43. Chicago: F. Tennyson Neely, 1894.

——. "The Fundamental Teachings of Buddhism." *Monist* 4:2 (January 1894): 163–75.

——. "Das Wesen des Buddhismus im Lichte der (Japanischen) Tendai-Schule." *Der Buddhist* 1 (1905–6): 341–44.

Badger, Reid. *The Great American Fair*. Chicago: N. Hall, 1979.

Bailey, Beatrice Bodart. "Kaempfer Restor'd." *Monumenta Nipponica* 43:1 (1988): 1–33.

Bandō Shōjun, ed. *A Bibliography on Japanese Buddhism*. Tokyo: CIIB Press, 1958.

——. "D. T. Suzuki's Life in La Salle." *Eastern Buddhist* 11:1 (August 1967): 137–46.

Barrows, John Henry. "Results from the Parliament of Religions." *Forum* 18 (September 1894): 54–67.

——. *Christianity: The World Religion*. Chicago: A. C. McClurg, 1897.

——. *The Christian Conquest of Asia: Studies and Personal Observations of Oriental Religions*. Morse Lectures of 1898. New York: Charles Scribner's Sons, 1899.

——, ed. *The World's Parliament of Religions*. 2 vols. Chicago: Parliament Publishing, 1893.

Batchelor, Stephen. *The Awakening of the West: The Encounter of Buddhism and Western Culture*. Berkeley: Parallax Press, 1994.

Beal, Samuel. *A Catena of Buddhist Scriptures from the Chinese*. London: Trübner, 1871.

——, ed. *Fo-Sho-Hing-Tsan-King: A Life of the Buddha by Asvaghosha Bodhisattva*. Oxford: Clarendon Press, 1883.

Beautiful Scenes of the White City and the Famous Midway Plaisance. Chicago: Laid and Lee, 1894.

Bellah, Robert N. "Intellectual and Society in Japan." *Daedalus* 101:2 (Spring 1972): 89–115.

——, ed. *Religion and Progress in Modern Asia*. New York: Free Press, 1965.

Benz, Ernst. "Buddhism in the Western World." In *Buddhism in the Modern World*, edited by H. Dumoulin, 305–22. New York: Collier Macmillan, 1976.

Bernauer, James, and David Rasmussen, eds. *The Final Foucault*. Cambridge, Mass.: MIT Press, 1988.

Best, Ernest E. *Christian Faith and Cultural Crisis: The Japanese Case*. Leiden: E. J. Brill, 1966.

Bigelow, William Sturgis. *Buddhism and Immortality*. Ingersoll Lecture, 1908. Boston: Houghton Mifflin, 1908.

Blacker, Carmen. *The Japanese Enlightenment*. Cambridge: Cambridge University Press, 1964.

Bocking, Brian. "Comparative Studies of Buddhism and Christianity." *Japanese Journal of Religious Studies* 10 (1983): 87–110.

Bonney, C. C. "The World's Parliament of Religions." *Monist* 5:3 (April 1895): 321–44.

Borgen, Robert. *Sugawara no Michizane and the Early Heian Court*. Cambridge, Mass.: Harvard University Press, 1986.

Brear, Douglas. "Early Assumptions in Western Buddhist Studies." *Religion* 5 (1975): 136–59.

Breckenridge, Carol A. "The Aesthetics and Politics of Collecting: India at World Fairs." *Comparative Studies in Society and History* 31:2 (April 1989): 195–216.

Brinkley, F. *Japan and China: Their History, Arts and Literature*. Vol. 5. London: T. C. & E. C. Jack, 1904.

Brown, Judith M. *Modern India: The Origins of an Asian Democracy*. Oxford: Oxford University Press, 1990.

Brownell, Clarence Ludlow. "Hongwangi and Buddhist Protestantism in Japan." *Transactions of the Asiatic Society of Japan, London* 6 (1902): 68–87.

Buel, J. W. *The Magic City: A Massive Portfolio of Original Photographic Views of the Great World's Fair*. Philadelphia: Historical Publishing Company, 1894.

Bukkyō daijiten (Encyclopedia of Buddhism). 10 vols. Tokyo: Sekai seiten kankō kyōkai, 1968.

Bukkyō Kakushū Kyōkai, ed. *Bukkyō kakushū kōyō*. 5 vols. Kyoto: Kaiba Shoin, 1896.

Burg, David F. *Chicago's White City of 1893*. Lexington: University of Kentucky Press, 1976.

Burnouf, Eugène. *Le Lotus de la bonne loi*. Paris: Maisonneuve et Cie, 1852.

——. *L'Introduction à l'histoire du Buddhisme Indien*. Paris: Maisonneuve et Cie, 1876.

Caldarola, Carlo. *Christianity the Japanese Way*. Leiden: E. J. Brill, 1979.
Carter, Paul A. *The Spiritual Crisis in the Gilded Age*. DeKalb: Northern Illinois University Press, 1971.
Carus, Paul. *Monism and Meliorism: A Philosophical Essay on Causality and Ethics*. New York, 1885.
——. "Monism and Meliorism." *Open Court* 8:5 (March 1889).
——. "Religion of Resignation." *Open Court* 3:48 (January 1890): 2051–52.
——. "Positive Science versus Gnosticism and Agnosticism." *Open Court* 4:2 (March 1890): 2120–22, 2145–47, 2189–90.
——. "Enter into Nirvana." *Open Court* 4:43 (December 1890): 2635–36.
——. *The Soul of Man*. Chicago: Open Court, 1891.
——. "The Religion of Science." *Monist* 2:4 (July 1892): 600–606.
——. "The Religion of Science." *Monist* 3:3 (April 1893): 352–61.
——. "The Dawn of a New Religious Era." *Forum* 16 (1893): 388–96.
——. "Science a Religious Revelation." In *The World's Parliament of Religions*, edited by John Henry Barrows, 978–98. Chicago: Parliament Publishing, 1893.
——. "The Relation of the Sciences to Religion." In *Neely's History of the Parliament of Religions*, edited by W. R. Houghton, 450. Chicago: F. Tennyson Neely, 1894.
——. "Karma and Nirvana: Are the Buddhist Doctrines Nihilistic?" *Monist* 4:3 (April 1894): 417–39.
——. "Christian Missions: A Triangular Debate before the Nineteenth Century Club of New York." *Monist* 5:2 (January 1895): 264–81.
——. "The World's Religious Parliament Extension." *Monist* 5:3 (April 1895): 345–53.
——. "Buddhism and Christianity." *Monist* 5:1 (October 1895): 65–103.
——. "The Philosophy of Buddhism." *Monist* 7:2 (January 1896–97): 255–86.
——. *Buddhism and Its Christian Critics*. Chicago: Open Court, 1897.
——-. "The Mythology of Buddhism." *Monist* 7:3 (April 1897): 415–45.
——. *The Gospel of Buddha*. 6th ed. Chicago: Open Court, 1898.
——. Review of Asvaghosha's *Discourse on the Awakening of Faith in the Mahāyāna*, translated by Teitaro Suzuki. *Monist* 11:2 (January 1901): 293–94.
——. *Amitabha: A Story of Buddhist Theology*. Chicago: Open Court, 1906.
——. "The Work of the Open Court." In *Twenty Years of the Open Court, 1887–1906*. Chicago: Open Court, 1907.
Chamberlain, Basil Hall. *Things Japanese*. London: John Murray, 1905.
——. *The Invention of a New Religion*. London: Watts, 1912.
Chang, Richard T. "The Question of the Unilateral Denunciation and the Meiji Government, 1888–1892." In *Japan in Transition: Thought and Action in the Meiji Era, 1868–1912*, edited by Hilary Conroy, Sandra T. W. Patterson, and Wayne Davis, 174–92. London: Associated University Presses, 1985.
Cheney, Annie Elizabeth. "Japan and Her Relation to Foreign Powers." *Arena* 8 (1893): 455–66.
——. "Mahayana Buddhism in Japan." *Arena* 16 (1896): 439–44.
Childers, R. C. *A Dictionary of the Pali Language*. London: Kegan Paul, Trench, Trübner, 1974.
Chisolm, Lawrence W. *Fenollosa: The Far East and American Culture*. New Haven: Yale University Press, 1963.
Christy, Arthur. *The Orient in American Transcendentalism*. New York: Columbia University Press, 1932.

Chudhadharn, H.R.H. Prince Chandradat. "Buddhism as It Exists in Siam." In *The World's Parliament of Religions*, edited by John Henry Barrows, 645–49. Chicago: Parliament Press, 1893.

Clausen, Christopher. "Victorian Buddhism and the Origins of Comparative Religion." *Religion* 5 (1975): 1–15.

Cohn, Bernard S. "The Command of Language and the Language of Command." In *Subaltern Studies IV*, edited by Ranajit Guha, 276–329. Delhi: Oxford University Press, 1985.

Colebrooke, H. T. *Essays on History, Literature and Religions of Ancient India*. New Delhi: Motilal Banarsidass, 1977.

Collcutt, Martin. *Five Mountains: The Rinzai Zen Monastic Institution in Medieval Japan*. Cambridge, Mass.: Harvard University Press, 1980.

——. "The Zen Monastery in Kamakura Society." In *Court and Bakufu in Japan*, edited by J. Mass, 191–220. New Haven: Yale University Press, 1982.

——. "Buddhism: The Threat of Eradication." In *Japan in Transition: From Tokugawa to Meiji*, edited by Marius B. Jansen and G. Rozman, 143–67. Princeton: Princeton University Press, 1986.

Conant, Ellen P. "The French Connection: Emile Guimet's Mission to Japan. A Cultural Context for Japonisme." In *Japan in Transition: Thought and Action in the Meiji Era, 1868–1912*, edited by Hilary Conroy, Sandra T. W. Davis, and Wayne Patterson, 113–46. London: Associated University Presses, 1985.

Concerned Buddhists. "*Bankoku shūkyō dai kai gi ni tsuite kaku shū kyō kai ni nozomu*". [A Request to the All Sects Council concerning the World's Parliament of Religions.] *Shūkyō*, April 5, 1893 (Meiji 26), 294–99.

Conroy, Hilary. "Western Parameters of Sino-Japanese Relations." In *Japan in Transition: Thought and Action in the Meiji Era, 1868–1912*, edited by Hilary Conroy, Sandra T. W. Davis, and Wayne Patterson, 193–204. London: Associated University Presses, 1985.

Conze, Edward. "Buddhist Philosophy and Its European Parallels." *Philosophy East and West* 13:1 (1963): 9–23.

——. "Spurious Parallels to Buddhist Philosophy." *Philosophy East and West* 13:2 (1963): 105–16.

——. "Recent Progress in Buddhist Studies." In *Thirty Years of Buddhist Studies*, 1–32. London: Bruno Cassirer, 1967.

——. "Problems in Buddhist History." In *Further Buddhist Studies*, 144–49. London: Bruno Cassirer, 1975.

Cooke, Gerald. "Traditional Buddhist Sects and Modernisation in Japan." *Japanese Journal of Religious Studies* 1:4 (December 1974): 267–330.

Cooper, Michael. "The Early Europeans and Tea." In *Tea in Japan: Essays on the History of Chanoyu*, edited by Paul Varley and Kumakura Isao, 101–33. Honolulu: University of Hawai'i Press, 1989.

——, ed. *They Came to Japan: An Anthology of European Reports on Japan, 1543–1640*. Berkeley: University of California Press, 1965.

Craig, Albert. *Chōshū in the Meiji Restoration*. Cambridge, Mass.: Harvard University Press, 1964.

——. "Fukuzawa Yukichi: The Philosophical Foundations of Meiji Nationalism." In *Political Development in Modern Japan*, edited by R. E. Ward, 99–148. Princeton: Princeton University Press, 1968.

Cutler, H. G. *The World's Fair: Its Meaning and Scope*. Chicago, 1891.

Dai jimmei jiten (Biographical encyclopedia). Tokyo: Heibonsha, 1955.

Davis, Sandra T. W. "Treaty Revision, National Security and Regional Co-operation: A Minto Viewpoint." In *Japan in Transition: Thought and Action in the Meiji Era, 1868–1912*, edited by Hilary Conroy, Sandra T. W. Davis, and Wayne Patterson, 149–73. London: Associated University Presses, 1985.

Davis, Winston Bradley. "The Civil Religion of Inoue Tetsujirō." *Japanese Journal of Religious Studies* 3:1 (March 1976): 5–40.

——. *Toward Modernity: A Developmental Typology of Popular Religious Affiliations in Modern Japan*. Ithaca: Cornell University, 1977.

——. "Buddhism and the Modernisation of Japan." *History of Religions* 28:4 (May 1989): 304–39.

De Harlez, Charles. "Buddhist Sects in Japan." *Dublin Review* 116 (January 1895): 25–45.

De Jong, J. W. "A Brief History of Buddhist Studies in Europe and America." *Eastern Buddhist* 7:1 (May 1974): 55–106; 7:2 (October 1974): 49–82.

De Silva, K. M. *Social Policy and Missionary Organizations in Ceylon, 1840–1855*. London: Longmans, 1965.

Dharmapāla, Anagārika [David Hevaviratne]. "The World's Debt to Buddha." In *The World's Parliament of Religions*, edited by John Henry Barrows, 862–80. Chicago: Parliament Publishing, 1893.

——. "Points of Resemblance and Difference between Buddhism and Christianity." In *The World's Parliament of Religions*, edited by John Henry Barrows, 1288–90. Chicago: Parliament Publishing, 1893.

——. "The World's Debt to Buddha." In *Neely's History of the Parliament of Religions*, edited by W. R. Houghton, 406–9. Chicago: F. Tennyson Neely, 1894.

——. "Buddhism and Christianity." In *Neely's History of the Parliament of Religions*, edited by W. R. Houghton, 803–6. Chicago: F. Tennyson Neely, 1894.

——. "The World's Debt to Buddha." In *Return to Righteousness*, edited by A. Guruge, 3–22. Colombo: Government Press, 1965.

——. "India and Japan." In *Return to Righteousness*, edited by A. Guruge, 651–54. Colombo: Government Press. 1965.

——. "Diary Leaves of the Buddhist Representative to the World's Parliament of Religions in Chicago." In *Return to Righteousness*, edited by A. Guruge, 707–12. Colombo: Government Press, 1965.

Diosy, Arthur. "Yamato Damashii: The Spirit of Old Japan." A paper read before the Ninth International Congress of Orientalists, September 4, 1891. Reprinted from *Imperial and Asian Quarterly Review*, July 1893.

Dornish, Margaret Hammond. "Joshū's Bridge: D. T. Suzuki's Message and Mission, 1897–1927." Ph.D. diss., Claremont University, 1969.

Dreyfus, Hubert L., and Paul Rabinow. *Michel Foucault: Beyond Structuralism and Hermeneutics*. Chicago: University of Chicago Press, 1983.

Dulles, Foster Rhea. *Yankees and Samurai: America's Role in the Emergence of Modern Japan, 1791–1900*. New York: Harper and Row, 1965.

Dumoulin, Heinrich, ed. *Buddhism in the Modern World*. New York: Collier Macmillan, 1976.

——. "Buddhism and Nineteenth-Century German Philosophy." *Journal of the History of Ideas* 42:3 (July–September 1981): 457–70.

D'Vivedi, Manilal N. "Answers of Orthodox Hinduism to Certain Religious Problems." In *The World's Parliament of Religions*, edited by John Henry Barrows, 333–39. Chicago: Parliament Publishing, 1893.

Earhart, Byron H. *Japanese Religion: Unity and Diversity*. Belmont, Calif.: Wadsworth, 1982.

Eden, Charles H. *Japan: Historical and Descriptive*. London: M. Ward, 1877.

Edkins, Joseph. *Chinese Buddhism: A Volume of Sketches, Historical, Descriptive, and Critical*. London: Kegan Paul, Trench, Trübner, 1893.

Eitel, Ernest J. *Handbook of Chinese Buddhism*. 2d ed. 1888. Reprint, Amsterdam: Trübner, 1970.

Eliade, Mircea. *From Primitives to Zen: A Thematic Sourcebook on the History of Religions*. New York: Harper and Row, 1967.

Eliot, Charles. *Japanese Buddhism*. 1935. Reprint, London: Routledge and Kegan Paul, 1959.

Elison, George. *Deus Destroyed: The Image of Christianity in Early Modern Japan*. Cambridge, Mass.: Harvard University Press, 1973.

Ellwood, Robert S., Jr. *Alternative Altars: Unconventional and Eastern Spirituality in America*. Chicago: University of Chicago Press, 1979.

Encyclopedia of Buddhism. Colombo, 1971.

Ernest, R. *Buddhism and Science*. Rangoon: Publications of the Buddhasasana, 2446 (Buddhist dating).

Fader, Larry A. "Zen in the West: Historical and Philosophical Implications of the 1893 Parliament of Religions." *Eastern Buddhist* 15:1 (Spring 1982): 122–45.

Fenollosa, Ernest F. "Contemporary Japanese Art." *Century* 46 (August 1893): 577–81.

——. *Epochs of Chinese and Japanese Art*. 2 vols. London: William Heinemann, 1913.

Fields, Rick. *How the Swans Came to the Lake*. Boulder: Shambhala, 1981.

Fisk, Adele M. "Buddhism in India Today." In *Buddhism in the Modern World*, edited by Heinrich Dumoulin, 130–46. New York: Collier Macmillan, 1976.

Flower, B. O. "Justice for Japan." *Arena* 10 (1894): 225–36.

Foucault, Michel. *The Order of Things: An Archaeology of the Human Sciences*. London: Tavistock, 1970.

——. *Discipline and Punish: The Birth of the Prison*. Hammondsworth: Peregrine, 1977.

——. "Nietzsche, Genealogy, History." In *Language, Counter-Memory, Practice*, edited by D. F. Bouchard, 139–64. Ithaca: Cornell University Press, 1977.

——. *The History of Sexuality*. Harmondsworth: Penguin, 1978.

——. "Questions on Geography." In *Michel Foucault: Power/Knowledge: Selected Interviews and Other Writings, 1972–77*, edited by Colin Gordon, 63–77. Brighton: Harvester Press, 1980.

——. "Two Lectures." In *Michel Foucault: Power/Knowledge: Selected Interviews and Other Writings, 1972–77*, edited by Colin Gordon, 78–108. Brighton: Harvester Press, 1980.

——. *The Archaeology of Knowledge*. London: Tavistock, 1982.

Fraser, Mrs. Hugh. *A Diplomatist's Wife in Japan*. London: Hutchinson, [1898?].

Fujii Jintaro, ed. *Outline of Japanese History in the Meiji Era*. Translated by K. Hathe and Kenneth Coton. Centenary Cultural Council Series, 7. Tokyo: Ōbunsha, 1958.

Fukuzawa Yukichi. *Autobiography*. Revised translation by Eiichi Kiyooka. New York: Columbia University Press, 1966.

Furuta Shokin. "Shaku Sōen: The Footsteps of a Modern Japanese Zen Master." Translated by Kudo Sumiko. *Philosophical Studies of Japan* 8 (1967): 67–91.

Gardener, Helen. "Japan: Our Little Neighbor in the East." *Arena* 11 (1895): 176–91.

Gates, Merril Edwardes. "The Significance to Christianity of the Discovery and the History of America." In *Christianity Practically Applied*, edited by E. M. Wherry, 34–56. Chicago: Evangelical Alliance, 1893.

Gluck, Carol. *Japan's Modern Myths: Ideology in the Late Meiji Period*. Princeton: Princeton University Press, 1985.

Gombrich, Richard F. *Theravāda Buddhism: A Social History from Ancient Benares to Modern Colombo*. London: Routledge and Kegan Paul, 1988.

Gombrich, Richard F., and Gananath Obeyesekere, eds. *Buddhism Transformed: Religious Change in Sri Lanka*. Princeton: Princeton University Press, 1988.

Goodman, Grant K. "Dharmapala in Japan, 1913." *Japan Forum* 5:2 (October 1993): 195–202.

Gordon, M. I. "Some Characteristics of Buddhism as It Exists in Japan Which Indicate That It Is Not a Final Religion." In *The World's Parliament of Religions*, edited by John Henry Barrows, 1293–96. Chicago: Parliament Publishing, 1893.

Grant, Robert. *An Historical Introduction to the New Testament*. London: Collins, 1974.

Grapard, Allan G. "Japan's Ignored Cultural Revolution: The Separation of Shinto and Buddhist Divinities in Meiji (*shimbutsu bunri*) and a Case Study: Tonomine." *History of Religions* 23 (February 1984): 240–65.

——. "Enduring Problems in the Study of Japanese Religions." *Journal of Religion* 70:1 (January 1990): 73–79.

Griffis, W. E. *The Mikado's Empire*. New York: Harper and Brothers, 1876.

Guruge, Ananda, ed. *Return to Righteousness: A Collection of Speeches, Essays and Letters of the Anagarika Dharmapāla*. Colombo: Government Press, 1965.

Gutzlaff, C. "Remarks on the Present State of Buddhism in China." *Journal of the Royal Asiatic Society of Great Britain and Ireland* 16:1 (1854): 73–92.

Halbfass, Wilhelm. *India and Europe: An Essay in Understanding*. Albany: State University of New York Press, 1988.

Hales, Peter Bacon. "Photography and the World's Columbian Exposition: A Case Study." *Journal of Urban History* 15:3 (May 1989): 247–73.

Hall, Ivan Parker. *Mori Arinori*. Cambridge, Mass.: Harvard University Press, 1973.

Hallisey, Charles. "Roads Taken and Not Taken in the Study of Theravāda Buddhism." In *Curators of the Buddha*, edited by Donald S. Lopez Jr., 31–61. Chicago: University of Chicago Press, 1995.

Hamilton, Annette. "Fear and Desire: Aborigines, Asians and the Australian Imaginary." *Australian Perceptions of Asia. Australian Cultural History* 9 (1990): 14–35.

Hanayama Shinsho, ed. *Bibliography on Buddhism*. Tokyo: Hokuseido Press, 1961.

Haneda Nobuo. *December Fan: The Buddhist Essays of Manshi Kiyozawa*. Kyoto: Higashi Honganji, 1984.

Hardacre, Helen. *Shintō and the State: 1868–1988*. Princeton: Princeton University Press, 1989.

Hardy, R. Spence. *The British Government and Idolatry in Ceylon*. London: Crofts and Blenkarn, 1841.

——. *Eastern Monachism*. 1850. Reprint, London: Williams Norgate, 1860.

——. *Manual of Budhism in Its Modern Development*. London: Williams Norgate, 1853.

——. *The Sacred Books of the Buddhists Compared with History and Modern Science*. Colombo: Wesleyan Mission, 1863.

——. *The Legends and Theories of the Buddhists Compared with History and Modern Science*. London: Williams Norgate, 1866.

Harootunian, H. D. *Toward Restoration: The Growth of Political Consciousness in Tokugawa Japan*. Berkeley: University of California Press, 1970.

——. *Things Seen and Unseen: Discourse and Ideology in Tokugawa Nativism*. Chicago: University of Chicago Press, 1988.

Harris, Neil. "All the World's a Melting Pot? Japan at American Fairs, 1876–1904." In *Mutual Images*, edited by Akira Iriye, 24–54. Cambridge, Mass.: Harvard University Press, 1975.

Harris, T. W. "Proofs of the Existence of God." In *The World's Parliament of Religions*, edited by John Henry Barrows, 306–14. Chicago: Parliament Publishing, 1893.

Hawks, Francis L. *Narrative of the Expedition of an American Squadron to the China Seas and Japan*. London: Macmillan, 1952.

Hay, William H. "Paul Carus: A Case Study of Philosophy on the Frontier." *Journal of the History of Ideas* 17 (October 1956): 498–510.

Heisig, James, and John C. Maraldo, eds. *Rude Awakenings: Zen, the Kyoto School, and the Question of Nationalism*. Nanzan Institute for Religion and Culture. Honolulu: University of Hawai'i Press, 1995.

Hewitt, Augustine F. "Rational Demonstration of the Being of God." In *The World's Parliament of Religions*, edited by John Henry Barrows, 256–69. Chicago: Parliament Publishing, 1893.

Hirai Kinzō. "The Real Position of Japan toward Christianity." In *The World's Parliament of Religions*, edited by John Henry Barrows, 444–50. Chicago: Parliament Publishing, 1893.

——. "Synthetic Religion." In *The World's Parliament of Religions*, edited by John Henry Barrows, 1286–88. Chicago: Parliament Publishing, 1893.

——. "Religious Thought in Japan." *Arena* 7 (1893): 257–67.

——. "The Real Position of Japan toward Christianity." In *Neely's History of the Parliament of Religions*, edited by W. R. Houghton, 157–61. Chicago: F. Tennyson Neely, 1894.

——. "Synthetic Religion." In *Neely's History of the Parliament of Religions*, edited by W. R. Houghton, 798–803. Chicago: F. Tennyson Neely, 1894.

Hirakawa, A., and E. B. Ceadel. "Japanese Research on Buddhism since the Meiji Period." *Monumenta Nipponica* 11:3 (1955): 221–46; 11:4 (1956): 397–424.

Hirschmann, Edwin. *White Mutiny: The Ilbert Bill in India and Genesis of the Indian National Congress*. New Delhi: Heritage, 1980.

Hoare, J. E. "The 'Bankoku Shinbun' Affair: Foreigners, the Japanese Press and Extraterritoriality in Early Meiji Japan." *Modern Asian Studies* 9:3 (1975): 289–302.

Hodgson, Brian Houghton. "Notices of the Languages, Literature, and Religion of Nepal and Tibet." *Asiatic Researches* 16 (1828). Reprinted in *Essays on the Languages, Literature, and Religion of Nepal and Tibet*, 1–34. Varanasi: Bharat-Bharati, 1971.

——. "Sketch of Buddhism, Derived from the Bauddha Scriptures of Nepal." *Transactions of the Royal Asiatic Society* 2 (1828). Reprinted in *Essays on the Languages, Literature, and Religion of Nepal and Tibet*, 35–64. Varanasi: Bharat-Bharati, 1971.

Hori, G. Victor Sōgen. "Japanese Zen in America: Americanizing the Face in the Mirror." In *The Faces of Buddhism in America*, edited by Charles S. Prebish and Kenneth K. Tanaka, 49–78. Berkeley: University of California Press, 1998.

Houghton, Walter R., ed. *Neely's History of the Parliament of Religions and Religious Congresses at the World's Columbian Exposition*. Chicago: F. Tennyson Neely, 1894.

Hoy, David Couzens. "Foucault: Modern or Postmodern?" In *After Foucault: Humanistic Knowledge, Postmodern Challenges*, edited by Jonathon Arac, 12–41. New Brunswick: Rutgers University Press, 1988.

Hume, Robert A. "Universal Christianity." Appendix to John Henry Barrows, *Christianity: The World Religion*. Chicago: A. C. McClurg, 1897.

Iglehart, Charles W. *A Century of Protestant Christianity in Japan*. Tokyo: Tuttle, 1960.

Inagaki Hisao. *A Dictionary of Japanese Buddhist Terms*. Kyoto: Nagata Bunshodo, 1985.

Inden, Robert. "Orientalist Construction of India." *Modern Asian Studies* 20:3 (1986): 401–46.

——. *Imagining India*. London: Blackwell, 1991.

Inoue Enryō. *Bukkyō katsuron joron*. Tokyo: Tetsugaku shoin, 1887. Reproduced in *Meiji bunka zenshū*, vol. 9, *Shūkyō*, 377–416. Tokyo: Tōyō University, 1954.

——. "Nihon shūkyō ron" (On Japanese religion). *Nihonjin* 1 (May 18, 1888): 12–19.

Inoue Tetsujirō. *Shaka shuzoku ron* (The history of the Shaka tribe). Tokyo: Tetsugaku shoin, 1897.

Iriye, Akira. "Japan's Drive to Great-Power Status." In *The Emergence of Meiji Japan*, edited by Marius B. Jensen, 268–329. Cambridge: Cambridge University Press, 1995.

——, ed. *Mutual Images*. Cambridge, Mass.: Harvard University Press, 1975.

Irokawa Daikichi. *The Culture of the Meiji Period*. Translated by Marius B. Jansen. Princeton: Princeton University Press, 1985.

Iwao Seiichi, ed. *Bibliographical Dictionary of Japanese History*. Translated by Burton Watson. Tokyo: Kodansha, 1978.

Jackson, Carl T. "The Meeting of East and West: The Case of Paul Carus." *Journal of the History of Ideas* 29 (January–March 1968): 73–92.

Jaffe, Richard M. *Neither Monk nor Layman: Clerical Marriage in Modern Japanese Buddhism*. Princeton: Princeton University Press, 2001.

Jansen, Marius B., ed. *Changing Japanese Attitudes towards Modernization*. Princeton: Princeton University Press, 1965.

——. "Modernization and Foreign Policy in Meiji Japan." In *Political Development in Meiji Japan*, edited by R. E. Ward, 149–88. Princeton: Princeton University Press, 1968.

——. *Japan and Its World*. Princeton: Princeton University Press, 1980.

Jansen, Marius B., and Gilbert Rozman, eds. *Japan in Transition: From Tokugawa to Meiji*. Princeton: Princeton University Press, 1986.

Japan Biographical Encyclopedia and Who's Who. Tokyo: Rengo Press, 1958.

Japanese-English Buddhist Dictionary. Tokyo: Daitō shuppansha, 1965.

Johnson, Allen, ed. *Dictionary of American Biography*. New York: Charles Scribner's Sons, 1929.

Johnson, Rossiter, ed. *A History of the World's Columbian Exposition Held in Chicago, 1893*. 4 vols. New York: Appleton, 1897–98.

Jones, Hazel. "Bakumatsu Foreign Employees." *Monumenta Nipponica* 29 (1974): 305–27.

——. *Live Machines: Hired Foreigners and Meiji Japan*. Vancouver: University of British Columbia Press, 1980.

Jory, Patrick. "Thai and Western Buddhist Scholarship in the Age of Colonialism: King Chulalongkorn Redefines the Jatakas." *Journal of Asian Studies* 61:3 (August 2002): 891–918.

Kaburagi Goro, Peter. "The Shintō Religion." In *The World's Parliament of Religions*, edited by John Henry Barrows, 1373–74. Chicago: Parliament Publishing, 1893.

Kaempfer, Englebert. *The History of Japan, 1609–1692*. Vol. 2. 3 vols. Glasgow: James MacLehose and Sons, 1906.

Kasulis, Thomas P. "The Kyoto School and the West: A Review and Evaluation." *Eastern Buddhist* 15:2 (Autumn 1982): 125–44.

Katz, Nathan. *Buddhist and Western Philosophy*. New Delhi: Sterling, 1981.

——. "Scholarly Approaches to Buddhism: A Political Analysis." *Eastern Buddhist* 15:1 (Spring 1982): 116–21.

Kawai Yoshigiro. "A Declaration of Faith and the Truth of Buddhism." In *The World's Parliament of Religions*, edited by John Henry Barrows, 1290–93. Chicago: Parliament Publishing, 1893.

Keene, Donald. *The Japanese Discovery of Europe, 1720–1830*. Stanford: Stanford University Press, 1969.

——. *Landscapes and Portraits*. London: Secker and Warburg, 1972.

Kenkyusha's New Japanese-English Dictionary. New ed. Tokyo: Kenkyusha, 1963.

Kent, John. "Religion and Science." In *Nineteenth Century Religious Thought in the West*, edited by Ninian Smart, J. Clayton, S. Katz, and P. Sherry, 1–36. Cambridge: Cambridge University Press, 1985.

Ketelaar, James Edward. *Of Heretics and Martyrs in Meiji Japan: Buddhism and Its Persecution*. Princeton: Princeton University Press, 1990.

——. "Strategic Occidentalism: Meiji Buddhists at the World's Parliament of Religions." *Buddhist-Christian Studies* 11 (1991): 37–56.

King, Richard. *Orientalism and Religion: Postcolonial Theory, India and "the Mystic East."* London: Routledge, 1999.

Kirita Kiyohide. "D. T. Suzuki on Society and the State." In *Rude Wakenings*, edited by James W. Heisig and John C. Maraldo, 52–74. Nanzan Institute for Religion and Culture. Honolulu: University of Hawai'i Press, 1995.

——. "Suzuki Daisetsu: zasshi, shinbun kei ronbun ichiran" (Suzuki Daisetsu: A catalogue of essays published in magazines and newspapers). *Hanazono daigaku bungakubu kenkyū kiyō* 27:3 (1995): 151–224.

Kishimoto Hideo, ed. *Japanese Thought in the Meiji Era*. Vol. 2, *Religion*. Translated by John F. Howes. Tokyo: Ōbunsha, 1956.

Kishimoto Nobuta. "Future of Religion in Japan." In *The World's Parliament of Religions*, edited by John Henry Barrows, 1279–83. Chicago: Parliament Publishing, 1893.

——. "Buddhism in Japan 1. The Religious Compound in Japan." *Open Court* 8 (August 1894): 4183–84.

——. "Buddhism in Japan 2. Northern and Southern Buddhism." *Open Court* 8 (August 1894): 4197–98.

——. "Buddhism in Japan 3. Sacred Literature." *Open Court* 8 (August 1894): 4202–3.

——. "Buddhism in Japan 4. Present Condition." *Open Court* 8 (September 1894): 4211–13.

——. "Buddhism in Japan 5. The Influence of Buddhism on the People." *Open Court* 8 (September 1894): 4243–45.

——. "Buddhism in Japan 6. The Zen and the Shin Sects." *Open Court* 8 (October 1894): 4232–34.

——. "Future of Religion in Japan." In *Neely's History of the Parliament of Religions*, edited by W. R. Houghton, 794–96. Chicago: F. Tennyson Neely, 1894.

Kitagawa, Joseph M. "Buddhism and Asian Politics." *Asian Survey* 2:5 (July 1962): 1–11.

——. "The Buddhist Transformation in Japan." *History of Religions* 4:1 (Summer 1964): 319–35.

——. "Obituary for Hideo Kishimoto." *History of Religions* 4:1 (Summer 1964): 172–73.

——. *Religion in Japanese History*. New York: Columbia University Press, 1966.

——. *The History of Religions: Essays on the Problem of Understanding*. Chicago: University of Chicago Press, 1967.

——. "Buddhism in America." *Japanese Religions* 5:1 (July 1967): 32–57.

——. "Two Creative Epochs in East Asian Buddhism." *History of Religions* 22:1 (August 1982): 85–93.

——. *The 1893 World's Parliament of Religions and Its Legacy*. Eleventh John Nuveen Lecture. Chicago: University of Chicago Divinity School, 1984.

——. *On Understanding Japanese Buddhism*. Princeton: Princeton University Press, 1987.

Kitahara Michio. "The Rise of Four Mottoes in Japan." *Journal of Asian History* 20:1 (1986): 54–64.

Kiyota Minoru. "Presuppositions to an Understanding of Japanese Buddhist Thought." *Monumenta Nipponica* 22:3–4 (1967): 251–59.

——. *Gedatsukai: Its Theory and Practice*. Los Angeles: Buddhist Books International, 1982.

Klostermaier, Klaus. *Survey of Hinduism*. Albany: State University of New York, 1989.

Kōsaka Masaaki, ed. *Japanese Thought in the Meiji Era*. Vol. 9, *Thought*. Translated by David Abosch. Tokyo: Ōbunsha, 1956.

Koschman, Victor J. *Mito Ideology: Discourse, Reform and Insurrection in Late Tokugawa Japan, 1790–1864*. Berkeley: University of California Press, 1987.

Kozaki Hiromichi. "Christianity in Japan: Its Present Condition and Future Prospects." In *The World's Parliament of Religions*, edited by John Henry Barrows, 1012–15. Chicago: Parliament Publishing, 1893.

——. "Christianity in Japan: Its Present Condition and Future Prospects." In *Neely's History of the Parliament of Religions*, edited by W. R. Houghton, 489–94. Chicago: F. Tennyson Neely, 1894.

——. *Reminiscences of Seventy Years*. Translated by Noriaki Kozaki. Tokyo: Christian Literary Society of Japan, 1933.

Kritzman, Lawrence D., ed. *Michel Foucault: Politics, Philosophy, Culture: Interviews and Other Writings, 1977–1984*. New York: Routledge, 1988.

Kung Hsien Ho. "Confucianism." In *The World's Parliament of Religions*, edited by John Henry Barrows, 596–604. Chicago: Parliament Publishing, 1893.

Kuroda Shintō. *Outlines of the Mahāyāna as Taught by Buddha*. Tokyo: Bukkyō gakkuwai, 1893.

Kuroda Toshio. "Shintō in the History of Japanese Religion." *Journal of Japanese Studies* 7:1 (Winter 1981): 1–21.

Laffan, Michael. "Mustafa and the Mikado: A Francophile Egyptian's Turn to Meiji Japan." *Japanese Studies* 19:3 (1999): 269–86.

Lancaster, Clay. *The Japanese Influence in America*. 1963. Reprint, New York: Abbeville Press, 1983.

Large, Stephen. "Buddhism and Political Renovation in Prewar Japan: The Case of Akamatsu Katsumaro." *Journal of Japanese Studies* 9:1 (Winter 1983): 33–66.

Layman, Emma McCloy. *Buddhism in America*. Chicago: Nelson-Hall, 1976.

Leonard, William Emery. "Paul Carus." *Dial* 66 (1919): 452–55.

Leonowens, Anna. *The English Governess at the Siamese Court*. 1870. Reprint, Singapore: Oxford University Press, 1989.

Lillie, Arthur. *The Popular Life of the Buddha*. 1883. Reprinted as *The Life of the Buddha* (Delhi: Seema Publications, 1974).

Ling, Trevor. *A Dictionary of Buddhism: Indian and Southeast Asian*. Calcutta: K. P. Bagchi, 1981.

Livingston, James C. "British Agnosticism." In *Nineteenth Century Religious Thought in the West*, edited by Ninian Smart, J. Clayton, S. Katz, and P. Sherry, 231–70. Cambridge: Cambridge University Press, 1985.

Lloyd, Arthur. "Development of Japanese Buddhism." *Transactions of the Asiatic Society of Japan* 30:3 (December 1894): 337–481.

——. *The Creed of Half Japan*. London: E. P. Dutton, 1911.

Lopez, Donald S., Jr. *Curators of the Buddha: The Study of Buddhism under Colonialism*. Chicago: University of Chicago Press, 1995.

Lovric, B. J. A. "How to Think about Thought and Understand Understanding Not Our Own." *Asian Studies Association of Australia Review* 10:1 (July 1986): 29–40.

Lowell, Percival. *The Soul of the Far East*. 1888. Reprint, New York: Macmillan, 1911.

MacFarlane, Charles. *Japan: An Account, Geographical and Historical*. London: Routledge, 1852.

Malalgoda, Kitsiri. *Buddhism in Sinhalese Society, 1750–1900: A Study of Religious Revival and Change*. Berkeley: University of California Press, 1976.

Marshall, Byron K. "Professors and Politics: The Meiji Academic Elite." *Journal of Japanese Studies* 3:1 (Winter 1977): 71–97.

Marshall, Peter. *The British Discovery of Hinduism in the Nineteenth Century*. Cambridge: Cambridge University Press, 1970.

Maruyama Masao. *Studies in the Intellectual History of Tokugawa Japan*. Translated by Hane Mikiso. Tokyo: University of Tokyo Press, 1974.

Matsugama Takayoshi. "Origin of Shintō." In *The World's Parliament of Religions*, edited by John Henry Barrows, 1370–73. Chicago: Parliament Publishing, 1893.

Matsunaga, Alicia. *The Buddhist Philosophy of Assimilation: The Historical Development of the Honji-Suijaku Theory*. Tokyo: Tuttle, 1969.

Mayo, Marlene J. "The Iwakura Embassy and the Unequal Treaties, 1871–1973." Ph.D. diss., Columbia University, 1961.

——. "The Nationalist Revolution in Japan. Review article of Beasley, *The Meiji Restoration*. Stanford." *Monumenta Nipponica* 29:1 (1974): 83–91.

McMullin, Neil. *Buddhism and the State in Sixteenth Century Japan*. Princeton: Princeton University Press, 1984.

——. "Historical and Historiographical Issues in the Study of Pre-Modern Japanese Religions." *Japanese Journal of Religious Studies* 16:1 (March 1989): 3–40.

McRae, John. "Oriental Verities on the American Frontier: The 1893 World's Parliament of Religions and the Thought of Masao Abe." *Buddhist-Christian Studies* 11 (1991): 7–36.

Merk, Frederick. *Manifest Destiny and Mission in American History: A Reinterpretation*. New York: Knopf, 1963.

Meyer, Donald H. "Paul Carus and the Religion of Science." *American Quarterly* 14 (Winter 1962): 597–609.

Mikkyō daijiten (Encyclopedia of Esoteric Buddhism). 6 vols. Kyoto: Hōzōkan, 1971.

Mitchell, Timothy. "The World as Exhibition." *Comparative Studies in Society and History* 31:2 (April 1989): 217–36.

Miyoshi Masao. *As We Saw Them: The First Japanese Embassy to the United States, 1860*. Berkeley: University of California Press, 1979.

——. *Off Center: Power and Culture Relations between Japan and the United States*. Cambridge, Mass.: Harvard University Press, 1991.

Moeran, Brian. "Making an Exhibition of Oneself." In *Unwrapping Japan: Society and Culture in Anthropological Perspective*, edited by Eyal Ben-ari, Brian Moeran, and James Valentine, 117–39. Honolulu: University of Hawai'i Press, 1990.

Morse, Edward S. *Japan Day by Day*. Tokyo: Kobunsha, 1936.

Mouer, Ross, and Sugimoto Yoshio. *Images of Japanese Society*. London: Kegan Paul International, 1986.

Mueller, J. H. "Are Our Christian Missionaries in India Frauds?" *Arena* 16 (1896): 806–7.

Muller, F. Max. "Buddhist Nihilism." In *Lectures on the Science of Religion*, 131–50. New York: Scribner, 1872.

——. *Dhammapada*. In *Lectures on the Science of Religion*, 151–300. New York: Scribner, 1872.

——. *Selected Essays on Language, Mythology, and Religion*. 2 vols. London: Longmans, Green, 1881.

——. *Lectures on the Origin and Growth of Religion as Illustrated by the Religions of India*. Delivered in April, May, and June 1878. London: Longmans, Green, 1882.

——. "Esoteric Buddhism." *Nineteenth Century* 33 (1893): 767–88.

——. "Greek Philosophy and the Christian Religion." In *The World's Parliament of Religions*, edited by John Henry Barrows, 935–36. Chicago: Parliament Publishing, 1893.

——. "The Real Significance of the Parliament of Religions." *Arena* 11 (1894): 1–14.

——. *Chips from a German Workshop*. Vol. 5. New York: Charles Scribners, 1900.

——, ed. *Buddhist Mahāyāna Texts*. Sacred Books of the East, vol. 49. Oxford: Clarendon Press, 1894.

Mungello, D. E. *Curious Land: Jesuit Accommodation and the Origins of Sinology*. Honolulu: University of Hawai'i Press, 1989.

Munsterberg, Hugo. *Zen and Oriental Art*. Tokyo: Tuttle, 1965.

Murakami Shigeyoshi. *Japanese Religion in the Modern Century*. Tokyo: Tokyo University Press, 1980.

Murphet, Howard. *Hammer on the Mountain: The Life of Henry Steel Olcott (1832–1907)*. Wheaton, Ill.: Theosophical Publishing House, 1972.

Mutsu Munemitsu. *Kenkenroku: A Diplomatic Record of the Sino-Japanese War, 1894–5*. Edited by Gordon Mark Berger. Tokyo: Tokyo University Press, 1982.

Nagai Michio. "Herbert Spencer in Early Meiji Japan." *Far Eastern Quarterly* 14 (1954): 55–64.

——. "Westernization and Japanization: The Early Meiji Transformation of Education." In *Tradition and Modernization in Japanese Culture*, edited by D. H. Shively, 35–76. Princeton: Princeton University Press, 1971.

Nagarkar, B. B. "The Work of Social Reform in India." In *The World's Parliament of Religions*, edited by John Henry Barrows, 767–79. Chicago: Parliament Publishing, 1893.

Najita Tetsuo and Victor Koschman, eds. *Conflict on Modern Japanese History: The Neglected Tradition*. Princeton: Princeton University Press, 1982.

Nanjio Bun'yiu [*sic*], ed. *A Catalogue of the Chinese Translation of the Buddhist Tripitaka, the Sacred Canon of the Buddhists of China and Japan*. Oxford: Clarendon Press, 1883.

Nanjō Bun'yū and Maeda Eun, eds. *Bukkyō Seiten*. Tokyo: Sanseidō, 1905.

Nelson, Andrew Nathaniel. *The Modern Reader's Japanese-English Character Dictionary*. Rev. ed. Rutland, Vt.: C. E. Tuttle, 1971.

Nidhi, Aeusrivongse. "A Preliminary Study of Central Thai Writings on Buddha's Life and Their Relationship to the Religious Movement of Early Bangkok." Unpublished manuscript, Department of History, Chiang Mai University, 1982.

Nishida Taketoshi. *Meiji jidai no shimbun to zasshi* (Newspapers and journals of the Meiji period). Tokyo: Shibundō, 1961.

Nishikawa Sugao. "The Three Principles of Shintō." In *The World's Parliament of Religions*, edited by John Henry Barrows, 1374–75. Chicago: Parliament Publishing, 1893.

Nishizaki Ichiro, ed. *Lafcadio Hearn: Oriental Articles*. Tokyo: Hokuseido, 1939.

Nitobe Inazō. *Bushido: The Soul of Japan*. New York: G. P. Putnam, Knickerbocker Press, 1906. Published in Japanese, 1899.

Noguchi Zenshirō. "The Religion of the World." In *The World's Parliament of Religions*, edited by John Henry Barrows, 440–43. Chicago: Parliament Publishing, 1893.

——. "Would Win Converts to Buddhism." In *Neely's History of the Parliament of Religions*, edited by W. R. Houghton, 156–57. Chicago: F. Tennyson Neely, 1894.

Norman, E. Herbert. *Japan's Emergence as a Modern State*. New York: International Secretariat, Institute of Pacific Relations, 1940.

Notehelfer, F. J. "On Idealism and Realism in the Thought of Okakura Tenshin." *Journal of Japanese Studies* 16:2 (1990): 309–55.

Nyanatiloka. *Buddhist Dictionary: Manual of Buddhist Terms and Doctrines*. Colombo: Frewin, 1956.

O'Flaherty, Wendy. "On the ASSR and Joseph Kitagawa." *History of Religions* 25:4 (May 1986): 293–95.

Okakura Kakuzō. *The Hōōden: An Illustrated Description of the Buildings Erected by the Japanese Government at the World's Columbian Exposition, Jackson Park, Chicago*. Tokyo, 1893.

——. *The Ideals of the East*. London: John Murray, 1903; New York, 1904.

——. *The Awakening of Japan*. New York: Century Company, 1903–4.

——. *The Book of Tea*. New York: Fox Duffield, 1906.

——. *Okakura Kakuzō: Collected English Writings*. 3 vols. Tokyo: Heibonsha, 1984.

Olcott, H. S. *The Buddhist Catechism*. 1881. Reprint, Adyar: Theosophical Publishing House, 1975.

——. *Colonel Olcott's Diary*. Vol. 4. 1883–91. Microfilm. New Delhi: Nehru Memorial Museum Library.

——. *The Golden Rules of Buddhism*. 1887. Reprint, Adyar: Theosophical Publishing House, 1974.

——. "On the President's Japan Tour." *Lucifer* 4 (March–April 1893): 243–48.

——. *Old Diary Leaves*. 6 vols. Adyar: Theosophical Publishing House, 1972.

——. *Applied Theosophy and Other Essays*. Adyar: Theosophical Publishing House, 1975.

Oldenberg, Hermann. *Buddha, sein Leben, seine Lehre und seine Germeinde*. Berlin: W. Herts, 1881. First English edition, London: Williams and Norgate, 1882.

——. *The Buddha: His Life, His Doctrine, His Order*. Delhi: Indological Book House, 1971.

Ooms, Herman. "Neo-Confucianism and the Formation of Early Tokugawa Ideology: Contours of a Problem." In *Confucianism and Tokugawa Culture*, edited by Peter Nosco, 27–61. Princeton: Princeton University Press, 1984.

——. *Tokugawa Ideology: Early Constructs, 1570–1680*. Princeton: Princeton University Press, 1985.

Peebles, J. M. *The Great Debate: Buddhism and Christianity Face to Face*. Colombo, n.d.

Peiris, W. *The Western Contribution to Buddhism*. Delhi: Motilal Banarsidass, 1973.

Perez, Louis G. "Mutsu Munemitsu and the Revision of the 'Unequal' Treaties." Ph.D. diss., University of Michigan, 1986.

Pierson, John D. *Tokutomi Sohō, 1863–1957: A Journalist for Modern Japan*. Princeton: Princeton University Press, 1980.

Piovesana, Gino K. "The Beginnings of Western Philosophy in Japan: Nishi Amane, 1829–1897." *International Philosophy Quarterly* 2:2 (1962): 295–306.

Prebish, Charles. *American Buddhism*. North Scituate, Mass.: Duxbury Press, 1979.

——. *Luminous Passage: The Practice and Study of Buddhism in America*. Berkeley: University of California Press, 1999.

Prebish, Charles, and Kenneth Tanaka, eds. *The Faces of Buddhism in America*. Berkeley: University of California Press, 1998.

Prothero, Stephen. *The White Buddhist: The Asian Odyssey of Henry Steel Olcott*. Bloomington: Indiana University Press, 1996.

Pung Kwan Yu. "Confucianism." In *The World's Parliament of Religions*, edited by John Henry Barrows, 374–439. Chicago: Parliament Publishing, 1893.

Pye, Michael. *Zen and Modern Japanese Religion*. London: Ward Lock Educational, 1973.

Pyle, Kenneth B. *The New Generation in Meiji Japan: Problems of Cultural Identity, 1885–1895*. Stanford: Stanford University Press, 1969.

Rafael, Vicente L. *White Love and Other Events in Filipino History*. Manila: Ateneo de Manila University Press, 2000.

Rajapakse, Vigitha. "Buddhism in Huxley's Evolution and Ethics." *Philosophy East and West* 35:3 (1985): 295–304.

Rambach, Pierre. *The Art of Japanese Tantrism*. London: Macmillan (Skira), 1979.

Reed, Edward J. *Japan: Its History, Tradition and Religions*. 2 vols. London: John Murray, 1880.

Reynolds, Craig J. "The Author Function and Thai History." *Asian Studies Association of Australia Review* 10:1 (July 1986): 22–28.

Reynolds, Frank E., and Jason A. Carbine. *The Life of Buddhism*. Berkeley: University of California Press, 2000.

Rhys Davids, C. A. F. *Buddhist Psychological Ethics*. London: Pali Text Society, 1900. Reprint, 1974.

——. *Compendium of Philosophy*. London: Pali Text Society, 1910.

——. *Buddhism: A Study of the Buddhist Norm*. London: Williams and Norgate, 1912; New York: Holt, 1912.

——. *Gotama the Man*. London: Luzac, 1928.

——, ed. *Manual of a Mystic*. London: Pali Text Society, 1916. Reprint, 1962.

Rhys Davids, T. W. *Buddhism: A Sketch of the Life and Teachings of Gautama, the Buddha*. 1878. Reprint, London: Society for Promoting Christian Knowledge, 1882.

——. *Buddhist Birth Stories*. London: Routledge, 1880.

——. Review of F. Max Muller, *The Dharmapada*. *Academy*, July 2, 1881, 12.

——. *The Hibbert Lectures, 1881*. London: Green and Sons, 1881.

——. *Buddhist-Sūtras*. Sacred Books of the East. Vol. 11. Oxford: Clarendon Press, 1881. Reprint, Delhi: Motilal Banarsidass, 1980.

——. *Mahavagga*. Part 11. Oxford: Clarendon Press, 1882.

——. *Buddhist India*. London: Unwin, 1903. Reprint, Delhi: Motilal Banarsidass, 1971.

——. *Buddhism: Its History and Literature. American Lectures on the History of Religions 1894–5*. London: G. P. Putnam's Sons, 1904.

——. *Dialogues of the Buddha*. 3 vols. London: Oxford University Press, 1908.

——. *Early Buddhism*. London: Constable and Company, 1908.

——. "The Early History of the Buddhists." In *Cambridge History of India*, 171–97. Cambridge: Cambridge University Press, 1922.

——. "What Has Buddhism Derived from Christianity? '22.2.1877.'" *Journal of the Pali Text Society* 7 (1913–23). In Centenary Facsimile Reprint, 37–53. 1981.

Ritter, George E. Albrecht. *A History of Protestant Missions in Japan*. Tokyo: Methodist Publishing House, 1898.

Roberts, Wm. C. "The Problems of Our Multifarious Population and Their Probable Solution." In *Missions at Home and Abroad*, edited by R. E. M. Wherry, 79–96. New York: American Tract Society, 1893.

Rocha, Cristina. "Being a Zen Buddhist Brazilian: Juggling Multiple Religious Identities in the Land of Catholicism." In *The Globalization of Buddhism: Case Studies of Buddhist Missions*, edited by Linda Learman. Honolulu: University of Hawai'i Press (forthcoming).

Rockhill, W. Woodville. *The Life of the Buddha and the Early History of His Order (from Tibetan Sources)*. Oxford: Clarendon Press, 1884.

Rogers, Minor L., and Ann T. Rogers. "The Honganji: Guardian of the State (1868–1945)." *Japanese Journal of Religious Studies* 17:1 (March 1990): 3–28.

Rydell, Robert W. *All the World's a Fair: Visions of Empire at American International Expositions, 1876–1916*. Chicago: University of Chicago Press, 1984.

Said, Edward W. *Orientalism*. London: Routledge and Kegan Paul, 1978.

——. "An Ideology of Difference." *Critical Inquiry* 12 (Autumn 1985): 38–58.

——. *The World, the Text, and the Critic*. London: Vintage, 1988.

——. *Culture and Imperialism*. London: Chatto and Windus, 1993.

Saint-Hilaire, J. Barthélemy. *The Buddha and His Religion*. London: Routledge, 1860.

Sanford, Charles L., ed. *Manifest Destiny and the Imperialism Question*. New York: John Wiley and Sons, 1974.

Sangharakshita. *Flame in Darkness*. Pune, 1980.

Sansom, G. B. *The Western World and Japan*. New York: Alfred A. Knopf, 1950.

Scheiner, Irwin. *Christian Converts and Social Protest in Meiji Japan*. Berkeley: University of California Press, 1970.

Schwab, Raymond. *The Oriental Renaissance: Europe's Rediscovery of India and the East, 1680–1880*. New York: Columbia University Press, 1984.

Schwantes, Robert S. "Christianity vs. Science: A Conflict of Ideas in Modern Japan." *Far Eastern Quarterly* 12 (February 1953): 123–32.

Seager, Richard Hughes. "The World's Parliament of Religions, Chicago, Illinois, 1893: America's Religious Coming of Age." Ph.D. diss., Harvard University, 1987.

——. *The Dawn of Religious Pluralism: Voices from the World's Parliament of Religions*. La Salle, Ill.: Open Court, 1993.

——. *The World's Parliament of Religions: The East/West Encounter, Chicago, 1893*. Bloomington: Indiana University Press, 1995.

——. *Buddhism in America*. New York: Columbia University Press, 1999.

Senzaki Nyōgen. *Like a Dream, Like a Fantasy: The Zen Writings and Translations of Nyōgen Senzaki*. Edited by Eido Shimano Rōshi. Tokyo: Japan Publications, 1978.

Shaku Sōen. "Letters of Soyen Shaku to His Teacher, Kosen Imakita." In *Like a Dream, Like a Fantasy*, edited by Senzaki Nyōgen, 91–99. Tokyo: Japan Publications, 1887.

——. "Arbitration Instead of War." In *The World's Parliament of Religions*, edited by John Henry Barrows, 1285. Chicago: Parliament Publishing, 1893.

——. "The Law of Cause and Effect as Taught by the Buddha." In *The World's Parliament of Religions*, edited by John Henry Barrows, 829–31. Chicago: Parliament Publishing, 1893.

——. "The Law of Cause and Effect as Taught by Buddha." In *Neely's History of the Parliament of Religions*, edited by W. R. Houghton, 378–80. Chicago: F. Tennyson Neely, 1894.

——. "Arbitration Instead of War." In *Neely's History of the Parliament of Religions*, edited by W. R. Houghton, 797–98. Chicago: F. Tennyson Neely, 1894.

——. *Bankoku shūkyō taikai ichiran* (An outline of the World's Parliament of Religions). Tokyo: Komeisha, 1895.

——. "Shūkyōka kondankai ni tsuite" (Report on a meeting of religious leaders). *Nihon shūkyō* 2 (October 1896): 173–77.

——. *Sermons of a Buddhist Abbot*. Translated by D. T. Suzuki. Chicago: Open Court, 1906.

——. "The Buddhist Conception of Death." *Monist* 17:1 (January 1907): 1–5.

——. *Seiyū nikki* (Diary of a journey to the West). Facsimile reprint. Edited by Inoue Zenjō. Afterword by D. T. Suzuki. Ofunacho: Tōkeiji, 1941.

——. *Zen for Americans*. Chicago: Open Court, 1974.

——. "Reflections on an American Journey." Translated by Wayne S. Yokoyama. *Eastern Buddhist* 26:2 (Autumn 1993): 138–48.

Shaku Sōen, John Henry Barrows, and F. F. Ellinwood. "A Controversy on Buddhism." *Open Court* 11 (1897): 43–58.

Sharf, Robert H. "The Zen of Japanese Nationalism." *History of Religions* 33:1 (1993): 1–43.

——. "Whose Zen? Zen Nationalism Revisited." In *Rude Awakenings: Zen, the Kyoto School, and the Question of Nationalism*, edited by James W. Heisig and John C. Maraldo, 40–51. Honolulu: University of Hawai'i Press, 1994.

Shibata Reuchi. "Shintoism." In *The World's Parliament of Religions*, edited by J. H. Barrows, 451–55. Chicago: Parliament Publishing, 1893.

Shimazuno Susumu. "Religious Influences on Japan's Modernization." *Japanese Journal of Religious Studies* 8:3–4 (September–December 1981): 207–23.

Shinohara Koichi. "Buddhism and the Problem of Modernity in East Asia: Some Exploratory Comments Based on the Example of Takayama Chogyu." *Japanese Journal of Religious Studies* 8:1–2 (March–June 1981): 35–50.

Sinnett, A. P. *Esoteric Buddhism*. 1883. Reprint, Adyar: Theosophical Publishing House, 1972.

Smith, V. A. *Fine Art in India and Ceylon*. Oxford: Clarendon Press, 1911.

Snider, Denton J. *World's Fair Studies*. Chicago: Sigma, 1895.

Snodgrass, Adrian. *The Matrix and Diamond World Mandalas in Shingon Buddhism*. New Delhi: Aditya Prakashan, 1988.

Snodgrass, Judith. "Strategies of Discourse: The Deployment of Western Authority in Meiji Japan." *Communal/Plural* 1:11 (1993): 27–45.

——. "Japan Faces the West: The Representation of Japan at the Columbian Exposition, Chicago 1893." In *Japanese Science, Technology and Economic Growth Down Under*, edited by Morris Low and Helen Marriott, 11–24. Melbourne: Monash Asia Institute, 1996.

——. "Colonial Constructs of Theravāda Buddhism." In *Tradition in Current Perspectives*, 79–98. Yangon: Universities Historical Research Centre, 1996.

——. "The Deployment of Western Philosophy in Meiji Buddhist Revival." *Eastern Buddhist* 30:2 (Spring 1997): 173–98.

——. "Retrieving the Past: Considerations of Texts." *Eastern Buddhist* 31:2 (1998): 263–67.

——. "*Buddha no fukuin*: The Deployment of Paul Carus's *Gospel of Buddha* in Meiji Japan." *Japanese Journal of Religious Studies* 25:3–4 (Fall 1998): 319–44.

Solomon, Ted J. "Soka Gakkai and the Alleged Compatibility between Nichiren Buddhism and Modern Science." *Japanese Journal of Religious Studies* 7:1 (March 1980): 34–53.

Southwold, Martin. *Buddhism in Life: The Anthropological Study of Religion and the Sinhalese Practice of Buddhism*. Manchester: Manchester University Press, 1983.

Soviak, Eugene. "On the Nature of Western Progress: The Journal of the Iwakura Embassy." In *Tradition and Modernization in Japanese Culture*, edited by D. H. Shively, 7–34. Princeton: Princeton University Press, 1971.

Spuler, Michelle. *Developments in Australian Buddhism: Facets of the Diamond*. Richmond: Curzon, 2002.

Staggs, Kathleen M. "In Defence of Japanese Buddhism: Essays from the Meiji Period by Inoue Enryō and Murakami Senshō." Ph.D. diss., Princeton University, 1979.

——. "'Defend the Nation and Love the Truth': Inoue Enryō and the Revival of Meiji Buddhism." *Monumenta Nipponica* 38 (1983): 251–81.

Stokes, Eric. *English Utilitarians and India*. Oxford: Clarendon Press, 1989.

Strong, John S. *The Legend of King Asoka: A Study and Translation of the Asokavadana*. Delhi: Motilal Barnarsidass, 1989.

Sumangala, H. "Buddhism: Southern Orthodox." In *The World's Parliament of Religions*, edited by John Henry Barrows, 894–97. Chicago: Parliament Publishing, 1893.

Suzuki, Beatrice Lane. "What Is Mahāyāna Buddhism?" *Eastern Buddhist* 1:1 (May 1921): 61–69.

Suzuki, D. T. "Notes on the Madhyamika Philosophy." *Journal of the Buddhist Text Society* 6 (1898): 19–22.

——. "The Madyamika School in China." *Journal of the Buddhist Text Society* 6 (1898): 23–30.

——. "Confucius." *Open Court* 13:11 (November 1899): 644–49.

——. "Asvaghosha, the First Advocate of Mahāyāna Buddhism." *Monist* 10:2 (January 1900): 216–45.

——. "The Breadth of Buddhism." *Open Court* 14:1 (January 1900): 51–53.

——. *Asvaghosha's Discourse on the Awakening of Faith*. Chicago: Open Court, 1900.

——. "Pooru. Kerasu shoden (Short Biography of Paul Carus)." In *Budda no fukuin*, 2d ed., 1901. Reprinted in *Suzuki Daisetsu zenshū* (The complete works of Suzuki Daisetsu), 25:507–9. Tokyo: Iwanami Shoten, 1970.

——. "What Is Buddhism?" *Light of Dharma* 2 (1902): 11–14.

——. "Mahayana Buddhism." *Light of Dharma* 2 (1902): 79–81.

——. "Individual Mortality." *Light of Dharma* 3 (1903): 67–72.

——. "A Buddhist View of War." *Light of Dharma* 4 (1904): 179–82.

——. "Philosophy of the Yogacara: The Madyamika and the Yogacara." *Muséon*, n.s., 5 (1904): 370–86.

——. "The First Buddhist Council." *Monist* 14:2 (January 1904): 253–82.

——. "The Essence of Buddhism." *Light of Dharma* 5 (1905): 73–75.

——. "A Religious Book of China." Translated with Paul Carus. *Open Court* 19 (August 1905): 477–93.

——. "Moral Tales of the Treatise on Response and Retribution." *Open Court* 19 (September–October 1905): 549–62, 604–21.

——. "Is Buddhism Nihilistic?" *Light of Dharma* 6 (1906): 3–7.

——. "Japanese Conception of Death and Immortality." *Light of Dharma* 6 (1906): 3–8.

——. "The Zen Sect of Buddhism." *Journal of the Pali Text Society* 5 (1906–7): 8–43.

——. *Outlines of Mahāyāna Buddhism*. London: Luzac, 1907. Reprint, New York: Shoken Books, 1963.

——. "The Seven Gods of Bliss." *Open Court* 21 (1907): 397–406.

——. "A Brief History of Early Chinese Philosophy." *Monist* 17:3 (July 1907): 415–50; 18 (April and October 1908): 242–85, 481–509.

——. "The Development of Mahayana Buddhism." *Buddhist Review* 1:2 (1909): 103–18.

——. "The Development of Mahāyāna Buddhism." *Monist* 24:4 (October 1914): 565–81.

——. *Essays in Zen Buddhism*. 1927. Reprint, London: Rider, 1949.

——. "Zen Buddhism as Chinese Interpretation of the Doctrine of Enlightenment: Buddhism as Understood by Zen." *Eastern Buddhist* 2:6 (1923): 293–347.

——. "Zen as Chinese Interpretation of the Doctrine of Enlightenment." In *Essays in Zen Buddhism*, 39–117. 1927. Reprint, London: Rider, 1949.

——. *Introduction to Zen Buddhism*. 1934. Reprint, London: Rider, 1960.

——. *The Training of a Zen Buddhist Monk*. Kyoto: Eastern Buddhist Society, 1934.

——. *Zen Buddhism and Its Influence on Japanese Culture*. Kyoto: Eastern Buddhist Society, 1938.

——. *Manual of Zen Buddhism*. Buddhist Society. London: Rider, 1950.

——. *Mysticism: Christian and Buddhist*. Ruskin House. London: Allen and Unwin, 1957.

——. *Zen and Japanese Culture*. New York: Bollingen, 1959.

——. "Introduction: A Glimpse of Paul Carus." In *Modern Trends in World Religions*, edited by J. M. Kitagawa, ix–xiv. La Salle, Ill.: Open Court, 1959.

——, trans. *Budda no fukuin*. Tokyo, January 1895. 2d ed., 1901. Reprinted in *Suzuki Daisetsu zenshū* (The complete works of Suzuki Daisetsu), vol. 25. Tokyo: Iwanami Shoten, 1970.

Suzuki Norihisa. "Nobuta Kishimoto and the Beginnings of the Scientific Study of Religion in Modern Japan." *Contemporary Religions in Japan* 11:3–4 (September–December 1970): 55–180.

Tachiki Satoko Fujita. "Okakura Kakuzō (1862–1913) and the Boston Brahmins." Ph.D. diss., University of Michigan, 1986.

Takakusu Junjirō. "The Amitāyur-Dhyāna-Sūtra." In *Buddhist Mahāyāna Texts*, edited by F. Max Muller, 159–201. Sacred Books of the East, vol. 49. Oxford: Clarendon Press, 1894. Reprint, Delhi: Motilal Banarsidass, 1968.

——. *I-Tsing: A Record of the Buddhist Religion as Practiced in India and the Malay Archipelago (AD 671–695)*. Oxford: Clarendon Press, 1896. Reprint, Taipei: Ch'eng Wen Publishing Company, 1970.

——. "Buddhism as We Find It in Japan." *Transactions and Proceedings of the Japan Society of London* 7 (1905–7): 264–70.

——. *The Essentials of Buddhist Philosophy*. 1947. Reprint, Honolulu: University of Hawai'i, 1956.

Takakusu Junjirō and Watanabe Kaikyoku, eds. *Taishō shinshū daizōkyō*. 100 vols. Tokyo: Taishō issaikyō kankō kai, 1924–32.

Takeda Kiyoko. "Apostasy: A Japanese Pattern." *Japan Interpreter* 2:12 (Spring 1978): 170–200.

Tamamuro Taijō. *Nihon bukkyōshi* (History of Japanese Buddhism). Vol. 3, *Kinsei kindaihen* (The early modern and modern period). Kyoto: Hōzōkan, 1967.

Tanaka, Stefan. *Japan's Orient: Rendering Pasts into History*. Berkeley: University of California Press, 1993.

Tateno Gozo. "Foreign Nations at the World's Fair: Japan." *North American Review* 156 (1893): 34–43.

Tennent, James Emerson. *Christianity in Ceylon: With an Historical Sketch of the Brahmanical and Buddhist Superstitions*. London: John Murray, 1850.

Thelle, Notto R. *Buddhism and Christianity in Japan: From Conflict to Dialogue, 1854–1899*. Honolulu: University of Hawai'i Press, 1987.

Thoreau, H. D. "The Preaching of Buddha." *Dial* (January 1844): 391–401.

Tobita Yoshibumi. *Meiji no kotoba jiten*. Tokyo: Tokyodo, 1985.

Toki Hōryū. "Buddhism in Japan." In *The World's Parliament of Religions*, edited by John Henry Barrows, 543–52. Chicago: Parliament Publishing, 1893.

——. "History of Buddhism and Its Sects in Japan." In *Neely's History of the Parliament of Religions*, edited by W. R. Houghton, 222–26. Chicago: F. Tennyson Neely, 1894.

——. "What Buddhism Has Done for Japan." In *Neely's History of the Parliament of Religions*, edited by W. R. Houghton, 779–81. Chicago: F. Tennyson Neely, 1894.

——. *Si-Do-In-Dzou (Japanese Mudras): Gestes de l'officiant dans les ceremonies mystiques des sectes Tendai et Singon*. Paris: Ernest Leroux, 1899.

Tokyo National Museum. *Umi o wattata Meiji no bijutsu*. Catalogue of exhibition *World's Columbian Exposition of 1893 Revisited: Nineteenth Century Japanese Art Show in Chicago, U.S.A.*, Tokyo National Museum, April 3–May 11, 1997.

Trachtenberg, Alan. *The Incorporation of America: Culture and Society in the Gilded Age*. New York: Hill and Wang, 1982.

Trompf, G. W. *Friedrich Max Muller*. Bombay: Shakuntala, 1978.

Trumbull, M. M. "The Parliament of Religions." *Monist* 4:3 (April 1894): 333–54.

Tsunemitsu Kōnen. *Meiji no bukkyōsha*. 2 vols. Tokyo: Shinjūsha, 1968.

Tsunoda Ryusaku, Wm. Theodore de Barry, and Donald Keene, eds. *Sources of Japanese Tradition*. New York: Columbia University Press, 1958.

Tweed, Thomas Anthony. *The American Encounter with Buddhism, 1844–1912*. Bloomington: Indiana University Press, 1992.

Tworkov, Helen. *Zen in America: Five Teachers and the Search for an American Buddhism*. New York: Kodansha America, 1994.

Uyemura Masahisa. "On Religion (Translation from the *Rikugo zasshi* by Rev. W. Dening)." *Chrysanthemum* (March 1881): 80–84.

Valliant, Robert B. "The Selling of Japan: Japanese Manipulation of Western Opinion, 1900–1905." *Monumenta Nipponica* 29 (1974): 414–38.

Varley, Paul, and Kumakura Isao, eds. *Tea in Japan: Essays on the History of Chanoyu*. Honolulu: University of Hawai'i Press, 1989.

Verhoeven, Martin. "Americanizing the Buddha: Paul Carus and the Transformation of Asian Thought." In *The Faces of Buddhism in America*, edited by Charles S. Prebish and Kenneth K. Tanaka, 207–27. Berkeley: University of California Press, 1998.

Vessie, Patricia Armstrong. *Zen Buddhism: A Bibliography of Books and Articles in English, 1892–1975*. Ann Arbor: University Microfilms International, 1976.

Victoria, Brian. *Zen at War*. New York: Weatherhill, 1997.

Wakabayashi, Bob Tadashi. *Anti-Foreignism and Western Learning in Early Modern Japan*. Cambridge, Mass.: Harvard University Press, 1986.

Walpola, Sri Rahula. *What the Buddha Taught*. London: Gordon Fraser, 1982.

Wargo, Robert J. J. "Inoue Enryō: An Important Predecessor of Nishida Kitaro." *Studies on Japanese Culture. Japan P.E.N. Club* 2 (1973): 170–77.

Watts, Alan. *The Way of Zen*. 1957. Reprint, New York: Vintage Books, 1989.

Webb, Mohammed Alexander Russell. "The Spirit of Islam." In *The World's Parliament of Religions*, edited by John Henry Barrows, 989–96. Chicago: Parliament Publishing, 1893.

——. "The Influence of Islam on Social Conditions." In *The World's Parliament of Religions*, edited by John Henry Barrows, 1046–52. Chicago: Parliament Publishing, 1893.

Welbon, Guy Richard. *The Buddhist Nirvāṇa and Its Western Interpreters*. Chicago: University of Chicago Press, 1968.

Wheeler-Barclay, Marjorie. "The Science of Religion in Britain, 1860–1915." Ph.D. diss., Northwestern University, 1987.

Wheelwright, Carolyn. "A Visualization of Eitoku's Lost Paintings at Azuchi Castle." In *Warlords, Artists and Commoners: Japan in the Sixteenth Century*, edited by George Elison and Bardwell L. Smith, 87–112. Honolulu: University Press of Hawai'i, 1981.

Wherry, E. M., ed. *Christianity Practically Applied: General Conference of the Evangelical Alliance, Chicago 1893*. New York: Baker and Taylor, 1893.

——, ed. *Missions at Home and Abroad: Papers and Addresses Presented at the World's Congress of Missions, October 2–4, 1893*. New York: American Tract Society, 1893.

Wickremeratne, L. A. "Religion, Nationalism, and Social Change in Ceylon." *Journal of the Royal Asiatic Society* (1969): 123–52.

Williams, Duncan Ryūken, and Christopher S. Queen. *American Buddhism: Methods and Findings in Recent Scholarship*. Richmond: Curzon Press, 1999.

Wilson, H. H. "On Buddha and Buddhism." *Journal of the Royal Asiatic Society of Great Britain and Ireland* 16:1 (1854): 229–65.

Witteman, A. *The World's Fair*. Chicago, 1893.

Wright, Brooks. *Interpreter of Buddhism to the West: Sir Edwin Arnold*. New York: Bookman Associates, 1957.

Yamazaki Masakazu and Miyakawa Toru. "Inoue Tetsujirō: The Man and His Works." *Philosophical Studies of Japan* 7. Tokyo: Japan National Commission for UNESCO, 1966.

Yamazaki Taikō. *Shingon: Japanese Esoteric Buddhism*. Boston: Shambhala, 1988.

Yatsubuchi Banryū. "Buddhism." In *The World's Parliament of Religions*, edited by John Henry Barrows, 716–23. Chicago: Parliament Publishing, 1893.

——. "Buddhism." In *Neely's History of the Parliament of Religions*, edited by W. R. Houghton, 323–24. Chicago: F. Tennyson Neely, 1894.

——. *Shūkyō taikai hōdō* (Report on the Parliament of Religions). Kyoto: Kōkyō Shoin, 1894.

Yokoi Tokio. "Christianity—What Is It?" In *The World's Parliament of Religions*, edited by John Henry Barrows, 1283–84. Chicago: Parliament Publishing, 1893.

Yokoyama Toshio. *Japan in the Victorian Mind: A Study of Stereotyped Images*. Houndmills, Basingstoke: Macmillan, 1987.

Yoshida Kyūichi. *Nihon kindai bukkyōshi kenkyū*. Tokyo: Yoshikawa kōbunkan, 1959.

Ziolkowski, Eric J. "The Literary Bearing of Chicago's 1893 World's Parliament of Religions." *Eastern Buddhist* 26:1 (Spring 1993): 10–25.

INDEX

Adler, Rev. H., 55
Akamatsu Renjō, 113, 119, 152–53, 155, 257, 297 (n. 22), 300 (n. 13)
Ālaya-vijñāna, 146
All Japan Convocation of Buddhists. *See* Zenkoku bukkyōsha daikonwakai
American Board of Missions, 193, 288 (n. 27), 309 (n. 102)
American imperialism. *See* Imperialism
Amida Buddha, 89, 216, 219
Amitāyur-Dhyāna-Sūtra, 110
Anātman, 6, 220, 234, 237
Anesaki Masaharu, 308 (n. 88), 317 (n. 28)
Ansei Treaties, 130. *See also* Treaty revision
Araya-shiki, 146
Arnold, Edwin, 7, 100, 211, 234, 235, 244, 248, 293 (n. 62), 303 (n. 41); *The Light of Asia*, 7, 101, 234, 235
Arya-dharma, 5, 85, 114, 204
Ashitsu Jitsuzen, 77, 82, 86, 126, 130, 131, 135, 174, 176, 177, 196, 202, 207, 209, 216–17, 218, 225, 249, 275, 289 (n. 58), 290 (n. 5), 300 (n. 4), 304 (n. 5), 307 (n. 69), 310 (nn. 16, 17, 18), 311 (n. 27), 312 (nn. 60, 67), 314 (n. 47), 321 (n. 61)
Asian Buddhist modernities, 8–12. *See also* Chudhadharn, Prince Chandradat (of Siam); Dharmapāla, Anagārika
Asoka, 63, 90, 190, 291 (n. 18), 308 (n. 79)
Association of Buddhist Sects, 118, 128
Association of Politics and Education. *See* Seikyōsha
Asvaghosha, 234, 240, 260, 261, 262, 263
Atheism, 186–87, 219–20, 232
Ātman, 229
Auxiliary Congresses, 45–46, 48–49, 65, 284 (nn. 2, 5)
Avalokitesvara, 218, 230
Avatamsaka sect, 266
Avatamsaka Sutra, 146, 301 (n. 33)
Azuchi castle, 43, 284 (n. 89)

Baker, Edward P., 24
Ball, Henry, 119
Barrows, John Henry, 48–49, 54–56, 58–64, 66–82 passim, 83, 85, 173, 178, 182, 184, 190, 191, 201, 202, 206, 210, 217–18, 224, 225, 226, 240, 260, 273, 284 (n. 9), 286 (n. 58), 287 (nn. 13, 17), 289 (nn. 45, 46, 58, 65), 304 (n. 1), 305 (nn. 23, 24), 308 (n. 86), 309 (n. 100), 310 (nn. 5, 13, 14, 19), 311 (nn. 27, 32), 312 (nn. 60, 67), 313 (n. 10), 318 (n. 7), 318 (n. 8)
Beal, Samuel, 103, 293 (n. 62)
Berkeley, Bishop George, 206
Bhūtathatā, 214–16
Bigandet, Rev. P., 103
Bigelow, William Sturgis, 113, 163, 199
Blavatsky, Madam H. G., 159, 161, 203, 303 (n. 32)
Blyth, Reginald Horace, 321 (n. 58)
Bodhi, 106–7, 294 (n. 85)
Bodhisattva ideal and social action, 218, 225
Bonney, Charles C., 48, 49, 50, 52–54, 55, 60, 65, 66, 68, 72, 76, 284 (n. 14), 286 (n. 42), 287 (n. 68), 288 (n. 17)
Brahmo Samaj, 289 (n. 42)
Budda no fukuin, 245, 246, 248, 249, 250, 252–53, 254, 257, 261
Buddha, 94, 217; as *cakravartin*, 105–6; in Eastern Buddhism, 188, 206–7, 216–17; in Southern Buddhism, 204–6. *See also* Amida Buddha; Gautama; Sakyamuni; Three Bodies of the Buddha; Vairocana Buddha
Buddhaghosha, 293 (n. 62)
Buddhism, Eastern, 10, 11, 115, 222, 223, 232, 250, 259–77, 314 (n. 43); and treaty revision, 179–81; not atheistic, 186–87; social action in, 188–89, 219, 221; and Asian modernity, 203–4; and

Sakyamuni's highest teaching, 207–9; as universal religion, 209–11, 221; western responses to, 212, 224–31; Buddha nature in, 213–15, 216–17, 218; and philosophical idealism, 213–15, 227–28, 275; interdependence and karma in, 215–16; meaning of Buddha in, 216–18; and compassion, 217–19; nirvana in, 218–19; as philosophical religion, 219; nature of self in, 219–20; as scientific, 221
—Japanese, 72, 86–87, 143, 145, 151, 153, 180, 186, 192, 210, 222, 263, 276, 288 (n. 39), 289 (n. 65), 296 (n. 9), 297 (n. 20)
—Mahayana, 7, 86, 87, 88, 92–94, 103, 109–13, 119, 121, 136, 145, 146–47, 150–52, 153, 161–63, 174, 180, 186, 191, 199–201, 206–9, 214; nirvana in, 217–20, 225; in Paul Carus's monism, 222, 223, 231–32, 240–42, 248; D. T. Suzuki on, 260, 262, 263, 264, 265, 271, 273, 276
—Theravada, 9, 86–87, 95, 108, 121, 136, 157, 159, 161, 162, 198–200, 204, 207, 221, 246, 263, 271, 272, 276, 291 (n. 23), 292 (n. 43), 309 (n. 1), 314 (n. 29)
—and science, 54, 211–13, 227–28, 229, 231, 233, 243
—in Ceylon, 4–5, 89–90, 91, 94–102, 107, 203–4
—in Meiji Japan, 13–15; early Meiji crisis, 116–18; learning from the West, 118–21; Meiji reforms, 118–21, 143; lay movement in, 126–27, 149–50, 218, 250; in modern society, 126–32; and the state, 127–29; revival and nationalism, 129–32; and treaty revision, 130, 172–98; and patriotism, 143–44; *See also* Buddhism, Eastern; *Shin bukkyō*
—in Western scholarship, 1, 2, 4–7, 8, 198, 286 (n. 46), 288 (n. 39); early scholarship on, 85–87; in travellers' tales, 87; and British treaty with Ceylon, 94–97; as atheistic Religion, 97–99; as philosophical humanism, 99–101; as materialist error, 102–4; as religion of self-reliance, 104–7; Darwinism, karma, rebirth and, 109; and Northern decadence, 109; as Theosophy, 160–64; and monism, 227–33
Buddhist All Sects Council, 135, 174, 179
Bukkyō kakushū kyōkai. *See* Buddhist All Sects Council
Bukkyō, 298 (n. 60)
Bunmei kaika, 121–22
Bunri rei, 117. *See also* Separation edicts
Burke, Edmund, 145
Burnouf, Eugène, 291 (n. 23), 293 (n. 63)
Bushidō, 267, 268, 269, 270
Busshō, 215
Byōdōin, 29, 34, 283 (n. 63)

Candlin, Rev. George T., 62–63
Carlyle, Thomas, 268
Carpenter, J. Estlin, 241–42
Carus, Paul, 11, 12, 15, 83, 107, 212, 222–44, 245–58, 259, 260, 261, 262, 264, 265, 267, 274, 275, 276, 288 (n. 21), 308 (n. 38), 313 (n. 1), 314 (nn. 31, 43, 44), 315 (nn. 64, 71), 316 (nn. 77, 91), 318 (nn. 1, 8), 319 (n. 10), 320 (n. 24)
Chamberlain, Basil Hall, 269–70
Chambers, Robert, 102
Cheney, Annie Elizabeth, 182, 184, 290 (n. 72), 306 (n. 40)
Christ as Buddha, 130–31, 236, 239, 256; as Maitreya, 231, 236
Christianity in Meiji Japan, 3, 298 (n. 60); and modernization, 121–24; and treaty revision, 133; and the Japanese spirit, 192; distinctive features of, 192–94. *See also* American Board of Missions; Doshisha; Kumamoto Band; Min'yusha
Chudhadharn, Prince Chandradat (of Siam), 10, 211, 215, 243, 312 (n. 59)
Clark, James Freeman, 121
Colenso, Bishop, 103
Columbian Exposition, 2, 16, 17–21, 25, 45–46, 50, 56, 175, 182, 196, 282 (n. 36), 284 (n. 6)
Comparative religion, 5, 56, 70
Comte, Auguste, 102, 121, 133, 140
Confucianism, 71–72, 128, 256, 290 (n. 65), 299 (n. 71), 300 (n. 2)
Confucius, 256, 266
Congress of Missions, 191
Conze, Edward, 290 (n. 7), 293 (n. 73)
Copleston, Bishop R. S., 158, 159
Court of Honor, 28
Crystal Palace Exposition, 45
Csoma, Alexander, 91
Cutler, H. G., 25

D'Alwis, James, 290 (n. 6)
D'Vivedi, Manilal N., 13, 57, 90, 286 (n. 44)
Daikyō, 133
Dainihon bukkyō seinenkai (Young Men's Buddhist Association), 127, 137–38, 298 (n. 48)
Daizōkyō, 206
Darwin, Charles, 102, 103
Darwinism, 211
Dhammapada, 234, 235

Dharma, 211, 216, 255
Dharmakāya, 214, 216, 218, 220, 231–32, 263
Dharmapāla, Anagārika (David Hevaviratne), 10, 12, 57, 62, 70, 75, 82, 157, 190, 202, 204, 205, 206, 209, 210, 240, 276, 307 (n. 61), 311 (n. 43), 313 (n. 84)
Dome of Columbus, 21–23, 25, 28, 284 (n. 14)
Doshisha, 3, 70, 122–25, 135, 179, 193, 194, 288 (n. 27), 300 (n. 76)

Eastern Buddhist, 262, 271
Eastern Buddhist Society, 271–73
Ebina Danjō, 297 (n. 33), 308 (n. 89)
Eitel, Ernest J., 231, 235, 237, 315 (n. 64)
Ekayāna, 198, 309 (n. 1)
Eliade, Mircea, 276
Elison, George, 295 (n. 112)
Ellinwood, Rev. F. E., 86, 217, 224, 225, 226, 260
Emerson, Ralph Waldo, 229, 275
Enlightenment (Buddhist), 106, 109

Faber, Ernst, 72, 288 (n. 33)
Fausböll, Viggo, 293 (n. 73)
Fenelossa, Ernest, 29, 43, 113, 139, 140, 142, 153, 156, 163, 199, 309 (n. 2)
Ferris wheel, 26–28
Fichte, Johann Gottlieb, 145, 146, 264
Five Aggregates, 146
Five periods (of the Buddha's teaching), 146, 207, 263, 301 (n. 33), 320 (n. 33)
Flower, B. O., 182, 184
Fo-Sho-Hing-Tsan-King, 234, 315 (n. 58)
Four Noble Truths, 294 (n. 94)
Friends of the Nation. *See* Min'yusha
Fukoku kyōhei, 117, 121
Fukuda Gyōkai, 126
Fukuzawa Yukichi, 122, 139, 142
Furuta Shokin, 250

Gandhi, Virchand, 75, 287 (n. 17), 288 (n. 38)
Gates, Merril Edwardes, 46, 284 (nn. 2, 3)
Gautama (Gotama), 77, 97–99, 105, 107, 110, 161, 188. *See also* Sakyamuni
Ginsberg, Alan, 272
Gogerly, D. J., 91
Gokoku airi, 125, 143–44, 174
Gordon, Rev. M. L., 70, 71, 74
Gospel of Buddha, 11, 12, 222–24, 232, 233–44, 261; in Japan, 245–58, 274, 276
Griffis, William Elliot, 112
Grossier, Abbé, 108

Haibutsu kishaku, 142, 296 (n. 8), 298 (n. 47)
Hara Tanzan, 126, 139, 140
Hardy, Rev. Robert Spence, 72, 94–99, 101–2, 103, 104, 226, 280 (n. 7), 292 (n. 40), 293 (nn. 63, 72)
Harris, Townsend, 185
Hartmann, Edward von, 133
Haskell, Caroline, 191, 224, 225
Hawaii: annexation of, 23–24; Japanese suffrage in, 181
Headland, Isaac T., 70
Hearn, Lafcadio, 275
Hegel, Georg W. F., 88, 139, 140, 142, 145, 146, 147, 214, 264
Higashi Honganji, 128–29, 139, 152, 178, 302 (n. 2)
Hikkaduvē Sumangala, 85, 158, 159, 161, 189–90, 204, 205, 206, 295 (n. 114)
Hinduism, 88–91, 100, 105, 288 (n. 41), 291 (n. 12)
Hirai Kinzō, 13, 68, 76, 77, 126, 129, 155, 157, 176, 179, 194, 196, 202, 254, 288 (n. 17), 289 (n. 45), 290 (n. 72), 302 (n. 2), 305 (n. 24), 307 (n. 58), 311 (n. 43), 314 (n. 43); on treaty revision, 79, 173, 181–91; on Japanese religion, 193, 210, 217, 218, 219–20
Hirata Atsutane, 117, 295 (n. 4)
Hōben, 301 (n. 26)
Hodgson, Brian Houghton, 91–92
Honji suijaku, 295 (n. 4)
Hōōden, 2, 17, 20, 180, 196, 275, 300 (n. 9); and Japanese civilization, 29–38; American responses to, 39–44; and Okakura's later writings, 267–68
Hōōdō, 283 (n. 63)
Horiuchi Jō, 176, 310 (n. 27)
Hoshin (*sambhogakāya*), 216, 231–32
Hosshin (*dharmakāya*), 214, 216, 218, 220
Hossō sect, 146
Hōsui. *See* Inoue Enryō
Hotoke, 186
Houghton, Walter, E., 201, 202, 240, 287 (n. 13), 312 (n. 60)
Hume, David, 145
Hume, Rev. Robert A., 286 (n. 43)
Huxley, Aldous, 322 (n. 63)
Huxley, Thomas, 104, 124, 206

Idolatry, 187–88, 288 (n. 41)
Ii Naosuke, 180
Ilbert Bill, 281 (n. 5)

Imperialism, 40, 45–64, 91–92, 147, 180
Imperial Rescript on Education, 133, 299 (nn. 71, 72), 308 (n. 89)
Indō busseki kofuku. *See* Mahābodhi Society
Inga no rihō, 202, 212
Inoue Enryō, 8, 9, 14, 125–26, 127, 130, 131, 132, 135, 155, 157, 166, 172, 174, 175, 201, 208, 214, 219, 245, 248, 249, 251, 268–69, 270, 271, 297 (n. 22), 298 (nn. 43, 61), 299 (n. 61), 300 (n. 4), 304 (n. 5), 305 (nn. 27, 29, 39), 306 (n. 40), 307 (nn. 64, 67), 311 (n. 53), 318 (n. 35); and Buddhist revival and nationalism, 137–54, 300 (n. 15), 301 (nn. 18, 20)
Inoue Tetsujirō, 140, 299 (n. 71), 300 (n. 10), 317 (n. 17)
Iwakura Tomomi, 296 (n. 17)

Jacobi, Friedrich Heinrich, 264
James, William, 272
Janes, Captain L. L., 123
Jayatilaka, D. B., 243
Jōdoshinshū, 112, 164, 177, 178, 202
Johnson, Rossiter, 49, 67, 75, 286 (n. 43)
Judge, W. Q., 303 (n. 32)
Jung, Carl G., 321 (n. 58)

Kaburagi Peter Goro, 192, 305 (n. 24), 309 (n. 89)
Kaempfer, Engelbert, 88, 111
Kamil, Mustafa, 269
Kanamori Tsūrin, 124
Kanō Eitoku, 43
Kant, Immanuel, 140, 145, 146, 214, 227, 264
Karma, 109, 211, 213, 215–16, 232, 234
Kasawara Kenjū, 119, 120, 297, (n. 21), 302 (n. 2)
Katō Hiroyuki, 139, 140
Kawai Yoshigiro, 279 (n. 3)
Kegonkyō (Kegon Sutra), 208, 301 (n. 33). *See also* Avatamsaka Sutra
Kegon sect, 320 (n. 33)
Kern, H., 293 (n. 73)
Kerouac, Jack, 272
Kishimoto Nobuta, 133, 191, 193, 308 (n. 88), 317 (n. 28)
Kitabatake Dōryū, 140, 300 (n. 10)
Kitagawa, Joseph M., 257
Kiyozawa Manshi, 140, 178, 300 (n. 10)
Kopetzky, Olga, 237, 315 (n. 65)
Kozaki Hiromichi, 3, 122, 123, 124, 193, 194
Kōzen Gunaratna, 164
Kumamoto Band, 122–25, 193, 288 (n. 27), 297 (n. 36)
Kumamoto Yōgakkō, 123
Kumiai, 193, 194, 300 (n. 76)
Kuroda Shintō, 202, 214–15, 216, 217, 220
Kuroda Toshio, 309 (n. 91), 310 (n. 16)
Kuru Masamichi, 29

Lanman, Charles, 293 (n. 73)
Legge, James, 70
Leibnitz, Gottfried Wilhelm, 145
Leonowens, Anna, 290 (n. 67)
The Light of Asia, 7, 101, 234, 235
Lillie, Arthur, 107, 205
Lloyd-Jones, Rev. Jenkin, 184
Locke, John, 145
Lotus Sutra, 298 (n. 49)
Luther, Martin, 89, 90
Lyell, Charles, 102

MacFarlane, Charles, 111–12, 294 (n. 94)
Mādhyamika sect, 266
Mahābodhi Society, 157, 176, 209, 305 (n. 10), 311 (n. 27)
Mahāparinibbāna Suttanta, 236
Mahāse'tu, 235–36
Mahāvagga, 235
Mahāvamsa, 90, 91
Maitreya, 231, 236, 237, 291 (n. 23), 306 (n. 32), 309 (n. 1), 314 (nn. 29, 44), 322 (n. 61)
Manas, 229
Manifest destiny, 23–28, 45–64, 282 (n. 26). *See also* Ferris wheel
Manifesto, 173, 174–76, 178–79, 194, 196, 202, 209, 210, 212, 213, 219, 250–51, 254, 262–63, 276, 295 (n. 1)
Manufactures Hall, 25–26
Matsugama Takayoshi, 192, 308 (n. 89), 309 (n. 91)
McFarland, S. G., 70
McMullin, Neil, 13, 128, 290 (n. 7), 291 (n. 32)
Meirokusha, 139, 142
Messianic mission, American, 50–52
Middle Way, 145, 146, 214
Midway Plaisance, 20–21, 26, 35, 48, 57, 58, 59, 67
Mill, James, 89
Mill, John Stewart, 124
Min'yusha, 149, 176, 297 (n. 35), 305 (n. 13)
Miyake Setsurei, 140, 300 (n. 10)
Mohottivate Gunananda, 158, 159, 163, 291 (n. 27)

Moksha, 217
Monier-Williams, Sir Monier, 121
Monism, 11, 222–44, 261, 316 (n. 84)
Monist, 227, 233, 254, 259, 262, 288 (n. 2), 315 (n. 57)
Morris, William, 268
Motoori Nobunaga, 117
Mozoomdar, P. C., 289 (n. 40)
Muller, F. Max, 7, 83–84, 90, 107, 110, 113, 119, 121, 202–3, 205, 226, 248, 290 (n. 6), 292 (n. 62), 293 (nn. 67, 70), 296 (n. 18), 313 (n. 15), 315 (n. 68)
Munsterberg, Hugo, 272, 321 (n. 57)
Murakami Senshō, 14, 251–52, 300 (n. 13)
Mutsu Munemitsu, 19, 20, 44, 306 (n. 38)

Nagarkar, 289 (n. 42)
Nakanishi Goro, 249, 298 (n. 43)
Nanjō Bun'yū, 110, 119, 120, 261, 296 (nn. 17, 18), 300 (n. 13)
Nantembō Tōjū, 321 (n. 47)
Neely's History, 76–79
Nehan, 202, 217–18
Nehankyō (Nirvana Sutra), 211
Nichiren sect, 112, 298 (n. 49)
Nietzsche, Friedrich Wilhelm, 88
Niijima Jō, 123, 288 (n. 27), 297 (n. 36)
Nirmanakāya, 216, 231–32
Nirvana, 86, 93, 94, 106, 107, 108, 109, 162, 188–89, 202, 217–19, 224, 225–26, 234; four kinds of, 217–18, 225, 312 (n. 70)
Nishi Amane, 137
Nishi Honganji, 118, 119, 120, 129, 152, 164, 302 (n. 2)
Nitobe Kokuzō, 267
Nivedita, Sister, 267, 268
Nogi Maresuke, General, 270, 321 (n. 47)
Noguchi Zenshirō (Noguchi Fukudō), 76, 126, 155, 156, 157, 158, 168, 176, 178, 179–80, 182, 186, 196, 289 (n. 45), 310 (n. 17), 321 (n. 52)
Nukariya Kaiten, 270, 321 (n. 48)

Ōbei, 273, 281 (n. 21)
Ōbei bukkyō tsushinkai (Society for Communication with Western Buddhists), 152
Ōbō-buppō, 128, 144, 298 (n. 54). *See also* Rāja dharma
Occidentalism, 11–12, 273–77
Oda Nobunaga, 43, 128
Okakura Kakuzō, 131, 140, 269, 300 (n. 9); and the Chicago Exposition, 29–30, 31, 34, 38, 43; anti-imperialist writings, 267; Zen and Bushidō, 267–68, 320 (nn. 35, 36)
Olcott, Henry Steel, 3, 15, 155–58, 179, 209, 223, 243, 245, 248, 274, 275, 302 (nn. 1, 2, 4, 5, 7, 8, 10), 303 (n. 13), 304 (n. 69); in Ceylon, 158–60; in Japan, 160–71
Oldenberg, Hermann, 88, 293 (n. 73)
Open Court, 224, 227, 233, 242, 254, 255–58, 259, 262, 288 (n. 21), 308 (n. 38)
Open Court Publishing Company, 227
Orientalism, 4–10, 75, 204, 222, 234, 272–77
Oshin (*nirmanakāya*), 216
O'Sullivan, John L., 23, 282 (n. 26)
Ōtani Kōsan, 165, 178
Ōtani University, 251, 300 (n. 10)
Otto, Rudolph, 272
Ōuchi Seiran, 126, 127, 130, 131, 132, 135, 140, 157, 174, 196, 300 (n. 10), 304 (n. 5)

Pali Text Society, 7, 104, 113, 203, 204, 271, 293 (n. 73), 294 (n. 85), 315 (n. 68)
Palmer, Potter, 42
Palmer, T. W., 39
Parinirvāna, 225, 236, 237
Paticca-Samuppāda (pratītya-samutpāda), 311 (n. 41), 312 (n. 59)
Patriotism: and Japanese Buddhism, 147–48
Pentecost, Rev. George F., 287 (n. 17), 288 (n. 38)
Perahera, 100–101
Perry, Commodore Mathew, 24, 32, 180, 294 (n. 105)
Philadelphia Centennial Exposition, 18–19
Phoenix Pavilion. *See* Hōōden
Prinsep, James, 90, 91, 94
Pung Kwang: on Confucianism, 71
Pure Land Buddhism, 219, 272
Pure Land sects, 277

Rāja dharma, 128
Rebirth, 109
Reed, Edward J., 112–13, 257, 295 (n. 114)
Reid, Thomas, 145
Renan, Ernest, 102, 119
Rhys Davids, C. A. F., 294 (n. 90)
Rhys Davids, T. W., 7, 86, 88, 90, 93, 94, 102, 104–9, 113, 114, 121, 203, 204, 205, 225, 226, 234, 236, 237, 291 (n. 18), 293 (nn. 67, 73, 74), 315 (nn. 62, 68)
Ricci, Mateo, 71, 88
Richard, Rev. Timothy, 71
Rinne, 202

Roberts, Rev. William C., 51–52
Roosevelt, Theodore, 23
Roy, Rammohan, 204
Ruskin, John, 268
Russell, Alexander, 319 (n. 19)
Russell, Ida, 319 (n. 19)

Sacred Books of the East (series), 226, 296 (n. 18), 315 (n. 68)
Saddharma-pundarīka-sūtra, 309 (n. 1)
Said, Edward, 4, 7, 11, 12, 293 (n. 73)
Saint-Hilaire, J. Barthélemy, 102, 103, 108–9, 226, 293 (nn. 63, 67)
Sakurai Keitoku, 113
Sakyamuni, 5, 8, 10, 73, 75, 86, 94, 97, 105, 145, 146, 147, 162, 164, 169, 199, 200, 205, 206, 207–9, 210, 216, 217, 220, 225, 231, 236, 237, 239, 246, 249, 252, 255, 263, 264, 292 (n. 42), 301 (n. 33), 306 (n. 32), 310 (n. 13), 314 (n. 45); as anti-Hindu hero, 88–91; as historical philosopher, 98–99. *See also* Gautama
Sambhogakāya, 216, 231–32
Samskaras, 232
Sangha, 149–50, 298 (n. 54)
Sano, Rev., 157
Saraswati, Dayananda, 204
Satori, 186
Schelling, Friedrich W., 145
Schleiermacher, Friedrich, 272
Schopenhauer, Arthur, 88, 133, 205, 234, 264
Seikyōsha, 8–9, 130–31, 132, 135, 138, 140, 147, 155, 166, 167, 174, 176, 177, 180, 297 (n. 35), 298 (nn. 60, 61), 300 (n. 4), 304 (n. 5), 305 (n. 13)
Senart, M., 293 (n. 73)
Sen no Rikyū, 270, 283 (n. 88)
Senzaki Nyōgen, 319 (n. 19)
Separation edicts, 117, 296 (n. 7)
Sesshū, 31
Seville Universal Exposition: Japanese art at, 43
Shaku Sōen, 12, 13, 62, 70, 76, 78–79, 82, 86, 109, 121, 136, 174, 176, 177, 178, 201, 212–13, 217, 218, 220, 224, 225, 226, 232, 245–62 passim, 269, 274, 276, 280 (n. 9), 289 (n. 45), 297 (n. 24), 298 (n. 48), 305 (n. 10), 306 (n. 4), 307 (n. 46), 310 (n. 12), 312 (nn. 54, 67), 313 (n. 84), 316 (nn. 1, 2), 317 (n. 35), 318 (nn. 7, 8), 319 (nn. 16, 17), 321 (n. 52)
Shaku Unshō, 126, 128
Shibata Reiichi, 279 (n. 4)
Shichinichi gōshūhō, 170
Shiga Shigetaka, 140, 150, 300 (n. 10), 301 (n. 47)
Shimaji Mokurai, 119, 126, 127, 130, 140, 155, 174, 177, 196, 249, 257, 297 (n. 22), 299 (n. 70), 300 (nn. 10, 13), 304 (n. 5)
Shimbutsu bunri, 117, 127
Shin bukkyō, 8, 115–16, 118, 125, 130, 136, 137, 141, 198, 262, 266, 267, 270, 273, 274, 295 (n. 2), 298 (n. 43)
Shingon sect, 127, 177, 275, 277, 309 (n. 2), 320 (n. 33)
Shinnyo, 214–15, 216
Shinri no ri, 143–44
Shintō, 116, 128, 137, 187, 189, 295 (n. 4), 298 (n. 50), 309 (n. 94); State Shintō, 133; Hirai on, 187, 188, 197; Christian delegates on, 191–93
Shitsu tan, 208
Shōjō nimon, 202, 219
Shōmu, Emperor, 127
Shoshū kaimei, 118
Shōtoku Taishi, 127
Shūkyō, 298 (n. 60)
Sino-Japanese War, 269
Slater, T. E., 288 (n. 41)
Smith, V. A., 81
Smithsonian Institute, 35
Snider, Denton J., 26–27, 28, 38, 39–40, 44
Snyder, Gary, 272
Social Darwinism, 2, 16, 20–21, 47, 61, 80
Sonnō gohō, 129
Sonnō hōbutsu daidōdan, 8–9, 132, 138, 144, 177, 299 (n. 68), 300 (n. 4), 304 (n. 5)
Sonnō jōi, 129
Sōseki Natsume, 126
Spencer, Herbert, 104, 124, 133, 139, 145, 193
"Storehouse consciousness," 146
Strauss, C. T., 221, 313 (n. 84)
Suchness concept, 263
Sunderland, Eliza, 69
Sūnyatā, 220
Suzuki, D. T., 12, 126, 243, 245, 246, 247, 248, 249, 250, 259–77, 316 (n. 88), 318 (n. 7), 319 (nn. 8, 10, 16, 18, 21), 320 (nn. 24, 27), 321 (nn. 47, 48, 49, 57, 58)
Swedenborg, Emanuel, 248
"Synthetic Religion," 186, 191

Takakusu Junjirō, 110, 119, 120, 261, 296 (n. 18), 297 (n. 22)
Tanabashi Ichirō, 140, 300 (n. 10)
Tanaka Kōho, 298 (n. 49)
Taoism, 71

Tateno Gozo, 18, 19
Tathatā, 215
Tejima, Commissioner, 38
Tendai sect, 127, 142, 146–47, 277, 309 (n. 2), 320 (n. 33)
Tennent, Sir James Emerson, 94, 96–97, 99–102, 292 (n. 40)
Tenshin. *See* Okakura Kakuzō
Terry, M. S., 69
Tetsugakkan, 141
Tetsugaku shoin, 141, 300 (n. 15)
Theosophical Society, 155, 156, 160–61, 164, 178, 179, 203, 272; Buddhist Division, 160
Theosophy, 160–64, 170, 213, 302 (n. 5)
Three Bodies of the Buddha, 78, 216, 217, 231–33, 263
Tison, Alexander, 289 (n. 46)
Toki Hōryū, 80, 82, 170, 174, 176, 177, 208, 209, 210, 211, 215, 216, 218, 219–20, 249, 274, 289 (n. 45), 299 (n. 62), 307 (n. 70), 310 (n. 16), 311 (nn. 45, 46), 312 (n. 67), 314 (n. 34), 321 (n. 61)
Tokugawa Ieyasu, 128
Tokunaga, Professor. *See* Kiyozawa Manshi
Tokusawa, Mr., 304 (n. 69)
Tokutomi Sohō (Tokutomi Ichirō), 124, 297 (n. 36)
Tokuzawa Chiezō, 164
Tokyo Fine Arts Academy, 29
Torrington, Governor, 99
Toyotomi Hideyoshi, 283 (n. 88)
Tōyō University, 141
Treaty revision, 2, 16–21, 43–44, 130, 172–97, 281 (n. 2), 282 (n. 2). *See also* Ansei treaties; Cheney, Annie Elizabeth; Flower, B. O.; Fukuzawa Yukichi; Ii Naosuke; Mutsu Munemitsu; Seikyōsha; Sonnō hōbutsu daidōdan; Tateno Gozo
Trikāya, 314 (n. 47); and Christian trinity, 231–33. *See also* Three Bodies of the Buddha
Tripitaka, 296 (n. 17)
Turnour, George, 90, 91, 94

Universalism: Christian, 54–56; Buddhist, 209–11
University of Chicago, 224
Upāya, 301 (n. 26)

Vaipulya sutras, 146
Vairocana Buddha, 219
Valentine, Milton, 69, 70, 82, 284 (n. 16)
Valignano, 88, 295 (n. 112)
Vivekananda, 12, 13, 57, 63, 75, 267, 273, 276, 322 (n. 63)

Wach, Joachim, 272
Warren, W. F., 57
Washburn, Rev. George, 287 (n. 68)
Watts, Alan W., 272, 321 (n. 57)
Webb, Mohammad, 290 (n. 1)
White City, 21, 28
Wilson, H. H., 94, 97
Wooded Island, 34–38
World's Parliament of Religions, 1, 4, 12–13, 14, 15, 17, 45–47, 50–52, 56, 58–59, 61, 65–84, 85, 113, 114, 136, 145, 157, 172, 173, 189, 198, 205, 220, 223, 242, 246, 247, 275, 276, 280 (n. 19), 297 (n. 40)

Yatsubuchi Bunryū, 82, 175, 176, 177–78, 179, 191, 201, 206, 208, 216, 217, 246, 288 (n. 17), 289 (n. 45), 305 (n. 17), 310 (n. 18), 314 (n. 47)
Yokoi Tokio, 125
Young Men's Buddhist Association (YMBA), 127, 137–38, 298 (n. 48)

Zaike bukkyō, 126, 178
Zen, 12, 13; decentering original Buddhism, 263–64; decentering Buddhist canon, 264–65; as positive, energetic, practical Buddhism, 265; as essence of Eastern Buddhism, 266–67; and Japanese Culture, 267–71
Zenkoku bukkyōsha daikonwakai, 196